GENERALLY SPEAKING

List of Publications

Fiction:

Ultimatum (1973)
Exxoneration (1974)
Exodus UK (1975)
Separation (1976)
Balls! (1976)
Periscope Red (1980)
Separation II (1981)
Triad (1981)
Retaliation (1982)
Starmageddon (1985)
Rommel & Patton (1986)
Red Arctic (1989)
John A.'s Crusade (1995)
Death by Deficit (1995)
Caged Eagle (2002)
A Richard Rohmer Omnibus (2003)
Ultimatum 2 (in progress)

Non-Fiction:

Practice & Procedure Before the Ontario Highway Transport Board
The Green North: Mid-Canada (1970)
The Arctic Imperative (1973)
E.P. Taylor (1978)
Patton's Gap (1981)
How to Write a Best-Seller (1984)
Massacre 747 (1984)
The Golden Phoenix: The Biography of Peter Munk (1997)
Mustangs Over Normandy (1997)
HMS Raleigh *On the Rocks* (2003)
Generally Speaking: The Memoirs of Major-General Richard Rohmer (2004)

GENERALLY SPEAKING

———

THE MEMOIRS OF

MAJOR-GENERAL RICHARD ROHMER

———

THE DUNDURN GROUP
TORONTO

Copy-Editor: Andrea Pruss
Design: Jennifer Scott
Printer: Transcontinental

Library and Archives Canada Cataloguing in Publication

Rohmer, Richard, 1924-
    Generally speaking : the memoirs of Major General Richard Rohmer.

ISBN 1-55002-518-X

1. Rohmer, Richard, 1924– 2. Authors, Canadian (English) — 20th century — Biography. 3. Canada. Canadian Armed Forces. Reserve Force of Canada — Biography. 4. Lawyers — Canada — Biography. 5. Canada. Royal Canadian Air Force — Biography. 6. Fighter pilots — Canada — Biography. 7. Journalists — Canada — Biography. 8. Canada — Biography. I. Title.

PS8585.O3954Z46 2004   971.064'092   C2004-904465-6

1   2   3   4   5   08   07   06   05   04

We acknowledge the support of the Canada Council for the Arts and the Ontario Arts Council for our publishing program. We also acknowledge the financial support of the Government of Canada through the Book Publishing Industry Development Program and The Association for the Export of Canadian Books, and the Government of Ontario through the Ontario Book Publishers Tax Credit program, and the Ontario Media Development Corporation's Ontario Book Initiative.

Care has been taken to trace the ownership of copyright material used in this book. The author and the publisher welcome any information enabling them to rectify any references or credits in subsequent editions.

J. Kirk Howard, President

Printed and bound in Canada.
Printed on recycled paper.

www.dundurn.com

Dundurn Press
8 Market Street, Suite 200
Toronto, Ontario, Canada
M5E 1M6

Gazelle Book Services Limited
White Cross Mills
Hightown, Lancaster, England
LA1 4X5

Dundurn Press
2250 Military Road
Tonawanda, NY
U.S.A. 14150

TABLE OF CONTENTS

CHAPTER 1
Catching Field Marshal Rommel

———◆———

L OOKING BACK OVER A REASONABLY long life I have decided that the one event I took part in that had the most impact and significance occurred in the late afternoon of July 17, 1944.

The place was Normandy. The event occurred during the Battle of Normandy, which lasted from D-Day on June 6, 1944, through to August 20, when the German 7th Army was defeated and the Falaise Gap was finally closed.

Field Marshal Erwin Rommel, arguably the most capable of all the German generals who faced the Allied forces in northwest Europe, was the commander of the German 7th Army and all of the forces facing the Allies (the Canadian, British, American, Polish, French, and others who had successfully assaulted the German forces in Normandy, breaching Hitler's Atlantic wall on D-Day).

By July 17, the Canadians and the British were pressing against Caen and were moving toward Falaise to the west of that city. The battle was tough and slow.

On that day, Field Marshal Rommel had left his headquarters on the northern bank of the Seine River at La Roche Guyon, west of Paris. His plan was to visit his Panzer Corps commander in Normandy, General Sepp Dietrich, a long-time crony of Hitler. Dietrich's headquarters were located in the village of St. Pierre sur Dives southeast of Caen. It was a long drive to Normandy, one that Rommel had taken many times with his driver, Corporal Daniel. It was Rommel's practice to sit in the passenger seat and do the map reading. The automobile was a huge Horch with a canvas top that on this day was down so that Rommel and Daniel and the three officers in the back seat, Rommel's aides, could keep a sharp eye out for *jabos*, Allied fighter aircraft whose pilots would like nothing better than to attack a German staff car.

By this time the Allied fighter aircraft — the Spitfires, Typhoons, Mustangs, Thunderbolts, and Lightnings of the United States Army Air Corps, the Royal Air Force, and the Royal Canadian Air Force — had complete command of the skies over Normandy. As Rommel approached the battle area, he knew that the danger of being attacked by an Allied fighter was high. But by this time he also knew that the Mustang I aircraft flown by the Royal Air Force (RAF) and Royal Canadian Air Force (RCAF) would not attack his car. These were fighter reconnaissance aircraft, their pilots being highly trained in visual reconnaissance, aerial photography, and the direction of artillery fire. A decision had been made by the commander of the Second Tactical Air Force (Canadian and British) in early July that highly specialized fighter reconnaissance pilots should not be put at risk by being permitted to attack targets of opportunity. In such an attack on tanks, guns, or other targets on the ground, the risk of being hit by anti-aircraft weapons was substantially increased. There were so many other fighter aircraft available and doing armed reconnaissance sweeps that if a target of opportunity was found by a Mustang I pilot he would simply radio its exact location back to the Group Control Centre (GCC), a radio station behind the Allied lines where the operator had multiple radios and frequencies and was in contact constantly with the fighter aircraft out over the enemy territory. The GCC operator would direct the appropriate fighter aircraft to the target, and then the attack would begin. German intelligence, who constantly monitored the radio talk of the Allied pilots, knew that the Mustang I (with its birdcage canopy hood looking very much like the Me109) would no longer attack a target of opportunity such as Rommel's Horch.

It was Rommel's intention to visit the front and let himself be seen by his troops on the ground to shore up their morale, notwithstanding the personal danger to himself. The Field Marshal was an extremely brave man, as his record from the First World War showed when he was awarded the Pour le Mérite, the equivalent of the Victoria Cross, when he was a young captain at the front.

Rommel arrived at the headquarters of Sepp Dietrich in mid-afternoon. The two generals conferred, discussing strategy and tactics. A few minutes before 4:00 p.m. word came from Rommel's headquarters that the Americans, under General Omar Bradley, had started an attack in strength in the St. Lô area. Rommel immediately made the decision to return to La Roche Guyon in order to run the battle against the Americans and give direction to his generals. Sepp Dietrich asked him not to go because of the danger from the jabos. But Rommel would have none of it. He had to get back to his headquarters.

With Corporal Daniel at the wheel, Rommel in the passenger seat, and the three staff men in the rear seats, Rommel was off at high speed heading east toward Livarot, a village about nine miles to the east of St. Pierre sur Dives. As he approached Livarot, Rommel saw a formation of fighter aircraft jabos in the distance to the north but heading toward his location.

He immediately ordered Daniel to turn south on a side road just to the west of Livarot.

At that moment I was leading the section of four fighter reconnaissance Mustangs that Rommel saw coming toward him from the north. I was flying at about fifteen hundred feet. I had brought my formation out of our base B8 at Magny between Arromanches and Bayeux about forty-five minutes earlier. I had proceeded east toward Dozulé in accordance with my briefed instructions and then headed south looking for tanks, vehicles, artillery, or anything else military that I could see en route. The trip to this point had been relatively uneventful except for some 20-mm and 40-mm flack that had been fired at us. The three Mustangs with me were spread out in battle formation about two hundred yards apart. The purpose of my team was to protect me, the leader, in the event of being attacked by Me109s or Focke-Wulf fighters.

As we flew south, approaching Livarot, to the west I saw ahead a huge staff car travelling at high speed south down a side road. I knew that the occupants could see us, but as I drew close and was about to pass it on the right side there was no indication that the vehicle was going to stop or take any kind of evasive action. The reason, of course, was that the occupants knew that we would not attack. As I passed the staff car I could see two men in the front and three in the back and the glinting of gold from the uniforms. I knew without question that the car was carrying some high-level "brass," although I had no idea who it was. I checked the location on my map for the exact pinpoint, then called Group Control Centre to give them the location of this wonderful target of opportunity, which I was not permitted to attack. We Mustang pilots with aircraft heavily armed with six .5-inch machine guns in the wings and two 30-mm guns through the propeller (believe it or not) were highly frustrated and furious, but we turned and headed back for our base at Magny.

I was to discover many years later that the man on the front seat of the staff car was Field Marshal Rommel and that as a result of my call to Group Control Centre two Spitfires were directed in to attack his Horch just after it turned onto the main road between Livarot and Vimoutier. The two Spitfires came in from the north. The first cannon shell hit Corporal Daniel and killed him. The car went out of control and hit a stump. At that moment Rommel was looking back over his right shoulder watching the approach of the firing Spitfire. When the car hit the stump his head hit the right windshield post, caving in the left side of his forehead. The Horch tipped on its side, throwing out Rommel as well as the three men in the rear seat, none of whom were injured. However, Rommel was at death's door. His people managed to get him to a nearby druggist, who gave him morphine, and then he was taken to a Luftwaffe hospital near Evreux. It

The Catching of Rommel, July 17, 1944.
Painting by Don Connolly.

would take months for Rommel to regain his health. The effect of my catching the field marshal, leading to the shoot-up by the Spitfires, was that Rommel was out of the war, a crucial turning point in the battle of Normandy and of the war in the northwest Europe.

To have had a substantial part in taking Field Marshal Rommel and his strong, legendary leadership out of the war is probably the single most significant achievement for which I can claim credit. On the other hand, and in retrospect, I am pleased that it was not I who shot up Rommel in his Horch.

Mind you, it was not until many years after the event that I was able to put together all of the pieces that told me that it was I who had caught Rommel.

After I reported the staff car on the radio I then turned and headed back west to our base at B8 and thought no more of the situation. I duly reported the sighting of the staff car to the intelligence officers at our squadron. It was recorded in the squadron's log that I had spotted a staff car. It was the one and only such vehicle that I saw in my entire 135 reconnaissance missions during my tour of operations. So its image was and still is clear in my memory. I had no idea that Spitfires had shot up the staff car. There was no liaison with the Spitfire squadrons, and so the matter just disappeared, if you will. As I recall, there was a rumour a couple of weeks later that Field Marshal Rommel had been severely injured in an accident. That was the end of the matter.

Subsequently, my personal flying log book was lost due to enemy action when our squadron moved from an airstrip near Evreux up to another airstrip, this time at Diest Schaffen in Belgium. The Dakota transport aircraft carrying our personal equipment went to the wrong place and was shot down. With it went that precious log book. But if I needed any references there was still the squadron's log book, which was kept by 430 Squadron's administrative staff and overseen by the squadron commander.

In 1975, as the newly appointed commander of the Air Reserve Group with the rank of brigadier-general, I attended a reunion of 430 Squadron at its headquarters at Valcartier, Quebec, where the unit was then flying the Kiowa helicopters. During that visit I was delighted to find that the original wartime squadron log book was still in existence and in the possession of the squadron. I asked for and was given a photocopy of the log, which recorded the story of each and every one of the missions that I had taken part in during my time with the squadron from September 1943 near Ashford in Kent, England, to the end of November 1944, when we were based at Eindhoven in the Netherlands.

In 1981 I completed and published my partly autobiographical story of D-Day and the Battle of Normandy under the title *Patton's Gap*, a reference to the Falaise Gap, which American General George S. Patton, Jr., ought to have been permitted to close commencing on the night of August 12, 1944. A few months after its publication I decided to do a novel based on the Battle of Normandy experiences of Field Marshal Rommel (of whom I was an admirer) and the great General George S. Patton, Jr., whom I had had the privilege of meeting on May 1, 1944. That meeting will be dealt with later.

The historical fiction book based on fact was *Rommel and Patton*. It was published in 1986.

In order to write the book I had to do a great deal of research, particularly on Rommel's life and experiences during the Battle of Normandy period. Of particular interest was the story of his being shot up on July 17, 1944. I read several accurate accounts of the event from both the German and Allied sides. At some point it occurred to me that I should look to see what I had been doing on July 17, 1944. I went to my copy of the squadron log book, opened it to the July 17 record, and discovered that I had reported "one staff car going south." As soon as I saw those words the image of that staff car instantly appeared in my memory. That had to be Rommel's staff car, the Horch.

It had to be Rommel, no question, except that Rommel had left Sepp Dietrich's headquarters at St. Pierre sur Dives at about 4:00 p.m. and had travelled only some twelve miles before he was shot up, but the log book told me that the time I saw him was shortly after 5:00 p.m. In other words, if the timing records were correct he had taken an hour to travel that short distance. Something was wrong. Rommel would have been thirty or forty miles away by 5:00 p.m. or shortly thereafter. My initial excitement at finding this enormously special connection with Rommel being taken out of the war turned into disappointment — until about two days later, when I discovered that the British were operating on double British summer time and the Germans were operating on European time. The difference between the two was one hour. So catching him at shortly after 5:00 p.m. double British summer time was exactly in accord with his departing from St. Pierre sur Dives at 4:00 p.m. European time. That staff car was indeed Rommel's.

What Goebbels, Hitler's propaganda master, had done was to let the world know that Field Marshal Rommel had been injured in an automobile accident in Normandy. There was no way he was going to admit that the great field marshal had been taken out of the war by enemy action. I wasn't aware of this Goebbels strategy until I was on a flight to Bermuda from Toronto to visit my friend Sir William Stephenson (the man called Intrepid). I was sitting beside a young businessman who was working in Bermuda. We struck up a conversation, and I told him that I was working on this particular book, whereupon he advised me that his father, who had been in the Second World War, had a newspaper clipping in the English language from 1944 announcing the death of Field Marshal Rommel. The German-originated clipping said that Rommel had died from injuries suffered in his accident on July 17, 1944. The clipping arrived at my office back in Toronto a few days later. It is an important story in itself and yet another of Goebbels's massive lies. Rommel did not die of injuries from his accident. He died from Hitler forcing him to take a cyanide pill.

Because of my personal link to Rommel and therefore indirectly to his demise, this briefly is what happened to him. Shortly after July 17, 1944, the notorious attempt to take Hitler's life at his Wolfshanze East headquarters took place. Hitler survived with minor injuries but immediately commenced slaughter all those who purportedly had taken part in the plot to kill him. Rommel was one of the suspects.

By early October 1944, Rommel was in the final stages of his recuperation at his home in Herrlingen near Ulm. He was fit again and ready to take command once more and had so notified Hitler. Instead of giving him a new command, Hitler sent two of his young generals to Rommel's home with a letter. In it, Hitler said that the Gestapo had convinced him that Rommel was part of the group that had plotted to kill him, and he therefore gave Rommel a choice. One of the young generals had a cyanide pill with him. Rommel was to take the cyanide pill and die. If he refused to take the pill he would be stripped of his rank forthwith and turned over to the People's Court for trial for high treason. His wife would not have his pension and his son, Manfred, who was then sixteen (later lord mayor of Stuttgart for many years), would not be protected. If he took the pill it would be said that he died of injuries from his accident. He would receive a full state funeral. His wife would have his pension and his son would be protected. Being a man of honour and integrity, Rommel left the house with Hitler's two men and drove off. He took the pill.

There is a peculiar footnote to the Rommel story. Soon after I joined my squadron in September 1943 some of my fellow pilots had noted the phonetic similarity between Rohmer and Rommel, with the result that I was soon being called in jest, "Rommel, Fox of the Desert." As it turned out, I had my unique meeting with my namesake some ten months later.

CHAPTER 2
Beginnings and Roots 1924–1936

———◆———

I WAS BORN ON JANUARY 24, 1924, and came from a solid, working-class, European mix. I was born close to the intersection of Queen and Herkimer streets in the steel city of Hamilton, Ontario. There is a cottage on the southwest corner of that intersection. The house of my Scottish grandfather, Thomas Wright, and his wife, Elizabeth Stewart Wright, faces Queen, the first residence south of the cottage on the corner. My young father, Ernest Herman Rohmer, and his lovely wife, Marion Margaret Wright, both originally of Hamilton, were living in Buffalo at the time. He was working in the Dunlop Tire factory building tires. Ernie was strong, intelligent, and an all-round athlete. How he and my mother met, courted, and married I have no idea. But with the slim work opportunities of the post–First World War period, it was apparent that Ernie's best opportunities to make a living were not in the steel mills of Hamilton but in the booming bowels of the Dunlop Tire plant in Buffalo, which was supplying tires to the infant but quickly growing automobile industry with Henry Ford's revolutionary mass-production line concepts.

My grandfather, Francis (Frank) Rohmer, was born somewhere in Ontario, probably in the 1880s. Frank was the son of Louis, who had come from Alsace Lorraine (which was either French or German at the time) to Ontario. We knew very little about Louis except that it was rumoured that he was a pastry chef, that he had worked in Stratford, Ontario, and that he had died a very strange death when Frank was quite young. At one time or another Frank operated a laundry in (of all places) Orangeville. When I arrived he was working as a tailor at a major Hamilton suit firm, Firth Brothers, while his wife and children were in Orangeville. Times were

Top: *At eighteen months old, in Buffalo, New York.*

Bottom: *At Gramma Rohmer's house in Orangeville, Ontario, 1927.*

always tough for Frank and his wife, Agnes Richardson Rohmer, who came originally from the Caledonia area near Hamilton.

We have a magnificent photograph of the Richardson family taken on the day of the Jubilee of Queen Victoria in 1897. In the centre of the formal photograph, properly dressed with appropriate British flags flying, are my great-grandfather, Matthew Richardson, and his wife. She was a large lady whose maiden name was Lyon. Her mother was a Jarvis, which means that we are related to the incredible Jarvis family that was so famous and powerful in that region and in Toronto. Standing behind my bearded great-grandfather and to the left in the photograph is my mustached grandfather, Frank Rohmer, and his bride. Also in the photograph is my great-uncle Walter (all of us in the Rohmer family look like Uncle Walter). Then there are two sisters of Agnes, with their diminutive

Richardson family photo.

husbands. The Richardsons were a proud United Empire Loyalist family, which allows me to use UEL in my post nominals, which I have yet to do.

This Jubilee photograph was taken four years before the birth of my father, Ernie, and probably two years before the birth of his older brother, Albert. Then followed the arrival of Ralph (Bob), Gertie, Minnie (who died early), Matt, and lastly Jack.

On my mother's side, her father, Thomas Wright, came directly from Inverary in Scotland to Hamilton, where he worked as a clerk for the Toronto, Hamilton and Buffalo Railway with its offices located north of their residence on Queen Street by about half a mile. By legend, Lizzie Stewart Wright came from a farming area in the region of Strathroy. She was a tall, imperious woman who in her later years dressed and became much like Queen Mary with her long, flowing purple gowns and huge hats. Thomas and Lizzie had three children, George, Lloyd, and Marion. During the First World War, George, who became a sergeant-major, was severely injured in one of the major battles in France, while Lloyd served as a dispatch rider in the same area overseas. George later became a fireman and then an engineer with the Toronto, Hamilton and Buffalo Railway.

All of these people were hard workers. None of them had education beyond high school, and indeed my father had to leave home and go to work after he finished the eighth grade. Those were tough times both at Queen and Herkimer and in Orangeville, where the Rohmer brood resided in a little cottage that's still there, #3 Third Street at the east end of town.

My parents decided that my mother should come back to Hamilton for my delivery so that I would be a Canadian citizen upon arrival. Maybe there were other reasons, but that appears to be the best one. So it was that on January 24, 1924, I was born at the intersection of Queen and Herkimer in the Wright house. The doctor who delivered me lived next door in that cottage on the corner. His name was Dr. Silcox. There was no money to pay him for his good services, so in lieu of cash I was given as my second name Heath, the maiden name of Dr. Silcox's wife. Where Richard came from I don't know.

My earliest recollections began when I was two. I can still see the first duplex that we lived in in Buffalo. Where, I have no idea. But once we moved the second floor of another duplex next to Riverside Park, which was close to the Niagara River, my memories became fairly strong.

When I was about three, Uncle Bob Rohmer came to pay us a visit all the way from Hamilton, where he was working. He convinced me that if I could put salt on a robin's tail I could capture that bird and keep it as a pet. That was a real challenge. My mother dressed me in a raincoat, a slicker as we called it, and a hat to go with it. I took the salt shaker and out into Riverside Park I went — and would you believe it I almost got a robin. My parents and Uncle Bob were watching from the dry safety of the house. That was probably the first time that I lived up to the motto that is in my coat of arms, "On to the next windmill" which translated into Latin is *ad proximum ventum pistrinum*. I would try many times more in life to put salt on a robin's tail.

It was in Riverside Park that I first saw an airplane. I have no idea what the machine was. Probably some holdover from the First World War. But as my three-year-old eyes watched this beautiful machine, I was captivated by what it was doing, flying through the air, making a lot of noise. I guess I must have realized that a person was flying in it. That was the beginning of my love affair with aviation and aircraft, an affair

The Rohmer coat of arms: "On to the next windmill."

that still turns me on, especially when I get my hands on the controls of an aircraft. I still fly a tail dragger, an Aeronca Champ, but only in the spring, summer, and fall. I still fly with great skill — to the astonishment of most people when they learn that I have not given up the particular prowess that I first learned back in 1942.

One other thing that I remember clearly from the Riverside Park duplex is that at Christmas when I was four years old my father bought me a beautiful, large-vehicled Lionel electric train. Pieces of it may still be with my brother, Ron. My father put that beautiful contraption together on its tracks, plugged the transformer into the wall socket, and, sitting at the controls, he ran that Lionel train by the hour. It was actually his train for me to watch, for him to enjoy. Why not? After all, he was working hard at the Dunlop plant, he was only twenty-seven years old, and if my Lionel train that he bought for me gave him pleasure that was fine with me.

There are two other remembrances I have of that time. The first was that my parents loved Italian spaghetti, and I can remember being taken to a large restaurant downtown in Buffalo for a feast of that delicious food and standing on the table at the restaurant, then digging into the strings and learning to twist them around a fork and a spoon.

The second was that I was sent out one day to the local store down the street to buy a chocolate bar. I came home with the chocolate bar, but unfortunately the vendor had made sure that this little blonde-haired person with the curly hair and really innocent face got the one bar that had worms in it. I can recall that this displeased my father enormously. I saw him march out the door of the flat with the choco-late bar in hand down toward the unwitting vendor. I have no idea what happened, but to have been confronted by my angry father that day the vendor would have been lucky to have survived a fist in the teeth or something similar.

So much for Riverside Park. Around that time I can recall my father brought home a yellow car. It was a coupe with a big Shell sign on the doors. He had met and been befriended by an entrepreneur by the name of Arthur Maddigan, who had the Buffalo franchise for Shell gasoline and oil products and had a service station not far away from where we lived. Maddigan had other stations as well. Father had left Dunlop and gone to work with Maddigan as a sales representative or manager, I'm not sure which. But it was a good enough position that he had this car. Not bad in those days.

Father talked Maddigan into financing him in the start-up of a new service station in Hamilton, Ontario. The pull of that place was strong. Another attraction in Hamilton was football, the playing of it that is. My father, Ernie, played baseball when he was in Buffalo but somehow he travelled back to Hamilton to play football with the Tiger ORFU (Ontario Rugby Football Union) team, which was one notch below the big-time Tigers. If we went back to live in Hamilton then he could play football to his heart's content.

So eventually the three of us made the move back to Hamilton, mov-ing first to an inexpensive house that we rented on the Hamilton beach strip, well away from the Cannon Street location that Ernie had selected for his first Rohmer service station site. It was in a large building on the

At the beach in Hamilton, age seven.

south side of Cannon Street near James Street, where railway tracks crossed Cannon. He installed the tanks and pumps then created an office in the building, and the service station opened with the support of Arthur Maddigan.

My father's first service station was a success. He soon opened another on Ottawa Street at Roxborough in Hamilton, where he launched a new retailing scheme whereby he gave a five-cent token by way of a rebate on every gallon of gasoline that was purchased. That token could be used to purchase anything else in the service station except gasoline, and particularly could be used to acquire premium dinnerware, toasters, electrical devices, drinking glasses … a whole host of stuff that he bought wholesale, usually from a Toronto outfit called Cassidy's.

Of course, in those days he could buy his gasoline from wholesalers at exceptionally good prices. His rebate promotion was highly successful. The volume of his sales skyrocketed. He opened up several other stations in Hamilton, including one at Cannon Street and Wentworth, which is where at the age of eleven I started to work pumping gas, topping up the oil in cars, cleaning windshields, and, yes, handling money. In 1928 and 1929 my father played for the Hamilton Tiger football team. He was a flying wing, playing on the other side of the snap from the great Hamilton football legend Brian Timmis. That year the Tigers were so successful that they won the Eastern Canada championship and then departed, complete with flannel trousers, dark blue blazers, and light grey Fedora hats, for the west to attempt to win the Canadian championship Grey Cup. Out they went, departing from the TH & B station off James Street South. I can remember crying because I thought I would never see my father again when he got on that train. It was the same station from which I would depart in early 1943, headed for England and the battle with Hitler.

The Hamilton Tigers won the Grey Cup and returned with great fanfare, celebrations, and parades, including diamond rings from the city council. My father's name was on everybody's lips in Hamilton, and I have to believe that his football fame assisted in bringing business to his service stations.

For myself, I wound up in public school at Adelaide Hoodless when my parents moved back from Hamilton Beach into the centre of the city, to a house on Blake Street. During our time in that house my father coached, managed, and really developed the Hamilton Tiger box lacrosse team. His brothers were major parts of the organization, which ultimately turned out to be a championship group. Brother Bob played goal (he was called the Masked Marvel), brother Matt, who had been an Olympic lacrosse player in Los Angeles, was centre, and Jack Rohmer, then about age sixteen, was the rover. Even though he had a bad knee, which had been broken badly in a football game in Ottawa in 1930, my father had stormed back and was able to play defence in addition to managing the team. Like the football squad, the Hamilton Tigers lacrosse team won the Eastern Canada championship. Then they all got on the train at the TH &B station and went west, successfully defeating all comers on the way out to Vancouver. They had a bloody five-game battle with the New Westminster Salmonbellies, which the

Here I am in the front of the photograph as mascot of the Hamilton Tigers, Mann Cup lacrosse champions of 1933.

Rohmer boys eventually won. It was a tough, vicious series followed closely and carefully by all Hamiltonians, who were just getting used to their radios. Like the football, the lacrosse games were played at the Hamilton Amateur Athletic Association grounds (HAAA) in the west end of the city, not far from (strangely enough) the intersection of Queen and Herkimer.

I have an identification scar over my right eye from the HAAA grounds. My Uncle Lloyd was driving me in a car along the narrow street on which the HAAA grounds front. There were a lot of cars parked, and a kid jumped out from between the cars. Uncle Lloyd slammed on the brakes, I was in the back seat, and my seven-year-old head slammed into the back of the front seat, opening up a cut over my right eye which our family doctor managed to sew up with a huge needle.

It was 1935. At the age of eleven I knew that something was wrong in the Rohmer household because from time to time I could hear my parents arguing with highly raised voices. It was a particularly uncomfortable time for me and for my tough young brother, who had arrived in 1931. Ron was tough indeed, strong, self-willed, and quite a determined little person.

Catastrophe struck our little family. I was told that my mother and father were going to divorce, whatever that meant. I soon found out it meant that my father and mother would no longer live together. It meant that my brother and my mother and I, with my grandmother, Lizzie Wright, who was undoubtedly a factor in the decision to divorce (an event that never occurred in the 1930s — I mean, no one got divorced) would move to California, as far away as possible from Hamilton. Grandmother Wright had relatives in Los Angeles. Grandmother would go and live with them, and mother, Ron, and I would find a place to live. It followed that my father would have to support us, which he did. My father, in his virile middle thirties, had found another woman, Jean Cline. His plan was to divorce mother and marry Jean, with whom he would have a child named Jane Rohmer.

I can still remember being seen off at the CNR station in Hamilton at the north end of James Street. Ernie came to see us off. It was a most unhappy, bewildering time.

We made our way through Chicago by train, then got on the Santa Fe railway headed for Los Angeles. It was a spectacularly beautiful train ride all across the country. At the wholesome age of eleven I really had no way of comprehending the nature of the split and the divorce and all of the things that went with it. All I knew was that my father had gotten rid of us and that we were going to make a new life in California.

My younger brother, Ron, and I at the Verdugo Road house in Pasadena, California.

When we arrived in Los Angeles, my mother, still a beautiful thing in her mid-thirties, was fortunate to find a house on Verdugo Road in Pasadena. It was rented from an older gentleman by the name of Mr. Fox who very quickly had big eyes for Marion Wright Rohmer, but that didn't interfere with our tenancy at his bungalow. I think he had a little house around the corner somewhere, so he didn't bother us all that much.

In the fall of 1935, it was time for me to go to school. I went to a pleasant public school headed by a motherly, grey-haired principal. My eighth-grade class was filled with kids who were twelve, thirteen, fourteen, most of them much taller than I. In fact, in the school class picture I look like a midget in comparison to all of them. But the girls looked after me and made sure everything was all right. The only problem I had with the school was that when they had assemblies in the morning, everyone was required to put hand over heart and swear allegiance to the American flag. For some reason I couldn't bring myself to do that. I was a Canadian, not an American!

In January 1936 I graduated from the public school with my class and went on to my first year of high school at Eagle Rock High School in Pasadena. It was a huge institution even then. Because I had little direction I elected to take all the easiest courses. One of the organizations I did join was the Reserve Officers Training Corps (ROTC), the famous American military body in all the high schools. One of the problems was that I was so small they didn't have a uniform that would fit me. I had a shirt that was all right and a pair of trousers that were shortened, but they didn't have a jacket small enough to be altered. And of course I had my wedge cap. I certainly enjoyed the ROTC time in the spring of 1936, particularly the marching and the handling of the old 303 rifle that one had to drill with. My biggest difficulty with the 303 was that when it stood beside me on the ground it was taller than I.

It was about this time that I became very unhappy in California. I didn't like the school situation, I missed Canada, and I missed the opportunity to see my father. In the past I had been a perfectly behaved little boy, but I suddenly started to rebel. One day I escaped out my bedroom window to do something that I had been instructed not to do. I suppose that the uprooting from Canada and being away from my father and all the turmoil that went with the dysfunctional family started me on a path of rebellion.

A young couple that managed the local motion picture theatre took pity on me and gave me a bit of unpaid work in their candy store and also in the theatre. I can remember in the theatre one Saturday afternoon sitting beside one of the Our Gang kids, Alfalfa. That was quite a thrill. But eventually I was so unhappy that Mother reluctantly agreed to consider moving back to Canada. Apparently she was quite lonely as well. So the decision was made that we would move back, this time not to Hamilton but to Windsor, Ontario, where her brother, Lloyd Wright, had been living for some years working successfully at Ford in the engineering department. And he had married Agnes Wellman, Aunty Agnes, a robust Windsor lady.

Eventually all the arrangements were made. We boarded the Santa Fe again and took it back to Chicago, then a train back to Detroit and Windsor, where Lloyd and Agnes were waiting for us. They had arranged for an apartment for Mother, Ron, and me on Goyeau Street near Jacksons Park. Lloyd and Agnes were not far away in a house and were able to take in my grandmother, Lizzie Wright, so she didn't have to live in the apartment with us. When mother tried to enroll me in the high school system in Windsor she discovered that my qualifications coming out of California were not good enough and I would have to go back into eighth grade. That was definitely not something I wanted to do.

Fortunately, she found that the Basilian priests of Assumption College had many American kids in their high school next to the Ambassador Bridge. The Basilians would take me, notwithstanding my lack of credentials. So I was enrolled at Assumption College in first year high school starting in the fall of 1936.

There were many wonderful priests and ecclesiastics (studying to be priests while teaching), but the man who took a great interest in me was one Father Vincent Guinan, a tall, round-faced Irishman, bald, with a red-haired fringe, probably around forty at that time. He was my algebra teacher but became much more than that. He decided that I should enter the public speaking contest against the school champion, Joe Fram. Father Guinan put me in the contest, then constructed a speech for me that began, "Under the spreading chestnut trees the village smithy snoozes, to him since 1923 have come no nags for shoeses." I don't know how my memorized speech ended, but I can tell you that my mother and her new-found boyfriend, Joe Junget (an American consulting engineer who was building the power plant at Ford's factory in Windsor), came to the public speaking contest to cheer me on. Between Father Guinan and mother and Joe's encouragement I managed to win the contest and beat Joe Fram.

That was the beginning of my so-called public speaking career, which in the law and the military and in other pursuits has often been extremely helpful in allowing me to make progress.

As to Father Guinan, I will revisit him in 1945 when he forcefully persuaded me to make a decision that would affect the rest of my life.

The next event was that Marion Wright Rohmer wanted to marry Joseph Junget. After some negotiating that I knew nothing about, my father agreed that I could come to Hamilton to live with him and Jean and their new baby, Jane. We were now into 1937. I had finished my high school year at Assumption College, and during the summer I made the move to Hamilton, where my father and Jean were living in an apartment on Wentworth Street South. Jean made a good effort to make me comfortable in the bosom of her family.

CHAPTER 3

Fort Erie and High School:
Kicked Out of the House

———◆———

B<small>Y 1937, MY FATHER,</small> E<small>RNIE</small> Rohmer, then a robust thirty-six-year-old, had developed a chain of gasoline service stations, operating under the name of Rohmer Service Stations Limited, into a group of four successful units in Hamilton, his hometown. That was quite an achievement in the middle of the Depression. He was famous in Hamilton from his Hamilton Tiger lacrosse exploits when they won the Mann Cup, the Canadian box lacrosse championship in 1933 (which was a major event in those days), and also for his football exploits when he played for the Hamilton Tigers and won the Grey Cup in 1929.

My father was now buying his gasoline wholesale in Buffalo through connections he had made there earlier when he was working for Arthur Maddigan.

In order to have much easier access to Buffalo, my father decided that he would move his family — his new wife, Jean Cline, my newly arrived half-sister, Jane, and me — to the small town of Fort Erie across the Niagara River from Buffalo.

Ernie found a suitable big old barn of a house just along the Niagara River Road to the north of Fort Erie at a little place called Cosy Dell. It was an old frame house separated from the river only by the Niagara Boulevard itself. To the west of the main house was an ancient water tower, its roof probably about fifty feet above the ground, quite an elaborate and unusual structure.

As soon as we moved into the Cosy Dell house I was installed in the local high school. I had gone directly from Assumption College first year of high school to Hamilton, where I had two or three weeks at

Central Collegiate, and then we moved to Fort Erie, so I was in second form, or grade 10.

My time at Fort Erie High School was to be a happy period that lasted through grade 12, or junior form. I would go to school to enjoy life and have a good time, but I was to rarely study or open a book during the years there. That was probably because of the environment that developed at Cosy Dell.

Soon after we moved into the house a lady called Mrs. Hildreth appeared as housekeeper along with her two daughters, both of whom were somewhat older than I. That was not a problem for me. I was lodged in a bedroom in the attic, well out of the way of any traffic on the lower floors. Then one day a strange woman arrived at the house. A short, grey-haired lady. I had no idea why she was there or who she was. Her stay was brief indeed — one day. The day after she left Mrs. Hildreth informed me that Jean was not well, and either the next day or the day after I was informed that Jean had died. I have never tracked the newspaper reports of the day or done any other research as to what happened, but my recollection will serve me for this purpose.

Evidently Jean had become pregnant shortly after we arrived at Cosy Dell. For some reason it was decided that she should have an abortion. Somehow my father must have found this grey-haired woman who offered that service. Where he found her I have no idea. She had come to Cosy Dell, done the operation, and left. What she left was Jean with an acute case of peritonitis, which killed her.

All this was way over my head except that, a few days after the event, after the police had been by to investigate, I found in the glove compartment of my father's car a note that he had written blaming himself for the event. The note was in preparation for his suicide or his departure from the scene in one way or another.

There was some form of court proceeding, probably an inquest. It was obviously a major event in the life of the people of the quiet town of Fort Erie. In the end, my father apparently was not charged. I do not recall what happened to the grey-haired woman who performed the abortion.

Looking back on the situation it is now clear to me that at my high school the teachers had developed a great deal of sympathy for little Richard Rohmer. Little I was, and at that point it must have been compelling for the compassionate team of teachers to be sorry for and protective of me.

The principal of the high school was a man who was to later (along with all of the rest of the teachers who had to deal with me) look after my interests. His name was Thompson. We called him Puffball, a term of endearment because he had a large girth. Then there was my favourite teacher, Miss Corrine Byers, later Mrs. Tostevin, who taught English and French. Orville Weaver was the science and chemistry teacher, who also coached the football and basketball teams. A red-haired man called MacKenzie taught mathematics, and a small, hugely deformed man with a wonderful personality, Frank Coombs, who was to marry the prettiest girl in town, taught Latin. It was one subject I paid attention to, and it has been very useful over my long life in terms of interpreting the meaning of English words. There were others in the teaching body who were of significance, but these were the main players so far as I was concerned.

After the furor over Jean Cline Rohmer's demise, my father spent a great deal of time in Buffalo, particularly in a nightclub called McVan's. He even took me there a couple of times, even though I was underage and, of course, had nothing to drink expect pop.

Indeed, the odd showgirl would turn up at the Cosy Dell location. After all, as I indicated, my father was a young, robust, athletic guy, good-looking, and he loved women.

But as to our own relationship, it was never close at all. In fact it was much to the contrary. His aspirations in a son were that he would be a big person like himself, totally athletic and able to play football, lacrosse, baseball, and everything else that was going — hockey, for example, in which he excelled. Instead of that, in those days, I was not what he expected in any way, shape, or form.

However, I did do the football thing in high school, playing on our junior team (we were all so young we didn't have a senior team). But my father would never come out to see us play against Welland or Ridgeway or Niagara Falls or anybody else, even though he had been a big football player himself. I played fullback and safety and if I do say so myself I didn't do a bad job. By 1940 our team won the Central Ontario Secondary School Association championship but were beaten out for the Ontario championship by Lindsay, a much bigger team, on an icy field in Toronto. Even that high level of achievement didn't attract my father to come and see what was happening on the football field.

I was on the school track team as well. Basketball was another area of involvement; I played on the school team through my entire period at Fort Erie high school.

Then there was the school play. The producer and director was the wonderful Miss Byers. She selected a play by Booth Tarkington. The production was *Clarence*, and the lead role was given to, guess who, Richard Rohmer. That was a most exciting time, going through the rehearsals with Anita Quested, Mary Schofield, and the others. My mother, then Marion Junget, made the effort to travel from Windsor to Fort Erie to see the play, and I can tell you I was most grateful to her for doing that.

Playing the main character in the Fort Erie High School production of Clarence *by Booth Tarkington, 1940.*

When I reached the age of sixteen my father decided that it was time for me to really go to work. He made me manager of his Fort Erie service station, a small, against-the-curb operation where I served gasoline while attempting to attend school at the same time. His priority was the service station and not school for me. He then opened another station in Stamford and I was plugged into it to take on the management, leaving Fort Erie to somebody else. In order to travel to work the first car I was able to buy was a Buick convertible, I think it was built in about 1929 or '30. It was a huge car with front and back seats and an engine that hissed to 40 miles per hour when it started to roar. It had huge spare tires mounted on each front fender. It was really something. My next car was a 1930 Ford with a rumble seat that spewed carbon monoxide into the driver's area at a great rate. Between those two vehicles I was able to drive precariously from Fort Erie to Cosy Dell and later to our new home at Black Creek on the Niagara Boulevard, roughly halfway between Fort Erie and Niagara Falls. On at least two occasions the carbon monoxide from the defective system in the Ford almost did me in late at night — put me to sleep, that is, and into the Niagara River. Close shaves, but it didn't happen.

My father had decided, when we were still living at Cosy Dell, that he would marry again. He found a really elegant Fort Erie lady, a widow (or was she divorced?) by the name of Marion Willson who came from a cultured family of border brokers with a brother, Ray Willson, who was a lawyer.

My father and Marion were married when we were still at Cosy Dell. She brought to the marriage an adopted daughter about my age. The presence of these two new women in the household was rather difficult for me to adjust to, to say the least. My new adopted step-sister's name was Sue. Shortly afterward, we all moved to Black Creek into a huge house there. It was fairly modern, with a big boathouse. It was much better than the Cosy Dell structure. At that point it was decided that my brother, Ron, seven years younger than I, should join the family. My mother and her Joe were about to move back to the United States, and Ron did not fit into her plans.

That experience for Ron was to be ultimately disastrous. He was in a home where there was no love shown for him. He was tough-minded and stubborn in any event. Ultimately, to more or less get rid of him, he was sent to Ridley College as a boarder, but, poor guy, he couldn't stand it there and his conduct was such that he was expelled. At that point in his life he had no one who loved him, and when I look at it it's a wonder he survived at all.

As for myself, finally the day of reckoning was close at hand. It was Christmas 1940. I was in Grade 12. Somehow I intercepted my Christmas report card. I think I had failed all six subjects. So instead of facing my father's unavoidable wrath I decided I would forge his signature to the report card. I am absolutely certain that Puffball Thompson and his people knew that the report card had been forged, but instead of blowing the whistle on me Mr. Thompson and his teachers decided that my interests would be best served by saying nothing to my father or to me, and so on I went merrily through to Easter 1941.

When the boom was lowered I was in Mr. Weaver's class at the front of the school building on the ground floor. I saw my father's car drive up to the front of the school. It was his Cadillac convertible, a beautiful machine which I had been allowed to drive from time to time. Out he stepped, dressed in his business suit with his white fedora squarely in place. He went up the walk toward the front door and disappeared from view. About fifteen minutes later he left. I knew what was coming.

A few moments later there was a knock on the door of Mr. Weaver's classroom. It was Mr. Thompson. He asked me to step outside into the hall.

He told me, "Dick, your father has finally found out that you signed your report card so I think you better go home and have a talk with him."

In retrospect, there was no doubt that Mr. Thompson had known from the very beginning that I had forged my father's signature. Puffball could see that I was happy in school even though my marks were dreadful, and I think that he understood what was going on. I immediately drove home to Black Creek. My father was waiting for me. After lecturing me strongly that I would never be good for anything he ordered me out of the house immediately: "Get some clothes and get out of here."

Which is exactly what I did.

Fortunately for me, our next door neighbour at Cosy Dell was a Fleet Aircraft Company executive by the name of Ab Silcox. A lean, wiry gentleman of dour mien but a kindly soul who had told me that if I ever needed a job to come and see him.

I was seventeen. Out of the house. And no money. I needed a job.

I immediately telephoned Mr. Silcox at Fleet and went out to see him. I was hired on the spot to do a clerical job in the purchasing office to start the next day.

I knew of a lady in Fort Erie who ran a boarding house. Yes, she had room for me, but I had to share it with another boarder by the name of Tex Wetherly, also a Fleet Aircraft worker but much older than I. Tex was a worldly fellow, mustache, full black hair, barrel-chested, a nice guy. So by the end of the day I had a job at Fleet and I had accommodation at the boarding house.

So far as my father and I were concerned we were finished with each other. He and his third wife must have been highly relieved to get rid of me. If they were, the feeling was certainly mutual.

I worked in my clerical job for about three months and then discovered that there was an opening on the floor of the factory in the unit that stripped down and rebuilt the Fleet Finch airplane. Fleet had produced it with great success as an elementary trainer for the Royal Canadian Air Force in the British Commonwealth Air Training Plan (BCATP).

Fleet was receiving back into its factory Fleet Finches that had run up hundreds of hours of flying time and had to be completely overhauled. Others had been damaged in minor crashes.

I had had no mechanical training, but in those turbulent days of 1941, when the whole of the nation was being galvanized into production of aircraft and weaponry and young men of the age of eighteen and above were joining up by the thousands, manufacturers such as Fleet had to take on people and then train them for the specific jobs that they were to do.

The work assigned to me was to learn how to install the Plexiglas coupe tops that covered the cockpits of the Fleet Finch. I had to first install the rails on each side of the cockpit then mount the Plexiglas sliding hoods with their wheels into the rail and adjust the whole mechanism so that the instructor pilot and the student could easily and quickly enter and exit the machine. Believe me, doing the job was no easy task, but I eventually started to get it right.

By the fall of 1941, Fleet was opening another factory at the Crumlin airport in London, Ontario. The plan was to move the Fleet Finch rebuild operation to London. I was asked if I would go there and continue my job. No question. I had no ties, and I was happy to do so. And so was Tex, now my good friend and, being so much older, my mentor.

So off we went to London. Tex had a contact who told him about a lady looking for boarders not far from Crumlin. So he made all the arrangements, and in due course we arrived at our new residence, where we were greeted by our seemingly elderly landlady (she was probably in her forties) and her husband. They were in a small bungalow with a spare room for their new tenants. It was the winter preceding Christmas of 1941 that we made our move. I can still remember clearly standing on the street corner of the main street just a few yards away from our house waiting for the bus in the mornings. It was cold, snowy, and uncomfortable. But I had a job, a raise in pay, and a comfortable place to live.

CHAPTER 4
Joining the Royal Canadian Air Force

W HEN JANUARY 1942 ARRIVED I decided to make the move to join the Royal Canadian Air Force. I had wanted to be a pilot ever since seeing my first airplane in Riverside Park in Buffalo at the age of three. Airplanes had fascinated and enchanted me all my life. That was my driving ambition. By this time it was my total wish to be able to join the Air Force, become a fighter pilot, and fly the already legendary Spitfires and Hurricanes. What a dream.

My birthday was January 24, 1924. Which meant that on January 24, 1942, I would be eighteen and the Royal Canadian Air Force would accept me — if, of course, I could pass all of the required examinations, particularly the physical.

About two weeks before my birthday I went to the London recruiting centre and began the documentation and processing, including the medicals, that were necessary to support my application for aircrew. To my great joy I passed everything with flying colours, and on the very day of my eighteenth birthday I was sworn in as a member of the Royal Canadian Air Force. That was undoubtedly one of the most significant turning points in my life because from that day my life has been shaped by the discipline of the military, the discipline of the fighter pilot, the discipline of being an officer of every rank starting from an aircraftsman second class (private) to a major-general in Her Majesty's Canadian Armed Forces, or air vice-marshal, my RCAF pre-Hellyer rank.

I said goodbye to my gang at the Fleet Aircraft at Crumlin, to Tex Wetherly, who was going to join the Air Force himself, and to my London landlady, and I was off by train to the RCAF's Manning Depot at the Canadian National Exhibition grounds in Toronto.

With the whole group of other raw, and I really mean raw, recruits I was taken into the maw of the great Cow Palace at the Exhibition grounds, where hundreds of us were billeted in double-decker metal bunks with a minimum of privacy and a maximum of things we had to do. Inoculations, uniforms, basic instruction on drills, how to salute, how to clean buttons and boots, what the ranks were, how to recognize an officer when you saw one, always to say "yes, sir" ... it was heavy-duty indoctrination right from the word go. But it was great and important fun.

We were all there for one purpose, and that was to fight the Hun and preserve freedom. The whole nation was involved in that single objective. No one questioned where the country was going and what our purpose was. All of us were proud, really proud, to be wearing the uniform of the Royal Canadian Air Force.

Aircrew were required to perform security guard duty at selected airbases around the country. You had to do a security guard stint of six or eight weeks before you could begin your aircrew training. It was a sort of penance ritual. About the end of February I was shipped off with a large contingent of fellow recruits to do security guard duty at the Royal Canadian Air Force main base at Trenton.

The Trenton airfield had been established before the war and was the crown jewel of the Royal Canadian Air Force as far as bases were concerned. In 1942 it was a Service Flying and Training School (SFTS), teaching recruit pilots to fly the two-seater, single-engine, low-wing Harvard trainer that had been bought from the Americans, with deliveries beginning even before the Japanese decided that the Americans were worthy of attack and visited Pearl Harbor on December 7, 1941.

I might add that in the group with which I went to Trenton, probably 40 percent were American boys who had come up to Canada to join up and who had been processed before Pearl Harbor. They had elected to stay on and be trained by the Canadians with a view to going back to the United States in a good position if they had their pilot's wings and possibly commissions as well.

Arriving at the Trenton air base we were given billets in the huge dormitories to the west of what is still the huge parade square in front of the administration building. We were briefed on our security guard duties and given our shifts of action. At an assigned time, we would be picked up from our billets and, taking the 303-calibre rifles that had been signed out to us, we would go off to one of the forty-foot towers that had been built around the perimeter of the airbase and from the perch at the top of the tower we would keep a watchful eye, be it day or night, on the area assigned to us. It was one person per perch. Of course it was cold, uncomfortable, and an unusual position for a novice teenager to be in. But that's what we had to do. About the only person I can recall from that period countless years ago was the great Jake Gaudaur, the Hamilton football hero who later reached heights in the Canadian Football League.

On the fabled parade square at Trenton we were soon under the heel, thumb, and command of the legendary Sergeant-Major Long John Silver, who marched us around mercilessly in our platoons of twenty or thirty. This happened day after day, until one day Long John Silver, a white-haired, portly gentleman (but tough as nails), who must have then been in his fifties, decided that I really looked too young and inno-cent to be out on the parade square. He assigned me to a clerk's job in the headquarters building, a respite which I was very pleased to have. It gave me a relief not only from the parade square but also from the dreadful drudgery of getting up in a watchtower and trying to stay awake while watching for subversives or the enemy, who might be infil-trating the repair depot that was our prime guarding place on the west side of the airport. On top of that, the girls in the administrative office were very solicitous of my welfare and so what had been a period of dark, dreary drudgery turned into a session of comfortable delight.

From the Trenton scene, with other graduates of the security guard system, our group was assigned to Number 1 Initial Training School (Number 1 ITS) of the Royal Canadian Air Force, located at the old Toronto Hunt Club premises at 1107 Avenue Road on its east side just north of Eglinton Avenue in Toronto.

Number 1 ITS was the first true step in the path to aircrew training. By that time April had arrived and we were ready for immersion again into parade square drills as well as into the basics of ground school instruction on various aspects of flying.

We were given aptitude tests and time "flying" in basic Link trainers, which were designed to give us some primitive feel of flying an airplane. We were put in the great machine, hurled around in a huge circle, and test-ed on our ability to withstand the force of gravity (or G-factor). We were examined for our eyesight. You had to have 20/20 vision, and you could not under any circumstances be colour-blind.

Number 1 ITS was an extremely important institution: there it was decided whether you would be trained as a pilot, a navigator, a wireless operator, or an air gunner. In those days the demand for aircrew was extremely high, as the flow of aircraft into the arsenal of the RAF and RCAF in the United Kingdom began to grow and the bombing

Leading aircraftsman Richard Rohmer in the summer of 1942 at #1 Initial Training School, RCAF, 1107 Avenue Road, Toronto.

attacks on targets in France, Europe, and in particular Germany were beginning in strength.

As it happened, I had a cousin of my mother who was in a senior administrative position at Number 1 ITS. His name was Tom White. Squadron Leader White, being one of the senior officers, was anxious to ensure that I received no special favours from him. But the tough drill corporal assigned to our flight and class was bound and determined that because I was a relative of White, I would get the toughest treatment that he, Corporal Anderson, could hand out. I tell you he gave me a terrible going over for weeks, but he didn't break either my spirit or the will to succeed. And I never did complain to Tom White, but was I ever a target!

We had two officers in charge of our class. One of them was another football legend in his own time, manager of the Argonaut football team and a great player, Lew Hayman. The other was a pleasant, round-faced, portly gentleman of flying officer rank by the name of Birge, who, I am sure, had no military experience until the day he put on his officer's uniform. It didn't matter. Between the tough-as-nails corporal and all of the instructors qualified in ground school instruction we received very good fundamental, preliminary aircrew and military training in the weeks that we were at Number 1 ITS. It was a good summer.

CHAPTER 5

Flying Training Windsor and Aylmer:
Wings and the New Pilot Officer

B Y HAPPY FORTUNE I WAS selected for pilot training and posted to Number 7 Elementary Flying and Training School (EFTS) at Windsor, Ontario. I had many ties there as a result of living in Windsor with my mother and brother in the middle 1930s.

At Elementary Flying and Training School in
Windsor in 1942. I am in the top row at the far left.

The Windsor EFTS school was equipped with the De Havilland Tiger Moth biplane, an excellent performer that, along with the Fleet Finch, proved to be the backbone of the British Commonwealth Air Training Plan for *ab initio* pilot training in Canada.

As a matter of dress we aircrew trainees were required to wear a white patch at the front of our wedge caps. That signified to the world and to the rest of RCAF that we were in the elite aircrew group. It was a good idea psychologically because it gave us a little mental boost. At Windsor we were in barracks probably of about forty men, once again in double-decker bunks with little privacy, but, after all, who needed it? The instructors, both aircrew and ground crew, were all civilian, except a flight lieutenant of the RCAF acting as a liaison supervising the quality and standards of the training.

We would receive approximately seventy-five hours of flying training at Windsor, going solo after about eight hours of dual instruction. Then after a period of several weeks to obtain that level of experience we would be sent off to the next level of training at one of the many Service Flying and Training Schools, where we would be trained on the single-engine Harvard and Yale aircraft. The alternative was to be sent to a twin-engine SFTS, which would have either the British Anson or the American Cessna. The Cessnas were in the western provinces, and the Ansons were in the east at such locations as Brantford.

My time at the Windsor EFTS was a most successful phase in my RCAF training. My instructor, Peter McKenzie, was an excellent teacher. We hit it off very well — so well, in fact, that at the end of the training session, having done tests in solo and aerobatics and instruments and everything else, I reportedly obtained the highest marks (on a final test flight done by Chief Instructor George Stewart) achieved by anyone during the time that the EFTS was in operation. The same with my ground school marks. What a far cry from the marks that I had achieved at Fort Erie high school. It's amazing what motivation can do for you — whether you're young or old.

The Tiger Moth was a beautiful machine on which to learn to fly. It was challenging, to say the least, in its tail-dragger demands. Tail-dragger, of course, means that when the aircraft is on the ground, its tail sits on the ground on its tail wheel or skid, as the case may be. Our Tiger Moths had skids, which meant that in order to steer the aircraft on the ground the brakes had to be utilized fully and heavily.

After a big graduation party at the hotel at the northeast corner of the main intersection just to the west of what is now the airport terminal building (the hotel is long gone), the members of our class were off to our various designated Service Flying and Training Schools. Our operational hangar at the Windsor EFTS is still standing and in operation. In 1995 I had the privilege of being the chief guest of honour and speaker at a reunion of all of those ancient souls who had gone through the EFTS during the Second World War. It was a heavily attended event that took place in and around the hangar and was a great success.

In the fall of 1942 I was posted to the SFTS at Aylmer, Ontario, where the deputy flight commander of A flight was waiting for me. He was a diminutive man with an ego double the size of his stature. He had looked over the records of those assigned to his flight from Windsor and decided that since he was the top instructor he should get the top student. Whereas Peter McKenzie and I had gotten on extremely well, my relationship with this little man was a disaster from the very beginning.

As our flying training progressed at Aylmer, it was arranged that I should have a different instructor because of the personality clash I had with the deputy flight commander. Everything began to work out very well. In the final stages of our training our class moved to the auxiliary airfield near St. Thomas, where we undertook our advanced flying training preparatory to receiving our wings. We had a large number of Australians in our class. They were a grand bunch with their very light blue uniforms, broad accents, and general flamboyance. One thing that stuck out in my mind from those days was that the Australians were either very good pilots or very poor. We lost at least three of them in crashes, and perhaps there were even more.

The aircraft in use at Number 7 SFTS Aylmer was the marvellous Harvard, the North American aircraft product that was the star single-engine trainer used by the RCAF in the British Commonwealth Air Training Plan. The yellow Harvard had a huge Pratt & Whitney engine, a retractable undercarriage, and it was as heavy as the Spitfire (perhaps heavier). It was a superb trainer in which to fly to get one's wings. By graduation time I had over one hundred hours on the Harvard. My flying and ground school marks were sufficient to earn me a commission as a pilot officer at the same time I received my wings in March 1943.

There was a defect in the system at that time: some of the graduates would receive commissions and others would be promoted only to the rank of sergeant. In other words, there was a vast class distinction that was unjustified and unfair.

As a result, a good many of my really outstanding classmates wound up as sergeants. In particular there was my close pal from Georgia, Frank (Gator) Osteen, a wry, taciturn, outspoken person who clearly turned off the officers who were assessing whether one had the qualities to carry a commission or not.

Gator was one of the several Americans in our class who had come up from the States either before or just at the time of the Japanese attack at Pearl Harbor. As an aside, in 1996, at a cocktail reception given by Barrick Gold and Peter Munk at the Toronto Club, the first President George Bush told me that he had decided to come up to Canada to join the RCAF and was all set to go when Pearl Harbor occurred. He, of course, went into the American Navy as a pilot and was ultimately shot down and rescued. Who knows, if he had made the move to Canada, George Bush, Sr., could well have been a class-mate at Windsor and Aylmer, and the list of U.S. presidents would have been somewhat different.

The dinner agenda and menu for the graduation festivities of my class on March 4, 1943, was sent on to me years later by one of our instructors, Flight Lieutenant Norwood. It is one of my treasures.

The protocol before the graduation dinner had to do with uni-forms. If you knew you were going to be getting a commission you had to get fitted and order a pilot officer's uniform. If you were going to graduate as a sergeant it was simply a matter of having someone stitch sergeant's stripes on each arm of your ordinary blue uniform.

For those who were to be commissioned there was immediate access to a Toronto tailor who set up shop in a hotel in Aylmer just about a week before graduation. As soon as I knew I was on the commission list, I went to be measured with the promise that he would have the pilot officer's uniform back to me in time for graduation. I can remember very clearly getting measured and feeling that I had won the world's top prize, which indeed I had. The plan was that as soon as the wing's parade was finished and the graduation dinner done, then we were out of there, out of Aylmer and ready to go. That meant the newly minted pilot officers had to have their uniforms ready to put on. As I recall, we had an allowance for the uniform, so financing this enormous change in garb was not a problem. On March 4, 1943, about one year and two months after I had survived all the examinations and entered the RCAF, I was a fully qualified nineteen-year-old RCAF Pilot Officer ready to go on to the next adventure.

That next adventure took place at the officer's mess of the RCAF station at Hagersville.

On a visit to Hamilton immediately after my graduation, the newly minted Pilot Officer Rohmer had accidentally met Flight Officer Ann Dunn of the marvellous Dunn family of Fort Erie. I had known all of them while I was going to high school there. Ann, who was five years older than I and a university graduate, was stationed at the RCAF training base at Hagersville. She benignly took it upon herself to invite this brand new pilot officer out to Hagersville for the graduation banquet of the class there. I accepted without any hesitation. After all, I had never been in an officer's mess before. Nor by this time had I had any hard liquor or even beer to drink!

Ann picked me up in her car at my father's house on Melrose Avenue in Hamilton and off we went. I was proudly dressed in my pilot officer's uniform with my flat hat on jauntily. It was a grand evening, virtually petrifying for me as I walked into an officer's mess for the first time. The place was filled with flying officers, flight lieutenants, squadron leaders, and even a wing commander! It was also an edifying evening at which I met the second-in-command of the Hagersville flying operations, one Flight Lieutenant "Mid" Middleton. I was in absolute awe of this powerful person, whom I distinctly remember leaning on the bar as he downed whatever it was that he was drinking at the time. Middleton and I were destined to meet again a year and a half later when he joined 430 Squadron when we were at an airfield called Diest Schaffen in Belgium. At that point our roles would be reversed, because by that time I would be one of the most experienced pilots in 430 Squadron, a fighter reconnaissance unit on Mustang I fighter aircraft. Middleton arrived to join the unit as a novice Mustang pilot. In the operations that we flew together I would be the leader and the instructor.

However, at that long-ago evening at RCAF station Hagersville, I had no briefing as to how to behave. I was just there and, as I said, in awe of Middleton and his experienced colleagues.

I happily survived that wonderful evening, arrived safely home, and awaited my orders, which soon came. I was instructed to proceed to Halifax and get properly equipped for an ocean crossing at the holding depot there and be prepared to sail to the United Kingdom.

My father and his wife, Marion, saw me off at the Toronto, Hamilton and Buffalo Railway station on James Street South. It was the same station where my father had returned from his Grey Cup victory in 1929 with the Hamilton Tiger football team and later in 1933 from his Mann Cup victory with the Hamilton Tiger lacrosse team champions.

I think that at that point my father could not have helped being at least slightly proud of me. I had my gorgeous blue greatcoat on with its epaulettes sporting my pilot officer's rank, my officer's flat hat, blue shirt, and black tie. I was a modern pilot officer to say the least. And nineteen years old plus two months.

When I arrived in Toronto on the TH&B Railway I had to stay overnight in order to catch the troop train out to Halifax the next morning. There was Ann Dunn again, and by this time I was acquiring a taste for beer. We had a grand evening at the Royal York, shook hands, perhaps there was a kiss on the cheek. Then she was gone to I know not where.

CHAPTER 6
Deadly Convoy Across the Atlantic

———◆———

A T THE HOLDING DEPOT AT Halifax I was assigned to be the senior officer out of six RCAF pilot officers designated to go on board a ship called the *Torr Head*. At least one man from my SFTS course, Jack Leach, an American, was part of our team. On the specified date all six of us boarded a tender vessel in Halifax harbour and went out to board the *Torr Head*, which turned out to be an old, small Irish freighter with an even older captain. He was a short, round, white-haired man who had been called out of retirement to be master of this vintage one-stacker vessel loaded with the Good Lord only knew what. We never did find out. Probably we were afraid to ask in case someone said we were loaded with bombs and other ammunition.

As the officer in charge of our Air Force team of six, I had to liaise with the captain and his first mate. After some discussion and giving of directions, we were led to our two-to-a-room cabins. We settled in with our kit bags and dressed in working clothes composed of our battledress jackets and trousers. The dress blue officer's uniform that I had bought was stashed away. A shirt with a scarf at the neck and drill boots were also in the order of dress. We wore our wedge caps instead of the flat hat, which was left below in the cabin. Everything shipshape, we were ready for our marvellous cruise across the Atlantic as part of Convoy X.

What we uninformed Air Force sprogs didn't know was that March and April 1943 was the time when the German U-boat packs were at their strongest, most vicious, and most deadly. I was about to spend the ten most frightening days I have ever experienced. The combination of terror of the U-boat attacks and being seasick was almost too much. What would have been totally too much would have been if the *Torr Head* had been sunk by a torpedo or by shells. We were to be targets of both.

As ship after ship in the convoy left the sanctuary of the Halifax harbour they manoeuvred into their assigned positions in the convoy, with the destroyers forming up on each side. Our convoy came together just outside the Halifax harbour. Then the whole mass slowly moved to the east as it began its transit across the Atlantic.

It was on the second day, when we were beyond air cover out of Dartmouth, that the U-boat attacks began in daylight. It was a terrible shock to see a ship to our right or left or ahead of us or behind blow up with a terrible, deafening explosion and smoke and fire as the single torpedo would hit it. As soon as the first attack began I scrambled up to the bridge with my life-jacket on to stand beside the diminutive, ancient captain and listen to his Irish cursing as the first ship went down and then the second and then the third. We were at the absolute mercy of that U-boat pack. We hauled in survivors from a boat from the first or second ship that went down. We had a torpedo run right by us, by our bow, on at least on three occasions. The destroyers would dart into the centre of the convoy and let off depth charges. Then at night the attack would continue with star shells being set up by the destroyers to try to find the surfaced U-boats. On one of those nights we could hear the guns from the U-boats and shells whistling by us.

I tell you, it was a long, terrifying experience. I never took off my life jacket from the time of the first attack until we arrived in the Liverpool harbour. I slept in it, washed in it, did everything with that life jacket on because you never knew from one minute to the next whether a torpedo was going to be into the *Torr Head*. Whether you were sleeping or in one of the heads (toilets) when that torpedo arrived, if it didn't kill you then you had to get on deck immediately and be prepared to get into one of the lifeboats or, for that matter, jump into the killing sea — with its temperature you could survive only a matter of a few minutes before the cold finished you off.

The loss of men, freighters, and precious cargoes out of our convoy was phenomenal.

But we did make it to Liverpool, with its bustling cranes and harbour filled by ships being unloaded with absolutely vital supplies: food, clothing, ammunition, guns, aircraft, fuel, everything necessary to keep the United Kingdom alive and ready to defend the British Isles. At the same time, the Brits had to stockpile and prepare on a long-term basis for the expected Allied invasion somewhere against the French coasts. But that was way off in the future, and we lowly pilot officers were concerned only with our own survival, food, drink, and lodging.

We said a fond and thankful goodbye to *Torr Head*, her captain and crew, and in particular the men in the galley who had prepared and served the meals on the way across (a large number of eggs were consumed). We were then sent off by train to Bournemouth on the south coast of England. The Royal Canadian Air Force had selected it as the town where it would find a sufficient amount of lodging for all of its people arriving in England, a sort of manning depot for aircrew and ground crew alike. Bournemouth was and is a famous seaside resort. It had any number of small hotels that had been commandeered by the RCAF, with, of course, the approval of the Royal Air Force, which really ran everything at that stage. At that point we knew very little about the battle for even the slightest amount of independence that had to be fought by the leaders of the RCAF. They were under the grinding, intolerant heels of the British Royal Air Force, who regarded the Canadians as low-life colonials.

As I waited for a posting out to an Advanced Flying Unit (AFU), life in Bournemouth for three or four weeks was relatively peaceful and civilized. There were concerts in the restaurant of the main department store in the centre of town next to the park. There were marching drills to keep us occupied and classes in Air Force matters and safety gas masks and all that sort of thing.

There was one exciting episode during my Bournemouth stay. I had walked along the roadway from the centre of town along the beach edge and cliff westerly up toward the hotel in which I was billeted. It was midday. The weather was clear and virtually cloudless. The temperature was moderate, so I did not have on my greatcoat. I looked out south from my vantage point on the cliff as I was walking. There coming toward me from the south, their propellers almost touching the water, was a squadron of Spitfires spread out in a kind of line-abreast formation. They were coming straight at me. Spitfires? In a split second I recognized that they weren't Spitfires but German Focke-Wulf 190s, fighter bombers. The purpose of their visit was to attack anything that moved and to drop their lovely bombs. By the time I put all this together they had already opened fire, fortunately not in my direct direction. I scuttled for a basement entrance, and as I ran I saw a young boy, probably about eight years old, in my path. I grabbed him and practically carried him down the steps to an open stairwell that I thought would give us haven. As the two of us got to the bottom of the stairs I looked up just as a 190 was going by. I could have reached out and almost touched the aircraft. There was the pilot looking down at me, the black German iron cross painted on the side of his sleek machine. In the distance the sound of bombs detonating could be heard along with a clatter of machine-gun fire. I did not hear any anti-aircraft weaponry because the attack was a successful surprise venture. The anti-aircraft crews had no time to man their guns. Then they were gone, all ten or twelve of them, as quickly as they had come, sneaking back south toward the French coast, probably turning east after they were out a short distance. They were hightailing it for their base in the Pas-de-Calais area, getting as far away from the British coast as possible so as to avoid interception by the ever alert Spitfire squadrons.

That was my first sighting of the vaunted German fighter aircraft, the Focke-Wulf 190. It would not be my last by any means.

While at Bournemouth we were subjected to a panel of senior pilots who were to select who was to be posted to fighters, bombers, coastal command, or whatever. The panel I was confronted with raised the question of my being an instructor, to which I responded that I was far too young (I looked to be about sixteen even though I was nineteen) and I would be far more valuable as a fighter pilot. Of course, they had in front of them my flying training records, which told them I might well make a good instructor at some Advanced Flying Unit or at some other no-thrill flying training activity. Fortunately, my argument was persuasive. They agreed with me and designated me to go into fighter aircraft but first of all to an AFU.

In a few days that's where I went. The location and the number of the AFU has escaped my records for the moment. It was a grass airfield somewhere in the middle part of the south of England. There we were trained on the single-engine Miles Master, a two-place (front/rear), wide-undercarriaged tail-dragger that was the advanced trainer for the Royal Air Force. Several hours were required in training on the Master before being sent off to an Operational Training Unit (OTU), where one would convert to the Spitfire or, as matters turned out for me, to the recently arrived Mustang I, a single-engine fighter built by North American Aircraft. Like all RCAF would-be fighter pilots I was focused on going to a Spitfire OTU and then to one of the Canadian squadrons located in the southern and southeastern parts of England with ready access to the English Channel and the coast of France.

But that was not to be.

CHAPTER 7
Introduction to the Mustang I Fighter

———◆———

ONE DAY IN THE MIDDLE of our training sessions a pair of beautiful new Mustang Is flew in and landed at our AFU. They were piloted by Canadians who had graduated from that same AFU a few months before.

We were invited to go and take a good look at the Mustangs. I must say I was really impressed with the huge, beautifully built aircraft that stood before me. One of the Mustang pilots was a flight lieutenant by the name of Jack Watts, a wonderful man who would later become very much a part of my life with 430 Squadron and post-war as well.

Jack was an affable, pleasant, sort of backcountry boy with a remarkable giggle that he thought was a laugh. He showed me all the features of the Mustang and its large cockpit. He persuaded me to apply to go to the Mustang Operational Training Unit, number 41 OTU at Hawarden near Chester in the west of England. If I went to 41 OTU I would be converted onto the Mustang and trained for visual reconnaissance (recce), photographic recce, and artillery direction in support of the Army. Jack Watts sold me on the Mustangs that day. I applied for and was posted to 41 OTU at Hawarden, and in June 1943 I arrived at that unit along with twenty-three other pilots to be converted.

The training was intense, especially the groundwork that introduced us to our main role of expert map reading and being able to pinpoint the location of tanks, guns, vehicles, or troops. There was also a low-level oblique (side-pointing) photography role, as well as vertical photography from a higher level. The third main task was the direction of artillery fire, for which we ultimately were trained in special missions at the Salisbury Plains, where we learned to range the 25-pounder guns. As with the Advanced Flying Unit, 41 OTU was a British Royal Air Force operation and so it was necessary for us Canadians to adjust to the environment of the RAF — the officers' mess, the billeting, the food, the discipline, the bar. Not a difficult task if you're nineteen and wide open for advice, instruction, and learning.

The first objective at Hawarden was to learn to fly the Mustang. Simulated training came first on the ubiquitous Miles Master, doing circuits with all the right speeds and engine indicators going that would be similar to the Mustang. Then it was a matter of committing to memory the Mustang I handbook, a very small document. Included were the takeoff, landing, cruising, and stalling speeds, the engine instruments, the rpm (propeller revolutions per minute) … everything that had to be absorbed. The throttle, stick, gun positions, rudder pedals, brakes, everything had to be memorized and the drills absolutely perfect. Then, by yourself, you were sitting in the machine, going through the starting procedures, starting the big Allison engine, everything functioning normally, oil pressure okay, oil temperature all right, fuel okay, controls free and moving well. The Mustang had been built for six-foot-two American boys. The rudder pedals with their toe brakes could only come back so far. So it was necessary for me to have two pillows behind my back in order to properly be able to reach the rudder pedals and to activate the brakes. Not a problem. My parachute was always snug and comfortable. Just taxiing the Mustang for the first time was an exceptional thrill. It was like driving a huge, brand new Cadillac or Jaguar, solid, smooth, a confidence-building experience.

Then it was time for the first takeoff. When the run-up of the engine was completed, we checked the mags and again all the temperatures and pressures. Everything was working properly, the tail wheel was locked, the underbelly air scoop was in the right position, and I was cleared to go. As I put the throttle to the engine and it went to full power the Mustang quickly gathered speed. I lifted the tail slightly, and before I knew it I was off the ground. Undercarriage up, throttle at full bore, I quickly reached climbing speed and was initiated into the beautiful, gorgeous Mustang. After completing the first set of required manoeuvres, the next and biggest step was landing for the first time. Throttle partly back, speed back, flaps down, undercarriage down, approach from a certain distance and height. No problem. The tail down in the proper tail-dragger position for a three-point landing and with a bit of a jiggle on touchdown my machine was on the ground rolling nicely. Flaps up, into the assigned parking bay. Turn into the required parking position, stop, shut the aircraft down. It was done, an incredible experience. There would be hundreds of takeoffs and landings and plenty of hair-raising experiences in the Mustang for me from that day in June 1943 through to the day I left 430 Squadron at Eindhoven in Holland, having finished my tour of operations. By then, the end of November 1944, I was thin, gaunt, and had added about five years in age in that year and a half.

The class of young pilots being converted onto the Mustang at Hawarden was made up of a motley crew from Czechoslovakia, the United Kingdom, Canada, Australia, and one lad called Tubby from New Zealand.

There was a silent-type Brit about whom we knew very little except that he was a cultured guy, probably close to thirty years of age, which meant that he was very old in the normal context of things. He was a flight lieutenant by the name of Jock Colville. Jock was a pleasant man who usually kept to himself and never spoke about his background. He and I got on very well, he being an almost fatherly type to me.

When we were at the auxiliary airport of 41 OTU out in the remote areas away from Chester and Hawarden we really got into flying the airplane, particularly at low level, I mean right on the deck, where we would often have to operate as fighter reconnaissance pilots. During our weeks at the auxiliary field we progressed rapidly in our skills in handling the beautiful Mustang airplane. However, on one takeoff I pulled up the undercarriage just a little too early. As the undercarriage was coming up, the aircraft sank slightly and the retracting right wheel touched the ground. However, I did not hit the pavement with my propeller. So I got away with it, as they say.

During the middle of our time at the auxiliary airfield it was appropriate to have a class photograph.

I can remember all of us gathering with lots of chatter in front of the camera. As it happened I wound up sitting beside Jock Colville, as the photograph will show. Beside Jock is my New Zealand friend, Tubby. Most of the other identifications have slipped my memory except for my American classmate from the Windsor beginning, Jack Leach, who is in the back row number four from the right.

#41 Operational Training Unit at Hawarden, England.
I am in the first row, far right, next to my friend Jock Colville.

When the course was completed we were all posted to our various squadrons. At that point there were three Canadian fighter reconnaissance Mustang squadrons: 400, 414, and 430. And there were a similar number of Royal Air Force units. Jock Colville was posted to one of those, 168 Squadron. I went to 430 Squadron, where my friend Flight Lieutenant Jack Watts was a flight commander; there were two flights, A and B, in each squadron.

I would not see Jock Colville again, although I spoke with him by telephone twice while I was in England in the 1960s, when he was Sir Jock Colville.

Sir Jock? Indeed, as I discovered much later, Jock was in fact Winston Churchill's private secretary.

Accepting Colville's pleading (Colville being a fully trained pilot and member of the Royal Air Force Auxiliary), the great man Churchill had agreed to let Colville take a leave of absence from his post as his private secretary so that he could train on the Mustang, join a Royal Air Force fighter reconnaissance squadron, and take part in the upcoming D-Day operations (still a long way off). Jock was not permitted to go on an operational sortie until D-Day because, if captured, he had far too much secret information. He took part in 168 Squadron's operations in the Battle of Normandy from June 6 to August 20 and then went back to serve his marvellous master at 10 Downing Street. 168 Squadron was based with my 430 Squadron and 39 Recce at our B8 airfield base at Magny in Normandy, but they had their own section of B8 and we never had contact with Jock and his RAF colleagues.

Years after the war Jock wrote a book about his time and experiences with Winston Churchill. In his book, Sir Jock took critical aim at the credibility of Sir William Stephenson, the famous Canadian spymaster immortalized in the book *The Man Called Intrepid* by William Stevenson.

As the fickle finger of fate would have it, and that's another story, during the last five years of Sir William's life in Bermuda he became my "father figure." My wife, Mary-O, and I spent much time with him. We were very close. We never spoke about Jock Colville.

Peculiar how the circle of life can link a person such as myself to Jock Colville on the one hand in the early 1940s and to one of his ultimate targets for denigration, Sir William Stephenson, in the 1980s and '90s.

In basic terms, Sir Jock maintained that contrary to all reports Sir William really never had any direct contact with Churchill, even though Sir William was given Churchill's full authority to act as the British spymaster in the United States and Bermuda during the crucial years of the war.

My theory about Colville's position is that Sir William's meetings with Churchill were in keeping with the operation of a true spymaster. In other words, they were covert, without record, and away from 10 Downing Street, so that in the event William Stephenson was caught or otherwise exposed in the United States prior to or after the Americans getting into the war, there could be no track back to Churchill at all.

Be that as it may, Sir Jock Colville had his place in history and in my life. He died in the 1980s.

When our fighter reconnaissance training at 41 OTU was completed, we were assigned to our respective squadrons. I was sent to 430 Squadron of the Royal Canadian Air Force based at the first Tactical Airfield at Great Chart near Ashford in Kent.

CHAPTER 8

430 Squadron at Ashford and Gatwick

———◆———

Two other Canadians on the course were posted with me to 430
Squadron. The two were Flying Officer Butch Butchart, a dour, taciturn, highly skilled bush pilot from the North Bay and Sudbury area
who was probably about thirty by that time, and Flying Officer Ed
Geddes, twenty-one, a round-faced, mustached, quiet type, a solid man
from the West. The three of us packed our bags and took the train from
Chester to London and from there to a town to the southeast of London
called Ashford in Kent.

We arrived at the Ashford train station in the late afternoon of
September 22, 1943, where we were met by a duty driver and truck from
our new squadron. In the back of the canvas-topped vehicle with our
bags we bumped along west from Ashford to a farmer's field near a place
called Great Chart.

The field was owned by one Lord Strobolgi and had been converted into the first tactical airfield of what was known as the Second
Tactical Air Force (2nd TAF). The long east-west field of the farm had
been graded by the bulldozers of British Army engineers to make a
smooth dirt airstrip. It would be a model for the kind that would be created in Normandy less than a year later.

There was also an intersecting north-south strip, but it was the east-
west that was the main runway.

When we arrived at Lord Strobolgi's estate it was about seven
in the evening, still lots of light. The beautiful Mustangs were lined
up on the south side of the airstrip in a long row. They belonged to
430 Squadron. The other two units, 400 and 414, were not present at
that location.

To the south of the row of Mustangs were the administrative tents, fresh and brown, standing like irregular mushrooms in a row.

Our driver took us to the big tent in the middle. The three of us went inside, expecting to find at least a few people ready to receive us, look after our documents, and tell us where to go. Instead there were two people at the several tables. One was a clerk and the other was a small boy who looked to be about twelve years old. He was about four feet tall, dressed in a flight lieutenant's uniform and wearing a wedge cap. Butchart whispered to me, "Who the hell is the mascot?" We soon found out.

He was the delightful Hart Massey, the brilliant son of the Canadian high commissioner to the United Kingdom, Vincent Massey. Hart had been afflicted by an ailment that had struck him at about the age of ten or twelve. A decision had to be made by his parents at the time: either an operation that would stunt his growth or the loss of his eyesight. His parents decided for the surgery. Hart was both an administrative and an intelligence officer. He was there to welcome us and to help us get directed to our accommodations, which were two-man tents set up in another area to the west of the landing strip.

But where was everybody? There was no one around! They were at the local pub, at least all our pilots were. By the time we had a quick meal in the mess tent it was getting dark. The decision was made that Massey would lead us to the pub. Flashlight in hand in the now gathering darkness, the intrepid Hart took us across fields along paths and over fence stiles. We had no idea where we were or for that matter where we were going except that it was to a pub. Finally, after trekking for about twenty minutes, there appeared against the black sky a silhouette of a tall building. Not a light was to be seen. It was the pub, out in the middle of nowhere, looming ominously but invitingly. Massey led us to the front door, opened it, and there down the hall, perhaps forty feet away, was a huge pub room from which was flowing the sound of many male voices lifted in song. As we marched down the corridor we could see that in the smoke-filled room ahead of us there were some fifteen or twenty pilots. They were the officers of 430 Squadron.

When we new boys entered the singing stopped and shouts of welcome took its place. These were our new brothers, and they welcomed us with open arms. There were Jack Watts, Dick Manser, Red

Moore, Frank Chesters (the squadron leader), Freddy Bryon, and Jack Cox, to name a few.

Our welcome completed, we dove into the tomato sandwiches, mild and bitter and lager, and cigarettes (because we all smoked in those days, it was the thing to do). And then it was back to songs, led by the great voice of the round and jolly Flight Lieutenant Dick Manser.

That was my introduction to 430 Squadron and the fine young pilots who comprised it. Many of them would not survive the upcoming operations: D-Day, the Battle of Normandy, and operations in northwest Europe. But at that moment in the pub near Ashford we all knew that every one of us would survive and nothing would happen to us individually or collectively, which is the only way that you can go into battle against an enemy who is bound and determined to kill you and is in possession of airplanes, guns, and weaponry capable of doing so.

Let me leap ahead to 1994.

It was the fiftieth anniversary of D-Day, a time of nostalgia, going back and revisiting old airfields and places in and around London and Normandy.

One of the objectives during that visit to England was to find the site of our 1943 airfield on Lord Strobolgi's estate. I really had no idea where it was except that my memory told me that it was to the west of Ashford. By coincidence my old and dear friend Macklin Hancock, one of the world's great land use planners and environmentalists, with whom I had worked many times, owned a historic family house at Ashford which we had been able to lease from him for the week that we wanted to spend in the area.

Mary-O and I arrived at Macklin's house, set up shop, and began the quest to find Lord Strobolgi's estate. Frankly, I didn't know where to start except that perhaps Mary-O and I should do a square search of the area to the west of Ashford in our rented car. In addition to finding Lord Strobolgi's estate, one of the objectives was to find that magic pub where I had first met my squadron fifty-one years earlier.

The first day of scouring the area to the west of Ashford produced no scenes that were in any way able to jog my memory. Nothing seemed to fit. Mary-O and I stopped a gentleman leading a horse on a back road to ask him if he knew anything about a wartime airfield in the area. Both he and the horse said nay (neigh) at the same time. He muttered the name of some local who had been around for a hundred years and said perhaps I should try him. That evening I tracked that worthy down by telephone. He told me that the person I should be in touch with was Bob Goddard, who lived at Great Chart. We looked up Great Chart on our maps. There it was, just to the west of Ashford. It looked like a tiny hamlet, which indeed it was.

My next telephone call was to Bob Goddard, and I hit pay dirt. "Oh yes," he said, "I remember the Mustangs very well." He continued, "I was at school when they first came in, I was ten years old and when the first ones landed we couldn't wait. Finally when school was out I ran the whole mile to the farm where they had landed. It was a bloody fantastic sight!"

Bob Goddard knew exactly where it was that I wanted to go. Arrangements were made for Mary-O and me to go to his farm the next day. His farmhouse is a building from the fifteenth century attached to a church of the same vintage. It has a huge house with fence all around it and two Doberman pinschers to preserve the sanctity of the place.

We were sure we were at the right location when out of the house emerged this six-foot-four giant of a man, a congenial, friendly soul with his huge farmer's boots and all the other paraphernalia that a true English farmer wears.

He greeted us warmly then instructed us to get into his Land Rover, and we were off. Within five minutes we were standing on a north-south road and what had been the east end of the east-west runway. It had totally disappeared when the place reverted back to its farm use after the squadrons that succeeded us there had departed (430 Squadron left for Gatwick in October 1943). The features of Lord Strobolgi's estate had not changed. The wooded areas were still in place, as were the fields (apart from the airstrip) where we used to go poaching with our shot-guns looking for Lord Strobolgi's partridges, with his gamekeepers shouting at us furiously. Finding Lord Strobolgi's estate was wonderful, but what about the pub?

Bob Goddard took us to three or four pubs that he thought were within walking distance of the airstrip, but none of them seemed to match. Even so, he was a magnificent host at the bar of each of the pubs. When I ordered lager at the first one Big Bob sniffed, "Gnat's pee!" True, but tasty. On the way back to Macklin Hancock's house I said to Mary-O, "There's something about one of those pubs that I would like to go back and examine tomorrow. The inside of the place is something that I don't remember. There's no corridor down the middle. And there are buildings on each side of it, but the pub that I went to was out in the open, out by itself."

So back Mary-O and I went the next morning to check things out.

The owner was behind the bar when we went in. We told him what we were looking for, and he immediately responded, "Oh, this is the place for sure. There used to be a corridor down to the room at the back but we took that out." The buildings that are there on each side of it now had been built since the war. They were the reason that I couldn't place it when I first saw it.

Without doubt this was the treasured pub that filled my mind with so many vivid memories of the night of September 22, 1943, and of my squadron mates, both those long gone and those still alive.

All thanks to Bob Goddard. In mid-October 1998 I telephoned Bob Goddard, still in charge of his great eight-hundred-acre farm (his father had been a tenant farmer on it when the Mustangs arrived). Bob was as delighted to hear from me as I was to speak with him. And he promised another trip to my local pub the next time we were there. According to Bob the pub had been "tarted up." You can do that tart thing to a pub, but not to people who had quaffed pints of gnat's pee there fifty-five years before.

As the end of October 1943 arrived, the decision had been made to move the squadron out of its tents and into winter quarters at an airport called Gatwick.

On the day the move was made, being one of the really junior members of the squadron, I was not permitted to fly the some thirty or forty miles to the west where Gatwick was located but was relegated to go by truck.

At that time the Gatwick airfield had no runways; it was simply rolling turf. There was an air repair facility hangar on the south side of the airfield where Wellington bombers were refurbished. About half a mile to the west was the mainline Brighton to London railway, which was the eastern boundary of the airport, and on the south side our dispersal building was located. That's where all our flying operations and administration were centred. The Commanding Officer and his clerical staff were located there. We pilots would congregate in and around the building waiting for instructions as to when and if we'd be flying that day. Our briefings took place there. It was the centre of our squadron life. Our aircraft were parked to the east of the dispersal building inside huge U-shaped berms of earth to protect against air attack.

There were no buildings on the north side of the Gatwick airport except for the abandoned grandstand of the racetrack that in former glory years had attracted hordes of people. Our billets and officers' mess were at the northeast corner of the airfield close to the railway station. The mess and billet structures were austere Royal Air Force single-storey buildings that had been put up in recent months. At least we had beds in our dormitory building, which was a single large room with perhaps a dozen beds and a coal-fired stove in the middle to protect us from the onslaught of the cold, damp British winter. Weather permitting, we would fly during the daylight hours, usually landing towards the west with our wheels almost touching the power lines of the railway track then touching down on the rolling turf.

I don't recall a Mustang crashing during a landing or takeoff at Gatwick. But I well remember the day when Freddy Bryon and Vince Dohaney, two two-hundred-pound lunkers, got into a Tiger Moth to joyride around the airfield. They had their pictures taken standing by the aircraft with their gloved hands making a "V for victory" sign. The next pictures were of the two of them again standing by the poor Tiger Moth, which was now a crumpled heap of wreckage. On takeoff it had leaped off the top of one of the airfield's many little hills without enough flying speed to keep it in the air. It promptly stalled, and with one wing down it crashed to the earth — and with the four-hundred-plus pounds of Bryon and Dohaney on board, it simply crumpled.

Victoria Station in London was about forty minutes to the north of Gatwick. Our billets were two minutes' walk from the railway station on the London/Brighton line. Frequently two or three of us would take an early evening train to Victoria Station and then it was on into Piccadilly Square and Soho to the bars and pubs there that catered to Air Force bodies — and in particular to fighter pilots.

All fighter pilots wore their blue dress uniforms with the top brass button undone. That signified that they were of the fighter pilot brotherhood as opposed to being bomber pilots or other lower life forms. My top button was always undone.

We would either take the last train back to Gatwick or, from time to time if a day or two or three of leave was permitted, go into town and stay at the Strand Palace or the Regent Palace in the middle of London. We would meet up in the bars and pubs with all sorts of fellow airmen, particularly Americans, because by this time the Yanks had arrived in strength in both Army and Army Air Force. And with them they brought tons of money, an attractive feature so far as all the young British women were concerned, particularly those around Piccadilly Circus.

For me, flying the Mustang in and out of Gatwick was always an exciting event. In particular, the day in November when I did my first operational sortie out across the English coastline over the Channel and into France was one of the more memorable days of my then very young life.

One of the problems I had when I joined the squadron was that at nineteen I still looked to be sixteen years of age. All the pilots were older than I and accordingly became very protective. This was true of the flight commanders as well. The result was that when it came time for me to do my first operational trip they were reluctant to let me go. It wasn't that I lacked any basic skills in flying or doing whatever was required of me as a fighter reconnaissance pilot, because I had been highly trained. It was simply the big brotherly (or was it fatherly?) attitude. Either way I was across the Channel long after Butchart and Geddes had gone for their first operational sorties against the Hun in France.

But I survived my first trip as a nervous number two, ardently protecting the tail of my leader as the pair of us roared across the Channel just above the waves to avoid radar detection and then pulled up to a lofty five thousand feet to cross the French coast, find our target, photograph it, and hare back to the welcoming shores of Mother England.

During the winter months our training missions far outnumbered operational sorties, but as we approached the spring, targets started to be assigned to us for photo recce in the Pas-de-Calais area. Whatever they were, they were important enough to be bombed in daylight by Mitchell or Boston squadrons. Then we would come in at four or five thousand feet or whatever altitude was selected for best accuracy with our vertical cameras (the huge camera was located pointing downward just behind the pilot's seat). The sites being attacked and photographed were given the code name Noball.

Our job was to fly directly over the Noball target at the height we were instructed. Over the site we would operate the camera, which took picture after picture for perhaps thirty long seconds until we turned it off. Back at base and after the film was processed the Army Air Photographic Interpretation Section (APIS) would examine the prints of the photographs to determine what damage, if any, had been done to the Noball targets.

430 Squadron went out on any number of Noball site photographic operations without anyone ever telling us what it was that we were photographing. We could see that the Noball sites were always in wooded areas. In the centre was a structure that looked like a hockey stick with the long handle of the hockey stick pointing west toward England and the blade of the stick pointing either south or north.

We went and did the Noball tasks assigned to us. We flew through tons of flak from the German anti-aircraft guns firing at us as we did our straight and level photographic runs. Usually there were two aircraft in a section with one person doing the photographing and the other as protective cover looking out for any potential attacking enemy fighters.

I was to find out what the Noball sites were on the night of June 12, 1944, when I was battered and bruised in the Regent Palace Hotel next to Piccadilly Circus.

CHAPTER 9
Winter 1943–1944 Operations Out of Gatwick

T HE WINTER OF 1943–44 at Gatwick passed by slowly with a few oper-ations for me thrown in to keep my fear factor going. Doing an operation wasn't so much a producer of fear at that stage but rather of high volumes of adrenaline and excitement as well as sharpening learn-ing faculties. Flying had to be good, both in tight formation and in bat-tle formation. In tight formation you were tucked in and flying two or three feet away from your leader. In battle formation you were about two hundred yards out from your leader, which required special flying tech-niques to keep up during turns. In battle formation, as a number two, your responsibility was to keep your eyes peeled for any bogies, any potential attacking aircraft. Believe me, that was a serious responsibility.

You had to be really conversant with your engine instruments, engine temperatures and pressures, fuel, air speed, rpm — your ability to scan all of those in a split second had to be good indeed. Except for these quick instrument scans, your eyes had to be outside the cockpit at all times. You had to be skilled in low-level photography using the oblique camera mounted on the left side just behind the cockpit at the level of the pilot's head. You had to get the target in place as it went under your wing and then came out from the trailing edge. You had to be on the money so that when the target appeared you had it right in the centre of the camera's lens. Then you would trigger the "camera on" switch. You could hear the camera hum in your earphones. Then "camera off" when you were past the target. The vertical photography was always a roll-the-dice situation because you would get yourself lined up on the target from way back, fly toward it, and as you were photographing you had to hope and pray that you were right over that invisible-to-you target.

More than anything when you got into your Mustang it had to be part of you and you part of it. Everything had to be in effect automatic, your brain process and the handling of all of the equipment, flaps, undercarriage, gun trigger on the stick, and the use of the gun sight sitting ahead of you. Then you had to be prepared for any emergency that arose. For example, if the electrical system began to fail you had to know how to attempt to fix it or cut it off totally. If your engine started to lose power, you had to know why, what was happening. If the propeller started to "run away" you had to know what to do.

Before I was finished my tour of operations at the end of November 1944 I had been put to the test several times.

One evening after dinner during that winter stay in Gatwick I was standing at the bar in our officers' mess believing I was by myself except for the bartender. At the far end of the bar around the corner a hand appeared from underneath with an empty glass. The glass hit the bar with an authoritative thud and a voice said, "A double scotch, please!" Had somebody passed out cold and was coming up for more from the floor? No, it was my good friend and scotch lover Hart Massey, who could stand at the bar and never be seen.

At Gatwick, January 1, 1944, age nineteen.

430 Squadron, New Year's Day, 1944, at Gatwick. Reading the letter from the mayor of Sudbury adopting the squadron as the City of Sudbury Squadron. I am sitting on the wing fourth from left.

Then there were about ten days of gunnery practice at a place called Peterhead on the northeast coast of Scotland. This was in January 1944. We flew our Mustangs up to this desolate Royal Air Force station, which was bleak, austere, frigid, cold, and highly unattractive.

The purpose of our trip so far north was to do air-to-air firing (practice, that is), shooting at drogues being pulled by tow aircraft. This was the only way that we could get some degree of skill in air-to-air firing. After all, the Mustang fighter, like the Spitfire and all others, was mainly a gun platform with the six .5-inch-calibre guns, three in each wing, and two 30-calibre firing through the propeller. Yes, firing through the propeller, a salute by the designers of the P51A toward the technology of the First World War.

The guns of the Mustang were focused at a range of 250 yards, where they all converged. The firepower was just that, powerful. So off a gang of us pilots flew to Peterhead, some in the Mustangs (all those that were serviceable) and the rest by Dakota (the workhorse American-produced transport).

Flight Lieutenant Jack Watts was the officer in charge of the squadron at Peterhead. Being a jovial and compassionate guy, Jack eventually became concerned about the hostile environment toward Canadians in the bleak Royal Air Force British officers' mess. After a few days he commandeered a huge canvas-covered truck into which all of us piled and went into the closest town, Aberdeen, for a pub crawl. Somehow Jack had neglected or intentionally decided that he wouldn't get permission from the Commanding Officer of the base to do this sortie into town. When we finally arrived back at RAF Station Peterhead the service police marched him off to the Commanding Officer. Fortunately, Jack was able to talk his way out of any harsh treatment, was severely reprimanded, and told not to do it again. Our hero was toasted at the bar by all of us.

Finally it was time to leave Peterhead, thank God! And go back to the comfortable clime of Gatwick.

On the way south we had to refuel, and arrangements had been made for us to stop at a Royal Air Force base north of London that was the home of the two Polish Spitfire squadrons. Because of the lateness of our arrival it was necessary to stay overnight, a decision that resulted in several hangovers the next morning (or as we called it, "severial").

In the officers' mess that evening the jovial Poles taunted us into a game of buck-buck. This was after several drinks at the bar. My recollection of buck-buck that night was that the members of the Polish team would line up in a row, each man bent over, his face turned away from the buttocks of the man ahead of him, whom he had grabbed from behind. This close association formed a chain of about ten bodies clutched together, backs to the ceiling, arms around the guy ahead. The opposing team, the Canadians that is, had an equal number of men. The first man ran at the line of Poles from behind and jumped as far as he could down the line, landing with a heavy thump on the back of the furthest victim he could reach. He was followed by the next Canadian member who went as far as he could toward the leader with a crashing thump. The intent was, of course, to break the back of the Polish line.

I want to tell you that this was a rough, mean, and cruel game of buck-buck. I think the Poles eventually won because they were skilled artists at the game, which clearly they practised night after night, whereas my gang were novices.

As for me, I was a coward. At a diminutive 145 pounds I was probably the smallest person in the room. So when the time came to play buck-buck I passed and simply acted as a cheerleader for Jack Watts, Dick Manser, and all the other idiots who were hammered by the flying Poles.

The Polish Spitfire pilots, God bless them, were incredible in the air and on the ground, great warriors. Historically their biggest problem in the air was that no one could shut them up. They kept talking to each other all the time, even in the heat of battle. When in a dogfight or the beginning of an engagement it is necessary to keep silence so that you can hear the squadron or wing commander giving his orders, or, for that matter, someone screaming at you to "break," which means take evasive action to the right or left because an enemy is up your jaxy ready to shoot.

As for the evening with the Poles, I think the only damage I suffered was the loss of half of my tie, which was cut off by some wild-eyed Polish pilot.

At Gatwick one day during March a pair of badly damaged American B-17 bombers returning from a mission to Germany landed at our airfield. The heavily torn machines and the injured crews brought home to us very vividly the carnage being wrought on the American daylight bombers in their horrendous missions into Germany, where they were being chewed up unmercifully by the Luftwaffe.

On another occasion two American Thunderbolt fighters came in looking for refuelling, having been on a mission across the Channel. As the pilots came into our dispersal they were talking to each other using their hands to show how they had fought with the German 109s successfully, or was it the FW 190s? Then they told us about the big victorious dogfight they had had. We were really impressed until someone noticed that the canvas covers on their guns had not been perforated by their machine guns. In short form, their guns had not been fired. Ah, well.

During bad flying days or when we were just waiting for flying assignments in our dispersal hut the routine was reading, talking, playing cards, usually Red Dog (I did not play cards and still don't), and talking about girls, home, yesterday's flight, or whatever. And, of course, smoking up a storm. The cigarettes were there in a chest in the centre of the room. To get a package, all free, all you had to do was open the chest, select the brand that you wanted to kill yourself with that day, and away you went. I started my smoking career at that time when I joined the squadron. I was to smoke heavily (in the range of about ninety cigarettes a day) until 1958, when my body couldn't take it anymore and I stopped. If I hadn't, these words would not be in the process of being written several decades later.

At this stage still at Gatwick we were a long way from even thinking about D-Day, whenever that was to be. Our operations across the Channel in France were not yet totally Army support oriented, as they would be from D-Day on. And so while there were Army liaison officers (ALOs) associated with our wing headquarters they were not involved in our pre-operational sortie briefings. The briefings outlined what objective the particular sortie was to carry out, such as photography for Noball sites or for a Rhubarb. Those were low flying missions ranging across the French countryside looking for trains or trucks or other targets of opportunity to shoot up. Those briefings were usually carried out by the squadron intelligence officer, the Commanding Officer, or the pilot designated to be the leader.

We never did operations with the whole squadron. The maximum number of aircraft on an operation would be four: two sections of two flying with one leader. The minimum would be two aircraft with the lead pilot designated to carry out the required activity, be it visual reconnaissance, photography, or artillery, with the number two man responsible for watching for enemy aircraft.

In a two-man sortie the briefing would include the track out to the English coast with a particular point of departure from the shore, then low level as close to the water as safely possible across to the French coast. That low-level flying was necessary to avoid radar detection by the Germans until we got to the French coast. Just before arrival at the coast we would climb to the designated height of three or four thousand feet or whatever was specified for carrying out the mission. Of course, if it was a Rhubarb we would simply stay right down on the deck as we crossed the coast and went in. Our routes inside the French territory were carefully designated with navigational landmarks specified to guide us along the way. At the briefing the leader would designate a takeoff time. Then we would gather our gear, pick up our parachutes and flying helmets with the face masks (with radio microphones — we never used oxygen because we could never get high enough). Then there was the solemn march out to our respective Mustangs.

A nervous whiz before climbing into the cockpit with one's parachute comfortably strapped on and in place. The pre-start check done with the ground crew standing by. Then flick all the switches, get the impeller going for the starter. Engage the propeller and engine at the right pitch sound of the starting gear and with great luck your engine would start with a great rumbling roar. Everything working correctly, the radio on, a check with the leader, and then the taxi out to the takeoff position. At Gatwick the takeoff was usually from east to west into the prevailing wind. Before beginning the takeoff run our tails were close to the railway track. Because of the difficulty of the rolling turf we rarely took off in formation at Gatwick but would do so singly, then play catch-up after the leader began to turn soon after he was airborne. The turning allowed us to catch up from behind and get into formation position with the leader fairly quickly.

Formation having been achieved it was then up to the leader to do all the navigating, almost all of it by map reading. Certainly that was the way as we flew from Gatwick toward our south coast crossing out point. But then we were over the English Channel and right down on the deck with no landmarks to latch onto. We used the gyro compass for navigation until we hit the French coast. Then it was back to map reading to the target or the designated Rhubarb area. As the two of us crossed the channel the heads of both pilots would be swivelling, looking out above to the right and left and to the rear (as far as possible) to watch for any attacking Focke-Wulf 190s or ME 109s. When we crossed the coast that head swivelling kept up, but at the same time we were immediate targets for anti-aircraft shells, be they 20-, 40-, or 88-millimetre that the Germans loved to lob at us. The 20- and 40-mm looked as though they were indeed being lobbed. As a rule we could see them coming because most of them were tracers, glowing objects that allowed the gunners to trace their path in the sky, the better to aim at and hit us.

The 88-mm gun, however, was quite a different beast. It was an anti-tank, anti-aircraft, anti-everything gun that was undoubtedly the best artillery piece anyone produced or used during the Second World War. It threw a high-speed shell with a flat trajectory, no tracers. As an anti-aircraft gun, it was radar controlled both as to its path to the target and the explosion height at which the target was flying. The moral of the story was that if you were in 88 country, to fly straight and level was to court deadly disaster. Either the 88 would hit you or explode close enough to put shrapnel into your machine. The members of 430 Squadron (in their Mustangs that rarely flew above five thousand feet) discovered the 88s in spades once the Battle of Normandy got underway on June 6, 1944, and we arrived at our Normandy airstrip B8 a few days after. Every day we had to transit the front lines from our B8 base at Magny southeast over the Caen area. Caen had such heavy 88 flack that we said we could walk on the stuff as it exploded in deadly black smoke balls all around us. But in discussing the Battle of Normandy at this point, I'm getting ahead of my story.

The spring of 1944 was upon us. It was time for 430, 414, and 400 RCAF squadrons to leave their respective winter airfields and billets and move into the mode of a mobile tactical airfield. There we were all housed in tents, including our mess and administrative quarters. Our technical people, with all their tools, equipment, spare parts, photography processing, and other special services, were put into vans and trucks, as were the offices of the airfield (129 Airfield — Canadian Group Captain Ernie Moncrieff) and the commander of 39 Reconnaissance Wing, Wing Commander Operations (Wingco Ops) R.C.A. "Bunt" Waddell. It was time to leave Gatwick and begin the final preparations for the invasion of France — the final countdown, if you will.

In the early spring of 1944, 430 Squadron became part of 129 Airfield assembled at Royal Air Force Station at Odiham (it is still there), to the west of London and north of the teeming British ports such as

Portsmouth, from which the invasion vessels would be departing to whatever destination was selected by the supreme commander, General Dwight "Ike" Eisenhower, and his senior land, sea, and air commanders (all British or American, no Canadians).

Odiham, a pre-war permanent force RAF station, had and still has all of the hangars, paved runways, and other infrastructure necessary for full-time peace and wartime operations.

The Odiham officers' mess was a two-storey structure with an elegant lounge and bar, dining facilities, and housing for those officers who were not encumbered by wives or family.

However, the sleeping/living quarters for 430 Squadron and the others in 129 Airfield were now back to the two-man tents we had had at Ashford. Each of us had his kit bag with clothes and shaving gear; a basin for washing body, shirts, undershorts, and socks; blankets and a pillow; and a sleeping cot. A mess tent plate and cutlery were also provided; they weren't necessary at Odiham, but they would be as soon as we were based in France, whenever that might be. Our sleeping tents were on the airfield to the east of the north-south taxi strip. Our administrative tent and our dispersal area were at the southwest corner of the intersection of the north-south taxi strip and the east-west runway. Our aircraft were clustered close by on the grass off the taxiway.

By this time 400 Squadron, the original Royal Canadian Air Force squadron (originally numbered 110), had been converted from the Mustang fighter recce role to the Spitfire Bluebirds. This was a high-altitude Spitfire, unarmed, painted blue like the sky, equipped with huge vertical cameras. This Bluebird Spit was long ranged and could fly higher than any armed Focke-Wulf 190 or ME 109. It was sent on tactical photographic missions to take pictures of bomb damage inflicted by the British and Canadian heavy bombers, the Stirling, Halifax, and Lancaster.

In April and May, 430 Squadron's activities out of Odiham into the coastal areas of France increased perceptibly. The squadron was tasked to take oblique photographs of French beaches, particularly in the Pas-de-Calais area, as well as in a remote sector called Normandy way to the south, clearly not a place where an invasion force would be sent. It was just too far away. But in any event the pictures had to be taken.

I can recall crossing out over Portsmouth on the way to France and seeing below me huge rectangular concrete structures being built in the water. They were massive in every respect, but there was no clue as to what they were. It was like the Noball sites. We weren't told about what we were seeing. That was appropriate, because if we were shot down in enemy territory and interviewed under duress that's the kind of information that German intelligence would be looking for.

We would find out what those huge concrete structures were on D-Day plus four.

CHAPTER 10

1975: Finding 430 Squadron's Log Book

———◆———

T HERE WERE THREE UNUSUAL RESEARCH "accidents" that allowed me to write my account of pre-D-Day, D-Day itself, and the Battle of Normandy.

The first of these was my finding of the wartime log book of 430 Squadron of the Royal Canadian Air Force. The log has a descriptive record of the daily activity of the unit and of every operational mission that was carried out during the period of its wartime existence. In fact, I was the author of a part of it.

Thirty-one years later, in my capacity as the commander of the Air Reserve Group of the Canadian Armed Forces, I was invited to a ceremony at Canadian Forces Base Valcartier, Quebec. 430 Squadron, equipped with helicopters, was to be presented with its Queen's Colour, a symbolic flag bearing the unit's badge and the names of the places where the squadron had won its battle honours. To qualify for presentation of the Queen's Colour, a unit must have been in existence for more than twenty-five years. I was the guest of honour and the only wartime 430 Squadron pilot to appear for the festivities. My wife and I were treated to much hospitality and courteous attention. We were taken on a tour of the squadron's facilities — the hangar, maintenance shops, administrative offices, and the aircrew's "waiting room," as we used to call it. That room I inspected with high interest, looking at all the pictures, paraphernalia, and trophies hanging on the walls. Sitting on a table at the side of the room was an unusual-looking book. It had a gray binding. It was large — about one and a half feet long, one foot wide, and three inches thick. My memory told me that it had the look of an ancient Royal Air Force record book I had seen many times before.

As I lifted the cover to look at the first page, I was astonished to find that this was 430 Squadron's original wartime log, complete with signatures! The discovery brought a moment of excitement as well as intense nostalgia. I leafed through the pages with their terse descriptions of our operational sorties, especially those of the D-Day period and the time of the closing of the Falaise Gap.

I had to have the original so I could photocopy it for my personal records. Would the Commanding Officer let me take it? Of course he would.

It was that discovery which made this section of my memoirs possible. My own personal log book covering the invasion period had been lost when a Dakota transport aircraft was shot down carrying our tents and personal gear from an airstrip near Evreux in France to another strip at Diest in Belgium. So I had no records of my own from those long gone days. Therefore, the find of the squadron log book was a surprising bonanza. In 1975, putting together an account of the Battle of Normandy had not even crossed my mind.

The second research accident has to do with finding two aerial photographs I had taken during 1944. As with my log book, all the important reconnaissance photos I had taken and been able to keep during the invasion period were lost. There was one particular photograph I wanted to find in the photographic archives in the United Kingdom. It was a picture taken on August 17, 1944, in the Falaise Gap. It was of a two-abreast column of German tanks, trucks, horse-drawn artillery, ambulances, and other vehicles moving in broad daylight without fear of any attack from the Allied Air Forces (this for reasons I will explain later). If I could find that picture it would explain with dramatic impact the scope and scale of the massive day and night exodus by the enemy out of the pocket in which we had the German Army trapped.

A search was conducted in the two institutions in the United Kingdom that might have had a negative of that photograph and all others taken by my squadron during the Second World War. The British are notorious hoarders, but that picture could not be found. In the meantime, I asked those of my wartime 430 Squadron colleagues I was able to track down, including Army intelligence officers associated with us during the period, if they had any aerial photographs from those days. I hoped that one of them might turn up something and that my special photograph would be in the lot. At a cocktail party in Toronto in the fall in 1979 I talked with Joan Waddell, the widow of the wing commander flying of 39 Recce Wing, of which 430 Squadron was a part during the summer of 1944. In those days Wing Commander R.C.A. "Bunt" Waddell was the flying boss of all of us, responsible among other things for our briefings and our overall operations, as well as being the man with his finger on the pulse of not only my squadron but also the other two Canadian units in the wing, 400 and 414 squadrons. Did Bunt have a box or collection of memorabilia from the Second World War? The answer was yes. I could go through it any time, which I did about a week later. My idea was that since Bunt had had access to all of the pictures taken by our squadrons, he might have taken a copy of my August 17 photograph and thrown it in with the others he thought worth keeping. There was only an outside chance. But it was worth a try.

I dug into Bunt's huge box of books, maps, bits and pieces of regalia, and other personal flying treasures. My hopes rose when I found a rolled-up bundle of about thirty air photographs, the very thing I thought I might find. A cursory look through the batch did not produce what I was looking for. Nevertheless, I decided I should ask to take them home with me so I could go over them carefully. Joan very kindly agreed.

That evening, during my third inspection of the bundle, I stopped at a picture that began to ring a bell in my memory. The picture was of a port. There was the shoreline. Beyond it was a town with docks and water in the centre. Surely that couldn't be Dieppe! I checked the date and the squadron number printed on the bottom of the photograph, then went to the squadron log book. They matched. It was mine! Even so, it was not the Falaise Gap prize I was seeking. The next run through the bundle caused me to stop at a blurred, indistinct photograph taken almost vertically at low level. There were six or seven tank-like objects on the ground. Tanks? I wondered if it was the photograph I had taken on the night I found the batch of tanks that almost caused Bunt Waddell to have me court-martialed. Impossible. It couldn't be. Back to the squadron log. It *was* mine, taken on a day that was significant for me, but far more so for General George S. Patton, Jr. It was August 1, 1944, the day that he and his magnificent Third Army became operational.

By this stroke of unexpected good fortune, and through the kindness of Joan Waddell, and the long-ago interest of Wing Commander (later Group Captain) Bunt Waddell, DSO, DFC, and an outstanding leader, my words describing two events are enriched by those photographs.

The third accidental find was Dirk Bogarde, the international film star, artist, and, latterly, best-selling author who had a role to play in the interpretation of the August 1, 1944, photo.

Dirk Bogarde.

During a visit to England in June 1980 I picked up a copy of Bogarde's second autobiography, *Snakes and Ladders*. It covered, among other times, his experiences during the Second World War. He had joined the British Army, was commissioned from the ranks, and, as his story went, trained as an Army photographic interpretation officer. He did? Interesting. We had half a dozen of them attached to our 39 Reconnaissance Wing. The APIS people interpreted the aerial photos we pilots took. Furthermore, his story recounted that he had joined 39 Recce Wing of the Royal Canadian Air Force at Odiham just before D-Day, and was with us through D-Day, France, Belgium, and Holland. He was? I didn't remember him. In those days he wasn't a film star, just a skinny twenty-two-year-old British Army officer. No reason to remember him. But, perhaps, just maybe there was.

Could Dirk Bogarde have been the man who interpreted that critically important (to me) photograph of tanks I took in the late evening of August 1, 1944? As soon as I returned to Canada I wrote to him at his residence in the south of France. I enclosed a copy of the relevant section of the manuscript of this book and a print of the August 1 photo I'd found in Bunt Waddell's memorabilia box. Was he the APIS officer I'd seen that night?

The day he received my letter he wrote a reply that was later followed up by another. Indeed Bogarde was my APIS interpreter.

"Right off I knew the Sortie-Snap," was his response.

Quite by accident the two of us had reached back across thirty-six years to a French farmyard and an APIS van of 39 Recce Wing enveloped in the uneasy beachhead battle zone darkness of the night of August 1, 1944. For me it was an uncanny but fortuitous link with that event and with Dirk Bogarde, a man who was exceptionally talented.

CHAPTER 11

Almost "Buying It" at Dieppe, April 24, 1944

———◆———

D IEPPE. THE TIME WAS 1815 hours on April 24, 1944. The place: over the German-occupied French coast at five thousand feet. The target: two ships reported to be in the harbour at Dieppe.

The sun's unobstructed rays beat down, warming the twenty-year-old pilot through the birdcage hood covering the cockpit of the Mustang I fighter aircraft.

Looking intently down past his green and brown camouflage-painted port wing, he was frantically scanning the thin layer of flat but lumpy cloud about two thousand feet below, searching for a hole through which he could catch a glimpse of the ground. A landmark had to be quickly found.

The youthful fighter reconnaissance pilot was on his first mission as leader. He had many operational sorties under his belt since he had joined his squadron in September 1943. But he had always been a number two, the follower whose task was to guard the leader's and his own tail against attack by enemy fighters. The leader was in command. He had to give all the orders, navigate, carry out the objective, and get his section of two, or sometimes four, aircraft safely back to base. He had a heavy responsibility.

So it was that the Mustang pilot, with the full weight of his first sortie in the lead, was somewhat nervous. He had a "bit of a twitch," as the airmen of the day called it. Furthermore, to make matters worse he had to take as his number two a Spitfire IX from another squadron. If he goofed or botched up the operation he and his own squadron would lose face. He'd never hear the end of it. The pressure was really on.

A Mustang and a Spitfire flying an operation together was a most unusual event. Two fighters, recce Mustangs from 430 Squadron of the

Royal Canadian Air Force, had been asked to accompany 411 Squadron, a Canadian Spitfire unit, on their bombing operation against two newly discovered freighters in Dieppe Harbour. The attack would be on the inner basin of that heavily defended port where so many Canadian soldiers had been killed, wounded, or taken prisoner in August 1942.

From their base at Odiham, southwest of London, the Mustangs had flown south in the late morning of April 24 to Tangmere, the Royal Air Force airfield on the south coast of England that had been turned over to a Canadian wing (three squadrons) of Spitfires.

At Tangmere, the Canadian wing leader, Wing Commander George Keefer, briefed the Spitfire pilots on their operation: dive-bomb and destroy the two freighters just arrived at Dieppe. The pair of Mustangs were to use their oblique aerial cameras to take glamour photos of the squadron of twelve Spits as they crossed the Channel in tight, close formation, every man in place. Immediately after the last Spit had dropped its bombs the lead Mustang, covered by his number two, would dash across the deadly Dieppe Harbour to photograph the blazing, exploding enemy vessels devastated by the accurately placed bombs of the diving Spitfires. That was the scenario as briefed.

Unfortunately, the engine of the lead Mustang refused to start at the moment designated by the wing commander for "pressing tits," that is, pulling or pushing all the levers and buttons necessary to start up the engine. A quick on-the-spot series of orders put the pilot of the second camera-equipped Mustang in the lead with a Spit IX from the squadron flying protection for him as his number two. When that adjustment was made the twelve aircraft of 411 Squadron took off, followed immediately by the lone Mustang and its single Spitfire protector.

There was only one problem for the Mustang pilot. His radio did not have a common operating frequency with the Spitfire squadron leader. Therefore he could not listen in on the radio instructions or chatter of the squadron. However, he was able to talk to his own Spitfire number two on the emergency frequency. In turn, the Spit pilot could then switch to his squadron's frequency to pass a message if need be.

One thing a fighter recce pilot was never supposed to do was get lost. Ordinary fighter pilots could do so and did so with regularity. But the fighter recce pilot was a highly trained specialist in navigation and map reading. He knew where he was at all times and could find a target in the far corner of a corn field if it was marked on his map by intelligence people before he took off. Well, that was the way it was supposed to be. The young Mustang pilot — he'd been lost once or twice but had always found his way home — was full of confidence. He wouldn't get lost. He would perform as if he were an old hand. Besides, all he had to do was follow the Spitfires. The squadron leader would get them to Dieppe. No problem.

The flight across the English Channel had been smooth. The late afternoon sky was cloudless. Visibility was unlimited. Some hundred yards off to the right of the squadron the Mustang pilot manoeuvred his aircraft to bring the Spits directly into the line of sight of his camera. From that position he took a dozen photographs of the clutch of fighters, all twelve nearly touching, flying together almost as one. Each pilot was doing his utmost to keep his aircraft in its exact tight-formation post so it would appear to be in perfect formation in the pictures. It would cost anyone out of position a round of drinks that night at the local pub!

The photography was finished by the time they were halfway across the Channel. The Spits opened up into battle formation, spreading apart to intervals of about fifty yards so each pilot could watch for attacking enemy aircraft.

As the French coast came into view a thin blanket of low cloud could also be seen. It began some three miles off shore, producing an apparently solid blanket of cover over the coastal lands where Dieppe was calculated to be.

The inexperienced fighter recce pilot, believing that he was superior in map reading to any Spit pilot, decided that he would try to be the hero by finding Dieppe through whatever cloud holes might miraculously appear in the cloud formation. He would then be able to tell the Spit leader, by this time presumably lost, where to go. After all, Mustang fighter reconnaissance pilots were highly trained in map reading, whereas Spitfire pilots were famous for their inability to keep track of their own whereabouts! The tantalizing prospect of finding Dieppe first and being one up on the Squadron Leader filled the young Mustang pilot's mind. Hence, he was frantically searching for a cloud hole below.

There was no hole to be found. He lifted his eyes momentarily to check the position of the Spit squadron that a few seconds before had been about a mile ahead of him.

The squadron had disappeared! The Spits were gone, vanished! Where were they? He *had* to find them.

If he couldn't ... It was unbelievable. How could he explain why he had lost an entire squadron! He would never be able to live it down. What a black!

As if by a miracle, about a mile ahead of him down at the level of the cloud about three thousand feet below, he caught sight of a Spitfire in its dive-bombing run hurtling vertically through a small aperture in the cloud. There were no other Spits in sight. It was the last one. That meant the rest of the squadron, all eleven of them, had delivered their bombs and were already heading out across the Channel for England.

Meanwhile, with no direct radio contact with the squadron commander, the Mustang pilot was left behind. Perhaps he could blame his failure on not having the Spit squadron's frequency on his own radio and so not being able to hear them. Any excuse would do.

It was impossible to take photographs through the cloud or through the hole the Spits had dived through because it was far too small. What to do? With little understanding of the potential dangers, he made his decision.

At the moment he had seen the last diving Spitfire he had been heading east. His Spitfire number two was two hundred yards to his right in battle formation. The radio instructions to the Spit pilot were terse: "I'm doing to do my photo run westbound along the beach. You stay well away out over the water."

The two aircraft, still heading east, began to descend. The Mustang pilot moved his throttle up to full power, putting his machine well ahead of the slower Spitfire. Checking his altitude as he approached the cloud layer, the fighter reconnaissance airman gently pushed the control column over to the left, swinging his huge fighter in an arc north over the cloud, now wispy and thin along the shore. He was still turning and descending. As the beach came into view, he was about three miles east of Dieppe and the towering beach edge cliffs that enclosed the town and its harbour.

Still down he went, the roar of his labouring engine louder than he had ever heard it. He checked his speed. It was higher than he had taken a Mustang before, just over 450 miles per hour. If he levelled out at three hundred feet and got in close to the beach he should get at least two or three good photos of the harbour and, with any luck, the ships the Spits had just attacked. At three hundred feet and a mile east of the entrance to the harbour, he levelled his Mustang and got set for his run in, ready to activate his camera by pushing the button on the control column. As he rocketed along, he could almost touch the high cliffs. He was ready, but not for what came next.

Suddenly it was as if the whole world had turned into a formidable display of horrifying fireworks. Every anti-aircraft gun in Dieppe started firing at him. An almost solid wall of white, burning balls were arcing comet-like toward him, enveloping his hurtling aircraft in a checkerboard of exploding light. Too late he realized that by the time the twelfth Spitfire had bombed the harbour, every German flak gun would be fully manned and red-hot. Petrified and trapped, the pilot had no choice but to press on. He just had to get at least one picture.

As the harbour flashed by to his left under the aiming marker painted on the trailing edge of his wing, he pushed the camera button. Now the hail of flak was so heavy and close he involuntarily ducked. He pulled his head down inside the cockpit, the goggles of his leather flying helmet almost touching his right hand, which clenched the control column. The instrument panel reflected the kaleidoscope of flashes from the anti-aircraft shells exploding all around him.

The Mustang sped past the harbour through the gauntlet of fire, the pilot expecting at any instant to be blasted out of the sky. He cursed the stupidity and inexperience that had put him in this deadly position. With the innate "gung ho" attitude of the young, he had seen himself as an invincible fighter pilot to whom nothing could happen, who could never be hit by flak, who could never be shot down. It couldn't be happening to him!

As quickly as the flak had begun, it stopped. He was beyond it, out of range. With great relief he began climbing northward in the direction of Tangmere, the fighter squadron nest from which he, his number two, and 411 Squadron had departed just a short time before.

My photo of Dieppe.

After landing at Tangmere and reporting to the Commanding Officer of the fighter Squadron (a unit which he himself would command in Canada in 1953, flying Vampire jet aircraft), the Mustang pilot flew back to his own base at RAF Station Odiham. Following a debriefing by an intelligence officer of 39 Reconnaissance Wing, of which 430 Squadron was a part, he was informed by the unit photographic section that only one photograph of Dieppe harbour had turned out.

Somewhat shaken by his experience, the author of the Daily Operations Log of 430 Squadron made this entry about his own trip that day:

> F.O.R.H. Rohmer, Yours truly, went out with some Spitfires from 411 Squadron, R.C.A.F. who bombed some shipping at Dieppe. F/L J.H. Taylor (Can.J.7426) was sup-

posed to have gone as No. 1, but because his engine wouldn't start, Flying Officer Rohmer took a Spitfire along as a No. 2, taking photographs of the Squadron on the way across. The bombing was done through a small hole above Dieppe, but it was too small to photograph through, so Flying Officer Rohmer, the clot, did a run across the mouth of the harbor at 300 feet just after the Spits had bombed. "Nachully" there was some flak but nothing came of it. One picture of the Basin came out but nothing showed up on it.

CHAPTER 12

The Flying Circus and Meeting General Patton

———◆———

> 8 May 1944 ADMINISTRATION: Flying Officer R.H. Rohmer (Can.J.24120) returned from Ramsberry and the Flying Circus today.
>
> 430 Squadron Log

WHAT THE SQUADRON LOG DID not say was that General Patton had inspected the Flying Circus that morning, May 8, 1944. Furthermore, the old boy had words with me!

The log does record that on April 28 I left our base at Odiham to replace Flying Officer Jack Cox (who was later shot down on D-Day) as a member of the Flying Circus of fighter aircraft then at Thorney Island, a Royal Air Force fighter station close to Portsmouth on the south coast of England.

My squadron had been working hard during the spring of 1944, both in operations and in training, honing our skills in aerial photography and low-level map reading. This was a special capability that required us to be able to pinpoint the location of trucks, tanks, guns, or whatever we discovered during our reconnaissance to an exact reference point, whether in the corner of a field or the centre of a town.

Another specialty was artillery reconnaissance (Arty/R) in which we directed the large guns to targets. Each of us had trained on the artillery ranges at Aldershot, learning the art of ranging the guns from the air. After D-Day it would be one of our roles to range the 155-mm and other big guns in circumstances where it was impossible for the Air Observation Posts (AirOPs) to operate in their tiny light aircraft, the Austers, because of their vulnerability to anti-aircraft fire. The plan was that we would then be called in. Sitting a reasonable distance back from the target at four or five thousand feet and supposedly out of range of the enemy anti-aircraft guns, we would be able to direct the fire of the four or six ranging guns, and when the shells were finally locked on to the target all of the guns assigned to the shoot would open up on it.

430 Squadron was equipped with twelve Mustang I aircraft, the original model of the famous fighting machine, the Mustang IV or P51D, which the Americans eventually developed into the long-range escort for their Flying Fortress bombers that smashed Germany by day. Built by North American Aviation of California, our Mustang Is cruised at about 260 miles per hour. They were equipped with an Allison engine with a cropped blower, that is, the engine's super charger was rendered inoperative, with the result that we had difficulty in operating above ten thousand feet. Moreover, the aircraft was large and heavy, making it impossible for us to turn inside a Messerschmitt 109 or a Focke-Wulf in a dogfight. The rule for the Mustang I was if bounced by an enemy fighter, do not attempt to dogfight because the German is bound to win. Instead, roll over on your back and dive with your engine at maximum emergency power. No German fighter could keep up with us. The Mustang, with its weight and superb streamlining, would leave any Me 109 or Focke-Wulf far behind at well over 400 miles per hour. That tactical rule was not always followed.

We were happy with our reliable fighters. They had started to arrive in 1942 to replace the less than satisfactory Curtis Tomahawks, 430 Squadron's original equipment. About the time I joined the unit at the tactical airstrip at Great Chart near Ashford in Kent in September 1943, the Mustang had satisfied everyone with its ruggedness, reliability, and comforting high speed. The only disappointments were its lack of dog-fighting manoeuvrability and its inability to operate effectively at high altitudes. It was a big, impressive fighter, a much larger machine than the Spitfires of the day. Painted in the dark greens of RAF camouflage and polished with loving care, the Mustang I was a sleek, beautiful airplane.

As I have described earlier, my appearance was a problem for me in my squadron: I was slight, thin, and had the face of a sixteen-year-old. I looked so young the squadron commander took a fatherly interest in me and could barely conceive of my being old enough to meet the threat of the deadly Hun.

If my youthful visage gave pause to my squadron commander, on Monday, May 8, 1944, it was to stop General Patton in his tracks, although by that time I had many missions under my belt and was rapidly becoming an experienced hand on the squadron. And, of course, having turned twenty the previous January, I was feeling much older and far more confident, even though I still looked sixteen.

After the gray winter at Gatwick, the squadron moved back into tents at the Royal Air Force base at Odiham. There we joined two other Canadian units, 400 Squadron with its Bluebird high-level photography unarmed reconnaissance Spitfires, and 414 Squadron, which was also a Mustang fighter reconnaissance unit. Our three Canadian squadrons were the operational arm of 39 Recce Wing. Once the invasion started, that wing was designated to work with the British Army as its reconnaissance and photographic eyes. The Royal Air Force recce wing counterpart on Mustang Is was to work with the Canadian Army. This Machiavellian twist of cross-ethnic fertilization was attributed to General Montgomery himself, the legendary leader for whom we would be performing all manner of dedicated services.

In the spring of 1944, someone at Supreme Headquarters realized that unless the people fighting the battle on the ground had some opportunity to have a prior look at the close support aircraft that would be working with them in battle, they might well confuse them with the enemy. This was particularly so with the Mustang, which had an uncanny resemblance to the German Me 109. In fact, it was so similar that I can recall being attacked over Holland in late 1944 by twelve American silver Mustang IVs who must have thought that because we had camouflage paint on our aircraft and a birdcage hood like the 109s we were, in fact, Germans. Probably to this day the American pilots who descended upon us from above like a group of famished hawks still grind their teeth when they think of those two Messerschmitts that got away by nipping into the nearest cloud. Thank God there was one close by.

In order to show our soldiers what their supporting airplanes looked like, it was decided to form a Flying Circus made up of all of the fighters, fighter bombers, and rocket-carrying Typhoons that were part of the Allied Tactical Air Forces. The Flying Circus, complete with a Dakota transport aircraft, would then travel around the English countryside, appearing on schedule over great gatherings of troops who would watch each of us fly by at a low level. Every one of the pilots thought it was marvellous to take part in a legalized "beat-up."

As the Squadron Log shows, I joined the Flying Circus at Thorney Island, a Royal Air Force base right on the water's edge on the south coast. In my trusty, polished Mustang, I landed there on Friday, April 28, with instructions to stay with the circus until May 8. On the Tarmac I could see one of every fighter the IX U.S. Air Force and the British 2nd Tactical Air Force had in inventory: the twin-boom, twin-engine Lightning; the squat, flat-nosed Thunderbolt; the Mustang IV of the Americans; the Spitfire and the rocket-carrying Typhoon of the British; and the not-yet-venerable U.S. Douglas DC3, known as the Dakota, which would carry paratroopers and tow gliders across to the invasion area in the dawn of D-Day.

That night there was a get-acquainted bash in the officers' mess, during which the participating pilots — British, American, and me, the Canadian — consumed more than enough mild and bitters (the flat British alcoholic brew that does indeed taste bitter) and lager beer to make absolutely sure through that the resulting haze of booze-enhanced camaraderie we got to know each other well. We had a grand time that night, particularly with the Americans. They were a happy-go-lucky gang having a ball. In fact, during the next few days they adopted me as one of their own to the point that I was allowed to fly their brand new Mustang IV. The rule book said I couldn't. The aircraft was USAAF. I was a Canadian. The machine was much different in the cockpit and in handling than my old Mustang I — more power, different engine, less weight. But what the hell! I had the chance, so why not? What a difference between the two.

The morning after our Thorney Island get-together party and a short recovery sleep, we had a briefing by the squadron leader in charge of the organization. After the usual thorough check of our airplanes, which consisted fundamentally of kicking one of the tires, the Flying Circus was airborne. Our ten-day tour took us from airfield to airfield and over massive gatherings of troops clustered in selected fields of English countryside, faces dutifully turned skyward as we roared by one by one, imprinting on their memories an indelible, unforgettable image.

At least, that's what we wanted to believe. We were sure that each man would say to himself, "Now I recognize that Thunderbolt and that Spitfire, that Typhoon and Mustang, that Lightning and Dakota. I swear that on or after D-Day I will not, repeat, will not shoot at them or anything that looks like them."

Without doubt there was great merit in the concept that if the Army saw us and were able to recognize us, they would not shoot at us. However, the post D-Day track record of the itchy-fingered, twitchy soldiers in the field clearly demonstrated that they would shoot at anything, no matter what it looked like and no matter what the insignia painted on the fuselage and wings — the American Star, the British Roundel, or the Iron Cross. But there was no doubt in our minds that each of us taking part in the Flying Circus was doing something highly beneficial for all our fellow tactical Air Force pilots who were part of the huge air armada that would sweep the skies of France in support of the liberating Allied armies.

The last stop on our extended tour was at Ramsberry, a Royal Air Force airfield near Liverpool. It was a flying training base and a very "tiddly" one. After our arrival late in the afternoon of Sunday, May 7, some officious RAF squadron leader violently objected to my unseemly dress. He thought I should have had on a shirt and tie. Instead, in true fighter form, I was wearing the only clothing I had with me, my Air Force blue battledress trousers and jacket (complete with wings and a rescue whistle at the collar) and a dark blue polka-dot scarf around my neck. My trousers were tucked into knee-length, sheepskin-lined flying boots. From the top of the right flying boot the handle of my dagger protruded. My hefty Smith & Wesson revolver was strapped to my right leg just above the knee, readily available should I need to defend myself against the Hun on the soil of France. The distraught squadron leader had no choice but to give up the battle when it was pointed out to him that fighter aircraft do not have baggage compartments and that I really had no choice but to dress as I was.

After that furor had settled down we trooped into dinner, during which it was announced that General Patton was going to inspect us the next morning at 0800 hours. That news created some excitement. We had not been inspected by a general before. We knew General Patton was known as "Old Blood and Guts," the American general who got into trouble slapping a soldier in Sicily. That summed up the extent of our knowledge of Patton.

At the appointed hour the next morning we were ready. Our aircraft were lined up wing tip to wing tip facing west at the west side of the grass-covered airfield. My machine was halfway down the line. Each pilot stood in front of his own aircraft. My Mustang, with its long, high snout, loomed up behind me. It was a clear, bright morning. The sun was at our backs, its light reflecting off the dew on the grass at our feet. A perfect day. At 0800 hours sharp a Jeep with its top down appeared on the roadway between the buildings in front of us, swung south, pulled around to the southernmost aircraft, and stopped. There he was, General Patton himself.

Standing rigidly at attention I turned my head slightly to watch as he climbed out of the vehicle, returning the salute of our squadron leader. Without further ado Patton began to walk down the line of aircraft, passing in front of each pilot. He did not stop to talk to any of my colleagues. But he did stop when he got to me! There he was, right in front of me. I was at stiff, ramrod attention, at my short tallest. My flat officers' cap was squarely on my head, polka-dot scarf neatly in place. The fifty-eight-year-old general was elegantly dressed. He had a wedge cap on his white-haired head. The left breast of his khaki battledress jacket was covered with a multitude of ribbons. Light tan riding breeks were above highly polished riding boots and silver spurs. On each hip was a revolver, the famed ivory-handled guns. He towered over me, all six-foot-two of him.

General Patton looked down at me, examining the boyish face. Then he looked up at the looming nose of the huge Mustang. Then back down to me again.

"Boy," he demanded, "how old are you?"

"I'm twenty, sir."

His eyes went up to the aircraft again, then back down to me. His right arm lifted as he pointed up to the airplane, but his eyes were still fixed on mine as he asked in his high-pitched voice.

"Do *you* fly that goddamn airplane?"

"Yes, sir."

With that he dropped his arm. "Son of a bitch," he said incredulously. With a shake of his head he turned and walked on.

CHAPTER 13
A Noball Operation, May 13, 1944

———◆———

13 May 1944 OPERATIONS: - the weather was fine during the day allowing six sorties to be flown ... F/L J.B. Prendergast and Flying Officer R.H. Rohmer flew to St. Omer to photograph three Noball targets. F/L Prendergast camera failed but targets were successfully photographed by Flying Officer Rohmer.

430 Squadron Log

THIS IS A DESCRIPTION OF a photo recce that the determined Jim Prendergast and I undertook on May 13, 1944. We were out to take pictures of three of those mysterious Noball sites. We still didn't know what they were, but I would find out on the night of June 12, 1944, one month less a day after this sortie.

Our task on May 13 was straightforward. The briefing officer informed us there were three Noball sites at St. Omer that we were to photograph. The targets had been bombed by Bostons earlier in the day. Our photographs would enable the APIS people to assess the damage, if any. The squadron had been doing Noball missions for several weeks, and in large number, but at no time were any of us informed what it was the bombers were trying so hard to destroy and we trying so hard to photograph. However, the pictures we took showed us that at each Noball site there had been fully or partially completed what looked like a section of roadway about one hundred yards long and about two hundred feet wide. At one end of this roadway there was a slight crook off to the side, making the whole installation look like a hockey stick with a shortened blade. In addition, there were new buildings erected in each construction area.

Another clue was that the Noball targets were concentrated in the Pas-de-Calais area, close to the Channel coastline. If it had been my job to interpret the photographs as well as take them I would also have been able to see that the handle ends of the hockey sticks were pointed toward London. One characteristic all of us were able to observe about the Noball sites was that the Germans built them almost exclusively in wooded areas — in orchards, forests, or copses of trees. It was as if they were trying to hide what they were building without knowing that it was impossible to conceal them from the prying, all-seeing eyes of our cameras and our high-altitude Bluebird Spitfires.

The routine for these missions was relatively straightforward. Prendergast, as the assigned leader, and I went over the maps on which our route across to France had been plotted. We discussed the direction of his run in on the target. He would fly at seven thousand feet directly over the Noball site. His aircraft would be straight and level so his vertical camera would be pointed at the objective. All three Noballs were close together and caught in one photo. To fly straight and level at the relatively low altitude made one a sitting duck if the area was protected by flak, especially by the deadly accurate German 88-mm anti-aircraft gun. The fire direction mechanisms on the 88s were such that the shells invariably exploded at our exact height. Even if they didn't hit you, they would come close enough to scare the hell out of you with their big, black, exploding clouds of lethal metal.

Prendergast's aircraft was rigged with an eight-inch vertical camera. Its small size dictated the height at which he had to take his photographs. My aircraft was equipped with a fourteen-inch oblique camera, installed just behind the cockpit pointing out to the left and slightly behind the tailing edge of the wing. I would have to be about two hundred yards off Prendergast's right so I could keep a protective eye on his tail to make sure we were not taken by surprise by any enemy fighters. Then just as he was completing his run directly over the target I would put my left wing down and fly my aircraft so the oblique camera would be pointed at the target just long enough to get a fast series of pictures. We began to prepare.

Our briefing and final discussion as to routes and operating procedures takes place in the large 39 Recce Wing operations tent at our base at RAF Station Odiham. We leave it and walk to our squadron's operations tent not far away to collect our helmets, goggles, gloves, and parachutes, which we drape over our right shoulders to carry out to the airplanes. Once there, the parachute, helmet, and goggles are put on and we climb into our respective aircraft. Prendergast is in Mustang N and I am in L. Those large identification figures are on each side of the fuselage between the cockpit and the tail section. With the assistance of our ground crews we strap ourselves into the bucket seats and start our engines. On go all the switches, including radio. I check its operation by talking with Prendergast, whose aircraft is sitting three places away from mine in the line, its prop turning over.

When the engine temperatures are up, another radio check and we taxi out onto the east-west Odiham runway. I follow a few yards behind Prendergast, each of us turning his aircraft from side to side so we can see ahead beyond the big, blinding nose of the Mustang. We stop for a final takeoff power run-up check. Takeoff clearance comes from the controller's hut. A green Aldis beacon points at us, brilliant even in daylight, saying "Go." We line up on the runway in formation. Prendergast is on the left. I have my left wing tip tucked in just behind his right for a close formation takeoff, the kind every fighter pilot likes to do. His right hand comes up, palm inward toward his face. He moves it forward and back twice, the signal to begin the takeoff. We start to roll. In a few seconds we are airborne. An automatic reach with the left hand for the undercarriage level pulls it to the "up" position. I watch Prendergast's wheels coming up and feel mine lock into place. I wait for the hand signal to lift the 15 degrees of flaps we have put down before takeoff. It comes. I move the flap selector to "up." I can see his flaps lifting until they are flush with the wing and clean. My wing tip is still tucked inside his as we turn west climbing. It is 1601 hours.

Prendergast straightens out on his south-southeast course, giving me the hand signal to go into battle formation. Immediately I pull out to the right. I will maintain that station during the entire operation, two hundred yards to the right or to the left, depending upon the turns that have to be made. However, on the target run I must be on his right.

At three thousand feet we level off, heading for Selsey Bill, the great peninsula on the south coat of England toward its eastern end. It is an excellent landmark for departures across the Channel and conversely an ideal low-level landfall on the way back. As we approach Selsey Bill, Prendergast starts to descend. Down to the deck we go as we leave the land and hurtle across the Channel just above the waves to avoid radar detection. I now activate my guns by turning the gun selector switch to "All." The two gun charger levers are pulled fully out and I am ready to fire if need be, using the illuminated gunsight just above the instrument panel directly ahead of me.

By this time we have started our watching procedures, for we could be attacked by enemy fighters at any moment. I check my station position with Prendergast's aircraft. I sweep my vision behind him, then forward in a clockwise motion ahead, and around in an arc back and behind to the right. My eyes search the horizon. Next I turn my head slowly to look directly overhead. My line of sight goes down again to the left rear behind the lead Mustang. And so the procedure is repeated constantly with regular checks into the rear-view mirror just above my head. It covers the blind spot that the Mustang I has to the rear due to its enclosed birdcage hood. Nothing is seen.

Radio silence is maintained as an operational necessity.

About five miles from the French coast Prendergast lifts the nose of his aircraft and we begin to climb, planning to cross the coast at seven thousand feet with a landfall at Quand Plage.

What is left of the regularly attacked German radar system will now pick us up on their screens. An alert will be given to the anti-aircraft batteries in our path, and the German fighter squadrons in the area will be notified. Whether they elect to respond remains to be seen.

We cross the coast at five thousand feet, still climbing. We are in the lair of the German Eagle. My head is really swivelling as I read every section of the sky for a sign of enemy fighters. In addition to keeping a sharp lookout, Prendergast is also doing the navigating and map reading. He must get us to the target and back. In a few minutes he is on the radio to me — no need for silence now — letting me know that the target is straight ahead at twelve o'clock. He'll be starting his photo run in about three minutes.

There are no clouds below us and above only high, scattered cirrus. A beautiful day, and therefore a dangerous one for us. We can be easily seen by high-flying enemy fighters. At seven thousand feet we're beyond the best operating height of the Mustang, so if we are attacked we are at a greater disadvantage than usual.

The next hazard is flak. Will the target be protected by 88s? If so, we're going to be in for a rough ride, especially Prendergast, who has to remain absolutely straight and level when he's taking his photographs. But there will be no flinching by Prendergast, whose reputation for coolness and determination has been solidly earned. As for me, I can weave and bob and still maintain my battle formation station and take my oblique photographs.

The moment of truth is at hand. Now the targets are one mile ahead. We are set for the run in.

Because there is no window in the floor you cannot see vertically down in the Mustang, so you must line up your aircraft using predetermined landmarks on each side of the target. Following those you then know without question that you're going to put the camera right over the target. So once he is lined up, Prendergast cannot see the Noball sites, but off to the side I can. There they are in copses of trees, the peculiar hockey stick forms gleaming white in their sheltering woods. The bombs that were aimed at the sites carved enormous holes in the countryside all around the copses. At one Noball a string landed across the stubby blade at the end of the stick. Whether it is damaged or not I cannot tell.

Prendergast is into his photographic run. I'm getting set to take my obliques just after he passes directly over the target. It is now or never for the 88s. Prendergast is over the target. Still no 88s. Now it's my turn. Taking the airplane over on its left side, with top right rudder I bring the Noball sites into the direct line of my camera by matching the targets with the camera-aiming mark on the trailing edge of my left wing. When I'm sure I have them I press the operating button on my control column. In my earphones I hear the electrical clicking each time the camera snaps a photo. After a few seconds, I pull the aircraft level and check my position in relation to Prendergast. I have come a little closer to him, so I pull out to the full two hundred yards. No flak. He advises me he's going back for another run westbound.

After a double crossover turn of 180 degrees we complete a second run over the targets. Still all is quiet. Nevertheless, it is time to get the hell out of there. Rubbernecking for enemy fighters we hightail for the coast, dropping down to wave level as soon as we hit the Channel. We double-check our IFF (Identification Friend or Foe) transmitters to make sure they're functioning. We want the radar operators in England to know that we are indeed friendly. As we approach the welcoming contours of Selsey Bill we climb up again to three thousand feet and go through the procedures of putting our guns on "Safe." At Odiham I do a stream — staying well back from Prendergast's aircraft — rather than a formation landing. We're back on the ground at 1730 hours, just under one and a half hours to France and back.

As we carry our parachutes and gear back to our squadron operations tent we talk about the trip. It appears to have been completely successful. Naturally we are both relieved that we got away with it without flak or fighters. At the 39 Recce Wing Operations tent we are debriefed by the same intelligence officer who briefed us. In the middle of the session we are informed that for Prendergast the trip was for naught. His vertical camera did not function, the result of an electrical failure. All that way at such high risk for nothing — unless my photographs turned out. They did. So our sortie was successful and well worth the effort.

On the night of June 12 we were to find out just how important the Noball sites really were and why it was so vital that they be destroyed. Our photographic reconnaissance was equally important, since it was the only way our intelligence knew whether or not the Noball targets had been destroyed, merely damaged, or completely missed.

CHAPTER 14
D-Day, June 6, 1944

———◆———

6 June 1944 OPERATIONS: D-Day. The first sorties were airborne before sunrise. This was the start of a very busy day, thirty sorties being flown in all. Flying Officer J.H. Taylor and Flying Officer R.H. Rohmer did a recce of all roads leading into Caen. Photos of transport headed toward Caen were taken.

430 Squadron Log

THE DAYS BETWEEN MAY 13 and June 5, the day before D-Day, were filled with an enormous number of photo recce missions. Bombing against those pesky Noball sites, whatever they were, continued apace. Similarly, 430 Squadron was tasked with photographing not only Noball sites (vertical) but also stretches of French beaches (oblique). We covered the Pas-de-Calais area close to England. Strangely (to us) we went far south to Normandy. We photographed major shore sections from Deanville west past the Orne River and Arromanches to the high cliffs north of St. Lô. Surely that area was too far away for a seaborne assault mounted from England. At least, that's what we low-life pilots thought. But we weren't the planners for Supreme Commander General Eisenhower. We were simply spear carriers.

Lo and behold, our long-distance photo missions across to Normandy had real meaning and enormous value and significance. When our airfield commander, and later in life a close friend, Group Captain Ernie Moncrieff, briefed us in the evening of June 5, he told us not only that D-Day was on for the next morning but also where.

D-Day! This was the moment we had all been waiting for, preparing for. During the last two weeks of May the pace of our operations had increased. More and more we were tasked for low-level photography of miles of beaches along several stretches of French coastline.

Along that same coast German radar installations capable of spotting ships on the English Channel were under vigorous air attack. They had to be knocked out. And we had to follow the bombers in with our cameras so the extent of the inflicted damage could be assessed.

Flying past Portsmouth on the way across to France during the last days of May and the beginning of June, I could see the multitude of ships large and small gathering there in ports all along the south coast. Troops, tanks, guns, and vehicles were at their assembly and marshalling points. For me it was a time of increasing excitement and anticipation. Like all our own pilots and ground crews I was as keen as mustard. We were on the verge of the promised assault on the enemy, the liberation of Europe and the defeat of the German Army. We were ready, pawing the ground.

On the night of June 5, Group Captain Ernie Moncrieff held a briefing for all the pilots of the three squadrons that comprised 39 Recce Wing to tell them that the invasion was on. On a huge map of the Normandy coast he outlined where the landings would take place. The Second British Army was assigned Gold, Juno, and Sword beaches stretching from the Orne River on the east to Port-en-Bessin on the west. The American First Army was assigned Omaha and Utah beaches to the west of Gold and partway up the Contentin Peninsula. 39 Recce Wing would therefore be concentrating its efforts in the Gold-Juno-Sword sector. Of particular concern was the area leading from the beachhead up to Caen, including the roads and railways leading into that city, because it was Montgomery's principal objective to reach and take Caen within the first twenty-four hours.

Every serviceable Royal Air Force and Royal Canadian Air Force heavy bomber would be airborne during the night, saturating the area immediately in front of the beaches, knocking out gun emplacements and other fortifications. Paratroopers would be dropped during the night. At first light, troop-carrying gliders would be landing in preselected areas well in from the beach. Our primary task would be tactical reconnaissance (TAC/R) flights to pick up movements of enemy tanks, troops, or vehicles and to spot the location of guns. All this information would be fed to Army headquarters and to the units in the field.

In addition, if we discovered major targets, such as concentrations of tanks, we were to radio our Group Control Centre and report the location, whereupon GCC would direct in Typhoon rocket-carrying squadrons or Spitfire fighter bombers. Some of the pilots from our sister squadron, 414, would direct the fire of the huge Royal Navy battleships that would be standing offshore. Their targets would be the heavy gun emplacements encased in concrete along the enemy coast.

H-Hour, the time designated for the British and Canadian troops to hit the beach, ranged between 0725 and 0745 hours. We would be over them.

Actually, the group captain's news that the invasion was on did not come as a total surprise. There had been standing orders that immediately before D-Day all our aircraft would be painted at the wing-roots and at the fuselage just ahead of the tail with broad black and white stripes, a further safeguard that the troops on the ground and the crews of ships would recognize us as friendly. On June 4 the order had been given to put on the stripes.

The group captain's briefing, the knowledge that D-Day was finally at hand, and the anticipation of taking part in this gigantic effort produced a euphoria probably much like that felt by the members of a professional football team before a championship game. We were "up."

After the briefing, our squadron's tasking for the morning was issued. I was assigned with Flying Officer Jack Taylor to do a tactical reconnaissance over the beachhead area, south to Caen, and for a short distance along the roads leading into that town from the south and southeast. Our takeoff time was to be 0600 hours. There were to be two sections of two ahead of us, each airborne at 0500 hours, also tasked to do TAC/Rs.

All six of us were quietly wakened in our tents at 0300. We dressed quickly and, without taking time to wash or shave, hurried to the mess tent. Our fabulous chef, Stradiotti, personally appeared to produce eggs, bacon, and coffee for us. After breakfast it was over to the Wing Operations tent to be briefed on our operations.

The two sections ahead of us took off in the darkness shortly after 0500. Both returned a few minutes after 0700. We were airborne at 0600 just before sun-up and, as the record shows, Taylor and I were the only people from 430 Squadron to be over the beaches at H-Hour.

In the semi-darkness we did a stream rather than formation takeoff. As soon as I was airborne, I began a turn to the left in order to place my aircraft inside of Taylor's banking to port about half a mile ahead of me. That way I could catch up with him quickly as our paths crossed. He was already in a gentle arc in the same direction toward a course that would take us south to exit the coast just to the east of Portsmouth. As I caught up with him, crossed under, and moved out to my comfortable battle formation position, the darkness was fast disappearing. But that day the sun was invisible, obliterated by a solid blanket of high, gray cloud that looked to me to be sitting above us at perhaps ten thousand feet. We knew the wind was strong, close to 20 miles per hour from the west. It wouldn't affect us, but it would undoubtedly play havoc with the men crossing the Channel in ships big and small.

As we approached the crossing-out point on the south coast the sight that lay before us was awesome. As far as the eye could see the sea was covered with ships in a vast, miles-wide, unending column reaching south to the horizon, plowing through whitecapped waves toward the Normandy shore. Ships coming in from ports to the east or the west of Portsmouth converged on the column about ten miles south of the coast. Even I could judge that we were flying over the largest armada that had ever sailed on any waters. While we still could not see the French coastline, we knew that the head of this enormous force of ships was sitting off the invasion beaches, its mighty battleships, cruisers, destroyers, and other assault craft spewing thousands of shells and rockets onto pre-determined targets in the final minutes before H-Hour.

While I was constantly checking the sky for enemy aircraft and occasionally catching glimpses of Allied fighter squadrons in the distance, it was impossible to keep my eyes off the amazing sight below us. The water was thick with ships rolling in the heavy seas, some of them towing protective barrage balloons to stave off low-level enemy aircraft attacks. From my vantage point everything appeared shaded by the diffused light filtering through the heavy cloud above us. Even the whitecaps had turned gray. The bobbing ships painted in their myriad patterns of dark, blending colours gave off a common grayness only slightly contrasted against the uninviting blackness of the wind-whipped channel waters carrying them.

Then we could see the outline of the Normandy coast dead ahead. Sitting over it was something we had not anticipated. It was a high, towering wall of broken cloud that had built up over the entire sector of Normandy beaches to be assaulted. That unexpected cloud barrier would make it next to impossible for the heavy and medium American daylight bombers to work effectively against the pinpoint targets they had to be able to see. Our fighter squadrons would have great difficulty in catching any marauding enemy aircraft because they could quickly take cover in the clouds. Allied fighter bombers and rocket aircraft would be similarly impeded, for, as we soon discovered, the uneven base of the cloud was only five hundred feet above the ground. Anybody flying under it would be highly vulnerable to flak and, for that matter, fire from machine guns and rifles. Furthermore, defending enemy fighters could use the low scud cloud as they manoeuvred into firing position on one's vulnerable tail.

Heading straight south for the beach just to the west of Ouistreham and by Lion-sur-Mer off my right wing tip, we dove down below the unwelcome cloud bank to cross the still vacant beach. Our speed was well over 400 miles per hour. Our eyes were peeled and our heads on swivels. It was Taylor's job to lead. He had to do the map reading and the reconnaissance. He would note the location of tanks, moving vehicles, and gun emplacements, as well as whether there was artillery or flak to be seen. If possible, he would photograph with his 14-inch port oblique camera the important items he observed.

Within two minutes we were over Caen, where the wall of cloud that sat over the beachhead had dissipated. We were able to climb rapidly to six thousand feet, a far safer altitude at which to operate. During the less than two minutes it had taken to fly at low level from the coast to Caen we had swept by fields littered with huge Horsa troop- and vehicle-carrying gliders. They had moved in the darkness in the early hours of the morning to attempt to seize the bridges over the Caen Canal and the Orne River. Some of the gliders were still whole, while others had wings ripped off or had crashed, totally torn apart.

As Taylor and I made our first run to Caen we could see brilliantly burning light anti-aircraft tracer shells slowly arcing up toward us, behind us, and on into the clouds above. Those first welcoming barrages were coming fairly close but were nothing to worry about. I always had a feeling of detachment and a they'll-never-hit-me attitude to the apparently slow-moving flak I could see on its way. It was no different that morning when I felt particularly fearless and invincible. But in the next weeks, my encounters with the accurate, invisible shells of the deadly German 88-mm aircraft guns and the high-velocity light flak that appeared on the battlefront changed my attitude to one of great respect and, on not a few occasions, unadulterated terror.

Thirty minutes were spent checking all the roads leading into Caen. Taylor saw some motor vehicles moving toward Caen on the main highway about five miles southeast of the city. Beyond that little movement was seen.

Then we turned back for the beaches, again diving down to low level to get under that wall of cloud. Arriving at the coast just to the west of Ouistreham, we swung west to follow the beach line about a half-mile inland.

It was H-Hour. Below us the terrain was crater-pocked from the thousand of bombs that had rained down during the night. New craters were being made before our eyes as shell after shell from the battleships, cruisers, and destroyers standing offshore smashed down under us. The devastating barrage was now lifting from the shore working inland in an attempt to destroy any enemy forces that might impede the imminent beaching of the first landing craft.

Out to sea we could see them coming, the first lines of landing craft filled with men, tanks, rockets, flak vehicles. Landing craft designed to explode any minefields were in the vanguard, the swimming Sherman Duplex Drive tanks wallowing behind like rectangular rhinoceros in the surf. They were almost there, almost at the point where bottoms and tracks would touch the sands of Normandy. They bobbed and plowed through the heavy waves about a hundred yards offshore, their gray-white wakes marking the growing distance between their sterns and the naval force that had escorted or carried them across the Channel during the stormy night. That mighty armada was now standing about three miles offshore with all its guns trained and firing at the beachhead and us.

From my cockpit I looked out into a horizon filled with the thick cordite smoke from the constant firing of hundreds of huge naval guns. So heavy was the blanket of smoke that it almost totally obscured the massive fleet. Through the heavy black pall, but made more visible and pronounced by it, I could see the flashes of the countless guns, like an unending line of twinkling Christmas lights winking on a dark, foggy night. That they were firing directly at us never even crossed my mind.

At Arromanches we turned around and headed back toward Ouistreham, arriving there just as the first landing craft and Duplex Drive tanks hit the beach under heavy fire from German machine guns and 88s. We could see the landing craft disgorging tanks and men into what was rapidly becoming a shambles as enemy fire concentrated on the beaches.

As we turned back once again toward the west the same scenario was developing where the 3rd Canadian Division was coming in on Juno Beach at Courseulles. Beyond them and to the west of Arromanches, 30 Corps of the Second British Army was beginning its assault.

Back and forth Taylor and I ranged over this incredible, lethal theatre of death and destruction. The turning point in the Second World War was taking place as we watched. We were witnesses to one of the monumental military events in the history of mankind.

So entranced and enthralled was I by the enormity of the scene that I failed to monitor my instrument panel regularly. When finally I did drop my eyes for a split second to run over my engine instruments, temperatures, pressures, and fuel, I was shocked. The fuel contents gauge on the floor to the right of my seat registered at the empty mark! And there I was, sitting over the Normandy beaches, at least one hundred miles from the coast of England. Time to get the hell home. Obviously I had been using a lot more fuel than the lead aircraft, otherwise Taylor would have turned back for England long before.

I radioed a fast call to him with a touch of alarm in my voice. We turned north immediately, climbing up and out over the thundering naval ships, levelling off at two thousand feet. I did not want to waste any fuel by climbing higher. The next step was to get the propeller into coarse pitch and engine power back for minimum fuel consumption. Then I quickly leaned out the mixture of fuel going to the engine to further minimize fuel consumption. This meant that my airspeed was about 150 miles per hour, roughly 100 less than our normal cruising speed. Taylor stayed with me. He did not cut his speed back but circled and weaved above me to give me protection against any potential enemy fighter attack.

Would I have to bail out? The last thing to do with a Mustang was to ditch it in the sea. It would not skim along the surface. Instead, experience had shown that the aircraft would go straight into the water just like the shark it resembled. The pilot would then ride it to the bottom, and that would be the end of the matter. No, if the engine quit I would bail out. At least I wouldn't be alone in the water; below me I could see nothing but ships of every type and kind plowing their way through the sea toward the Normandy coast. You could practically walk on them they were so thick.

The needle of the gas gauge was now on the left edge of the empty mark. Time to run through the bailout check: *If the engine quits I will pull back the red emergency handle on the starboard window rail and push straight up on the hood. If it works that will get rid of the hood. Next stage, check on my Mae West and the pull handle that will release the CO_2 to inflate it. Remember to grab the parachute release handle as you step out. Well above the waves, turn the round parachute release handle to release. Bang the handle to get rid of the parachute harness a split second before hitting the water. Make sure the lanyard from the dinghy pack on the parachute I'm sitting on is attached to the Mae West so the pack won't float away. The dinghy will have to be inflated quickly so I can get into it as fast as possible. Everything checks. If I run out of gas I'm ready.*

As soon as we left the French coast I sorted out in my mind where I would head. I wanted the closest airport I could find. I knew where it was and told Taylor of my intentions.

When I was about ten miles from the English coast the needle on the gas gauge was well below the empty mark. Miraculously, the engine was still grinding away. I had a few words with the airfield controller at my chosen destination to explain my emergency situation. Immediately he gave me clearance for a straight-in landing on the north-south runway. Into the final approach, wheels down, flaps down, approach speed 120, rounded out, throttled off, touchdown on the button end of the runway. I turned off at the first taxiway on the right. The engine coughed. Coughed again. Then quit.

It was 0809 hours on D-Day, June 6, 1944. The point of touchdown was Thorney Island, that happy place where I had joined the Flying Circus six weeks before. Within three and a half hours I would be leading a section from Odiham across the beachhead for a tactical reconnaissance of the Bayeux area.

CHAPTER 15

The Regent Palace Hotel Caper and the Arrival of the First Buzz Bomb, June 12, 1944

12 June 1944 OPERATIONS: An artillery shoot was flown by F/L J. Watts with Flying Officers F.P. Bryon, T.H. Lambros and R.H. Rohmer as cover. In French coast Cabourg. Targets to be engaged were enemy artillery. Due to our own guns not being ready, only first target was engaged, which was southeast of Caen. Out French coast Cabourg.

430 Squadron Log

FROM JUNE 6 WE PILOTS and ground people of 430 Squadron and everyone in 129 Airfield and 39 Recce Wing worked our tails off from three in the morning until midnight. What an exciting time for this twenty-year-old and all of my air and ground colleagues. And out there on the ground in Normandy, the brave people we were working for and supporting, the Canadian and British armies, were consolidating the enormous ground they had taken from the Rommel-led Germans with hard, bloody fighting.

It was a stressful and exhausting time for everyone.

That artillery shoot had seen Watts, Bryon, Lambros, and me airborne out of Odiham at 1315 and back again at 1515. After debriefing I had to hurry to change from my usual battledress flying gear into my light blue Royal Canadian Air Force "walking out" uniform (with shirt, tie, polished brass buttons, and the ever-present flat hat) and to pack my smallest bag with a change of underwear, black socks, and shaving kit — not really needed except for the toothbrush — before the five-thirty train left for London.

A one-day "spot of leave" had been granted to three pilots from each of 39 Wing's three squadrons. We had been working almost around the clock since D-Day, usually getting up at 0300 or 0400 for breakfast, briefing, and first-light sorties. Flying was finished late in the day, and debriefings often lasted until after dark. It was a demanding and dangerous time, although in our squadron we had been remarkably fortunate in that we had lost only one pilot, Flying Officer Jack Cox. He was shot down on D-Day when the formation four that he was in was attacked by four Focke-Wulf 190s.

Our Wingco Ops, Bunt Waddell, decided it was time to get a rotational system of one-day leaves going to relieve the high tension under which we had been working.

Naturally it was to London that this first gang headed, all nine of us. Most had made bookings at the Regent Palace Hotel, that renowned gem of British hostelry that sits cramped in on a triangular piece of land on the northern rim of that famous British battleground, Piccadilly Circus. There the aptly named Piccadilly Commandos operated by day and (mainly) by night, lurking in every cranny and doorway, from which they assaulted innocent soldiers, sailors, and airmen with salvos of enticements.

On arriving in London, our hard-flying team emerged into the pitch dark of the blackout and leaped into reliable square-box London taxis that were waiting, their hooded headlights dimmed. From the railway station we went straight to the Regent Palace. After a quick registration and throwing of bags in rooms we were off on a tour of our favourite clubs, a handful of nearby places where membership was limited to la crème de la crème, the Canadian and British fighter pilots, those men with the traditional distinction of wearing undone the top brass button on their jackets. All bomber and coastal commander crews and other lesser types were excluded.

Following a long evening tour, which took us first to the basement bar of our hotel, then to the Chez Moi Club, and finally to the Crackers Club, we arrived on foot at the front door of the Regent Palace, much the worse for wear. By now there were only six people in our team, the biggest of whom was Flight Lieutenant Jack "Sailor" Seaman, a tall, square, quiet hulk of a young man. On the other end of the scale I was by far the smallest, weighing in at 145 pounds, and not as high as Sailor Seaman's left shoulder.

As we approached the front door in the dim shadows of the blackout there came into view a woman standing near the entrance. She was on the west side of the Regent Palace's pie-shaped piece of land, which came to a point just a few feet south of the door. Ranged behind her was her stable of ladies of the night. Some eight of them were lined up along the curb.

In a flash our team lined up opposite them, and loud tongue-in-cheek (on our side) haggling began. Being by nature a fierce fighter, I decided that the best place for me to stand was directly behind the protective big body of Sailor Seaman. From that supposedly safe vantage point I entered the shouting fray, from time to time by sticking my head around Sailor's left shoulder to mouth something provocatively rude at the madam, then ducking back behind his large frame.

I had just made one of my brave vocal forays and retreated behind Sailor when he suddenly stepped aside. There facing me, about one and half feet away, was the madam. With experienced skill she cocked her clenched fist and smashed me full in the mouth. Under the force of the blow I staggered backward. Fortunately for my reputation, I did not fall. Astonished and in no little pain I pulled myself together, marched back to where she was standing, planted my feet, and returned the right smash. Whereupon she tottered backward, falling into the arms of her charges. That exchange of blows ended the session forthwith.

With the aid of my roommate, Flying Officer Joe "Splash" Roussel, I made my way up to the room, hand over an extremely painful mouth. When I got into the bathroom to put cold water on my face, the mirror told me the bad news. My lips were swollen like an orangutan's. That wasn't the end of the evening for my friends, but it certainly was for me.

Later that night, contemplating my misery of too much booze, compounded by thick lips, my ears picked up the sound of an unusual aircraft engine. Pilots were sensitive to the sounds of the engines of the myriad aircraft that populated our skies in those days. I certainly was. I had never heard this one before, but I knew it was an airplane, a low-flying one at that. Its noise was deep, guttural, throbbing and, as it approached, loud, pulsating with such force that it made the windows shake. As the machine came overhead in the darkness I threw open the window to scan the black sky. I could see nothing. The unusual aircraft was out of my line of sight, but its noise was all-enveloping, ominous.

Suddenly there was silence. Complete silence, almost as deafening as the noise that had stopped. That was strange. An aircraft low over the centre of London and the engine stops? It wasn't that it sputtered and wound down. It stopped abruptly. Most peculiar. In a few seconds the silence was shattered by a powerful explosion that lit up the sky. The first V-1, the infamous flying bomb, had arrived. It was the precursor of hundreds that Hitler was to shower upon London until the launching sites in the Pas-de-Calais area were overrun by the Allied forces much later.

Now the secret was out. Even we fighter reconnaissance pilots could be told. The Noball sites we had been photographing in France in the last months were launching pads for the V-1. Those hockey sticks were ramps, up which the ignited engines of the V-1s drove the pilotless flying bombs in a direct line toward the heart of London. Now there was no doubt in our minds about the importance of the attacks on the Noball sites and our supporting work. Without the confirmed destruction of a vast number of the launching ramps as well as the V-1 assembly and storage locations by USAF, RAF, and RCAF bomber attacks, the devastation of the V-1 onslaught on London might well have been sufficient to change the course of the war.

The order that brought the V-1 flying bomb crashing down at Bethnal Green in London was issued by Hitler himself, immediately after he had been informed by his staff that Allied landings were underway in Normandy. He commanded Jodl to pass the code word *Junkroom*, the signal to begin launching the devil's own device against the people of London. In themselves the V-1s were symbols of the lengths to which the strategists of the Second World War were prepared to go in order to bring the enemy to its knees, thereby achieving the ultimate victory.

The V-1 was a flying bomb. It was a pilotless, almost impervious winged projectile launched from specially constructed sites scattered around the Pas-de-Calais area within about one hundred miles of the centre core of London. It could reach any part of the 692 square miles of Greater London. There its precisely calculated fuel supply would run out. At that instant the thundering, pulsing roar of its paraffin-powered ramjet engine would abruptly stop, filling the air with the silence of the imminent death and devastation that would inevitably occur with its mindless impact.

The V-1 had a wingspan of about 17 feet and a length of 25 feet, a range of between 120 and 140 miles, and an optimum operating height of 1,000 to 4,000 feet. It flew at speeds over 400 miles per hour. In its bulky nose it carried a warhead of one ton of high explosives. In theory its carefully measured fuel load was sufficient to take it from the point of launching in France to the Tower of London, give or take two minutes of flying.

Of the first ten V-1s that were launched on the night of June 12, five crashed immediately after the launch, one went missing, and the other four (including the one I heard in London that night) reached England. Notwithstanding this feeble start there was no reason to believe that the battle against the V-1 sites at their manufacturing plants and storage areas had been totally successful. By mid-June the picture was much different. In one twenty-four-hour period commencing at 2230 hours on June 15 more than two hundred flying bombs were launched from the Noball sites. One hundred and forty-four reached England. Of those, seventy-three crashed on Greater London, wreaking enormous destruction.

In the end, 8,617 flying bombs were launched from France. Of those, approximately 2,340 arrived at the London civil defence region, killing 5,500 people, seriously injuring some 16,000 more, and destroying thousands of buildings.

As if the V-1 was not enough, the first V-2 rocket fell on London on Friday, September 8, a frightening projectile that arrived without warning and exploded. The detonation was followed by the sound of the rocket as the noise caught up with the missile, which had been travelling well beyond the speed of sound. By April 7, 1945, 1,190 V-2 rockets had been successfully launched against London. The arrival of 1,115 of those was recorded, some 501 falling in the London civil defence region.

CHAPTER 16

430 Squadron Moves to B8 at Magny in Normandy

———◄——►———

29 June 1944 OPERATIONS: At long last the weather broke sufficiently for the squadron to move to B8 landing strip, near Bayeux, Normandy. We had been waiting for this for several days. S/L F.H. Chester led the squadron in three sections. Landing was made at B8 without incident. The Orderly Room and Pilots room was established in three upstairs rooms of abandoned Château Magny and the squadron was ready for work. In the afternoon TAC/R's were flown by Flying Officer's J.A. Lowndes and K.K. Charman and by Flying Officer's T.H. Lambros and R.H. Rohmer. Fires were seen in Evreux and M.T. were spotted.

430 Squadron Log

MOBILITY WAS THE ESSENCE OF all the airfields in the 2nd Tactical Air Force, including ours, 129 Airfield, which accommodated the three squadrons of 39 Recce Wing. Everything we had — personal possessions, tents, kitchen equipment, servicing hangars, tools, parts, absolutely everything — had to be capable of fast movement from one operating base to the next.

Mobility meant moving all of these things, either by truck or in vans, each specially designed and equipped for the particular use assigned to it, such as a headquarters van or photo processing truck, as well as signals, medical, orderly room, central maintenance for the aircraft, and the like. Sleeping accommodations, messes, and supplementary space for the specialized vans were in the standard form of the ubiquitous canvas tent, man's primitive and only partially effective shelter against penetrating rain and piercing cold, and no defence at all against falling shrapnel. Our personal kit bags, sleeping, and messing tents were usually carried by a Dakota aircraft so that the pilots could set up shop the same day they arrived at the new base, while the vans and trucks of the rest of the mobile airfield proceeded by road (except for the initial cross-Channel move by ship), usually taking some days in the process.

Pilots had to be able to operate their fighter aircraft from the paved runways that the old RAF stations such as Odiham, Tangmere, and Thorney Island possessed, from rolling grass turf, as at Gatwick, or from untreated earth strips that the blades of the bulldozers of the Royal Engineers would carve out of a farmer's field or though his orchard. The first experimental tactical airstrip had been bulldozed out on a farm near Ashford in Kent, where 430 Squadron was located when I joined it in September 1943. The next strip on which we were to land was our first battle airfield in Normandy, named B8.

The airstrip the Royal Engineers had cut out for us at B8 lay to the northeast of Bayeux at Magny, about three miles from the outskirts of the legendary Norman city. B8 was a single strip running east and west to accommodate the prevailing winds. The surface was a brown, light loam that had been easily levelled by bulldozer blades across about three thousand feet of flat, cleared agricultural land, planted at the time in grain crop. Close to the edge of the strip and near its west end stood a large, gray, two-storey stone residence, more in the style and size of a manor house than a château, as the scribe of the squadron log, an obvious romanticist, had called it. Château Magny had been abandoned. The residents had been given the opportunity to move out all their furniture and possessions before the engineers had finished their construction work.

I was part of the second group to land at B8 on June 25. There were three of us: Bill Golden, Danny Lambros, and me. We touched down on the new airstrip shortly after noon. The bulldozers were still working around the edges of the strip, but no other vehicles were in sight. No tents had been erected, nothing was there except a huge stock of piled jerry cans full of aviation gasoline, the stuff we needed. It was a warm, sunny summer day, with lots of blue sky and just fragments of clouds.

The moment of landing, of touching down in France for the first time, was inspirational. It was the kind of emotion that those who are fortunate enough to arrive at a truly new frontier must have when they enter its threshold. We were there! Being on French soil at last was also tangible evidence that all of us, Army, Navy, and Air Force, had succeeded in bringing off at least the initial beachhead conquest. Together we had secured a tenuous foothold inside Fortress Europe, the preserve of the most formidable of Germany's fighting generals, Field Marshal Erwin Rommel.

As soon as our tanks had been topped with gasoline we were airborne again for our tactical reconnaissance into the area of Argentan through to Alençon. We flew south at five thousand feet, crossing over the enemy lines northeast of Caen in battle formation. Each of us had begun flying as if we were on a roller coaster, swinging from side to side, then up and down, changing altitude in a range of some five hundred feet. We had learned that without this constant change of line and altitude, those incredible German 88 anti-aircraft guns would be putting their vicious black shells either into our aircraft or close enough that we would hear them explode. The rule was, "If they're close enough that you can hear them explode you're in real trouble." Even so, as we crossed the enemy lines either going out or coming back in that dense, heavily defended sector, the roller coaster movement was no guarantee against being hit.

From June 25 to 29 we continued to operate from our base in England, but it became standard squadron practice to land at B8 to top up with fuel before going on. 129 Airfield and all its personnel, vehicles, and equipment finally arrived at B8 on Thursday, June 29, and immediately set up shop to receive and maintain the full complement of 39 Recce Wing's aircraft, some twenty-six Mustang Is and twelve Bluebird Spitfires. By that time most of the Mustang pilots had been into B8 at least once, so we were getting used to its approaches and the characteristics of the airstrip itself. Therefore, when 430 Squadron arrived at B8 in a squadron formation of ten, followed by the airlift party in a Dakota escorted by our other three Mustangs, our complement of twenty pilots was delighted to see that the trucks, vans, tents, and officers and men of 128 Airfield were already in place.

The incoming aircraft were directed to dispersal areas along the south side of the strip stretching from mid-strip to its western boundary. The aircraft were parked near the maintenance vans, tents, and other sub-units of the airfield that were also concentrated on the south side both to the east and west of Château Magny.

The château, perhaps a hundred years old or more, was L-shaped, with the long arm of the L running north and south and the short arm parallel to the runway, the west and north walls making the 90-degree join. A large bedroom on the second floor at the north end of the building was captured by the pilots as our "waiting room."

*Château Magny. The pilots' waiting room is on the
second floor at the far right of the building.*

A pilots' waiting room was a place where we did exactly that — wait. The wait was for a call from Ops, the Operations Headquarters of our wing. When the Wing HQ received tasking requirements from Second British Army (Demsey's) Headquarters for a TAC/R, Photo/R, Arty/R, or whatever, the Army liaison officers and our Wingco flying staff would sort out what had to be done, how, and by whom. That sorted out, a telephone call would be made from the Wingco Ops van to the waiting room, where the on-duty pilots would be gathered. There the duty flight commander — the same twenty squadron pilots were divided into two flights, A and B — would receive the call and designate which of the waiting pilots would carry out the sortie. Those chosen would then trudge off to the Ops van to be briefed. Shortly after that they would be airborne.

The traditional waiting room had perhaps a dozen and a half hard, collapsible chairs (like card table chairs) and two or three long, portable tables on which to play cards or write. On the walls would be a dartboard, pictures (Betty Grable legs type), and a notice board complete with flying advice and rude but current jokes. In modern times a pilot's room might be called a lounge. Not in those days. It was a waiting room, nothing more, nothing less.

The remainder of the morning of June 29 was spent sorting out the issue tables and chairs that we would need in the pilots' room in Château Magny. We checked the hand-crank telephone from our room to the Operations van, from which calls would come telling us who was needed and what time to report to the headquarters for briefing.

Our pilots' room, which was about thirty feet by twenty feet, had large, shuttered windows that swung open on each side of the fireplace in the north wall and in the west wall. Between them we had an excellent view of the airstrip, the better to watch the comings and goings of our own aircraft and those of the other squadrons. It was particularly nerve-wracking to watch some hapless colleague bring in a Mustang, badly beaten up by flak, to land without flaps or belly-up or with only one leg of its undercarriage down. Then, of course, there was the fascination that all airmen have with simply watching aircraft landing and taking off, especially the landings, some of which are a series of bouncing touchdowns, others smooth, three-point perfection. Anyone who made a bad landing certainly heard about it.

We were never quite certain what had happened to it, but apparently at one time there had been another wing attached to our Château Magny building on its northern wall. We knew it had been there because attached to the outside of the north wall at ground level immediately below the large window to the east of our fireplace sat a toilet, open for the world to see. A drainpipe followed the wall down from the second floor to the back of this toilet, then into a septic tank. However, because we had no running water the second floor toilet was not serviceable. We would have to use the outside throne. Airmen's ingenuity quickly prevailed. Walls, a flap as a door, and a roof, all of canvas, were improvised, and the outside toilet quickly came into service. As will later be seen, it was not without its hazards.

At the same time, other squadron pilots were milling about in an ancient apple orchard that had been selected as the spot where our sleeping and mess tents would be located. It was behind a stone fence north of the airstrip at its western end, within easy walking distance of our château. Pitching our tents among the trees was a wise decision on someone's part, as we would soon discover.

The milling about was caused by the need for careful selection of one's tent location in the orchard because for the first time we had to pick a spot where we could dig slit trenches, two to a tent. In the trenches we would put our sleeping cots. Then we put out tent up over the pair of trenches.

My own digging session was delayed because I had to fly a tactical reconnaissance operation with Danny Lambros. We went east to Evreux, well beyond the front lines. There we spotted many fires burning in the town and several motor transports on adjacent roads. However, we were back at base shortly after 1400 hours, so there was plenty of time to get on with the slit trench digging and put up the tent. Flying Officer Ed Geddes, who was to share the tent with me for the rest of our stay at B8, and I struggled with the erection of our canvas edifice. Finally we had it in place in time for an unappetizing first supper in France.

During that initial night the German bombers were out in force, prowling the beachhead in the darkness, attracting all manner of anti-aircraft firing. Quite apart from this noise we began to hear strange whistlings that some clever soul quickly identified as falling shrapnel. The tons of anti-aircraft shells being lobbed skyward toward the Hun, having exploded, had to come down. Our orchard was getting its fair share and was to receive it every night of the weeks that we were there. While we saw very little of Jerry during the day, as he was active under the protective cover of darkness, except when bad weather forced him to stay on the ground.

Another happening caused all of us to go back to the shovels the next day to make those slit trenches much deeper. The squadron log entry for June 30 deals gently with the event, but it scared the hell out of most of us, making us realize beyond a shadow of a doubt that we were no longer living in comfortable, protected England but rather in the battlefield.

430 Squadron Log Book June 30
General: We are quite happy with the general setting
here. Our living tents are pitched under the trees in a
very pleasant orchard. There is an abundance of drinking water and the tinned rations are quite good. The
first night in France was quite peaceful except in the
early hours of the morning when lone F.W. 190 came
screaming across the Airfield followed by Spitfires and
bursts of anti-aircraft fire.

While our log-keeper, Flying Officer Ed Winiarz, ignored the night's
bomber and anti-aircraft activity when he used the words "quite peaceful," even he was observed digging in deeper the next day.

Far more disturbing for the squadron pilots, now at a grand total
of eighteen, was that we had lost four people in the previous twelve
days. It's a devastating experience to see a close friend perish before
your very eyes, or to be told he is missing or shot down and will
never be back.

I was fortunate. I lost only one man in my 135 operational sorties. We had just taken off when he reported to me on his radio that
he had a glycol (engine coolant) leak. I turned my head to the right to
check his aircraft. Sure enough a gray-blue cloud of vapour was
streaming back from his engine, enveloping the cockpit. I shouted
at him to go back and land. He turned toward the airstrip, but the
aircraft never recovered from its bank to the right. Instead it went
over on its back and straight into the ground, where it exploded in a
ball of flame.

When I landed minutes after I was shaking from head to toe. Out of
my aircraft, I was in tears, probably as close to a mental collapse as I have
ever been. The man who had disappeared from this earth in an inferno
was my friend, a pal. Grief, horror, and shock combined with an understanding that there but for the grace of God ... Would I be next? Of
course not. It could never happen to me.

From D-Day through to the end of June, the fighting was bitter,
intense, and virtually stalemated. Would the stalemate be broken?
Would we break through, break out? Those were questions that we

pilots could only speculate on. It was up to General Montgomery to make it happen. He would have to use all the intelligence and forces at his disposal against a determined, highly experienced German Army under the brilliant Rommel, whom Montgomery had already defeated once on another continent.

As we settled in at B8 and Château Magny we sensed from what we could see from the air every day that our stay would be long and that the risks ahead would be high. We could also see that the volume of war equipment supplies and material being brought into the beachhead was enormous. Almost all of it was coming in through one Mulberry port the invading force had brought with it.

On June 10, as we crossed over the Normandy beach at Arromanches, we had seen the first clues about the use of the huge concrete structures we observed before D-Day sitting in the water in the Portsmouth area. They were pieces of Mulberry, an artificial harbour. There were two of these gigantic, ingenious structures. The one at Arromanches was to serve the British and Canadian armies, and the other, off the American beaches to the west, would provide for Bradley's forces.

As soon as Churchill became Prime Minister on May 10, 1940, he began to push for the design and construction of landing craft and artificial harbours, without which the return to France four years later could not be achieved. In 1943, at the Quebec conference of Churchill and Roosevelt and their military staffs, the worrisome matter of supplying the armies across the invasion beaches was settled. There would be two artificial ports, each with a capacity comparable to that of Dover. They would be built in sections, towed across the Channel as quickly as possible after D-Day, and sunk in pre-selected sites.

Hitler was convinced the invasion forces would have to seize a large port at the beginning of their attack in order to receive the vast volume of supplies necessary to support an Army. Accordingly, he had designated all major ports in northwest Europe as "fortresses" that would be held until the exhaustion of every last possibility of defence. What he was not aware of was that as a result of the Dieppe disaster in the summer of 1942 the Allied tactic was changed to attack ports not frontally but from the rear. In the Dieppe raid, Canadian and British troops had been sent in directly against the beaches of that port in a frontal assault. They had been slaughtered by an alerted German force whose guns commanded the beaches from above.

Nor was Hitler aware that at the outset of the assault the Allies would achieve surprise by bringing their own ports with them. When shown aerial reconnaissance photographs of the enormous concrete caissons sitting in the waters on the south coast of England, he recognized that they had to be quays. However, he believed they would be used to replace the dockage his engineers were to destroy in any Channel port that was attacked. If the Führer or his staff had guessed their true purpose, his generals would have been able to narrow down the potential landing sites to those that could receive Mulberries. That would have taken them to one place: Normandy. There they would have been able to concentrate their defensive forces behind Rommel's Death Zone.

The caissons of steel and concrete we pilots had seen were the Phoenix units. To build the Mulberry ports, 146 of these were required, from 10 of the smallest at 1,677 tons each through six sizes to the largest, 60 of which were needed at 6,044 tons each. Commencing D-Day plus four, some seventy ancient freighters and old warships were towed across the Channel and sunk as breakwaters for the Mulberries. They were Gooseberries. Linking the Phoenix units to shore were floating bridges called "whales."

As planned, the Mulberries were put in place rapidly and were in operation at both the American and the British-Canadian beaches. However, the weather of the worst summer since 1900 was to play havoc with the supply system. In a severe storm that lasted from June 19 to 22, the American Mulberry harbour was destroyed. At the same time, about eight hundred landing craft, tugs, freighters, and other vessels were either sunk or damaged severely. The devastation was far greater than on D-Day. With the destruction of the American Mulberry most of the burden of supply for all forces ashore, up to twelve thousand tons a day, fell on the Mulberry at Arromanches. The nearby tiny fishing harbour of Port-en-Bessin had been cleared and opened but was of little value. With only one major port, which was highly vulnerable not only to the inclement weather but also to destruction by German forces, it became imperative for the Americans to seize the major port of Cherbourg as quickly as possible.

The Americans took Cherbourg on June 26.

CHAPTER 17

The Battle for Caen

———◆———

7 July 1944 OPERATIONS: No sorties were flown until the afternoon when an Artillery Shoot was done by F/L E.S. Dunn with F/L J.B. Prendergast, Flying Officer's K.G. Gillmor and H.L. Wolfe* as cover. The first target, a bridge, was successfully engaged before engaging the second target. Two aircraft were hit by flak and damaged. As F/L Dunn was slightly injured the task was abandoned. Later, Flying Officer V.C. Dohaney engaged the second target successfully after our artillery silenced the flak. Flying Officer's J.N. McLeod,** R.H. Rohmer and D.A. Whittaker flew as cover. Three sorties were airborne late in the evening to observe road movements immediately after the bombing of Caen by Lancasters. It became dark before the bombing was completed and no observations were made. Caen itself was a mass of flames.

430 Squadron Log

NOT RECORDED IN THE SQUADRON log that day was one unusual operation having to do with fire, but not the enemy's. During the morning, Dohaney and other card-playing friends were at a game of Red Dog in the pilots' room on the second floor of Château Magny. They were waiting for the weather to clear and the Ops phone to summon them for briefings. I watched the Red Dog game for a while, smoking the occa-

---

* Wolfe was killed in Normandy in July 1944.
** McLeod was killed in December 1944 in Holland.

sional cigarette, as did almost all our gang. It was the practice to throw still lighted butts out the closest window. Once in a while they were ground out in a grimy, makeshift ashtray on the long, folding issue table that was the centerpiece of the large room. Feeling a strong call of nature I went downstairs and out the north door, pulled back the canvas flap of the Château Magny throne room, and proceeded to sit therein, first having checked to ensure that there were no enemy bees down the hole.

We had discovered their presence a few days before when one of my squadron mates had been hit from below in a sneak bee attack, which, fortunately for him, turned out to be his most severe war injury. However, my reconnaissance into the depths of the throne satisfied me that none of the buzzing enemy was present. So, bare-bottomed, I perched, sitting there for a goodly length of time reading some nondescript magazine that was part of the throne room equipment.

Suddenly, from above me there were shouts of alarm and panic. Almost at the same instant a torrent of water was poured down on me from the window immediately above by some avid pilot turned fireman. Some idiot had thrown a burning butt out the window. It had landed on the throne room roof and had eventually set it afire, unbeknownst to me. As the smoke curled up, one of my keen-eyed colleagues had either seen or smelled it and had leaped into action. Water buckets were stationed at all rooms of the Château as a precaution against fire. So, without any warning to me, my saviour proceeded to dump the contents on the fire. The water went directly through the hole made by the blaze and landed on me. I was soaked and shocked at the same time. Cursing wildly and showing absolutely no gratitude I pulled my wetted self together, stormed upstairs to the pilots' room, only to find my colleagues in paroxysms of laughter, tears in their eyes, doubled up. I was not amused, even less so when one of those ribald turkeys gasped through his laughter that they all thought I needed a bath anyway.

The artillery shoot undertaken by Pappy Dunn on the late afternoon of July 7 was part of the prelude to a massive ground and air assault upon Caen in order to finally take that stronghold thirty days after the originally scheduled date of capture, June 6. Montgomery was under tremendous pressure from the British press and from Churchill to get moving, pressure that would still be there and increasing during the first days of August.

Dunn's formation was airborne at 1600 hours. They were back on the ground at 1735 hours. One hour and ten minutes later another section of four was airborne to tackle the second target again. Flying Officer Vince Dohaney was in the lead with Jack McLeod, Dennis Whittaker, and me as cover. As we crossed the enemy lines to the west of Caen the cloud was still solid at five thousand feet. We would have to stay well below that altitude. As with Dunn's formation, we would be within perfect range of the light flak.

However, this time arrangements had been made with our artillery to saturate the flak installations with a massive barrage just before Dohaney began his shoot. If we were going to be successful and survive, that flak had to be neutralized. After ranging with a single artillery battery, an entire division of guns would fire on the pilot's order "Apple Pie," delivered on time and on target. The deadly flak was silenced as thousands of rounds cascaded down on the German guns. Dohaney then got busy with his shoot on the bridge. It was successfully completed in half an hour. The bridge was down, and we were back on the ground at 1935 hours, just fifty minutes after we took off.

Fortunately, the injury to Pappy Dunn when he was hit by flak that afternoon was not serious. But the increasing amount of flak being thrown at us — 88-mm, 40-mm, and anything else the Germans could find — was beginning to cause concern. Flight Lieutenant Jack Watts's aircraft had been hit by an 88 while he was leading a TAC/R in the Caen area on July 4. The 88 had hit the hydraulic line. All the fluid had escaped, making his flap system inoperative, with the result that he had to make a no-flap landing, touching down at about 100 miles per hour, a high speed that rapidly ate up the entire length of airstrip, forcing him to ground loop when he ran out of runway.

On July 8, two aircraft in another formation led by Watts were hit when they encountered intense flak twelve miles southwest of Caen. The Germans called our Mustangs *bluthunds*, or bloodhounds, but we were beginning to feel more like sitting ducks.

The weather also conspired against us throughout the month of July. The bad weather started on July 1 when no tasks at all were flown due to low cloud and rain. From the third through the sixth operations were severely restricted, but when they were possible they had to be conducted at low level because of the height of the cloud, ranging from one thousand to two thousand feet. By contrast, on July 6 there was no cloud and visibility was unlimited. However, on the seventh we were back to overcast 10/10 at five thousand feet. If we were to conduct operations at all the continuing low cloud forced us beneath it, within range of anything that could be fired — rifles and machine guns as well as anti-aircraft guns. Moreover, the accuracy of the enemy at the lower altitudes was greatly improved, except when we were at treetop level. Occasionally we made a run at that height into a specified pinpoint target, but as a rule reconnaissance and photography required us to operate from five thousand to seven thousand feet. On days when the 10/10 overcast ceiling was about that height we were silhouetted perfectly against the dull gray sky and could be easily tracked by anti-aircraft gunners or readily spotted by any Focke-Wulf 190 or Me 109 pilot flying at a lower level.

There was no choice. The tactical and photographic reconnaissance operations and the artillery shoots simply had to go on. The British, Canadians, and now the Poles for whom we performed our tasks were slugging it out toe to toe with the Germans in an attempt to reach Caen. Our eyes, our photographs, and our reports were absolutely essential to them. Or so we believed.

The bombing attack and our artillery shoots that day on the bridges south of Caen were indeed part of Montgomery's plan to finally capture Caen. It was still his strategy to keep pushing against the Germans in the Caen area in order to hold the maximum number of enemy troops, tanks, and guns at the eastern end of the bridgehead. He would thereby allow the Americans the fullest opportunity of success when the time arrived for their attempted breakout on the western flank. Montgomery had hoped that these breakout attacks would be underway by July 3, but General Omar Bradley, the commander of the American First Army, found his forces still contained in the flooded, marshy country in the Carentan estuary. It was a totally unsuitable area for deployment of the major assault forces necessary for the breakout thrust. As it developed, Bradley would not gain such a deployment area until he reached the general line of the

Periers–St. Lô Road on July 18. In fact, he was not able to launch his breakout attacks until July 25.

There was enormous pressure on Montgomery to capture Caen. Thirty days later the objective he was to have captured on D-Day was still not in his grasp. He simply had to wrest that key objective from the Germans. The powerful, experienced enemy was dug in and well organized in mutually supporting positions in a number of small villages that lay in an arc north-northwest of Caen. Because of the strength of the German defences, Montgomery decided to ask for the first time for the assistance of Bomber Command of the Royal Air Force, which contained a large number of Royal Canadian Air Force units. Bomber Command agreed after much negotiating as to the details of the plan for this operation, the first of its kind.

The target area assigned was on the northern outskirts of Caen, a rectangle four thousand yards wide and fifteen hundred yards deep. It contained major defensive positions and an enemy headquarters. The intent of the air bombardment was to destroy these positions and the supporting artillery and to cut off the lines of supply to the enemy's forward troops. The bombardment was to take place between 2150 and 2230 hours on July 7. It would be followed by a ground attack, which was to begin at 0420 hours the next morning and would be carried out by three divisions: 3 Canadian Division in from the northwest, 59 Division from the north, and 3 Division from the northeast. They were to converge on Caen, clear the main part of the town on the west bank of the Orne, and take the river crossings. This was the plan.

The only part of it that we lowly pilots knew about was that there was to be a massive bomber attack on Caen, that our shoots that day had something to do with it, and that the bombers were coming in at ten minutes to ten. So far as we were concerned this was a show we just could not miss. I didn't. I saw it all, not from the air but from the ground. Since B8 was some miles away from the target area, three of us had decided to get into a jeep and drive east, find a point of high ground where we could see Caen in the distance, sit back, and watch the show.

By the time we heard the drone of the first bombers out over the Channel, the 10/10 cloud cover that had plagued us over Caen just a little

At B8, France, July 1944.

more than two hours before had moved out. There was no cloud. This would allow the heavy bombers to come in at a much higher altitude, thereby better able to avoid being hit by the vicious onslaught of the German 88 batteries that ringed the Caen area.

In a few moments the lead Pathfinder aircraft appeared, crossing inland just to the east of us, between Ouistreham and Lion-sur-Mer, the same point of entry Taylor and I had used on D-Day one month and one day earlier. Strung out behind and above the Pathfinders, who went in at a much lower level in order to drop their guiding flares on the target rectangle, came a long, seemingly endless column of Lancaster and Halifax bombers, some 460 of them. They were flying not in any formation but separated by altitude and spacing to avoid hitting other aircraft with falling bombs.

The roar of the powerful engines of the enormous air armada was like the roll of incessant drums as the lead aircraft released the first bombs to open the unprecedented, concentrated attack in a sky already turned black by the exploding shells of the German 88s. In the far distance we could see brown-black fountains of earth and smoke lifting into the air in the target area as the bombs landed. In a few seconds the noise of the first explosions reached us, a thunder-like sound that would continue for forty minutes as each attacking bomber released its huge load, approximately five tons of mixed 500-pound and 1,000-pound bombs. On they came, wave after wave. Many suffered direct hits from the 88s, falling from the sky like great birds brought to ground at the end of a hunter's gun. Running the deadly gauntlet of anti-aircraft shells in broad daylight, a new experience for the British and Canadian bomber pilots who operated at night, must have taken all the courage of every man in every crew. Still they pressed on, delivering their bombs with deadly accuracy, a result that was not always achieved in later tactical bomber operations in support of Army attacks in the Caen area. But on the evening of July 7, with British and Canadian troops held back some six thousand yards away from the target area, the bombers were right on.

No enemy fighters were seen from where we stood. But midway during the passing of the unfaltering procession of bombers, a Mosquito aircraft, which we guessed to be one of the Pathfinders, came fluttering down from above the bombers. It was spinning slowly, lazily, completely out of control. With an enormous, ground-shaking thump it crashed to earth about a mile south of us. What had hit the Mosquito we had no idea.

Finally the last aircraft of the column delivered its load in the fast gathering darkness, its bombs descending into a flaming cauldron of burning buildings and crater-pocked terrain. The work of the bombers was done.

The air attack had had a devastating effect on the German troops, some of whom were found still stunned long after the event. To the north of the town, enemy troops were cut off and as a result received no ammunition, gasoline, or food; one complete regiment in the eye of the storm of bombs was completely wiped out.

On schedule the next morning, the three divisions, two British and one Canadian, moved in on Caen. After tough fighting for the next two days, that part of the town lying to the north and west of the Orne had been taken. The enemy remained in occupation of Faubourg-de-Vaucelles on the south side of the river.

The operation had been a success for Montgomery. He was thirty-four days behind schedule, but he finally held Caen.

My acquaintance Lieutenant-General George S. Patton, Jr., was in France. Exactly thirty-two years before, Patton and his wife had done an extensive tour of Normandy while on their way home from the Olympic Games at Stockholm, where he had competed in a military contest called Modern Pentathlon. He wound up fifth in a field of thirty-two contestants. Now he was going to participate in another form of physical competition for which he was equally well trained and experienced.

On July 6, George Patton's own D-Day, he had attended the usual morning briefing at Braemore House, then driven to the nearby airstrip with three members of his staff, his personal luggage, and his constant companion, Willie the bull terrier. There they climbed into the C-47 transport, which was already loaded. Patton's jeep was tied down at the rear of the aircraft.

At 1025 hours Patton and his party were airborne. It was almost a year to the minute from the time he had left Algiers for the Sicily that he and his then equal, Montgomery, would conquer. Now he would be simply one of Montgomery's Army commanders, taking directions from him. The only trouble was, Patton did not have an Army in the field. Some of the units of his Third Army were operating under General Omar Bradley in his First Army. Patton would get them back on the day the Third Army became operational. But when that would be was by no means certain at that point.

Escorted by a clutch of P-47 fighters, the C-47 made an uneventful trip across the Channel to a narrow airstrip behind Omaha beach. As soon as the aircraft was on the ground and shut down, Old Blood and Guts stepped out of the aircraft to be greeted by several hundred American soldiers. Naturally it was expected that he make a speech. When his jeep was out of the aircraft he mounted it and began, his shrill, high-pitched voice reaching out across the crowd of khaki. Jokingly he told his audience that he was the Allies' secret weapon. In a serious vein he cautioned them that his presence there was indeed secret and they could not tell anyone they had seen him in France.

Then, in typical emotional, blood-firing, stimulating Pattonese he shouted, "I'm proud to be here to fight beside you. Now let's cut the guts out of those krauts and get the hell on to Berlin. And when we get to Berlin, I am going to personally shoot that paper-hanging goddammed son-of-a-bitch [Hitler] just like I would a snake."

CHAPTER 18
Thirteen Holes in My Mustang, July 13, 1944

———◆———

> 18 July 1944 GENERAL: This afternoon "brown type"
> pilots began to make their appearance. Reason: all pilots
> were being issued with Khaki battledress to be worn
> when flying for purposes of identification.
>
> 430 Squadron Log

F OR THE SIGNIFICANT EVENT THAT happened on July 17, 1944, I
refer you back to the opening chapter and the story of the catching of Rommel. Now to July 18, and then to why thirteen is a lucky number for me.

Fortunately for us, the khaki battledress mentioned in the above log excerpt was American, consisting of lightweight, comfortably cut summer shirt and trousers and a zippered jacket. However, they were not issued gratuitously. We had to go to the nearest American unit and buy them. The alternative was to purchase the heavy British battledress, which no one did. Although the use of khaki was optional and not mandatory, most people made the switch for the summer season at least, and for good reason.

At a distance it was quite easy to confuse the Air Force blue of the Canadian and British battledress with the field gray of the German uniform. Many pilots and other aircrew had bailed out or survived a crash landing in enemy lines at points where the concentration of fighting was not as heavy as it was in the Caen area. Unfortunately, some of them had been mistaken for Germans and were fired upon by our troops. They would not have been shot at if their clothing had been khaki coloured, either British or American.

To minimize this obvious risk, some practical Air Force officer at higher headquarters issued permission to wear khaki with appropriate rank badges. I was one of the first to make the switch. As it happened, I never had the opportunity to try to make my way back through the enemy lines, but if I had there would have been no question that I was, at least for the moment, "a brown job."

As it was, I looked like an American officer, except for my blue Royal Canadian Air Force flat hat, which, of course, I didn't wear while I was flying. If I had bailed out or crash-landed in enemy territory I would have appeared as an American.

I wore khaki U.S. summer-weight trousers, a shirt complete with a lieutenant's bar (my RCAF rank of flying officer was equivalent) on the collar front, and a zippered jacket with the rank bars on the shoulder. That was my flying ensemble until September, when we arrived in Belgium to cold, wet weather.

One of my closest "near misses," which had occurred only a week before on Thursday, July 13, put me in the frame of mind to take up the khaki option as soon as it was offered. The remarks in the squadron log are terse:

> 13 July 1944 OPERATIONS: Weather was still unfavorable until mid-afternoon when an area search was flown by Flying Officers R.H. Rohmer and J.N. McLeod. Small numbers of MT [motor transport] were seen at various points and photos were taken. Heavy, accurate, intense flak was encountered at Evrecy and Flying Officer Rohmer's was hit in several places, damage Category "B."

With Jack McLeod as my number two, I was airborne a few minutes after 1500, again having to work below a solid cloud base sitting at six thousand feet. Our assigned route took us southwest of Caen, where I checked predetermined roads and areas immediately adjacent to them for trucks or tanks or anything military I could find. Two miles south of Villiers I found some unusual objects that I could not identify. I took some shots with my oblique camera that the photographic interpreter could puzzle over later. In addition, small numbers of motor transport were seen and recorded at various points.

Proceeding westbound over Evrecy, only sixteen miles south of our base at B8, I had my aircraft straight and level for a few seconds. After all, I was well clear of the dreadful concentration of 88s in the Caen area and was in a sector where little flak had been reported. There was no evidence of any flak coming at me or at McLeod. No warning of any kind.

My confidence was shattered by a tremendous blast accompanied by the instant appearance before my eyes of a jagged hole in my left wing. It was about a foot in diameter. I was impressed.

Without waiting for the arrival of the next shell, which I was sure would be on its way to where I would be in the next one or two seconds, I hauled sharply over to the right on the control column and pulled back on it. I didn't bother to look over my shoulder to see how close the next round had come. Now there was only one place to go — straight back to base, but roller-coastering all the way until I was over our own territory.

Once I was safely behind our lines I did a complete check on my controls. They were still operating. Had the shell or piece of it that had ripped the big hole through the wing hit the spar? Evidently not, because there was not indication of any buckling of the surface of the wing's skin. It hadn't hit the gasoline tank from what I could see. The only question left was if there was any damage to the hydraulic system that would prevent me from getting the flaps or, for that matter, the wheels down. I asked McLeod to slip underneath me to check over my underside for any damage to the fuselage or the bottom of the wings. He took a look and reported back to me that apart from the big hole everything looked good.

Calling ahead to our airfield traffic controller, Squadron Leader Harold Day, ensconced in his little shack at the edge of the airstrip, I declared an emergency, asking for straight-in clearance from the west. It was immediately granted. I approached our strip from the south, swinging out to the west, getting my air speed back to 120 miles an hour. The moment had come. Would the undercarriage work? If it didn't it would mean a wheels-up belly landing, uncomfortable, rough, and dangerous at best.

With my left hand I selected "down" on the undercarriage lever, shoving it toward the floor. The hydraulic pressure looked okay, but I wasn't sure. In a moment I felt the undercarriage unlock. In a few seconds I felt the legs lock down one after the other. As they did, the green undercarriage lights switched from red to green. My wheels were okay, down and locked.

The final uncertainty was the flaps. Speed back to 110. Again with my left hand moving out from my left hip I reached for the flap lever, moving it to the "down" selection. Instantly I could see the flaps moving. The aircraft's nose tipped slightly down as the lowering flaps took hold. No problem.

I touched down and completed my landing normally, swinging off the strip to the south and taxiing my Mustang directly to the tents of the maintenance section. The aircraft would be in their hands for some time, if indeed it could be repaired. As I was marshalled into the parking area I could see people emerging from all directions. There was always enormous interest in the type, location, and amount of damage when an aircraft was hit, and, of course, in how close the pilot had come to "buying it." In this instance, as the pilot, I too was interested in how close.

Close enough. In addition to the big hole in the wing there were twelve other hits by fragments, a total of thirteen on the thirteenth of July. I've regarded thirteen as a lucky number ever since. The piece that had come closest to me had gone through my Plexiglas canopy, entering on the left side, passing about an inch over my head, and exiting out the top right — justification for my being short and having to use two pillows behind me in the bucket seat of the Mustang in order to reach the rudder pedals.

My battered aircraft, AP18 carrying the letter O, was repairable. After extensive work it was back in operation thirteen days later on July 26 when Flying Officer Ed Winiarz flew it on a successful photo reconnaissance mission. Personally, I needed no repairs. My clash with the flak had occurred at about 1510 hours. By 1705 I was back in the air on a TAC/R 135 operation from Caen to Alecon. Two of our aircraft went unserviceable, one with a malfunctioning radio and the other with a generator that packed up. So did we. The operation was abandoned over Caen. July 13, 1944, was that kind of day.

Some fifty-five years later I discovered that I had developed a reputation among our ground crew members. One of our master photographers/photo experts, Bob Dumouchelle of Windsor, Ontario, published a book on his wartime adventures with a focus on his period with 430 Squadron during the Battle of Normandy.

Bob Dumouchelle was a leader of the team that loaded and installed our Mustang cameras each day, removed them after missions, then developed and processed the film for interpretation by the Army APIS and use by appropriate Army units. Fact or fiction, or grossly exaggerated, this is the way Bob Dumouchelle saw me during our operations out of Magny, B8:

> Most of our pilots were very young. One pilot who I admired very much — he was a hero really — was a baby-faced twenty-year-old kid named Richard Rohmer. He looked so young we called him Junior or Dick. ("Look, guys, don't call me Junior — I'm Flying Officer Rohmer!" We called him that anyway, though I don't today.) Richard went in where others feared to tread and more than once the squadron would return without him. When questioned, the pilots would state that no one could get into the target area — it was suicide! Eventually Richard's plane, full of holes, would come staggering across the sky and land on the edge of the runway with a plop. The aircraft was scrapped, though we'd salvage the cameras, and Richard would have brought back the best pictures of the enemy positions.
>
> After one of those difficult sorties, Richard clambered into the camera truck with Matson and me and got very emotional. Now I was all of twenty-two and Matson was twenty-seven — we were old men compared to him. Richard said he was so frightened flying over the target — they were throwing everything up at him. No matter how far down in his cockpit seat he crunched he was afraid the flak was going to get him.
>
> Yet he forced himself to go out again and again. A very brave man. He was awarded the D.F.C. — the Distinguished Flying Cross.

CHAPTER 19

Almost a Court Martial —
Saved by Dirk Bogarde

———◆———

1 August 1944 OPERATIONS: Haze, mist and poor
visibility prevented any flying until late afternoon. The
last TAC/R, Photo/R of the day was flown by Flying
Officer R.H. Rohmer with Flying Officer C.P. St. Paul.
No cloud. 50 tanks in Bois du Homme. 20 M.T. at
7446. Miscellaneous MET at scattered points. General
appearance of movements. Enemy reaction Nil.

430 Squadron Log

CLEM ST. PAUL AND I were airborne out of B8 in the late evening
at 2040 hours on a tactical reconnaissance covering assigned
points between Le Beny Bocage and Aunay-sur-Odon, about twenty-
five miles due south of our Bayeux base. The area contained a great
deal of high ground in a region where some of the hills were over a
thousand feet high.

A map on which the bomb line was drawn was handed to me
during our pre-flight briefing in the Ops van. The bomb line was put
on by our Army intelligence people. Anything we saw beyond the
bomb line we could assume was enemy and could be reported on the
air to Group Control Centre for attack by our aircraft. On the contrary, anything seen inside the bomb line was deemed to be Allied
and could not be reported on the air (because the Germans monitored our broadcasts) and could not be attacked. That was the firm
order. The bomb line went through Le Beny Bocage, swinging to the
north and then easterly to the north of Aunay-sur-Odon. The sector
I was to reconnoitre was in a pocket, or bulge, in the bomb line.

Therefore I knew I was working close to the front line, but no information was given to me about the structure of the battle that was going on at the time.

Still pivoting with 2 Canadian Corps at Caen, now as far south as Bourguebus, Montgomery had determined to push the Second British Army line on the west, and the American First Army abutting it, south from the Caumont area. The objective was to reach the general area of Le Beny Bocage. The main attack of the British force would be mounted by 30 Corps on the left and 8 Corps on the right. The area I operated over that night was fronted by 43 Division on the right and 7 Armoured Division (both British) on the left, to the southwest of Villers-Bocage. My bomb line was drawn through the town, curving to the west and swinging south to Le Beny Bocage.

The attack had started on the 30 Corps front at 0600 hours on July 30. By August 1, Le Beny Bocage had been cleared by 8 Corps. Its 125th Division on the left had repulsed several counterattacks. 7 Armoured Division of 30 Corps was moving on the left flank heading toward Aunay-sur-Odon.

When St. Paul and I arrived over the assigned area in our Mustangs the battle was raging below us. Unfortunately, I knew next to nothing about the tactical situation on the ground.

What I did know was that it was rapidly getting dark. I would have to get my recce done and get home as quickly as possible. We did not have landing lights on our airstrips. They would have attracted the enemy.

There were nine specific points assigned to me. As soon as they were covered I headed for home. Flying north over Montigny at about two thousand feet the flash of a gun in the darkening ground mist ahead of me and to my right caught my attention. I went into a gentle bank to see what was firing. To my astonishment I found I was sitting over dozens of tanks, probably the greatest number I had ever seen in one place in a battle situation. Some were moving, some were sitting, many were firing their guns. It was an incredible sight, one extremely exciting for a young bloodhound. The long guns hanging way out over the front of the tanks signalled only one thing to me. They were German Tigers! Perhaps if there was a Typhoon squadron airborne nearby, even at that late hour, they could come in and have at them. There was only one problem. The horde of tanks was well inside and to the north of the bomb line. The bomb line told me that anything to the north of it was ours and could not be reported on the radio or attacked. That was the rule.

But those were Tiger tanks down there!

I made the decision. I called Group Control Centre on my VHF radio. GCC responded immediately. My report of the tanks and the pinpoint of their location was delivered somewhat excitedly and acknowledged calmly. They were in Bois du Homme about one and a quarter miles southwest of the main intersection at Evrecy highway. That done I again turned for home in the closing darkness, but not before doing one final thing. I circled, tipped the Mustang over on its side, and pointed my oblique camera at a clutch of the tanks moving northward. My right thumb pressed pictures. I knew it was unlikely that they would turn out because it was so dark, but I did it anyway — then hightailed it for B8 with St. Paul still faithfully covering my tail in battle formation.

It was dark when I entered the Ops van to be confronted by our Wing Commander Flying, Bunt Waddell. He did not mince words. Those tanks I reported to Group Control Centre were *our* tanks. Army intelligence had no knowledge of any German tanks in the area but knew ours were there in strength getting ready to attack. By talking on the radio to Group Control Centre and reporting the tank location I had given vital secret information to the German intelligence people. They monitored all of our broadcasts. On top of it all, the tanks were inside, repeat inside, our bomb line and didn't I know the rule was that anything inside the bomb line was ours! I had compounded the situation by breaking that rule. Surely with my experience I ought to have known better. Monty's head-quarters and Dempsey's people at Second British Army HQ were furious. I could expect severe disciplinary action.

God, was I in trouble! Being shot at by the enemy was far less frightening than to be descended upon by one's own Wing Commander Flying and the entire British Army.

When I protested that I was sure the tanks were German Tigers, Bunt Waddell simply waved it off, saying it was not possible. There just weren't any in the area. The British Army intelligence people were absolutely sure. That was the end of the matter. I was to report to him first thing in the morning. Would I be court-martialled? There was no doubt he was thinking about it.

Now there was only one thing that could save me. The photographs. They were my only chance for salvation. But I was positive they wouldn't turn out. It had been far too dark and hazy when I took them. Tail between my legs I left the Ops van and hurried through the darkness to the photo developing unit just a few steps away. By this time they would have the film out of the camera and would be processing it. I burst in, breathlessly telling Corporal Bob Dumouchelle, the NCO in charge of the unit, about the predicament I was in. He calmed me down, saying that he had already started the developing process.

I impatiently waited, practically hanging over his shoulder as the prints emerged. They were still wet as we looked at them. My spirits lifted. We could see tanks, six or seven of them. Not clearly, mind you, but we could see them. I couldn't tell what they were, Tigers or our Shermans or whatever. But, by some miracle I at least had photographs with something on them.

Off again I went into the darkness, the wet prints in my hand. This time I headed for the Army Photographic Interpretation Section van close by. Bursting in on the startled APIS duty officer, who was unaccustomed to seeing a pilot in his place of business at that time of night, I quickly explained the situation, produced my photographs, and asked him to make a judgment. What were those tanks?

With no great haste he took the films, put them together in front of him, and picked up the main tool of his trade — a pair of stereo lenses, which, when placed over two in-line photographs, gave him a three-dimensional view of the objects in the photographs. By this time I was in a terrible state of anxiety. But still he was in no hurry. Studying the images below him he emitted two or three contemplative grunts. Then, laconically, and without even looking up he said, "They're Tigers."

Thank Christ! I could have kissed him, but I had only one thing on my mind. Thanking him profusely I gathered up the prints and was out the door, heading back through the black night to the Ops van just as quickly as my legs could carry me. It was about ten to eleven, but Wing Commander Waddell was still there. With triumphant relief I placed my Tiger treasures in front of him, repeating the judgment of the APIS officer. Bunt Waddell was pleased, and I believe he was just as relieved as I was. He would get on to Dempsey's headquarters as quickly as possible. "However," he reminded me sternly, "do not let it happen again. The bomb line is the bomb line is the bomb line!" I got the message.

The APIS officer who gave me the Tiger interpretation was a young British lieutenant, Dirk Bogarde, who later became an international film star, an excellent author, and a talented painter. In correspondence we exchanged in the fall of 1980, he wrote, "I ... remember the tremendous 'flap' that happened the moment we discovered that there were Tigers in the blasted bombing line! Naturally we hadn't seen them because no one expected them to be there anyway. And if *you* had not seen one burst of fire we might never have known until far too late. As it was, and as you know, the road to Falaise was the road of death ... and very unpleasant it was too: from the ground!"

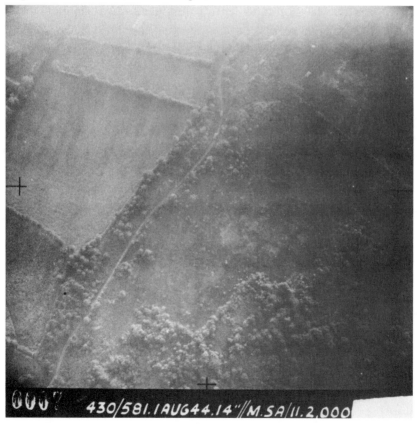

August 14, 1944. My photo of tanks interpreted by Dirk Bogarde.

8 August 1944 OPERATIONS: In spite of the haze and
general poor visibility, thirteen TAC/R's were flown today,
all successful. Information gleaned from these TAC/R's
was quite considerable. The largest concentration was
twenty plus tanks observed by Flying Officer Rohmer in
his morning TAC/R. Possible tanks among houses and
trees at 812425. 1 in flames at 863441.

430 Squadron Log

The area I worked that morning was just to the south of Mont
Pinçon, almost to Flers. The reported burning tank was at the front
line of the advancing 43 Division of the British 30 Corps stretching
east from Mont Pinçon to Thury Harcourt. While at that moment
there was no way I could identify the enemy tanks I saw, I later
learned that they were of 12 SS Panzer Division, that day engaged in
strong counterattacks against 59 Division attempting to take Thury-
Harcourt from the northeast.

As we ranged around enemy territory with our eyes glued to the
ground it was becoming increasingly obvious to us fighter recce
pilots that the enemy forces were being compressed. The Americans
were swinging around toward LeMans, some ninety miles southeast
of Caen, completing their left hook easterly across and under the
German Army.

As the compression of German forces accelerated, so did their need
to move tanks, vehicles, guns, and equipment in the full light of day.
Thus forced to expose themselves to the American, British, and Canadian
Tactical Air Forces, they became increasingly vulnerable to the crushing
power of the Allied fighter bombers and rocket-firing aircraft.

The massive German counterattack at Mortain in the U.S. sector,
which was started on August 7, was outside the assigned front of the
Second British Army, which our Canadian 39 Recce Wing supported.
Nevertheless our two fighter reconnaissance squadrons made substantial
finds of German tanks and equipment en route to the Mortain area, which
were then immediately attacked by Typhoons and Spitfires. An outstanding example was a recce operation carried out by our own 430 Squadron.

In mid-afternoon on August 2, Flying Officer Danny Lambros, accompanied by Flying Officer Clem St. Paul, had taken photographs in the Conde area some fifteen miles west of Falaise. Lambros's naked eye had not seen what his oblique camera had picked up and the interpreters were able to see when they took a good look at his photographs. What they found were about sixty Panzers and twenty motor transports. Within a half-hour of Lambros's landing at B8 at 1620 hours, word had gone out about the discovery. The Typhoons with their armour-penetrating rockets were immediately sent in. The result was that thirty-seven of the tanks were destroyed and most of the German vehicles. Quite an achievement for the bloodhounds, working as a team with our gutsy Typhoon pilots.

Shortly after three in the afternoon of August 3, Flying Officer Vince Dohaney and I made an airborne decision that, probably to our good fortune, we were not able to execute. With Dohaney leading, Jack McLeod as number two, and I, myself, leading the cover section with Flight Lieutenant Iverson, we were off at 1440 hours to do a TAC/R on roads from Tinchebray to Mayenne to Domfront to Vire. The weather was good, with no cloud. Dohaney saw three possible Sherman tanks about five miles northeast of Vire and six motor transports on the road just to the north of Mortain. As we were about to turn northward to return to base we spotted a huge gaggle of German fighters — Focke-Wulfs and Me 109s. They were slightly higher. We deduced instantly that they were going home. They were a long way from their bases in the Seine area, so we knew they were flying with no fuel to spare. When they crossed in front of our path we would still be about a mile north of them. Therefore, if we wanted to attack them, we would have to swing in behind them and try to catch up.

Four Mustang Is attacking some forty German fighters flying their peculiar, loose, all-over-the-sky gaggle formation? Why not? Clearly they were short of fuel. The last thing they would want to do was dogfight. Perhaps we could pick off some stragglers. Dohaney's voice came over the radio asking me tersely, "Should we?" My response was immediate. "Let's go." Dohaney called for close-in battle formation and put his power up to 45 inches of boost and 3,000 rpm, which all of us copied. We were off, blood racing, guns cocked and at the ready.

As we turned onto an arc intercept course the huge mass of fighters gave no indication they were aware of our presence. Or if they did know we were there, they could probably assess what we were just beginning to realize. There was no way we could catch them. When we did get into line directly behind them we were still about a mile back and below — and they were pulling away.

Well, we tried, and it would make a good "line shoot" when we got back to Château Magny.

CHAPTER 20

Enemy in a Pocket: Beginning the Falaise Gap

———————◆———————

12 August 1944 OPERATIONS: in spite of hazy conditions thirteen TAC/R's and one photo R were flown, one
task being abortive due to technical failure. No movements of major importance were seen.

430 Squadron Log

FROM AUGUST 10 THROUGH 12, heavy fighting was raging to the
north and south of the pocket forming around the German
Army. The battle to the west at Mortain continued. The enemy, badly
scarred by the devastating attacks the rocket Typhoons and fighter
bombers inflicted on his tanks and motor vehicles, seemed to have
finally decided that he would not move in daylight hours unless
absolutely necessary.

Of eleven tactical reconnaissance operations 430 Squadron carried
out on August 10, seven reported "no movements seen." Of the six operations carried out on August 11, three reported "no movement." And of
twelve operations on August 12, there were six so reported.

Furthermore, for some reason our direct taskmaster, Dempsey's
Second British Army staff, seemed either to have bogged down or there
was a new man on staff who did not know how to use the reconnaissance
squadrons at his disposal. For the first and only time the squadron log
recorded a situation like this: "Very few tasks were received from Army
this morning; consequently, no sorties were flown until this afternoon."

There was a dearth of tasking notwithstanding that the sky was
cloudless, visibility was excellent, and there was a hell of a lot of fighting going on out there.

Of the tactical reconnaissance operations on August 10 in which movement was reported, one was into the Mortain area, where the Germans were throwing all their weight in the counterattack thrust ordered by Hitler. This was to be the only Mortain recce that 430 Squadron was tasked to do during the period of the German assault that had started on August 7. The sector belonged to the Americans, who were successfully holding off the onslaught of the German Panzer divisions pulled in from the Caen/Falaise area and elsewhere. It was likely, however, that by the morning of August 10, Montgomery wanted to have one of his own "eyes" take a look at the situation rather than relying totally on reports from his Americans.

Thus at 0835 hours, with Flying Officer Ken Gillmor as cover, I was airborne out of B8 headed for Mortain. It was an excellent flying day. Visibility was unlimited except for 5/10 scattered cloud at fifteen hundred feet. In the Mortain sector immediately behind the German lines there was clear evidence of the heavy battle that was still being fought. I saw much scattered activity but no concentrations of vehicles or troops. So my report on debriefing after returning to B8 at 1015 hours had to be general: "Considerable movement and MET observed in the entire area."

In the next few days, strapped in our Mustangs flying at low level over the pocket, we would watch the Germans gather, form columns of vehicles in broad daylight, and drive "on towards the Seine ferries" through the Falaise-Argentan Gap that General Patton could have closed on August 12 and 13 when two of his armoured divisions arrived at Argentan; unfortunately, he was ordered not to close it.

On August 12, when I circled in the smooth late evening air in a cloudless, hazy sky halfway between Falaise and Argentan, I saw the war from a vantage point allowed only a few. But if I could have soared higher with the penetrating eyes of an eagle I would have seen all the forces in the Battle of Normandy arrayed before me.

Three miles to the north of Falaise, astride the road to Caen, I would have seen the flashes of the guns of the 2nd and 3rd Canadian Infantry Divisions, all fighting in a regrouping action, behind which they would mount a new operation, Tractable, an attack that could not get underway any earlier than August 14.

To the south, some seven or eight miles from where I was circling, was the town of Argentan. The distance between the Canadians standing astride the road to Caen, a few miles north of Falaise at Quesnay, and Argentan was a formidable twenty miles. In Argentan I would still have been able to see German troops. But on its southern approaches and to the west and east, I would have been able to see tanks and armoured vehicles of General Patton's XV Corps moving north under General Haislip. More particularly, they were Leclerc's 2nd French Armored Division on the west and to the southeast the American 5th Armored Division under General Oliver. Ahead of them, straight north up the road to Falaise until my eyes reached the rear of the horde of German armour and guns fighting off the Canadians to the north of Falaise, I would be able to see only a few enemy forces — a mere handful of tanks, guns, and troops to stand in the way of the advance of Patton's armour under Leclerc and Oliver. Virtually nothing.

Then looking far to the west toward Mortain, I would have seen the beginning of the German Seventh Army starting to withdraw under the permission of the Führer, granted that day. The Mortain counterattack had failed, but not before Hitler had thrown into the bulging pocket enormously valuable reinforcements of tanks, guns, and troops in a last-ditch effort. In that pocket to the west of me, and north beyond Falaise, was what was left of the whole of the German Seventh Army and the remnants of its Panzer Army. The pocket was enormous. Hundreds of thousands of men, thousands of vehicles, hundreds of tanks, an entire Army, all were in a pocket with only one mouth, the Falaise Gap. I was circling over it at the moment. It was twenty miles wide. Through it the first of the escaping, retreating German vehicles were beginning to move.

The opportunity to complete the encirclement was at hand, the very objective that Bradley and Montgomery had agreed upon a few days earlier. But there was no way the Canadians, the Poles, and the British Army could break through north of Falaise to rush south past Falaise to Argentan; they were pinned down where they were.

No, if the ring was to be closed with the two German armies inside the pocket, it would have to be done by Patton and it would have to be done forthwith. In a signal at 2130 hours on August 12, Haislip, the commander of XV Corps, notified Patton that he was about to capture his last assigned objective, Argentan. If Patton would authorize XV Corps to proceed north of Argentan, Haislip was ready to move the American Armored Division through Leclerc's French Division at Argentan for the drive north to meet the Canadians.

Patton's response was prompt. In a message at 0440 hours on August 13, Patton instructed him to push slowly in the direction of Falaise along the Argentan-Falaise road, which would also be the left boundary of his advance. On arriving at Falaise, Haislip was to "continue to push on slowly until ... contact [with our allies] was made."

When a 5th Armored Division patrol had attempted to advance north on the morning of August 13, they were stopped by German guns from the high ground north of Argentan, which inflicted damage on both the French and American attacking groups. In the afternoon a patrol from Leclerc's division entered Argentan, reaching the centre of town, but on the arrival of German tanks, it quickly retired. Neither of the probes north was in strength, although all the necessary American armoured force was in place to easily move through the German defenders.

Meanwhile, the six tanks that Butch Lowndes had seen at about 0900 the morning before moving easterly on the main highway about ten miles west of Argentan had arrived in the Argentan sector. They were elements of 1 SS and 2 Panzer Divisions. The 116 Panzer as well with infantry and artillery had also arrived late on the thirteenth. Even so, it was obvious to the German commanders that three emaciated Panzer divisions would not be able to hold for any length of time. The slim defensive line could have been eliminated at the bidding of the XV Corps units at Argentan.

On the morning of August 13, General Dietrich, the commander of Fifth Panzer Army, sent to the headquarters of Army Group B a signal that clearly stated the precarious posture of the German forces at that moment:

> If the front held by the Panzer Army and the Seventh Army is not withdrawn immediately and if every effort is not made to move the forces toward the east and out of the threatened encirclement, the Army group will have to write off both armies. Within a very short time

resupplying the troops with ammunition and fuel will no longer be possible. Therefore, immediate measures are necessary to move to the east before such movement is definitely too late. It will soon be possible for the enemy to fire into the pocket with artillery from all sides.

Astonishingly enough to me, the German line at Argentan did hold, not because of the defences in place but because Patton was told to stop further movement to the north. Patton then informed Haislip he was not to go north of Argentan and he was to withdraw any of his elements that might be "in the vicinity of Falaise or to the north of Argentan."

The directive that Patton was ordered to give created the notorious Falaise Gap. It was probably one of the most costly, controversial orders given in the European theatre during the Second World War.

As a result of that order and the subsequent creation of the Falaise Gap, in the next six days I watched thousands of vehicles, armour, horse-drawn artillery, and troops move through the Gap, making their way to the ferries of the Seine and sanctuary on the banks beyond, ready and able to fight another day.

What that order meant in terms of escaping German forces could only begin to be measured after the closing of the Falaise Gap during August 19 and 20, a full week after the decision had been made to create it.

CHAPTER 21

Reconnaissance over the Falaise Gap and its Closing

————◆————

17 August 1944 The last light sorties observed large amount of tanks, M.T. staff cars, etc. moving east out of the Falaise-Argentan pocket. At the same time, news was received tonight of 100 American tanks in Versailles.

430 Squadron Log

FROM AUGUST 13 ONWARD, THE pace of the enemy's withdrawal had accelerated rapidly as the Gap continued to remain open. TAC/Rs of the pocket began on August 13 with "impression of considerable activity in Briouze" and "in the Argentan-Falaise area 44 MET." On August 14, "40 plus MET moving northeast out of Laigle and movement in Laigle itself," and in the Domfront area a "column of tanks and MET, 50 MET in field." On August 15, "20 plus MET in convoy at Domfront"; "In the Evrecy, Laigle area 30 MET"; and "Open MET had passengers who waved white flags on approach of aircraft."

During a TAC/R of mine that day at about 1630 hours, I watched with amazement from an altitude of about one thousand feet as horse-drawn guns and armoured cars moved eastbound in the area about thirty miles to the west and north of Argentan. I reported "25 ambulances on the road" ten miles west of Argentan, also headed east. The enemy was out in the open and was being hit very hard by fighter bombers of the XIX United States Air Force and by our Typhoons and Spitfires. The large number of ambulances we were seeing quickly gave rise to the suspicion that the Germans were painting the protective red crosses on their military vehicles in order to save themselves.

During the late evening of August 13 I had been tasked to lead a TAC/R well to the east in the Dreux/Evreux area in the flat country leading toward the Seine. St. Paul, Winiarz, and Iverson were with me. It was a clear evening with high cirrus clouds and good visibility of up to twenty miles and beyond. We were flying at three thousand feet, about twenty-five miles outside the bomb line well into enemy territory. In the Dreux area, I picked up the dust of a large number of rapidly moving vehicles ahead of me but slightly to the right. They were still too far away to identify. Before I was in a position to pinpoint their location I checked my map. They were at least thirty miles beyond the bomb line. Therefore they had to be German!

In the front of my mind was the rough lesson I had learned about bomb lines two weeks earlier. This time, however, I was satisfied that I could with impunity ring up Group Control Centre to bring in the Spitfires and Typhoons. First I had to be sure the target was big enough to warrant it.

As we got closer I could see they were tanks going hell-bent, dust billowing behind them as they charged in column down a flat French side road eastward toward Seine. I estimated that there were about twelve of them, certainly a number that justified a call for the fighter bombers and rocket aircraft. Pinpointing their location I was just about to call GCC when my eyes told me there was something a little different about those tanks. They didn't look like Tigers or any other German tank I had seen.

My God, they were Shermans! But they were thirty miles beyond the bomb line! I later learned that they were Patton's tanks charging for Dreux, leaving Normandy, the pocket, and the Falaise Gap far behind. Incredible! I did not call GCC.

On August 17 all the squadrons in the British- and Canadian-manned 2nd Tactical Air Force operating out of Normandy received a controversial order that was attributed to Montgomery's headquarters. The bomb line was to be moved well east of the Gap between Falaise and Argentan. From that moment forward, none of the Typhoons and Spitfires of the British 2nd Tactical Air Force or the Thunderbolts and Lightnings of the IX United States Air Force could attack any enemy vehicles, troops, or other targets of opportunity within the pocket or the Gap. So far as we could see there were still tens of thousands of troops in the pocket, which was now becoming severely compressed. Tanks, horse-drawn artillery, ambulances, and vehicles of every kind were moving in broad daylight toward the Gap under our very eyes. As 83 Group Intelligence Summary of Operations No. 67 stated (our 39 Recce Wing was part of 83 Group), "we were debarred from attacking the Western-most enemy."

For all the pilots this was an astonishing order. It gave the Germans carte blanche — without fear of attack, they had time to gather their tanks and vehicles into orderly columns and then drive and march out of the pocket and the Gap toward the Seine. However, once they reached the open area a few miles to the east of the Gap they lost the bomb line protection and were subject to air attack.

We fighter recce pilots believed that if there was any problem with pinpointing or identifying enemy targets, whether they were one hundred yards or fifty away from our own troops on the ground, we, the ace map readers, the bloodhounds, should have been given the job of leading in the Spits, Thunderbolts, Lightnings, and Typhoons. We should have been the battleground Pathfinders. As we saw it, that solution would have been a far better practical alternative than taking the unbelievable route of denying our massive tactical Air Forces the opportunity to attack and destroy German forces now in full, organized retreat out of the pocket through the Gap.

While the order prohibiting air attacks in the Falaise Gap might have been incomprehensible to me, it certainly was not to the Army elements that had been bitten by our own aircraft. On August 19, the 51st (Highland) Division of 1 British Corps lodged a complaint to 21st Army Group about attacks that had occurred the day before. They complained of forty separate incidents resulting in twenty-five vehicle casualties and, more important, fifty-one personnel casualties.

However, it was the Polish Armored Division that had been truly suffering. At the time it was said that the Poles, fighting to the left of the Canadians coming down the Falaise road, had been attacked by our own Spitfires or Typhoons in the close quarter of the converging battle. Not only had these brave fighting men suffered heavy losses during the bomber raids on August 8 and 14, but they were also being hammered by our tactical aircraft. In the late hours of August 18 the division's headquarters reported, "Units and brigade headquarters have been continually bombed by own forces. Half the petrol being sent to 2nd Armoured Regiment was destroyed through bombing just after 1700 hours."

During the three-day period from August 16 to 18, 72 Polish soldiers were killed and 191 wounded through attacks from our own aircraft, while throughout 2 Canadian Corps, 77 were killed and 209 wounded. As a result, the Canadian Army headquarters lodged a strong demand for measures to be taken so that such incidents would not happen again.

Two other factors influenced the decision to issue the order that tied the Air Forces' hands. The first was the Army commander's typical inability to understand fully the capability of the Air Forces available to do his tasking. This inability leads to distrust, particularly when the Air Force has, as has been seen, made some grievous, costly errors in its close, heavy bombing support of the Army assaults. It is true that at the time of the Falaise Gap the Canadians, British, and Poles had had more than their share of short bombings in daylight by Bomber Command and the USAF. They were understandably furious with the Air Force. However, in our opinion as the people in and over the battlefield, the answer was not to emasculate us but to task the air commanders to come up with a solution that would ensure there was no repeat of the close-quarter attack on the Poles.

The second factor came from the many reports by the fighter recce pilots and others of an overabundance of sighted ambulances, for example, my own report on August 15 when I counted twenty-five vehicles with red crosses on them eastbound on the main highway ten miles west of Argentan. Major-General Francis de Guingand, Montgomery's chief of staff, later gave this explanation for moving the bomb line away and forbidding the Allied fighter bomber and rocket aircraft from attacking:

> We were kept pretty busy with the various problems connected with the battle of the "pocket." The co-ordination of air support was the most difficult of them all. When once the area had become reduced there was a great danger of the Tactical Air Forces supporting each Army Group becoming mixed up. It was very difficult to select

bomb-lines that would suit everyone. Eventually the task
of co-ordination was given to Coningham.

During this time pilots reported a large proportion
of the enemy's vehicles were carrying Red Cross flags
and emblems. It was obvious that this was merely a ruse
to avoid having their transport attacked. I believe these
flags were even seen on tanks. What were the pilots to
do? The decision was to avoid attacking them, for it was
thought that the Germans in their present mood might
well take reprisals against our prisoners and wounded.
A difficult decision, but probably the right one.

That line of reasoning might have been valid at Montgomery's
headquarters, but to the young pilots, cruising back and forth over the
bulging pocket, our guns and rockets turned off, the result was simply
that we could not believe anyone could give such an order. However,
given it was, and it was obeyed. The cost in vehicles and enemy troops
that might otherwise surely have been destroyed or forced to surrender
was enormous. As a gross error in tactical battlefield judgment, the
August 17 order must qualify as one of the gravest in the utilization of
assembled air power in the Second World War.

The earlier decision that had kept Patton's forces from proceeding north
from Argentan on August 12 and 13, thereby creating the Falaise Gap,
when combined with the injunction against pocket and Gap attacks by
the fighter bombers and rocket aircraft of the Allied Tactical Air Forces,
thwarted the first opportunity the Allies had during this retreat operation to cut off and destroy a whole Army. The second opportunity was
thwarted on August 19.

On that day I would be witness to an event that was to demonstrate
the costliness and stupidity of the order debarring air-to-ground attacks
in the pocket and the Falaise Gap.

CHAPTER 22

Montgomery at Fault for the Falaise Gap

———◆———

19 August 1944 OPERATIONS: Flying Officer R.H. Rohmer and Flying Officer E.F. Geddes TAC/R 13:00/13:45 10/10's at 5,000'. Visibility 10–15 miles. Column of armor 250 plus moving east 232233. 100 plus moving east at 220240. 10 tanks 181228. 20 tanks at 190172. 10 vehicles at 196215.

430 Squadron Log

O N AUGUST 17 AND 18, the flood of Germans through the Falaise Gap was in full flow. At last light on August 17, Flight Lieutenant Gill had reported in the Argentan area "300 tanks, staff cars, ambulances on all roads, general direction east through entire area." The morning of August 18 brought a report from Flight Lieutenant J.R. Manser: "All roads leading into Vimoutiers from south and southwest completely jammed with MET. Crossroads at 468510 same condition." Vimoutiers was fifteen miles northeast of Argentan, and the reported crossroads was at Exmes and lay ten miles due east of Argentan. Other reports from our aircraft over the Falaise Gap reported "all roads active with enemy tanks, guns, MET moving east"; "200 MET moving east and southeast"; "200 MET and tanks crossing river and moving east four miles south of Vimoutiers"; and "1,000 plus vehicles jammed in area" north of Argentan.

From the Falaise Gap east to the Seine, the main roads were filled with tanks, vehicles, and guns desperately fleeing from the pocket. Flight Lieutenant E.S. Dunn reported hundreds of MET moving east toward the Seine River crossing of Bonnieres, northwest of Mantes-Gassicourt.

The enemy was in full flight. Furthermore, he was escaping through the Gap that had been open for seven long and, for the Allied forces, costly days, and he was now free from Allied air attacks in the pocket and Gap.

With Flying Officer E.F. Ashdown, I arrived over the Gap shortly after 1300 hours in the afternoon of August 19, flying low at about a thousand feet. I was astonished by what I saw. Crossing the main road to Falaise three miles northwest of Argentan at Ocanges was a column of every imaginable type of vehicle, a mixed bag of trucks, horse-drawn artillery, tanks, ambulances — anything that could move. They had been gathering around Château Cui. They were two abreast on a dirt road leading northeast toward Pommainville. The head of the column was stopped at a fork in the road about four hundred yards east of the paved Falaise-Argentan road. The body of the double column of vehicles stretched snake-like westward across the Falaise-Argentan road toward the small village of Commeaux. Around it the enemy had been gathering in the fields and under trees over the previous twenty-four hours. They were now moving, jockeying into position, forging their way onto the roads leading into the tail of the seemingly endless column.

As its head at the fork in the road there were two staff cars. At my low altitude, I could plainly see their occupants standing beside them,

Château Cui at Ocanges on the Falaise/Argentan Road.

apparently attempting to decide which road to take. There before me was the largest, most vulnerable target of opportunity I had seen or would ever see. If they were not attacked and destroyed the enemy troops and their equipment below me would move out and escape to fight again another day.

But my number two and I could not attack. We fighter recce pilots still flew under the injunction that prevented us from going after ground targets. Even worse, the Army's order prohibiting any attacks against the enemy in the pocket or the Falaise Gap was in full force. Therefore, it was futile to call up Group Control Centre to report the column because the Air Force had been rendered impotent. There was no choice but to watch as the occupants of the staff cars got back into their vehicles and the column began to move out unimpeded along the south fork in the road. The intelligent Germans below me had long since deduced that through some incomprehensible decision made by their enemy, they were, at least for the moment, safe from any air attack. They could probably no more believe the incredible decision than I could sitting above them.

Instead of being destroyed upon the spot that entire column snaked its way out of the Falaise Gap. Two days later, in a jeep, I went down four miles of the roads it had followed. There was not a single destroyed or damaged vehicle, no evidence that the enormous, fleeing force had passed that way except for the bloated carcasses of a few dead horses along the roadside and one destroyed Tiger tank.

Whatever the justification for the prohibitory order, the sight of that long, two-abreast German column moving out of the Falaise Gap was a spectacle I will never forget. It was an event that should never have been allowed to happen.

On the evening of August 19, elements of U.S. General Hodges' V Corps met Polish tankers to complete the encirclement of the German Seventh Army and parts of Fifth Panzer Army, an estimated 125,000 men.

On August 20, the Falaise Gap was completely and finally closed.

The Battle of Normandy, which had begun on D-Day, June 6, was at its end.

I have a firm opinion on who it was who stopped Patton at Argentan, thus creating the Falaise Gap. Historians who weren't there and those who weren't even alive then can argue against my thesis all they want. But sorry, chaps, I was there.

As it happened, Brigadier E.T. Williams, one of Monty's own staff, was with de Guingand in the latter's van at Montgomery's headquarters when the order was given. American military historian Dr. Forrest C. Pogue interviewed Williams on May 30 and 31, 1947, just three years after the event. Williams enjoyed a high reputation for having a remarkably clear and accurate memory. Pogue took notes of what Williams told him. It will be recalled that 2nd French Armored was Leclerc's armoured division under Patton. Under instructions from Patton, Leclerc had pushed on slowly toward Falaise from Argentan on the evening of August 12. These are Pogue's notes:

> Falaise Gap — Remembers was in Freddie's (deGuingand) truck near Bayeux when 2d French Armored made its swing up and crossed the road towards Falaise. Monty said tell Bradley they ought to get back. Bradley was indignant. We were indignant on Bradley's behalf. DeGuingand said, "Monty is too tidy." Monty missed closing the sack. Freddie thought Bradley should have been allowed to join Poles at Trun. Bradley couldn't understand. Thought we were missing our opportunities over inter/Army rights. However, it should be pointed out that Monty regarded Bradley as under his command; therefore his decision was not made on the basis of inter/Army considerations. Master of tidiness. He was fundamentally more interested in full envelopment than this inner envelopment. We fell between two stools. He missed the chance of closing at the Seine by doing the envelopment at Falaise.

The argument can now be made that even if Bradley gave the order without getting Montgomery's permission, the reality is that

Montgomery was the commander of all of the field forces, including Bradley. At Bradley's headquarters there were British liaison staff from Montgomery's headquarters, the 21st Army Group. Montgomery would have been informed immediately by this liaison staff of Bradley's order to Patton on the night of August 12 to get back to Argentan and to respect the division lines between the British and Canadian armies on the one hand and the American on the other. That line went east and west through Argentan and had been opposed by Montgomery.

It would have been in Montgomery's power to overturn Bradley's order. Montgomery the commander failed or refused to overturn the order when he knew, or ought to have known, that Haislip had a chance to come up from the south of Argentan toward Falaise, meet the German forces from behind, and entrap the entire 7th German Army, which was to the west in the Mortain sector.

Therefore, even though in later writings Bradley said that it was his order and not Montgomery's, it was Montgomery's responsibility and his failure to override Bradley that caused the creation of the Falaise Gap and all its horrendous consequences.

So the Falaise Gap was closed. It was time for me to have a wisdom tooth looked after. On August 21 I went to the van of our wing dentist. Using the most primitive dental tools (a hammer and chisel) but sufficient local anesthetic, he extracted both of my wisdom teeth. The resulting swelling made me look like some sort of a chipmunk. The next step was to send me off on leave back to England. But that didn't happen before I had the opportunity to go with our air liaison officer, Captain Hugh Morris, in a jeep to Château Cui in the Gap area where I had seen the hundreds of German vehicles assembled and then moving down the road. (I revisited that château in the summer of 2003 during the period when the Juno Beach Centre was opened. And I followed the same path across the Falaise-Argentan road.)

It was the road where I had seen the whole column stopped and had failed to use my intelligence in dropping a message to them to either surrender or be blasted to kingdom come. There were bloated dead horses all over the place, feet in the air. Then we went east across the main Falaise-Argentan road to the point where I had seen the head of the column. There were vehicles and bodies all over the place. To our cautious surprise we found an abandoned German Opel car painted with a red cross on its top. Would the Opel operate; would the engine run; could we "appropriate" this car for our own purposes? Wary of booby traps we gingerly examined the car top to bottom. I got in, and lo and behold it started. With this proud new possession under control I followed the jeep back to our airfield. Ed Geddes, who was with us on this foray, shared the ownership of the vehicle. I left our prize with him when, after my cheek swelling was somewhat reduced, I went for a week's leave in England accompanied, or was it chaperoned, by the wonderful Dick Manser.

It was a Dakota that took us to Northolt airport. I had prudently acquired a bottle of Scotch (I still drank Scotch in those days). To my horror, when we arrived at Northolt there was an officious customs officer who demanded that I pay duty on the bottle of British Scotch, which I think was Johnny Walker. Can you believe it? I paid.

So ended the Battle of Normandy for Richard Rohmer.

CHAPTER 23
Belgium and Holland and My Shoot
at the Bridges of Venlo

———◆———

M<small>Y RECORDS DON'T SHOW ME</small> where I went for that one-week leave, probably to the centre of London.

In any event, it was back to Northolt to get on the Dakota to be taken back to Normandy. No problem, except that when we arrived at our airfield everyone was gone. I mean really gone — vans, tents, airplanes, nothing was there, not even a note as to where the squadron had gone. All that Dick Manser and I knew was that the whole battle area had moved far to the north.

What to do? The Dakota had to get back to England, so the pilot left Manser and myself with our baggage at the abandoned airstrip. For some inexplicable reason an ancient RAF York transport aircraft, a high-winged, fabric-covered machine, appeared at our airfield. Manser and I talked our way on board. The captain was heading north in this rickety old twin-engine machine, his ultimate destination being Brussels.

Brussels! Had our forces moved that far north in a week? Well, if he was going there we had no choice. Off we went with wings flapping like those of a goose. It would soon be dark, so the pilot decided to land at what he thought was an airstrip in the First World War sector at a place called Amiens, one of the more famous bloody battle areas of that great conflict. The Amiens field was open. We landed with a great crash and bang. It was dark, so we slept in our seats in the aircraft with food coming from ration tins that the crew had with them.

In the morning we were airborne again in the ancient York heading for Brussels and the airfield just to the north of the city.

What Dick Manser and I did not know was that Brussels had been liberated just the day before.

When the York arrived at the Brussels airport there were two squadrons of RCAF Spitfires there under the command of one of Canada's most outstanding Second World War pilots and leaders, Wing Commander Dal Russell, DSO, DFC.

His staff looked after us in a kindly, if not patronizing, way because the Spitfire pilots thought that they were so much better than we Mustang drivers. So far as we were concerned it was the other way around.

We were informed that our squadron was in a farmer's field back in France at a place called Evreux, west of Paris and at least a hundred miles to the south of Brussels. Until air transport could be arranged we would have to do our best and stay in Brussels. Tough deal. So into the centre of Brussels we went in a vehicle supplied by Russell's team. This was the first day after the liberation and the whole of the citizenry of that magnificent city was in the streets celebrating. It was an unbelievable situation. Manser and I were treated like heroes. We found accommodation in one of the hotels on the main square and from that point joined in the festivities. Beer, wine, hugs, kisses, cigarettes, cheering, shouting, flag waving. It was a phenomenal day and evening. We even saw the Mannequin Pis, who was still in liquid operation, believe it or not.

The next hungover day we were back at the airfield, where a Dakota transport was scheduled to come in to pick us up to take us to 430 Squadron at Evreux.

In due course the Dakota arrived, Dick Manser and I got on board with our baggage, and the Dakota headed south. Our new airfield at Evreux was a bleak farmer's field, flat and full of stubble from whatever the crop was that had just been taken, probably wheat. It was a most boring location, but Paris was not far away. The Opel car had survived the long journey up from Normandy at the skilled hands of some unknown driver. Skilled because the generator appeared to have stopped working, which meant that either the battery was fully charged or the car wouldn't work.

Undaunted, Ed Geddes and I decided we would do a foray into Paris to check out the Champs Élysées, the bars, dancehalls, and anything else that might offer an evening of productive activity.

The Opel got us to Paris all right, but we couldn't get back to the base that night because of that generator problem. So we had to stay overnight, which we did at some obscure fleabag that was inexpensive.

But we did see the Champs Élysées and we found an active dance-hall. We behaved ourselves with great honour and distinction through the entire episode.

Our operations at Evreux were confined strictly to ferrying photographs taken by 400 Squadron from their great, high-flying Bluebird spitfires. We would fly the treasured photographs up to Brussels. There they would be delivered to APIS people who would then interpret the photographs. The intelligence was immediately passed to Montgomery's headquarters, 21st Army Group, or wherever else the information had to go.

Then 430 Squadron was ordered to move to a Belgian grass airfield at Diest Schaffen, a town to the east of Brussels, a move that was quickly accomplished.

When our Dakota left Evreux for Diest Schaffen, all our equipment was on board, including my log book as well as my revolver in my kit bag. Instead of going to Diest the Dakota was ordered to go to the UK, where all our stuff was unloaded at some airfield, I know not where. The Dakota then was dispatched to do some other operational activity. Some days later either that Dakota or another picked up our stuff in England and flew off to deliver our much needed and precious cargo. However, the captain of the aircraft took it to the wrong Diest, a Diest that was in enemy territory. The result was simple. The Dakota was shot down, and all our possessions went with it. So much for my log book and my revolver, let alone my good blue uniform, trench coat, and all the other important clothing and living articles that I desperately needed. As to the precious revolver, there was much form filling out as well as apprehension as to whether I would be court-martialled for having lost my weapon. That never happened, but it could have.

At Diest Schaffen a tent quickly went up for use as our pilots' waiting location, but fortunately we were able to get into buildings for sleeping quarters and for our mess and bar. Thank God, because the days at Diest Schaffen were largely wet with the heavy September rain. The precipitation made it difficult to conduct operations because the bad weather turned us off. On top of that, the incessant moisture made the airfield rather dangerous to operate from.

At this point the British Army was about to conduct Market Garden, the Montgomery-inspired operation north to Arnhem and Nijmegen. It would be an operation best described as a total disaster. The great man, now a field marshal, thought that he could send his force up a single road from Belgium and cross the Maas and Rhine Rivers at Arnhem and Nijmegen. But he would first send in his airborne parachute troops, the tough, largely untested force that he had not used to this point except on D-Day.

Much of our work for the next weeks would revolve around Arnhem and Nijmegen and the entire British sector to the west and east of those locations. In mid-September I had one of my more exciting moments. Bill Golden and I had been doing a reconnaissance over Arnhem and Nijmegen. I was leading and was told to land at the airbase at Eindhoven, which had only recently been captured from the Germans. The runways at Eindhoven had been repaired, and Spitfire and Typhoon squadrons were operating from the airfield. In fact, the Typhoons with their rockets were taking off and, within sight of the airfield, were attacking targets on the ground. That's how close the fighting was to the airfield.

The purpose of landing at Eindhoven instead of Diest was to deliver my reconnaissance report and any photographs I might have taken to the Air Force and Army intelligence people located there. We landed at Eindhoven at about 1100 hours. We were instructed to go to the west side of the airfield, where a Typhoon squadron was located, and to park there.

We did exactly that. Then we were told that a truck would take us across the airfield so that we could be debriefed by the Army people at their location on the east side. No problem.

We got into this huge two-ton van with its canvas top. We jumped into the back part under the canvas. I was standing because, in simple terms, there was no place to sit. The truck started east across the airfield. From the vantage point at the back of the truck I could see all manner of aircraft flying in the circuit and around the airfield. Then I could see fighter aircraft coming toward us from the west at low level. Someone in the truck with us said, "Ah, look at the Spitfires coming at us." I said, "Spitfires, hell, they're ME 109s!"

At this point we were travelling at about 30 miles per hour. I could see this ME 109 coming straight at us. He was going to open fire. No question. That's what he's there for. To hell with this. Just as he was in range I elected to jump out, going 30 miles per hour or not. It didn't matter. As I jumped the 109 pilot opened fire, but, thanks be to God, at the last moment he aimed at a parked aircraft that we were passing just to the south of our truck's path. I could hear the gunfire as I was rolling on the pavement expecting to be hit at any second. It was all over in a few seconds. The 109 was gone. I had some bruises but no broken bones. But I can tell you it was a scary, scary moment.

I was airborne and in the Arnhem area when the great parachute drop was made there in September. It was a spectacular sight, with the Dakotas disgorging the paratroopers, whose huge, white chutes blossomed as they left their aircraft. The sky was filled with them, the cream of the British Army floating down into what was to turn out to be probably one of the greatest single massacres of the war. In 1960, Mary-O and I went back to Nijmegen and Arnhem and to Eindhoven. At Arnhem we

Flight Lieutenant Jack Watts and I with a Spitfire XIV
at Eindhoven, Holland, November 1944

went to the cemetery where the British paratroopers are buried. What a pathetic sight. The film *A Bridge Too Far*, in which my saviour of August 1, 1944, Dirk Bogarde, starred, told the story very well indeed.

430 Squadron finally moved from Diest Schaffen to Eindhoven on the fourth day of October. The airplanes and our dispersal (the pilots' shack) were at the northwest corner of the airfield. Our sleeping quarters were in a big, two-storey brick building across a canal at the northern sector of the airport. I would be stationed at Eindhoven until I finished my tour at the end of November.

The decision had been made to retire the Mustang I and to convert the squadron onto the Spitfire XIV, the superb, high-powered, five-bladed new version of the Spitfire. The conversion of 430 Squadron pilots began in the middle of November. But because I was so close to finishing my tour, with probably 130 operational sorties at that point, I elected not to convert onto the great machine. I was very thin, worn out, and was being dragged down by an infected tooth. My focus now was to finish my tour and get back to England. During that period there were two sorties that solidly stick in my memory.

The first was a search for V2 sites.

The Germans were hard at work lobbing V2 rockets across the Channel into London from the part of Holland that they still controlled. These were the ingenious product of the German scientist Werner von Braun and his colleagues.

The V2s needed a very small launch pad, not a permanent installation, and for that reason they were mobile. The pad could be taken to any given site quickly and put in place, the rocket erected and fired.

The V2 was particularly deadly. It would go up several miles then come down in a long arc. It would travel well beyond the speed of sound. At the receiving end in London you would first hear the explosion, and then the sound of the rocket arriving, like the clatter of a freight train, would follow. I had been close enough in London to a couple of these V2 arrivals to know exactly what they sounded like.

By the way, I forgot to say that while we were at Diest, one rainy day the flap of our dispersal tent opened and in walked none other than the man whom I had met on my first visit to an officer's mess, Flight Lieutenant "Mid" Middleton, the newest pilot on our squadron. I quickly identified myself and decided that, with my total and experienced seniority on the squadron, I would be the one to initiate him into the operational mode. In other words I would be his mentor. I am not sure that that was a comfortable experience for Middleton, but that's the way it went. And so whenever the opportunity arose I would take him as my number two, whether it was on an artillery reconnaissance or photographic or just straight visual.

So it was that on the sixth day of November I was tasked to depart Eindhoven and fly into a German-held sector to the north of Arnhem to search for V2 launch pads. Several had been fired from that area in the previous days. Middleton was my number two. It was a clear day with clumps of cloud at about two thousand feet. As we headed north I looked up and could see high above the silver glint of American B-17 bombers flying west, returning to England from whatever mission they had been on well to the east of us in Germany. By this time the American bombers were being escorted wherever they went by the long-range Mustang P51D, the highly efficient direct descendant of the ancient Mustang that Middleton and I were flying. They were all silver (aluminum), had the Rolls Royce-Packard Merlin engine and teardrop hoods, and were much lighter than our airplanes. When the Americans redesigned the Mustang, some sixteen hundred pounds had been stripped out of the fuselage. They were deadly.

I had noted the high bombers in my memory bank but thought nothing more about it, at least for the moment. We arrived at a spot that I wanted to look at carefully. So I began to circle, Middleton turning with me. It was his job to watch out for any attacking aircraft and to let me know immediately if he saw anything so that I could prepare to break and avoid being attacked. As I was turning left, for some reason I looked up vertically. There, over my right shoulder, straight above us coming down like hawks out of the far blue was a squadron of American Mustangs. They had spotted us and obviously decided that, because we looked like ME 109s and were painted dark, not silver the way they were, they were going to attack us. Middleton hadn't seen them. But I had. That was all that mattered. I immediately transmitted on my radio to let him know they were coming, shouting, "Prepare to break! I'm heading for that cloud!" By the grace of God there was a cumulus cloud very close to us. I headed for it, Middleton with me. We got into it just before the Mustangs could get into range. We made it into the safety of the cloud just in the nick of time. We would have been mincemeat at the hands of those American boys, who were sure that they had a couple of German 109s, notwithstanding the black and white D-Day markings still on the airplanes. If they had caught us we would have been gone.

The cloud saved us, but only just.

The second sortie that solidly sticks in my memory was what I now call the Shoot at the Bridges at Venlo.

It was a bleak, chilly, sunless day. There was a cover of high, impenetrable cloud at about eight or ten thousand feet. It sat like the rounded grey lid of a cold pot over the vast Netherlands countryside that lay flat and desolate around our airfield at Eindhoven.

It was Sunday, November 19, 1944. The nation of the beleaguered Dutch, so long occupied and suppressed by the hated troops of Nazi Germany, was slowly being liberated in bloody fighting by the Canadian Army in the Amsterdam sector, up against the North Sea. On the eastern sector, the British Army's assault against the area of the bridges at Arnhem and Nijmegen in Operation Market Garden, which began on September 17, had been costly to the extreme.

By mid-November the British Army was pressing the enemy hard in the area to the south of Nijmegen and Arnhem and east of Eindhoven toward the Maas River, where the bridges at the large Dutch city and rail centre of Venlo lay astride the river.

As the British mounted and maintained their attacks, the enemy retreated. Troops with their vehicles, tanks, artillery, and other equipment were trying desperately to cross the Maas.

But there was only one escape route. It was across the twinned railway and motor vehicle bridges that stood at Venlo. The decision was therefore made by Field Marshal Montgomery (still very much in command of the British and Canadian forces) that the bridges at Venlo had to come down. It was of absolute urgency and necessity that they be destroyed.

How to accomplish the task?

The first choice was by Air Force bombers. They would have to attack in daylight because the target was so difficult to hit. Precision bombing was required, and it would have to done from a great height because, to protect the bridges, the Germans had placed hundreds of their accurate, deadly 88-mm anti-aircraft guns in and around Venlo.

There was an alternative available to Montgomery. It was to utilize, for the first time, a Super Heavy Gun, an American-made, British-operated 8-inch artillery piece with a very long range. The massive shell had enormous destructive power. Fortuitously, such a Super Heavy Gun was within striking range of the bridges at Venlo. It was the gun of the 4th Battery of the No. 3 Super Heavy Regiment, Royal Artillery — British, of course.

The 4th Battery and its big gun were deployed in a field at Loon, some twenty-five thousand yards from and almost due west of the twin bridges at Venlo. That was a distance of 14.2 miles, yet within shooting range of the Super Heavy Gun.

There was one yellow caution raised. A Super Heavy Gun had not yet been fired in the Northwest Europe campaign. And if it were to be used, it would have to be ranged, its fire directed, by an Air Force pilot, a fighter reconnaissance airman experienced in artillery direction. But obviously such a pilot would have had no experience in doing an Arty/R over such an enormous distance and with a gun of that size.

Montgomery made the decision. Priority would go to the Super Heavy Gun and the fighter recce pilot who would do the ranging. There were only two fighter recce squadrons available. They were 414 and 430 Squadrons, both RCAF, of 39 Recce Wing, then based at Eindhoven.

It was a pair of Mustang pilots, the leader and his number two who, would carry out the shoot.

Montgomery's tasking regarding the bridges at Venlo was passed from Army Headquarters to HQ of the 2nd Tactical Air Force and thence to the Wingco Ops of 39 Recce Wing, Bunt Waddell, an excellent airman and leader.

For undisclosed reasons, Waddell selected from his nearly fifty available pilots an almost tour-expired (133 sorties), worn out, twenty-year-old to do this spectacular, first-ever, exceedingly important shoot. His name was Flying Officer Richard Rohmer (J24120). In the photograph taken at Eindhoven in November 1944, I am the gaunt person standing at the right. My number two was to be Flight Lieutenant E.F.J. Clark, known to the world as "Knobby."

I am (top right) with Gillmor, Geddes, Bricker, and Wilson of 430 Squadron at Eindhoven Airport, November 1944.

By a remarkable, happy coincidence that fell upon me in 1985 I am now able to tell the story of the shoot at the bridges of Venlo complete with maps, log books, and photographs. To the coincidences later.

Bunt Waddell and a Canadian ALO briefed me thoroughly, with Clark listening to every word. The targets were the twin bridges at Venlo. They were about five hundred feet long, stretching across the Maas River. The enemy was getting an incredible number of troops and huge amounts of material across them. Montgomery wanted them down right away.

I would be ranging a Super Heavy Gun. First time out for it. It was fourteen miles back from the target. Time of flight of the shell would be incredibly long, about fifty-five seconds. I couldn't believe it! The line of flight of the shell would be almost due east and the bridges' path across the Maas was east-west. So I would be ranging on a hair. I had to hit the hair using a gun fourteen miles away! Unbelievable.

Waddell cautioned me about the flak at Venlo. I had been there several times. You could almost walk on the exploding 88-mm shells. With luck I could see the fall of the Super Heavy Gun shells from a distance outside the Venlo 88-mm range. Maybe.

I was given the radio frequency of the Super Heavy Gun battery. Once contact was made with the radio operator, I would give him all my commands, corrections, and instructions.

When the briefing was over, Bunt Waddell underscored the importance of the operation by promising me a bottle of champagne if I hit the "goddamn" bridges. That was the best incentive I'd had since I had started my tour of operations with 430 Squadron as a sprog pilot in September 1943.

As the 430 Squadron ops record book shows, Clark and I were airborne in our Mustangs over Eindhoven at 1350 hours and headed east toward Venlo, climbing to the working altitude I had selected of four thousand feet. That height would give me a good opportunity to see where the shells were landing while we stayed out of range of the 88s.

We circled, and I switched to the designated radio frequency and transmitted, "Queen Baker this is Peco Blue Leader. Do you read me? Over." The response from QB was instant. It was a crisp, clear, "veddy British" voice coming in at strength five by five. Perfect.

I explained to the voice the procedure I wanted. Given the time of flight of the shell to the target, I would give the order to fire when I was within easy sight of the target so I could see the shell land. But at the same time I would be far enough out of range of those deadly 88s when the shell hit the ground. The timing for "Fire!" was therefore my call. I would give QB a ten-second warning before calling for them to fire. That settled, I then headed again toward the bridges. Knobby Clark was two hundred yards out off my starboard wing and slightly behind. There were the bridges, the target hair at twelve o'clock, dead ahead.

If I called for them to fire in about ten seconds I would be in the perfect position to see the first shell land. I gave the warning to QB. Would the first shot land on the bridges, on the east bank of the Maas or the west? Would I see it land at all?

"Fire!" I shouted into my face mask microphone. "Fire!" was the immediate response from QB as he repeated my order. His transmitter open, I could hear the blast in my earphones of the shell being fired. The radio operator then said, "Shot," which meant that the shell had been launched at the target. I then had some fifty seconds to get myself into position to pinpoint the spot where that first shot fell. At ten seconds before the shell hit QB warned me, "Splash!"

There it was! The explosion was massive. Smoke and debris and flame billowed up in a huge cloud. The shell had hit right in what I thought was the town square on the east bank of the Maas. The devastation was ... well, I'd never seen anything like it.

I turned and headed west again in order to stay away from the 88s. My correction decision was made after I plotted the shot on my special scale map.

"QB, drop four hundred," I ordered. That was four hundred yards to be taken off the elevation of the gun so the next shot would land on the west bank of the Maas within a few yards of the entrance to the bridges. My objective was to "bracket" the target as to distance. Drop four hundred. Up two hundred. Drop one hundred. Up fifty. Bracket until I had the shells dropping exactly as to distance.

Then it was to be the same bracketing as to the line from the gun. When the distance bracketing was finished the shells were falling to the left of the fifty-foot-wide twinned bridges, the "hair," by about forty yards. Right eighty. Fire — splash. Then left forty should put it right on line.

When I finished ranging at 1525 hours, after firing fifteen rounds in an hour and fifteen minutes, I had the shells landing within a few feet of the centre span of the bridges. They were missing the "hair" by a hair's breadth.

We couldn't stay any longer. We were running out of fuel, and I could see a gaggle of medium Mitchell bombers heading north toward the Venlo bridges, their obvious target. We left and landed back at Eindhoven at 1545. It had taken one hour and fifty-five airborne minutes to do the bridges at Venlo.

All I had to show for it was a hit on the western approach to the bridges and some near misses. My condensed report in the squadron operations book was: "Venlo. 6110's cloud 8,000'. Visibility unlimited. Bridge E.904091 engaged, after corrections 10 rounds landed within 20 yards, believed one direct. Shoot discontinued on arrival of friendly bombers. Large explosions seen at E.88908. Moderate accurate heavy flak E.8009."

Nevertheless, Wing Commander Waddell was generous enough to present me with the prize bottle of champagne. Knobby Clark and I polished it off in short order.

But wait! Word filtered down from high headquarters the next morning that the battery had used my ranging to keep firing at the bridge all night — and the bridge was down!

Two days later, on November 21, 1944, Knobby Clark and I climbed into our Mustangs again to go and take a confirming look at what we and the British Super Heavy Gunners had accomplished. It was late in the day, 1620 hours when we were airborne. Visibility was bad then good, anywhere from three-tenths of a mile to ten miles. But it was good enough to see what I wanted to see. As the ops book says I reported, "Railway bridge E903090 appears to have one span down."

The bridges at Venlo.

*The bridges at Venlo, destroyed by Super Heavy
artillery fire November 19, 1944.*

No question. The Super Heavy Gunners and I, with the intelligent assistance of their radio operator, had knocked down the bridges at Venlo. The enemy's only escape route had been destroyed.

CHAPTER 24

George Cooley and the End of My
135-Mission Tour of Operations

———◆———

THAT SORTIE TO CHECK THE state of the Venlo bridges was my final operational mission. It was number 135, and so back to England I went, the shoot at Venlo but a memory, no photographs, no written reports, no logs. Nothing. It was only a memory until I received a letter dated February 11, 1985, from one George Cooley of Kew, Richmond, in Surrey, England. This is where the coincidence comes in. These are the extracts from the Cooley letter that laid the groundwork for the coincidence:

> Dear General Rohmer,
> Following my recent retirement I have been delighted to read your book, *Patton's Gap*. As a member of RQRA of the British 11th Armoured Division, I was a VHF/HF operator (Artillery Reconnaissance) with an Army No. 22 set coupled to an RAF TRII43 set and worked with the RCAF 39 Recce Wing on numerous occasions from shortly after the D-Day landing until the crossing of the River Elbe towards the end of the war. In the early days of the campaign I seemed to be working exclusively with Mustangs whilst later it was with Spitfires.

Cooley makes comments about *Patton's Gap*, then goes on with this conclusion:

> I was disappointed that the magnificent work carried out by unit like yours of 2TAF never achieved the pub-

licity I felt it deserved. I recall, for example, an artillery reconnaissance exercise during which a direct hit was obtained on the road bridge at Venlo by a Super Heavy Artillery for which I was providing the radio link and a big ammunition dump's being hit during a shoot just prior to the Rhine crossing.

In conclusion I would like to congratulate you upon the presentation of the facts in your excellent book upon the Normandy operations.

An amazing coincidence! Cooley was the radio operator, the intermediary between me and the Super Heavy Gun battery, the man in the middle who made it happen. Here it was, 1985, some forty-one years after Venlo when, out of the blue, this letter arrived.

My reply was dated March 4, 1985. In it I use the words "out of the blue" to describe his letter and his reference to the shoot at the bridges at Venlo, for which he was providing the radio link.

Your out of the blue reference to that event is remarkable because it was I who did the shoot. At the moment the exact date and time in November is not available because my squadron log book (mine was lost by enemy action) is snowbound at my summer residence. When I get into it in the spring I will send you a photocopy. In any event I can recall quite clearly the Venlo shoot for a host of reasons.

From that exchange of letters, a pile of correspondence has grown over the years. George Cooley, brilliant scientist and good friend, has selflessly done an enormous amount of research into records, documents, and photographic files that can now be blended into the story of the shoot of 4 Battery of 3 Super Heavy Regiment, Royal Artillery, on November 19, 1944. The photographs and documents attest to this thorough research. The pièce de résistance is a photocopy of two pages of the war diary of 3 Super Heavy Regiment, RA, for November 19, 1944. The description of the shoot is vividly told. Of particular interest to me are the last three lines of the long single paragraph report: "The CO [Lieutenant-Colonel J.B. Hyde-Smith] received a photograph later from Brig. Mathew, CCRA 8 Corps. showing one span down and with a note attached saying 'Dear Smee, look what you done!'"

Apart from the brigadier's grammar and the identity of "Dear Smee," I am still searching for any mention that the shoot on the bridges at Venlo was ranged by a Mustang fighter reconnaissance pilot, let alone a colonial Canadian!

So ended my tour of operations with 430 Squadron after 135 operational missions. At the end of November I said goodbye to my 430 Squadron brothers and took the Dakota scheduled run back to England. I had instructions in my pocket to take a week's leave and then report to the Commanding Officer of 41 OTU, still at Hawarden near Chester. There I would finally become an instructor, teaching the fighter reconnaissance skills that I had acquired in my fourteen months of operational experience.

But as to the Venlo story, it is not yet finished. Venlo will be revisited in the year 2000, and with it the acquisition of a new friend, the legendary Prince Bernhard of the Netherlands.

CHAPTER 25
Instructing at 41 OTU and Return to Canada

———————

MY INITIAL STAY AT 41 OTU at Hawarden was brief. I was immediately posted to the fighter gunnery instructors school at a remote place in northern England called Catfoss. This was the RAF's famous air-to-air combat teaching centre where tour-expired fighter pilots were sent — if they were aces having had at least five victories against the enemy during their tour of operations — to learn the techniques of teaching air-to-air gunnery at Spitfire or Typhoon fighter operational training units.

Catfoss was to be my first experience in the wonderful Spitfire aircraft. The unit was equipped with Spit Vs, and for the purpose of dual instruction with the Miles Master, a tail dragger trainer made largely of wood with a huge radial engine. The instructor had the rear seat. It could be elevated very high, and the rear coupe top could be pulled up into a 45-degree position so the instructor could see well out ahead when the tail of the aircraft was down either on landing or taking off. I had flown the Miles Master at the Advanced Flying Unit training that I had taken before being posted to 41 OTU in 1943. But it was the Spitfire that was the real thrill. Moving from the Mustang to it was like moving from a Cadillac to a lightweight Ford Roadster.

The officers' mess and sleeping quarters were in an enormous Victorian mansion close to the airfield itself. The pilots on course shared a huge room with their assigned beds and dressers. There were about ten of us, and I was the only Canadian. The rest were British. The lectures that were involved and the flying of the Spitfire made the course at Catfoss most worthwhile. For the first time I was able to get into some vigorous aerobatics. The most challenging manoeuvre we had to do in the Spitfire was to attack a Wellington bomber flying at two thousand feet. In the Spitfire and "on the deck" you would approach the Wellington from the side (90 degrees) then pull up underneath it and, inverted, begin firing with your camera. I can tell you that being upside down at two thousand feet was quite a new and exciting position for me to be in. Quarter attacks, inverted attacks, deflection shooting with cameras, and live shooting at drogues, all of this went on for a period of several weeks in the cold, damp climate of northern England (which produced for me my usual chest infection, but this time I was not hospitalized).

It was at Catfoss that I celebrated my twenty-first birthday on January 24. Our flight commander, a squadron leader, discovered that it was my birthday. Generous man that he was he produced a barrel of beer for a party after dinner to the delight of my classmates and, of course, me. I was the first one carried off — or was it dragged off? — to our dormitory once I was beyond the capability of walking, or doing much else for that matter.

There was a second celebratory occasion when the cask of beer was again brought in. It was February 14, 1945, when to my utmost surprise and pride and joy I read in the *London Times* newspaper's honours list that His Majesty, King George VI, had seen fit to award me the Distinguished Flying Cross. I had the beautiful white cross ribbon with its purple stripes mounted under my wings before the end of the day.

For some inexplicable reason I never did get to an investiture at Buckingham Palace. However, I did receive the DFC in the mail. It now is displayed with my other decorations, orders, and medals in the Wings Room of the Royal Canadian Military Institute on University Avenue in Toronto. At the time of writing I am fortunate enough to have more orders, decorations, and medals than any other Canadian citizen. As I say to my rich friends and associates, such as Conrad Black, Galen Weston, and other outstanding entrepreneurs, "You guys have all the money but I have all the decorations."

When the training at Catfoss was completed it was then back to 41 OTU at Hawarden. Shortly thereafter the unit moved to the Aldershot area, where my instruction of students in gunnery became intense. Those who passed through the operational training unit were destined to go on to Canadian and British Spit XIV squadrons doing fighter reconnaissance from Holland with the intent to move with the British and Canadian armies as the final assault into Germany got underway.

My time at 41 OTU was relatively straightforward and uneventful, with one exception in terms of experience. Many of our students had been flying instructors in Canada, mostly on the Harvard trainer. So I, for one, anticipated that they would be quite competent in the Master aircraft with yours truly sitting in the back seat. I quickly found out that some of my students, even though they were highly experienced instructors themselves, were not particularly proficient when they were flying the Master. In fact, it was so bad that I found people veering off to the left or right when landing or taking off, and I promptly decided that when we were taking off or landing I would fly the aircraft. They could fly it once we got airborne, and I could talk with them about how the attack should be carried out.

By the time April rolled around I was getting bored with this instructing business and decided that I would like to get back on operations. My 430 Squadron colleague Jim Prendergast, being quite senior, had been given command of 414 Squadron, so I approached him with the request that he might consider inviting me to his new unit. Since we were then pretty heavy-duty competitors and had been at all times during our association on 430 Squadron I'm not sure that Jim was particularly keen about my request. In any event, that whole scenario was interrupted by VE day, May 5, 1945, when German generals signed surrender documents at Wageningen, Holland, in the presence of Prince Bernhard of the Netherlands and Field Marshal Montgomery.

Now the focus was on the Japanese area of battle. Plans were soon laid asking for Canadian volunteers from the European war to go back to Canada and retrain for the ultimate attack against the Japanese island fortress. Like thousands of other pilots and aircrew and ground crew I put my name in as a volunteer. The result was that I was shipped home to Halifax on one of the ancient troop ships, managing (as I had over two years before) to be heavily seasick during the voyage.

CHAPTER 26

Return to Assumption College, Windsor, and the Whiteside Family

I ARRIVED IN HALIFAX IN late June 1945 and then proceeded by train back to Hamilton, where my father and his wife, Marion, were living on Melrose Avenue in the east end of the great city.

Ernie Rohmer's gasoline service station business, which had been booming at the time the war started, was virtually gone. Pre-war he had had four stations in Hamilton and one in each of Fort Erie, Ridgeway, and Stamford.

Unfortunately, in order to build his chain of service stations, Ernie Rohmer had taken on a great load of debt. With the war came something new in marketing, the rationing of gasoline, which meant that his sales volumes were cut back dramatically, his cash flow dried up, and his ability to service his debt disappeared. While overseas, I had given him a loan of virtually all of the money I had saved from my pay. I don't recollect how much it was, but it was in the low thousands. Whether my money was critical (I assume that it was), suffice it to say that he did have one station left and it was a new one in Kitchener, Ontario, at Gaukel and Joseph streets. He also had a flourishing tire recapping business, Vitacap, going on in that city.

By the time I arrived home my father's negative attitude toward me had softened somewhat. He invited me into the business with him in Vitacap to try that out while I was waiting for my orders in relation to starting on my retraining for the assault against Japan.

At the beginning of August there was tremendous news. The United States had dropped the atomic bombs on Nagasaki and Hiroshima. The Japanese surrendered. As for my part, I have always been most grateful to Uncle Sam's President Truman for doing the atomic bomb thing. To have tried a frontal assault on Japan in the face of a determined Japanese defence would have been one of the greatest bloodbaths of the twentieth century. If we had had to go at them directly, thousands of young Canadians, including me, would undoubtedly have been sacrificed and gone. So I am most grateful to the Americans for those atomic bombs.

The Second World War was definitely at an end. The next step was to be discharged from the Royal Canadian Air Force. That ceremony took place for me in September 1945 in the form of a parade at, of all places, Manning Depot at the CNE.

I was totally uncertain as to what I should do in terms of civilian employment. My father had arranged a job for me with Jack Stradwick, a friend of his who was in the flooring and tile business in Hamilton.

By the time the beginning of September had arrived I had not started to work at Jack's store. I was still on discharge leave but decided that I would drive to Windsor in the old Chevrolet coupe that my father had acquired for me before I arrived back in Hamilton. At Windsor I would visit my mother's brother, Lloyd Wright, and his wife, Agnes, and also pay a visit to Father Vincent Guinan, my old algebra teacher at Assumption College, and some of the other priests who had been so good to me back in the middle 1930s. That trip was taken before I was discharged, so I was still in uniform, flight lieutenant, DFC, and all that sort of thing.

That trip to Windsor was the critical turning point in my life.

When I arrived, Uncle Lloyd and Aunt Agnes — he was an engineer at the Ford Motor Company and had served in the battlefields of Europe in the First World War — greeted me with open arms. They were in a duplex they owned on Askin Boulevard not far from Assumption College. My plan was to stay with them for two or three days, see the people at Assumption College, and then go back to Hamilton to start to work at Stradwick's store. On the second day of my visit I decided to seek out Father Guinan and whoever else of the priests and former ecclesiastics that I knew. When I arrived at the towering Assumption College building that provided the residences for the priests and the administrative offices I was both delighted and surprised to find that Father Guinan was now the president of the institution. Father Guinan could not hide his pleasure in seeing one of his protegés again.

Father Guinan, with his round, red Irish face topped with his bald pate and fringe of graying red hair, was garbed in his normal working clothes, his black cassock topped by the stiff white collar. He looked exactly as I remembered him from ten years earlier. After all, he was the man who had taught me algebra and public speaking and I was one of his prize-winning students. He invited me into his office and we began what turned out to be a conversation that changed my life. I told him what I was doing in Windsor, visiting my aunt and uncle, and that I had come to Assumption College to see him, Fathers Mulvihill, Armstrong, and whoever else was around from the old days. That small talk out of the way, Father Guinan pounced on the subject that was at the front of his mind.

"Now, Richard, what are you going to do with yourself?"

"Well, my father's lined up a sales job for me with a friend of his in the tile and flooring business in Hamilton."

"That's good." Father Guinan nodded. "Anybody can be a flooring and tile salesman, but you're going to go to school!"

"Well, I really hadn't thought about doing that."

"You have to go to university, that's all there is to it."

What could I say? After a little more discussion Father Guinan accompanied me down the hall to see the registrar, Father John Murphy, a man who was to become a dear and close friend of mine and of the Whiteside family as well. Father Guinan performed the introductions. Then he left me to Father John's mercies, which were very few at that moment. He closely questioned me on my academic qualifications. I had to tell him that I had only part of my junior matriculation, that I had failed the majority of the subjects, how and why it had happened. His conclusion was that I would have to go to cram school. That meant that I had to go back to high school to take my grade 13 and cram it into a period of six months.

No way! Disappointed, I went back to Father Guinan's office and said, "Father John says I have to go to cram school. Look, I'm a flight lieutenant, DFC, and I'm ready to get on with my life but I'm not going back to high school let alone a cram school. Forget it!"

Father Guinan thought about that for a minute or two. Leaning back in his swivel chair, hands behind his head, he asked, "How old are you?"

"I'm twenty-one."

"Good!" His hands were now on the desk, giving it a little pounding of enthusiasm. "Good. I can take you on as an adult student. You won't have to go to cram school. You can pick up three subjects of your choice right now. That will take you through to Christmas, then you can pick up three more. You can take Dr. Barath's aptitude test. It's a three-day affair. That will tell you for what you're best suited. Now go back to see your aunt and uncle on Askin Boulevard and tell them you're moving in with them. You can pay them room and board out of your sixty-dollar a month veteran's allowance. And that's it!"

Which is exactly what I did. Agnes and Lloyd were delighted to have me. Married late in life, they had no children, and on top of that I could drink straight gin with them snifter by snifter with an after bite of lemon to ease the taste.

I took the three-day aptitude test of Dr. Barath as administered by a red-haired student priest by the name of Mike Goetz. The conclusion of the testing, as I recall, was that I could take up the law or medicine or anything that stayed away from blunt mathematics. As it turned out, I would opt for the law, as many of my classmates did.

So it was that I went to university instead of working for Jack Stradwick.

If there ever was a single turning point in my life it was my meeting with dear old Father Guinan. If it had not been for that wonderful man I would have spent my life as a tile salesman. Well, I suppose there's nothing wrong with being a tile salesman, a perfectly honourable profession.

Assumption College, an ancient Basilian institution, was one of the several colleges of the University of Western Ontario. The courses at Assumption were designed to produce graduates in the Bachelor of Arts category. No sciences, just plain, ordinary arts: English, philosophy, history, the languages, that sort of thing.

Our classes were held in wooden wartime huts that had been erected just to the south of the main residence for priests and ecclesiastics and that also served as the administrative centre. The huts had been moved there from 7 EFTS at the airport when the flying school had shut down.

Assumption College was ancient territory to me, having gone to Assumption High School in 1936 after my mother and brother and grandmother and I returned to Canada and took up residence in Windsor. We had moved into a semi-detached, two-storey building at the northeast corner of Peter Street and Indian Road, just one block to the west of the Ambassador Bridge and about two hundred yards away from Assumption College and High School. As it happened, at the southeast corner of Peter Street and Indian Road was the residence of T. Walker Whiteside, KC (King's Counsel), and his family. I had met John, the son, a year younger than I, and his little sister, Mary-O. I think I was around twelve at the time.

When John and Mary-O's sister, Deanne, was born on March 29, 1937, Mary-O was so excited about that event that she went around to all the neighbours and knocked on their doors to tell them about her new sister. Mary-O knocked at our front door, and I must confess I don't remember precisely the event. Nor do I remember her running smack into a tree on the Whiteside property. I did remember her somewhat from those mid-1930 days. Tall, gangly, full of energy … but then she was so much younger than I that I really didn't pay much attention to her. John Whiteside, of course, was a different matter since we were contemporaries. He had served in the Canadian Navy as a radar technician. When I finally got into my first classes at Assumption College in October of 1945 I discovered that John was one of the students in the arts course but a year ahead of me, along with Peter Cory, an RCAF bomber pilot veteran. How they managed to be a year ahead I'm not really sure, but they were.

As Father Guinan had instructed, I started at Assumption in October. Our instructors were excellent. My veteran's allowance was sixty dollars a month, from which I paid my room and board with Aunt Agnes and Uncle Lloyd in the upper flat of their Askin Boulevard house. Those two marvellous people were very generous to me during the whole time when I must have been a real pain in terms of their own privacy and lifestyle.

Aunt Agnes was a great basic cook. My favourite meal, which she produced at least once a week, was macaroni and cheese with tomato and meat sauce. Wow, I could eat the whole thing and usually did, a great big bowlful. The result was predictable. When I went to live with them in

October of 1945, I weighed about 150 pounds. There is photographic evidence to show that about nine months later I weighed 190.

There were several important events that occurred in that period at Assumption College. The first was meeting Mary Olivia Whiteside once again. I can recall the event quite clearly. I was walking along University Avenue toward Assumption College from Askin when a huge black car coming toward me pulled up alongside. In the passenger seat was a most attractive young lady I had recently met by the name of Carolyn Carson, whose father was an executive with distiller Hiram Walker & Sons. In the driver's seat of what turned out to be her grandfather's automobile was Mary-O Whiteside. Carolyn made the introductions as I peered through the open passenger side window across at this interesting-looking young girl who at that point in the fall of 1945 had just turned eighteen. She appeared to be supremely indifferent to my presence, but having identified her as John Whiteside's sister and remembering her from the old days, I started to be intrigued by that beautiful young person behind the wheel.

Within a few days I had screwed up enough courage to telephone and ask if I might take her to the movies. While Mary-O sounded rather reluctant, she nevertheless agreed, and so that's where we began.

By this time the Whiteside family had moved to the huge home built by her grandfather, John Rodd, KC, in the 1920s. He had died just a few months earlier. It was situated southwest of Sunset Boulevard and Riverside Drive, overlooking the Detroit River. As I understand it, Grandfather Rodd had provided in his will that unless his daughter Olivia lived in the house after he died then it would have to be sold. The difficulty was that Olivia's husband, T. Walker Whiteside, KC, Mary-O's father, had taken grievously ill just a few months before I entered the picture, with horrendous problems in the intestinal area of the colon. To compound matters he was given a blood transfusion directly from his long-time close friend Henry Schade, a diminutive, dynamic man who headed up The Sterling Drug Company in Windsor. The problem was that Henry's blood and Walker's were not compatible. As a result, Walker went into shock and almost died during the night. He slowly recovered, but later, during an operation at Cleveland Clinic, Walker suffered a major stroke which paralyzed his left side and impaired his speaking ability. In addition, he required another operation known as a colostomy, which meant that the refuse from his body had to be collected in a bag. The first time I saw Walker he was in the front bedroom of the Sunset Boulevard house flat on his back, paralyzed on his left side, unable to get up. It was doubtful then that he would ever walk again. That was my introduction to this magnificent man who was to become my father-in-law.

What Olivia had done to her father's house was to make it into a duplex, a rather splendid one at that, with all of the magnificent accoutrements that Grandfather Rodd had put into the place. Olivia and Walker had the upstairs flat, which had rooms on the third floor.

The entrance to their unit was from the porte cochère on the east side of the building. Then it was up stairs with elegantly carved handrails to the second floor. There was a large high-ceilinged hall at the top of the stairs. On the right was Olivia and Walker's bedroom, with bathroom en suite, overlooking the river to the north. Beyond that was the living room and then the sunroom, where most of the actual communal living occurred, with its windows facing west and north. To the south of that room was the kitchen, so that the sunroom doubled as the main dining room. Off the hall to the south was a large bedroom on the west side and a bathroom facing the hall. To the left walking toward the bathroom was a large library filled with Walker's books and his desk, which was a finely crafted table with curved and sculpted legs. To the right was another bedroom. From the main hall were the steps to the third floor, which comprised three bedrooms for the once-upon-a-time help and a bathroom as well.

It was apparent that with Walker's severe illness his ability to earn income was really at an end, at least at that time it was. And believe it or not, Walker, the great golfer and very active man, was only forty-nine years old, just a young person through my eyes today as I write. But at that time he appeared to me to be quite old. In addition to John, Mary-O, and Deanne there was another family member, Olivia Whiteside's maiden aunt, a long retired school principal, Olivia Mark, in her eighties. She was called *Tante* (pronounced "tauntee") for aunt.

In due course I was spending more and more time at the Whiteside house, even when, in the early stages, Mary-O was still having dates with "other people." Happily that scenario didn't last very long.

My studies at Assumption College were as Father Guinan had predicted. I picked up three arts subjects when I began in October 1945 and then at the beginning of the next year I picked up another three. No need to go to cram school!

My studies were successful in all subjects but of course not hugely successful, which means that I managed to get a pass grade in all of them. Spanish, history, French, philosophy, and happily no mathematics.

For me, one of the highlights of Assumption College was the close relationship I was able to develop (as did John Whiteside and Mary-O's parents) with the principal teaching priests of the Basilian order at Assumption College, in particular the marvellous Father John Murphy, the registrar and an exceedingly brilliant teacher. Then there was Father Garvey, a proponent of Thomas Aquinas's philosophy and, in my respectful opinion, mind-stretching thinking. Father Mallon was the Spanish guru. Father Lebel did the English literature thing. Then we had an English teacher from the United States, a tall, gaunt man who spoke with a peculiar accent who went on from Assumption to be one of the outstanding academic literary figures in the United States. The almost everlasting Father Ruth was there as well as Father Swan, Father Mulvihill, and a host of others, including Mike Goetz, who was an ecclesiastic (a person studying to be a priest) and who later became a priest.

As the years went by, I became involved with the student council, ultimately becoming president of my class. For some strange reason, even though I was not a Roman Catholic (through the Whiteside family I had become a member of the Anglican church), I was invited to be the valedictorian of the graduating class of 1948. On the June day that we graduated from Assumption College (a preliminary action before we went to London, Ontario, to receive our degrees at the convocation of the University of Western Ontario that same month) the president of the class of '48 and other officials of the class gathered on the lawn to the west of the main classroom building immediately after the graduation ceremonies, there for the purpose of planting a tree. We didn't know what the tree was. It was simply a small tree ready to be planted. As the five of us gathered there was fortuitously a photographer from the *Windsor Star* present to capture the event. The photograph appeared in the paper the next day. It showed all of us, including Father John with his cap and gown on, shovel working, while we graduates stood and watched. In the distance to the northwest could be seen the ancient Assumption Church and beyond it the Ambassador Bridge.

I was to find that photograph in the 1980s when I was Chancellor of the University of Windsor, of which Assumption College had become an important founding part. Through that photograph I was able to find that tree, which had grown over forty years into an ancient, gnarled Catalpa beauty.

During each of the summers that I was at Assumption College, my income being only sixty dollars a month from the government of Canada as my veteran's allowance, it was necessary to seek other employment in order to make ends meet. During the summer of 1946 through the good offices of Walker Whiteside I was able to get a job at the Hiram Walker plant in Walkerville. My work was in the bottle receiving warehouse, and believe me it was tough going. Railway cars would be brought in to the side of the building, and the crew, of which I was a part, would then begin unloading the cases of empties. They would then have to be taken into this cruddy old building, which was about four storeys high, and stacked in accordance with the brand of whisky or other spirit that was going to be put into them. For example, Canadian Club was probably the best known rye whisky produced by the Hiram Walker firm. The Canadian Club bottles, big and small, would go into a particular area and the cases stacked one on top of the other right up to the ceiling, which was somewhere in the range of fourteen or fifteen feet high. It was tough, hot work, supervised by old sweats who had been with the company for years. During all of the period of their employment they had had reasonable access to the company's liquid products, through breakage or spillage or whatever means they could use to get at it.

For me that was quite a summer. I never got into any of the booze and I don't think I learned a thing from the older persons who were slugging away and had for years.

The next summer was quite different. In the fall of 1946 I was approached by the then Commanding Officer of the onshore naval station in Windsor, HMCS *Hunter*. The officer had been informed by headquarters that the first naval Air Reserve squadron was going to be formed and it would be at Windsor at HMCS *Hunter*. The aircraft to be supplied would be the ancient Fairey Swordfish, a plodding, antique biplane that had been produced in the 1930s and managed to survive the war flying from carriers against German battleships in the English Channel and elsewhere, dropping torpedoes and suffering enormous casualties because they were so slow moving.

The question put to me was would I care to join the naval reserve, come on board at HMCS *Hunter*, and act as the first Commanding Officer of this squadron to be formed? The answer was an enthusiastic "yes" because I would be able to fly once again. I would also be able to earn some dollars during the year and in particular in the summer when training opportunities would be offered at Halifax at the Stadacona training base. In other words, I would have a full summer of employment during my university time off.

I had to transfer from the Royal Canadian Air Force Reserve where, like tens of thousands of others, I was still in place although not serving. I would transfer to the Navy with the same rank that I held on my retirement from the RCAF, namely lieutenant, having been a flight lieutenant in the Air Force. So it was that I obtained my uniform, got all the papers processed, and, in 1946, became Lieutenant (N) Richard Rohmer, DFC, of the Royal Canadian Naval Reserve with my wings sewn on my left sleeve above the gold braid rather than on my left chest.

There were no aircraft on the horizon. None planned for arrival. So the Commanding Officer, in order to gainfully occupy my time, asked me if I would be good enough to see to the creation of the first University Naval Training Division (UNTD) the Canadian Navy's then new concept of getting university students into the naval reserve and training them to be officers over a period of years.

I agreed to that request and set out to organize the first University Naval Training Division at *Hunter*. I recruited from Assumption College about fifteen young men. On my left in the photograph taken of this new group, with his naval cap at a jaunty angle and being very thin, was a young man called Tom Smith. In later years Tom, one of the most loquacious, intelligent men you could have found, would be an energetic member of the naval reserve and would work in labour relations with, among other things, Imperial Oil. Tom ultimately succeeded me as

The University Naval Training Division was started at Assumption College in Windsor in 1947. I am in the middle of the front row.

Chief of Reserves with the rank of rear admiral, and he carried a lot of weight in the community in terms of both his size and influence. He probably weighed 140 pounds when the photograph was taken, and when he was Chief of Reserves in the 1980s he was probably in the range of about 230 or 240. Both his girth and his intelligence were heavy-weight. In fact, he served as senior naval reserve advisor with the rank of commodore when I was Chief of Reserves and so our relationship continued on to the very end of my active service in the military. Tom Smith departed this world in about the year 2000.

The summers of 1947 and 1948 I spent at Halifax and in particular at HMCS *Stadacona*, the main training base there. I must confess that I did not at any time feel comfortable in the naval environment. While I was of the executive officer class, because I had come from the Air Force and wore my wings on my sleeve I really did feel out of place and uncomfortable. And in the end, when it was time to go to law school at Osgoode Hall in Toronto in 1948, I did not continue my naval reserve activity.

During my two seasons at *Stadacona* I was on a ship once. As I recall it was a destroyer in the Halifax harbour. We went out for a short cruise. That didn't impress me at all. What did impress me was my visit to the naval airbase at Dartmouth during my second summer. I was able to go to the operating squadron there, which was flying, of all things, the Fairey Swordfish. On the squadron was a lieutenant whom I had met in London, England, during the war who had left the Air Force to join the Navy. We had a wonderful discussion about old times, and then he offered to let me fly the Swordfish. I had explained to him that I had maintained a limited commercial flying license at Windsor Flying Club in 1946 and 1947. He was satisfied that I could still handle an airplane. He took me out to an ancient Swordfish sitting on the ramp. We walked around it, and he told me all about its attributes: what its takeoff, cruising, and flying speeds were, its approaching speed on landing, what the revolutions per minute of the engine would be, how to handle the gasoline supply, all the basic essentials necessary to fly the machine. He got into the cockpit, showed me the control column, rudders, brakes, throttle, pitch control, all the things that were essential in the flying of this ancient creature. He then started the Swordfish as I stood on the wing root watching what he was doing.

That done, he got out of the aircraft. I put on the parachute and got in. I happily flew that wonderful airplane around Halifax and down the coast for probably an hour and a half then came back and landed. No problem.

That was my only flight in a Royal Canadian Navy aircraft. None of the studying of the handbook for hours. None of the matter of having lectures on how the airplane would handle and all that good stuff. It was simply that Lieutenant Falls was there at the right time and the right place and so was I. Lieutenant Robert Falls would rise to become Chief of the Defence Staff Admiral Falls in the late 1970s, at the very time that I became Chief of Reserves Major-General Richard Rohmer. He would be my boss at National Defence Headquarters light-years into the future.

By the way, there is a photograph of the young Lieutenant Richard Rohmer taken at *Stadacona* at about the time of the flight under the supervision of Lieutenant Falls. On the back of the photograph were some private words of love and affection that I had written to my fiancée in Windsor, Mary Olivia Whiteside. I will not attempt to repeat what those words were, and for whoever reads this it's none of your business.

Suffice it to say that Mary-O and I had decided, even though we were both nearly destitute, that we were meant for each other and that we were going to get married. Mary-O had decided to go to teachers' college in London, graduate, and get to the business of teaching. Her grandfather Rodd had wanted her to go into the law, and in fact Mary-O had made preliminary arrangements to go to Queen's before her father took sick. But his illness put such a tremendous drain on the family resources that there was no way that she would be able to go to university. In the end she opted for the route of becoming a teacher, which she ultimately did very well.

During her year at the Normal School in London, she attended classes and boarded at the same house as her friend Marnie Moynes (later Marnie Gatfield, wife of the esteemed Windsor doctor Bill Gatfield, who was either about to go to or had gone to Queen's to study medicine and play great football). There was an incident when I went to London for a weekend, hopefully to have a date with her, as did one of her other suitors by the name of John Jasperson, the son of friends of the Whiteside family. Colonel Jasperson had been a law partner of Walker Whiteside and had gone to war with the Essex Scottish, which he ultimately commanded. Indeed, he was in command of the Essex Scottish when the catastrophe called the raid on Dieppe took place in August 1946. The unfortunate Colonel Jasperson was a prisoner of war until the end. The Jasperson family home was in Kingsville. Bon Jasperson, who had been in the Navy, was attending Assumption College, so I was acquainted with him. Bon was to eventually become engaged to and then marry Carolyn Carson, the young woman who had introduced me to Mary-O.

As it happened, on this weekend in London Bon Jasperson was there with his brother John. During the evening, all of us were together, Mary-O and Carolyn, Bon and John, and yours truly. Somewhere during the course of the evening Bon and John got into a horrendous fist fight that moved in the darkness over several front yards. Finally, with all the shouting and punching, someone called the police, who arrived and carted all three of us off to the hoosegow. After much talking and explaining, the police decided that they wouldn't lay any charges and they would release the ferocious Jaspersons into my custody on their promise that they would not begin to pound each other again. That was to be my first experience in a police station and my first with members of any police force. There would be all manner of associations with the police that would arise in the far distant future.

My recollection is that on bended knee I asked Mary-O to marry me. This was in the library of the Whiteside family house sometime during 1948 when I was going to start my law school course at Osgoode Hall in Toronto. Both Olivia and Walker Whiteside had given their tacit approval on a couple of conditions, neither of which I can remember. From the beginning of my involvement with the family until 1948 Walker had made great progress and a wonderful effort to get back on his feet. I am proud to say that I spent a lot of time with him, helping him get out of bed, get up and down the stairs, and just get back on his feet. It took weeks and months of effort on his part, but finally it was done. The paralysis on his left side never really left him. He had to have a cane at all times and walked with some degree of difficulty. His speech improved enormously, and eventually he was able to get back to the office, although not on a full-time basis by any means.

For Mary-O and me the next step was to put together an engagement ring. I was as poor as a church mouse, and so the best I could come up with was an idea for a small diamond on a small ring. However, Olivia came to the rescue and produced a family heirloom in the form of a large, beautiful ruby. Birks on Ouellette Avenue put the ring together, the ruby in the centre and two small diamonds on each side. When that significant symbol was ready to be picked up the next step was the formal engagement. That little ceremony again took place in the library when I slipped the gorgeous ring on Mary-O's third finger of her beautiful left hand.

The decision was that Mary-O should teach for a year, which she did in the Windsor system at Harry E. Guppy Public School, teaching very young kids. The wedding would take place at the end of June or perhaps the beginning of July of 1949, after I had finished my first year of law school. The problem was that if I failed that year I would have to go back and see if I could get a job at Stradwick's tile store in Hamilton or wherever. So that was the long-range plan, and we began to work it all out as the months went by.

CHAPTER 27

To Osgoode Hall Law School and 400 Squadron

M Y ASSUMPTION COLLEGE CLASSMATE ELMER Awrey and I decided that we would attempt to room together as we both went into our first year of law school at Osgoode Hall in Toronto. Elmer was a very affable fellow whose father was the distinguished Crown attorney in the Windsor area. We found a Toronto rooming house that met our modest requirements. It was a block or two to the west of St. George and north of Bloor. We had the only room on the third floor with two beds and a dresser, which we shared, and a window opening to the south across to the matching window of two young ladies who apparently were taking some course somewhere close by. We never did meet, but we sometimes saw a lot of one another.

The classes at Osgoode were led by Dean Caesar Wright, who was about to revolt and go to the University of Toronto to form a law faculty there. Caesar Wright was big on casebooks and teaching torts. The entire class would meet in an enormous room now given over to a change room for barristers. All 350 of us were in the first year, and almost 90 percent were veterans hardened or softened by their experiences in the Second World War, some keener than others to be lawyers.

The fall, winter, and spring of that 1948 to 1949 school year was no-nonsense all around when it came to studying and application to what we intended to do with our legal opportunities.

Plans were laid for the Whiteside-Rohmer wedding to be on Saturday, July 2, 1949. In the spring all arrangements started to be made, with selecting the usual dresses and shoes and hats for the bridesmaids, arranging for the reception at the Essex Golf Club, organizing the Church of the Ascension on University Avenue, creating the guest list, and all the other innumerable details that had to be looked after. As for me, I was virtually out of the loop because the planning was done by Olivia with great assistance from Walker and, of course, Mary-O herself.

Finally the great day arrived. We still had not received the results of the examinations from Osgoode Hall, so we still didn't know whether I had passed or not. If I had failed to pass then my education would terminate and with it would go that magic ninety dollars a month allowance that I would receive as a married veteran. Be that as it may, we were in the position of going forward!

On July 2, a great gathering of guests arrived at the church, including the *crème de la crème* of Windsor business and professional people. I have no idea how Olivia and Walker, constrained as they were financially, were able to put together such a wonderful wedding for us.

Historically it was the hottest day of that summer. One of the problems we had at the church as well as at the reception was that the candles decided that they would lose their strength and tip over in the intense heat.

At the chosen hour Walker Whiteside brought my exquisitely beautiful bride up the aisle dressed in a superb wedding gown with her grandmother Rodd's veil hiding her very young face. In the presence of the assembled throng we exchanged our vows and our rings. Mine was that of my Scottish grandfather, Thomas Wright. Then the throng was off to the wedding reception at the Essex Golf Club clubhouse that Walker Whiteside had had such an important part in putting together, building, and organizing back at the end of the twenties. In fact, his filming of the construction of the clubhouse is a historic treasure that we have translated to video and will give to the Essex Golf Club as part of its historic records.

Of course, Mary-O's entire family was in attendance. My father and his wife, Marion (of Fort Erie), were there along with my then very young and skinny hockey player brother Ron.

The picture of the two of us cutting the wedding cake says it all.

Of course, we had no money for a honeymoon, but we were able to use my father's extremely modest summer cottage buildings at Port Dover, where we had visited several times before. In fact, Walker and Olivia had rented a cottage in Port Dover during the previous summer, 1948, so that the parents of the engaged couple could become better acquainted, the same applying to the engaged couple as well.

We enjoyed a "grand" honeymoon at Port Dover and over in the Hamilton area and then it was time to get established in Toronto, where Mary-O was fortunate enough to have secured a job at the Toronto School Board teaching at a school in the east end of the city in a rather low-income, tough area.

After shopping around we found a basement apartment north of the Danforth at Main Street. It was very expensive, I think it was in the range of about thirty-five dollars a month, furnished. We were there a few months while Mary-O was getting settled into her teaching job and I was back at Osgoode. I had passed my exams! But we found the place too expensive, so we wound up on a street called Firstbrook off Kingston Road in part of a semi-detached house. The semi-detached piece we were in was ten feet wide. We had the front room upstairs on the second floor, which was our bedroom/sitting room, and at the back of the building we had a former bedroom that was our kitchen, where I did my studying and Mary-O did her class preparation. In the room in between our kitchen and our bedroom/living room was another bedroom. It was occupied by the baby of the family from whom we were renting. All of us shared the single bathroom, which was at the top of the stairs next to our kitchen. Cramped as the space might have been the price suited us very well. It was seven dollars a week for rent.

Travel for us was by streetcar. An automobile was out of the question.

Life nevertheless went swimmingly with Christmas and Easter visits to Windsor and family. The spring law school examinations went all right but not quite as well as I had hoped. I passed all right, but in order for me to continue to receive my wonderful ninety dollars a month I had to have an average of 66 percent. As the numbers had it I was in the range of 65.1 percent. I therefore had a crisis.

I can recall attending upon the new dean of the law school, whose name was Smalley-Baker, the man who succeeded Caesar Wright. He was a tall caricature of an English barrister with big pot-belly, striped trousers, spats on his shoes, a flushed, red, round face, and a distinctive British accent even though he was Canadian. He had been an academic in the UK for some time and had picked up all of the mannerisms, which suited his dignity.

I pleaded my case in regard to the marks and bless his heart old

Smalley-Baker did make the upward adjustment for me that got me into that magic 66 percentage. So we survived the summer of 1950, but with some outside revenue from a source that delighted me (and that Mary-O acceded to).

While still at Assumption College in 1948, I had gone to the Windsor airport to see the Vampire fighter jets of 400 Squadron of Toronto performing in an air show and had been mightily impressed by what I'd seen. In the spring of 1950 I decided to approach the Commanding Officer of 400 City of Toronto Squadron, with its offices at the RCAF station at 1107 Avenue Road, the same place where I had taken my initial training during the summer of 1942. I met with the Commanding Officer, Wing Commander Archie James, a most pleasant man who had spent the wartime period as a senior instructor in the British Commonwealth Air Training Plan. I don't know what advice Archie received from anyone, but he did agree to take me on, and so in June of 1950 I joined 400 Squadron, but not with the rank of flight lieu-tenant, which I had had when I'd transferred to the Navy back in 1946. No, since I was coming back from the Navy I would have to lose all of my seniority and my rank. I would be required to rejoin the RCAF *ab initio* with the rank of pilot officer and seniority as of June 1950. The rank of pilot officer is equivalent to the lowest commissioned officer rank of second lieutenant in the Army. I was a little miffed by the rank reversion, but I swallowed my pride and went for it.

The squadron met for parade nights at 1107 Avenue Road, usually on a Thursday night. Then 400 Squadron flew its De Havilland Vampire jet fighters out of the air base at Downsview on the weekends.

The squadron and all of its characters, pilots, administrative and engineering officers, and ground crew quickly became a very important part of Mary-O's and my social life, with weekend dinners and enter-tainment at the very comfortable officers' mess in the Avenue Road building, which had originally housed the Toronto Hunt Club.

By this time Mary-O and I had to scrape enough money to buy a well-used, ancient automobile so that, among other things, I could get to 1107 Avenue Road during the week and out to Downsview on the weekends. The added income from my reserve pay for my work with the 400 Squadron increased our total income by a sufficient percentage to enable us to make the big purchase. From the squadron there was one other pilot who was living in the east end of Toronto. That was Dag Phillips, a wartime Spitfire pilot and a gregarious and gentle person with whom I shared rides out to Downsview on many an occasion. Our favourite route was to somehow get up to Don Mills Road (which was then a narrow, two-lane country road) and drive up it past the intersection of Eglinton and then Lawrence and on up to Wilson Avenue. There we would hang a left and go straight over to Downsview. That whole route was open farm country. There was nothing along the way except farmers' fields. Little did I know that by the end of the fifties I would have a substantial hand in shaping the development that was very quickly emerging in that sector of the rural Township of North York.

CHAPTER 28
Flying Vampire Jets and Starting Law Practice

IN 400 SQUADRON I QUICKLY checked out again on the Harvard two-seater trainer with which the squadron was equipped. In short order I had sufficient number of hours in that machine so that in 1950, by the time 400 Squadron went to its two-week summer camp period at Chatham, New Brunswick, I was ready to be checked out on and fly the single-seater Vampire fighter jet. And what an experience that was, going solo on a jet fighter for the first time. The only way you could deal with a Vampire was to go solo because there were no two-seaters. You did your simulated takeoffs and landings and handling of the aircraft in the Harvard, pretending it was a Vampire. When you had passed all of your checks and memorized your drills and most of the material in the Vampire handbook you were ready to go.

It was a clear morning at Chatham when I nervously climbed into the Vampire jet with my parachute strapped on, pushed all the buttons and pressed all the levers, turned on all the switches, and did everything necessary to start the aircraft. That done I closed the coupe top, waved the chocks away, then eased the throttle forward with the jet engine whine winding up and increasing in velocity and noise until it screamed behind me. I taxied out onto the end of the runway (the button), completed my final checks, and got radio clearance from the tower to take off.

I lined up the little Vampire at the centre of the runway then poured the coal to it, opening the throttle fully. On its tricycle undercarriage — the first time I had flown an aircraft with tricycle gear — the pickup of ground speed was quick with lots of thrust that pushed me against the back of the seat. I rolled down the runway, speed accelerating rapidly, and at the required flying speed I pulled back on the stick to lift my

Vampire off the ground. Next was to haul up on the undercarriage lever, which retracted the wheels, and I was fully airborne and off and climbing rapidly at an increasing speed. I was a jet fighter pilot!

This was far different from flying the Mustang and the Spitfire and certainly from the Harvard. What an exciting event for me, and how lucky I was to have been able to join 400 Squadron and to get myself back into the air flying that state-of-the-art Vampire jet fighter.

I flew around the Chatham area for about a half an hour doing various familiarization manoeuvres. Then it was time to undertake the ultimate test — the landing. Speed checked back I entered the circuit, flaps partially down, then the undercarriage down, monitoring the speed to ensure it was where it was supposed to be, in the range of about 120 miles per hour, then downwind left on the base leg and then final approach, flaps fully down, check the green lights for the undercarriage locked in position — on final and my touchdown was completed without crashing. In fact, it wasn't bad at all by way of a landing. The whole flight had gone perfectly, and I would spend many hours training in the Vampire during that two-week summer camp. In the mess on the evening of my solo I was required to buy a round of drinks for everyone in the squadron who was belly-up to the bar.

There were several real characters in 400 Squadron at that time: Squadron Leader Roderick Illingworth Alpine Smith, DFC and Bar, who had been a Spitfire pilot in Malta and a squadron commander in Europe; Flight Lieutenant Gordy Driver (who was subsequently killed in an Air Canada crash at Montreal); Bill MacKenzie, a regular force flying officer; Dag Phillips, who went on to spend his professional life flying for charter aircraft operators and private owners; Squadron Leader John Perry, DSO, who was to become a druggist and then became terminally ill with brain cancer within the next two or three years; Bill Stowe, a quiet young man who became an acoustical engineer; Squadron Leader Al Fleming, who was to later become the Commanding Officer; Flying Officer Yates; Flying Officer David Russell, whose father was a retired air commodore; Flying Officer Ab Vickers, who later became a minister in some faith or another; Flying Officer Garth Horricks; and Flying Officer Wilf Curtis, son of the then chief of the air staff. Early in the fall I was promoted to the rank of flying officer once again, and then at the beginning of 1951 my rank of flight lieutenant was given back to me. So in about six months I had moved from pilot officer to flight lieutenant. Not a bad progression.

Chief of the Air Staff Air Marshal Wilf Curtis and his team in Ottawa decided that there should be another auxiliary squadron formed at Toronto. On January 1, 1951, 411 Squadron was officially re-established. Having been part of a wartime Spitfire squadron, Rod Smith was promoted to the rank of wing commander (Army equivalent lieutenant-colonel) and given the task of forming the squadron and recruiting all of the personnel: pilots, engineering, and administrative, both officers non-commissioned and otherwise. Rod invited me to join him as a flight commander to help in all aspects of the recruiting and organization and chose John Perry, who had been a distinguished Pathfinder pilot, to be his second-in-command.

The three of us moved into our newly allotted offices at the east end of the arena at 1107 Avenue Road (it had originally been a horse arena for the Toronto Hunt Club but had been expropriated at the beginning of the Second World War and converted into a parade building). At that time, only six years after the end of the Second World War, we had no difficulty in finding and recruiting all the people we needed. Unfortunately, John Perry quickly began to show signs of the illness that was ultimately to take his life, and he was not able to perform the duties that he was expected to undertake as second-in-command. I immediately filled that vacuum, and by early spring Rod Smith asked me to take over as second-in-command, at which point I was promoted to the rank of squadron leader (Army equivalent major). Having started out as a pilot officer with no seniority as of June 1950 and to be promoted to squadron leader some nine or ten months later was a matter of no little degree of satisfaction.

Summer camp for 411 Squadron that year was held at the Royal Canadian Air Force station at Deseronto near Napanee. It had been an auxiliary field for the big base at Trenton during the war. With its wartime hangars and short runways it was a convenient place to attempt to train and convert onto the Vampire our new recruits, all of whom were survivors of the British Commonwealth Air Training Plan. Many had been operational pilots on Spitfires, Typhoons, and the like. It was not as if we were taking people off the street and attempting to train them. However, after a five- or six-year lapse of flying, some of them, not many, were not as proficient at flying as they had once been, and others were simply not comfortable with the risks they were now taking in flying a first-line fighter jet.

Make no mistake. In 1951 the two Vampire squadrons at Toronto had first-line responsibilities for air defence in the event of any Soviet bomber attack against southern Canada. The squadrons were no flying club. They were RCAF units high in personal danger and risk.

As a result, a few of the pilots whom we recruited in the spring and early summer of 1951 decided soon after they had flown and become familiar with the Vampire to get out of the squadron. Even so, 411's 1951 summer camp at Deseronto was most successful. All of our newly recruited pilots were flying the Vampire.

Squadron Leader Rohmer in Vampire jet
of 411 Squadron, Deseronto, 1951.

In the middle of the summer camp period Rod Smith and I were invited to take part in a squadron formation flight of the Hamilton squadron, also based for its summer camp at Deseronto. There was a major challenge for Rod but a lesser one for me. The squadron was equipped with the great wartime fighter, the P51D Mustang. It was a far different machine from the Mustang I that I had flown seven and eight years before. Rod Smith had never flown a Mustang of any type. The squadron formation of twelve aircraft would depart Deseronto and proceed northwest to Centralia, then swing around in a great circling arc to come back to base.

Smith and I decided that was no problem. We could easily handle the challenge.

After a full briefing of the squadron by Group Captain George Frostad (he who had thrown down the gauntlet), we were set to go. After signing it out, I went to the Mustang assigned to me. Parachute on, I climbed into the cockpit in which I had spent a little time reviewing the location of the various levers and gauges and instruments, including the flying instruments. Everything looked familiar, and so I was all set to go. I even knew how to start the machine! But one thing I wasn't able to do was to master the new safety harness. It was quite different from anything I had seen before.

By the time we had to start engines I still hadn't been able to get my harness clamped together. What should I do? Abort the flight because of my own finger trouble? Or bluff it and fly the Mustang even though I couldn't get my safety harness done up? Naturally I decided to press on regardless.

Well, I can tell you that between us Rod Smith and I put on a superb demonstration of squadron close formation flying, at which we were both highly skilled.

The weather was gorgeous, the group captain led the squadron with accuracy all the way around, and the mission was a great success.

Then it was time to land. Not having put a Mustang on the ground for several years in a tail-dragger undercarriage position, and without my safety harness done up, I managed my landing with a bit of an unwanted bounce. But I didn't crash, so it was a safe landing. In the joint squadron officers' mess that night there were great rounds of drinks bought by the new macho Mustang pilot Rod Smith and by the retread, yours truly.

When I look at the group picture of 411 Squadron pilots at Deseronto I must say that at the time of this writing almost all of those handsome young men are gone — with the exceptions of my great pals C. Richard Sharpe (now Colonel Sharpe) and Bob Buckles. Rod was deafened in one ear in 1952 by walking close past a Vampire whose engine was running up. He died in 2002. Crozier Taylor was killed in 2003 by an incurable disease. And Buckles has suffered a gentleman's stroke but is still going. In January 2004 I once again passed my private pilot's licence medical and continue to fly line an Ancient Bird, an Aeronca Champ of the Collingwood Classic Aircraft Foundation.

During the Deseronto summer camp period in 1951, Mary-O and I had rented a cottage on the water at Napanee. We would have any number of members of the squadrons and their wives or girlfriends around, so there were lots of parties and dinners during that most pleasant time. 411 Squadron was truly re-formed and up and running.

With the others in my class at Osgoode Hall law school, the class of 1951, I was gowned with my tabs and winged collar and made a solicitor of the Supreme Court of Ontario. This was done in the Convocation Hall at Osgoode Hall in the presence of the Treasurer (the head person) of the Law Society of Upper Canada and the gowned benchers of the Law Society, the governing body of the practitioners of law in Ontario. The call to the bar as a barrister would come later.

This was a hot day. It was early June. The spectators up in the gallery behind us included my father and his fourth wife, Marjorie, mostly called Marnie, a diminutive little woman out of Hamilton whom he had married after the divorce from Marion of Fort Erie. Partway through the hot ceremony I looked up to the balcony and saw my father and Marnie had disappeared. As we found out later, it was time for them to go and have a cool beer. Well, why not? The main thing was that Mary-O was there, as always, supportive and sweating it out, or should I say perspiring it out, even though Ernie couldn't stand the pressure.

The practice of law required a substantial input of money if one was going to open one's own office, which is the way I elected to go, hoping against hope that I could find enough business to pay the overhead.

The first office location was over Fran's Restaurant at Eglinton and Yonge. I had met Fran, a great big bear of a man who had opened his successful restaurants. As I recall, he had come from Buffalo to Toronto and was doing very well. In his building at Eglinton and Yonge on the northeast corner there were very small office spaces above the restaurant. I did a deal with him to have space and at the same time do some minor legal work for him. There were also real estate deals and wills and small things of that kind to be done for members of 400 and 411 squadrons, who were prepared to take pity on me in terms of making a go of my practice.

Fortunately, Mary-O was still teaching and bringing in the real money.

Finally, I realized that I would have to make some sort of change of venue to earn enough money to break even.

Perhaps selling life insurance might be the answer. I joined the on-commission sales staff of Canada Life with their offices under the management of John Monroe, a former football player. I think I managed to sell one insurance policy, and that was to Ernie Rohmer, who was somewhat back on his feet and had repaid my wartime loan some time before that. At the Christmas party of Canada Life, held at someone's home, bonuses were handed out. Mary-O was with me. We opened our envelope with anticipation of a great boon and discovered that we had ten dollars as our reward.

Enough already! It was time to move on. Get a position with a law firm.

Meanwhile, from 1950 onward, my main interest wasn't really the law. It was my involvement with the Royal Canadian Air Force Auxiliary Squadrons, first with 400 Squadron then with 411.

CHAPTER 29

Wing Commander and
CO 400 and 411 Squadron

———◆———

I T WAS DURING THE SUMMER of 1951 that the first string of tragedies hit 400 Squadron. The chain of events and deaths that followed would have a profound effect on my future in the RCAF Auxiliary.

The first tragedy was on a flight from Deseronto back to the base at Downsview during which Flying Officer Dewar Laing, who was at the controls, and Flying Officer Garth Horricks, flying in a Harvard, inexplicably went straight in and crashed, killing both of them. Whatever the cause, the two pilots were dead. Dewar Laing was a Windsor lad who was the son of a doctor; his parents were friends of Mary-O's parents. Garth Horricks was a regular force pilot and a brilliant, pleasant man who liked to get into the sauce. His wife had just given birth, or was about to. All in all it was a horrendous tragedy that began to send up red flags in the RCAF command structure about flying safety in 400 Squadron.

We were back in Downsview for the fall of 1951 when the next two events occurred.

I should point out that 400 Squadron and 411 Squadron shared the same Harvards and Vampires and flew on alternate weekends. The 400 Squadron commander at the time was Wing Commander Al Fleming.

The first event was during the Canadian National Exhibition and the second was just a few weeks after that.

Each year at the CNE there is a huge international air show. The first of these was, I believe, somewhere at the end of the 1940s, probably about 1949 or 1950. In any event, in the summer of 1951 the RCAF regular force gave an invitation to both 400 and 411 squadrons to provide a pilot to perform as the Red Knight at the CNE air show. The requirement was to do solo aerobatics along the waterfront, where the air show still is carried on to this day in the presence of a huge crowd gathered to watch the performances. As second-in-command of 411 Squadron, and after discussion with Wing Commander Rod Smith, I decided I would be the representative of my squadron. In 400 Squadron, the person designated was Flight Lieutenant Don Brown. Don was a tall, gangly fellow, round-faced with a brown mustache, a good-looking man with a young wife and family. He had been a bomber pilot during the war. I have no idea what his experience was as an aerobatic fighter pilot, or if he had any experience at all.

It was time to practise the routine that I was going to do. I would do a loop, then a Cuban 8 (which meant a half loop with a roll off on the top then down at a 45-degree angle and another half loop with a roll off on the top and then down to the surface again), not going below a hundred feet above the ground or, at the CNE, the water level. That manoeuvre looked like the number eight, hence its name.

Then, as a finale, there was to be an inverted flypast. My plan was to approach the waterfront from the west just out beyond the breakwall, flip over on my back, do the flypast, come back in level flight, and then depart for Downsview.

The Vampire had one serious defect: when the aircraft went upside down, the fuel system ceased to function as there was no pump to pump the fuel into the jet engine. As a result, if you were upside down for more than about six or seven seconds, the engine would begin to "flame out" (produce no power), and if you didn't get off your back immediately the engine would in fact flame out and there would be no way of restarting it in the air, certainly not at a low level. I decided that when I was practising at Downsview I would ask Squadron Leader Hank Reeves, our regular force support contingent's Commanding Officer, to be in the control tower to coach me by radio through the manoeuvres, in particular the inverted one. Mary-O was in the tower with Hank.

The first time I tried the inverted manoeuvre I started to count to seven, but after what I thought was about five seconds the shout came on the radio from the tower, "Get off your back!" The engine was already beginning to flame out, the clue being a grey cloud of jet fuel vapour coming out the tail of the aircraft. I couldn't see it from the cockpit. I practised this several times, finally getting it to the point where I was on my back for no more than four seconds, which gave a bit of a demonstration of inverted flying, and then went out of it. When all the practising was done, I declared myself ready to perform.

I would do the opening day at the air show, which was a Friday, and Don Brown would do the next day, the Saturday.

I can clearly recall going through my sequence with the loop, the Cuban 8, and whatever else I was doing, and then came the pièce de résistance, the inverted flypast. I turned at the west end of the "stage" over what was then the Palace Pier and then turned eastward on my track in front of the crowd, down low at about a hundred feet. Then I was over on my back. There was one major problem instantly. When I went over on my back the nose was down, which meant that I was heading for the water just a few feet below. With all of my might I pushed on the stick, bunting the aircraft so that it came up to the level position on the horizon. But I knew that I had been within a split second of going straight into the water. It scared the hell out of me, the great Red Knight! But obviously I got away with it and got out of my inverted position after four seconds. No flame-out!

It was that same day that Don Brown went out to Downsview, got in a Vampire, and began to practise his routine. Unfortunately, he did not have anyone in the control tower monitoring what he was doing and talking with him, particularly when he went into the inverted phase.

What happened was very simple. At whatever altitude, perhaps five thousand feet, he put the Vampire on its back in the inverted position. He probably began counting to ten, which is what the pilot's book said was his limit upside down before the engine flamed out. There was no one on the ground to tell him to get off his back. He experienced an immediate flame-out. Being near the airfield at Downsview, he attempted to do a forced landing back on the runway, obviously without power. As he approached the runway he had to come over a barn or some other structure. At that point he lost flying speed and stalled; the aircraft then went straight into the ground and Don Brown was gone, with all the traumatic consequences for his wife and kids, the pilots and people of both squadrons, and all their families.

As soon as I had word of Brown's crash, I called the regular force people at Trenton who were responsible for organizing the Red Knight display and told them that the auxiliary squadrons would not continue. If they wanted to have a Red Knight, they should provide a full-time regular force pilot, and accordingly, I would not perform again.

That was the third death in 400 Squadron within a relatively short period of time and another flight safety problem. From a safety point of view, Don Brown had obviously failed to have someone in the tower assisting him as I had with the practice manoeuvres.

Then, in the late fall of 1951, the ultimate accident happened for 400 Squadron.

The Commanding Officer, Al Fleming, was leading a section of four Vampires in close formation. He called a turn and began it when Flying Officer Yates, flying with him, turned the opposite way and the two collided in mid-air with no chance whatever to get out of their respective airplanes. The ramifications of that tragedy were devastating.

After the funerals were held and all of the causes and details were investigated, there was only one objective that had to be achieved: 400 Squadron had to be revamped. It was not long thereafter that the regular force group captain in place at the time in Toronto, Group Captain Ab Hiltz, called me into his office at 1107 Avenue Road. His request was that I should go back to 400 Squadron as its Commanding Officer. My mandate would be to do whatever I thought necessary to ensure that 400 Squadron pilots stopped killing themselves. Those were his words, and I understood exactly what he meant without any question. Hiltz had already talked to Rod Smith, who had probably made the recommendation that I should take over the squadron.

For me there was really no choice. I accepted on the understanding that I had a clear mandate to take whatever steps necessary to achieve the objective.

In any event, at the age of twenty-seven, I was now Wing Commander Rohmer (equivalent rank in the Army or today's Air Force is lieutenant-colonel), having joined 400 Squadron a year and a half earlier as a lowly pilot officer.

The first decisions I made in order to carry out the group captain's mandate were that first, I would personally check ride every pilot in the squadron, and second, any pilot who was not originally a fighter pilot, including bomber pilots or professionals flying for Trans-Canada Airlines, would be required to leave the squadron because those two flying modes were incompatible with a first-line jet fighter squadron operation.

I immediately began the check ride program by sitting in the back seat of a Harvard and having each and every auxiliary pilot of the squadron fly the airplane for me. As a result, I terminated the activity of close to half of the members of the squadron, Second World War fighter veterans all. When I had made the decision several of them said to me, "Thank you for that, I didn't know how to quit and wanted to very badly." The psychological effect of the five 400 Squadron deaths was profound. The men I grounded were not quitters. As it happened, my decision gave them an honourable way out. They must have been under tremendous pressure from their wives or sweethearts to leave the unit.

As for the Trans Canada and/or wartime bomber pilots, there were just probably two or three of those. When I gave notice of termination I had an intense reaction from one of them, a Trans Canada captain by the name of Ross Stevenson who years later became the Air Canada captain who challenged tooth and nail the validity of the company's sixty-year-old compulsory retirement rule for pilots.

Ross violently objected to my arbitrary decision in a confrontation in my office at 1107 Avenue Road. However, I stuck by my guns. I had no choice. I told Stevenson if he wanted to appeal my decision he could take it to Group Captain Hiltz. That was the end of the matter, and Ross was gone. But not without retaining a great deal of residual animosity toward me for what he considered to be an unfair decision.

However, in the rush and pressure of the situation at the time, one person escaped my attention. He was David Russell, the son of Air Commodore Russell, a distinguished airman who had served in both the First and Second World Wars. At the time I took command of 400 Squadron, David was on a Mustang conversion course at Hamilton, Ontario, and so was away from my squadron and in effect out of my jurisdiction. To this day I do not know why he was taking the Mustang conversion course. My impression of David from my earlier time on 400 Squadron was that being a post-war produced pilot he did not possess the experience that the old hands brought to their flying capability. If he had not been away on course, I would have had a check ride with him.

The chances were strong that he might well have failed that test in terms of staying with the unit.

Be that as it may, the final tragic disaster occurred. I received urgent word from Hamilton that David Russell had crashed his Mustang on landing. The aircraft had overturned and burned. David Russell did not survive.

It was my lot to then have to telephone his father to give him the dreaded news and then to go and see the air commodore in his residence in Hogg's Hollow in Toronto. It is and always has been an unbelievably bad experience for all of those who carried the responsibility of informing parents of the unexpected demise of their beloved children. It was devastating for the air commodore and a dreadful experience for me. It was a time for yet another funeral, but this was the first one where as Commanding Officer I had the responsibility for its arrangement and conduct, but with the full support of every remaining member of the unit.

In a sense I had failed to stop the killing in 400 Squadron. On the other hand, David Russell was beyond my jurisdiction at the time he died. My regret was, of course, that I had overlooked David Russell, or perhaps I had simply decided to wait until he got back to the squadron from Hamilton, at which time I would have put him through his paces. He was gone, but his departure at Hamilton merely served to strengthen my intention to do what I had to do to bring the squadron to the highest possible level of flight safety, operational capability, and discipline.

Early in 1952 I received an unwritten, roundabout invitation from Chief of the Air Staff Air Marshal Wilf Curtis, whose son, Wilf Jr., was a member of 400 Squadron and a competent pilot, young and ambitious. At the time, Canada was preparing its new squadrons of F86 fighters for action as part of NATO in Europe. The need for experienced fighter pilots as Commanding Officers of those units was apparent, and the post-war regular force was short of such bodies.

By this time, I had been practising law for some eight months or so, having been called to the bar of Ontario in June of 1951. That qualification, combined with my then current track record with both 400 and 411 squadrons, must have caught the air marshal's attention. The roundabout invitation to me was that I should join the regular force, retaining my permanent rank of wing commander. At the age of twenty-eight, that would have very likely given me an advantage in age over all the regular force wing commanders of the day of some six or seven years.

It would not be surprising that I found that proposal to be extremely attractive. Getting started in the practice of law was very difficult indeed. I had a beautiful wife to support. And I would continue to do what I had always wanted to do, my first ambition, which was to fly.

As I tell the story (but Mary-O denies), when I took the proposition home to her it was not attractive to her, not one bit. No matter what the rank was, she had seen enough of the structure of military life to convince her that she did not want to be trapped in the social and political webs of the Air Force of the day. As I tell the story she said to me, "Go ahead and take the proposition. But if you do you'll have to get a new wife to go with it!" Mary-O denies taking that position, but even if I acknowledge that my recollection might well be defective on the point I let it be known that I would not accept such an offer. In later years I was well pleased that I had not.

If I had accepted it and become a squadron commander in Europe my colleague wing commanders, all much older than I, and the senior officers at RCAF headquarters in Ottawa would very likely have done everything in their power to destroy me on the way up so that the "on the way up" would be converted into an "on the way out."

The end result in later years — much later — was that as commander of the First Air Reserve Group and then Chief of the Reserve Force in Canada I would enjoy the best of both worlds, with the exception, of course, that reserve officers, be they generals or otherwise, do not earn or receive pensions for their prolonged, often dangerous, efforts on behalf of Her Majesty the Queen. Pity!

CHAPTER 30
Roy Thomson, Lord Thomson of Fleet

———◆———

ROY THOMSON, RADIO STATION OWNER and newspaper publisher from northern Ontario, entered my life in 1952. From his storybook rags to riches tale beginning in northern Ontario, Roy had moved to Toronto, where I first met him. His partner was a totally flamboyant entrepreneur by the name of Jack Kent Cook. I met Roy through a most aggressive Windsor native who had moved to Toronto to attempt to earn his fortune. His name was Jim Larkin. Jim, a young, blond, eyes-flashing kind of lad, always out to make a deal, had somehow run across Roy in Toronto at just the time when Roy Thomson had decided that instead of building his publishing and radio empire he would enter politics and very quickly run the country. Larkin told him that he needed someone with political background and a lot of experience (of which I then had a scintilla) to be his campaign manager for the purpose of winning the federal nomination for the Conservative Party in North York.

I had just started the practice of law in an office over Fran's at Eglinton and Yonge, with no clients but Fran himself. At the same time I was Commanding Officer of 411 Squadron at Downsview. And I was a member of the Progressive Conservative Association somewhere, but not yet in Don Mills, which was still to be started let alone built. Jim Larkin took me in tow to meet Roy Thomson in his office on Bay Street.

Roy and I hit it off very well. I undertook to be the manager of his campaign to win the Conservative nomination for North York.

As it happened, the other contender was Nelson Boylen, who had been the reeve of the Township of North York for many years.

The nomination meeting was to take place in the public school on Wilson Avenue opposite the Toronto Cricket Skating and Curling Club.

I dragooned every member of 411 Squadron I could get my hands on, officers and men and women, to be become members of the riding association so they could turn up and vote at the nomination meeting.

Everything went according to plan.

On the night in question we all gathered in the Armour Heights Public School auditorium. Its floor was filled with folding steel chairs that were eventually filled with people, including large numbers of 411 Squadron bodies.

The politically experienced candidate, Nelson Boylen, a tall, gaunt farmer, gave his speech. Everybody clapped politely.

Then it was Roy's turn. The stumpy, gray-haired man from the north with his Bay Street business suit and thick glasses mounted the stage, went to the lectern, then delivered his speech.

Frankly, it was the most egotistical delivery — as he recounted his great achievements — that I had ever heard. It was to the point of being embarrassing. The only thing I remember about Roy's speech specifically was that he quoted Mahatma Gandhi saying, "There go my people I must follow them, for I am their leader." But, as I say, it was such an egotistical flow of words that by the time he was finished I was really embarrassed in the presence of my squadron and everyone else we had been able to gather to make sure that Thomson won. If I could have, I would have crawled under a chair, but with those chairs there was no place to crawl.

Roy Thomson won the nomination with a vast majority of votes and went on to run in the election that year to lose — to his great benefit — decisively. As a result Roy was able to pull all of his entrepreneurial talents together and go to the United Kingdom. There he won his fortune in the newspaper publishing and in television and eventually became Lord Thomson of Fleet, with its hereditary title that his son, Ken, now bears.

After the nomination meeting, I did not participate in the election, so I lost track of Roy except for his famous ascendancy in the UK, where I tracked what he was doing from time to time.

In 1976 I decided I would write a novel called *Exodus UK* in which I would deal with the thesis of what would happen if the economy of the United Kingdom collapsed. Where would the 50 million people from that island, or at least a portion of them, go to escape the poverty and difficulty that would arise if the UK's economy did in fact collapse? What about research?

I decided I would visit Lord Thomson in his Toronto offices, located just south of the Toronto City Hall on Queen Street in, believe it or not, the Thomson building. By the way, I had visited him in his offices on Fleet Street, London, between this point and the time that we got him his nomination. So I had kept in touch.

On the appointed day and hour, I arrived at Roy's office on the top floor. The office was located overlooking Bay Street. It was small and frugal. Roy was courteous and jovial, peering at me through those thick glasses.

I told him what the thesis of the book was: that the economy of the UK would collapse and then what. What would he do if that occurred? was my question.

Roy reached in his top right drawer, pulled out a loose-leaf binder, and threw it across the table at me, saying, "If you look at that book it contains my holdings all over the world now. Those holdings are so broad that if the economy of England and the United Kingdom collapsed I would just go straight on no matter what my holdings are in the UK at this point. In other words I have companies everywhere. Sure, I would be hurt to some extent, but believe me I would survive!" Then he bent forward and spoke to me confidentially, "As a matter of fact, Richard, I have an embarrassment of riches on my hands. A Middle East sheik and I are joint owners of an oil and gas field exploration play in the North Sea. We've just been told that there is oil and there is gas in this field. Now I have to cough up tens and tens of millions of dollars and pounds for my partnership deal so that we can get on with the exploration development. I mean I'm going to have to produce cash, piles of cash. I'm going to have to sell companies to raise money, do whatever I have to do to cash in on this oil field." Which is exactly what Roy did in the months after our meeting.

After filling me in on his view of the question of what he would do in the event the UK economy collapsed, he asked, "Have you seen Ken's art collection?"

I replied that I hadn't (of course I hadn't), whereupon Roy said, "Okay, follow me." Out the door of his office he went, and I followed him down the corridor. When he opened an office door there sat his son, Ken, at a clean desk. Roy said, "Ken, Richard would like to see your art collection," to which Ken responded positively and quickly. Within moments he had taken out his keys and unlocked the art gallery door. What followed then was a tour of the most magnificent collection of all manner of international art, the prime parts of which were his Kreighoffs. We spent half an hour going through his treasures. Did Roy leave and say, "I'll see you later"? No way. The old boy padded along behind us, very proud of his son and of the magnificent art collection. When it was all finished, I thanked Roy and left.

I had already planned a trip to England to meet various people there to talk about the same question: what would happen if the economy of the UK collapsed?

Now keep in mind that Roy Thomson never, but never flew, first class. True to his Scottish blood, he always went steerage.

When I arrived at the Toronto International Airport to take my Air Canada flight, who was there in a wheelchair with his homburg on, in the custody of an attendant who was to see him get on the aircraft? None other than Roy Thomson, Lord Thomson of Fleet.

I went up and said, "Roy, what the hell are you doing — obviously flying first class?"

"Well, Richard, I haven't been feeling all that well and I have to get back to England. So with the state of my health I thought it would be better if I went first class."

This time I went to steerage (as usual) and Lord Thomson was located in the first class section at the front of the airplane. As we taxied away from the terminal (obviously Terminal 1), the chief purser came back to me in the lightly populated airplane — I think Roy was the only one in first class — and said that Lord Thomson would be obliged if I would come and sit with him after the evening meal was served.

My message back to Lord Thomson was, "I would be delighted." In due course, I made my way up to the first class cabin. There he was with his thick bottle glasses reading a newspaper held close to his face.

Well, we had a wonderful crossing together, disturbed only by the presence of the chief pilot of Air Canada, whose name I have long since forgotten. He was not flying the aircraft that night, thank God, because when he appeared to present himself to old Roy the chief pilot was clearly somewhat into the booze. Even so, Roy and I had a marvellous time chatting each other up until we arrived at Heathrow. That was the last time I saw Roy Thomson, Lord Thomson of Fleet. He died a few weeks thereafter. His title and enormous fortune, which has multiplied many times since, passed to his son, Kenneth Thomson, Lord Thomson of Fleet.

In my opinion, Roy Thomson was an absolutely brilliant, intense, concentrated businessman. He was focused on all his goals. He was a great Canadian. I was most fortunate to have had an association with him and to be one of his admiring friends. I have always been pleased that he did not win that 1952 federal election seat.

If he had, there would have been no Lord Thomson of Fleet by the name of either Roy or Kenneth.

CHAPTER 31

The Air Force, the Lang, Michener firm, and the Arrival of Catherine

———————⬩———————

I N THE SUMMER OF 1952, 400 Squadron was gradually rebuilding after the drastic cuts in personnel that I had made. New pilot recruits were being brought on board and trained, and the organization was proceeding to my satisfaction and that of the Group Captain. However, an unexpected event occurred that would take me back to 411 Squadron as Commanding Officer.

My great friend Wing Commander Rod Smith, still commanding 411 Squadron, had a misadventure. He walked in front of a Vampire on the ramp when the pilot was revving up the jet engine, its high-volume shriek filled with all manner of damaging decibels. The noise severely damaged Rod's right eardrum, causing a deafness that has pursued him all of his life. Quite apart from the pain and physical difficulty, Rod was no longer able to fly and so had no choice but to give up command of his squadron.

This happened just a short time before both 400 and 411 squadrons were to go to their two-week summer camp, this time at the RCAF base at St. Hubert, Quebec.

Command of 411 Squadron was assumed by the second-in-command, Squadron Leader Doug Givens, a wartime pilot and professional test pilot for De Havilland. Givens was competent enough but was grossly overweight, a factor that quickly began to have an impact on his ability to exercise command. It very quickly became apparent to me — I was keeping a watchful eye on Givens's performance at 411 Squadron — that he would not be able to cut the mustard. Unfortunately, there was no one in 411 Squadron under Doug Givens who had the experience at that moment to take over command, although the highly capable Flight Lieutenant Bill Goodson ran the squadron under my watchful eye until the new C.O. was appointed. At 400 Squadron I had decided that Squadron Leader Bill Stowe, a quiet, wartime experienced, post-war trained engineer, would do just fine as a Commanding Officer. I therefore recommended to the group captain — by this time a reservist by the name of Group Captain George Gooderham — that I should return to 411 Squadron to take Rod Smith's place and that Bill Stowe be promoted to wing commander and take over 400 Squadron. My recommendation was accepted, and so I returned to 411 Squadron, the first officer to command both units. My decision was tough on Doug Givens, but as I saw the situation, there really was no alternative.

Both squadrons went through their 1952 summer camp training sessions in St. Hubert in good style. Prior to going to St. Hubert, the squadrons had been based temporarily at Mount Hope, the airport at Hamilton, while runway repairs and rebuilding were being done at Downsview. Those repairs were out of the way, and so when summer camps were finished we took our aircraft back to our normal base at Downsview where, as usual, every second weekend flying training continued and every Thursday night parades were held at 1107 Avenue Road.

After taking over 411 Squadron, I confirmed that Flight Lieutenant Bill Goodson, who was to become a life-long close friend, would continue to be flight commander and second-in-command. He was a highly experienced, level-headed, and stable wartime fighter pilot who brought good leadership qualities and sound judgment to his new post.

Another 411 Squadron member who was also to become a life-long close pal was C. Richard Sharpe. Sharpe had performed a remarkably effective tour of operations on RAF Liberator bombers in the Burma area during the war. Because he was a four-engine type and not a fighter pilot originally, and for the reasons that I had already exercised in culling out 400 Squadron, I kept an eagle eye on his flying. I gradually became concerned about his landings and eventually decided that enough was enough. So I eventually asked Dick Sharpe to give up his flying and take an administrative post with the squadron. He reluctantly but loyally agreed, and as it turned out, his eyes were not serving him well, which had to do with his landing of the tricky little Vampire. Which leads me to a story that took place in Trenton, Ontario, in the fall of 1952.

I took 411 Squadron to the Trenton airbase on a long weekend for an air-to-ground firing exercise that was designed to give us training in firing our Vampires' cannons at ground targets in a range on the shore of Lake Ontario to the southwest of Trenton.

As a senior officer, I was lodged in the main mess at Trenton in appropriate quarters, while my pilots were in one of the big barrack blocks to the west of the main parade square. I'd lived in one of those same barrack blocks when I had been on the station for guard duty ten years earlier in 1942. So I knew the structure of the buildings, about four storeys high with great long corridors from one end to the other, perhaps 150 or 200 feet, with rooms off each side.

The floors of the corridors were either concrete or tile, the whole structure being concrete. They would make an excellent bowling alley if the opportunity arose.

As it happened, the opportunity did arise. I was in my room fast asleep when at about two o'clock in the morning the station duty officer awakened me to tell me that my officers in the barrack blocks had discovered a cache of another kind of blocks, namely ice. Where they got them from I will never know. But they were using these ice blocks as bowling balls and were raising drunken hell and causing a great commotion about which there were voluble complaints from the normal residents of the barrack block. I quickly dressed and was driven over to the scene of the crime, where I raised absolute bloody hell. Here we were, a bunch of reservists in the Taj Mahal of the Royal Canadian Air Force at Trenton, and we were behaving like a bunch of baboons. Tails between their drunken legs, my charges stopped their idiocy and went to bed.

I had ordered that all squadron pilots and officers report for duty at eight o'clock in the morning, as well as ground crew. At that time the pilots could be briefed for their gunnery activity, the aircraft loaded with ammunition, and the day's training operations would be underway on time. It was a Saturday morning with thick fog covering both the ground and the alcohol-bothered brains of some of my pilots who turned up on time. But two people in particular failed to arrive at eight o'clock. They were Flight Lieutenant Harold "Grizzly Bear" McGill, a sturdy wartime pilot who had elected to be the squadron adjutant, and his new assistant, one Flight Lieutenant C. Richard Sharpe. By the time eight-thirty arrived neither of them had put in an appearance. So in the presence of no flying because of the fog I said that we would have a little disciplinary activity. We would have McGill and Sharpe routed out of their beds and drunken stupors and brought to the briefing room that the squadron had been allocated for the weekend. It was in the huge hangar area on the north side of the east-west highway that divides the Trenton base.

With assistance I cut out large Lenin stars and had them mounted with string so that they would fit over the neck and hang at the chest. They were symbols of the "Hero of the Soviet Union," which was at that time our dedicated and hated enemy. I then cleared a large table and put on top of it a folding chair. Around my uniformed neck I put my personal Hero of the Soviet Union Star, then sent some likely person across to the barracks to get McGill and Sharpe out of the pit and dressed and escorted over to our newly created "court" to be tried for failing to appear.

It took about half an hour for the accused pair to appear under escort. After hearing the evidence against them and recognizing that they were still performing under the influence of far too much booze consumed the night before, in recognition of their great work on behalf of Mr. Stalin, I conferred upon each of them the award of Hero of the Soviet Union. With high dignity I slipped their stars over their reeking heads. A photograph forever commemorates that significant event. The man in

Wing Commander Rohmer installing Flight Lieutenant Richard Sharpe and Flight Lieutenant Harold McGill as Heroes of the Soviet Union, Trenton, 1952.

the middle is my dear friend C. Richard Sharpe, who was just beginning his career at Simpson's, the department store. Richard went on to be one of Canada's most successful executives, ultimately serving as the chairman and chief executive officer of Sears Canada for many years as well as on the board of the CIBC, Bell Canada, and other major corporations. We are with Dick and Peggy Sharpe at their digs or ours frequently, winter, summer, fall, and spring. Sharpe, CM, recently retired as the honorary colonel of 436 Squadron, which flies Hercules transport aircraft based at that same place, Trenton, Ontario. By the way, the tired Hercules transport aircraft that flew the ambulance, Mary-O, and me to Tortola in 1975 is still flying out of Trenton. The Government of Canada refuses to replace the clapped out Hercules.

Harold McGill went on to continue an enormously successful career until his retirement from National Cash Registers. I used to hear from him when I had a new book out, but Harold "Grizzly Bear" McGill is now gone.

Bill Goodson went on to become a publisher of the *Montreal Star* until its demise then went to the cities of Stowe and Burlington in Vermont, where he acquired a huge printing company that he ultimately sold. And in the course of time he was Colonel William Goodson, Honorary Colonel of 401 Air Reserve Squadron in Montreal, a post he has relinquished.

For me, the period 1950 to 1953 in the Air Force with both 400 and 411 squadrons was a time of considerable stress. By early 1953, Mary-O and I were living in the Lawrence apartments in East York. In the fall of 1952, it was time to start a family. That was the plan, and everything worked. I can remember our excitement when we had a positive pregnancy test at a drugstore on Bayview Avenue and then went to the movie theatre close by on the east side. My career as a lawyer after my call to the bar in 1951 was just getting underway after a bit of a slow start.

At the end of 1952 I was fortunate enough to be hired by the prestigious Bay Street law firm of Lang, Michener & Cranston. The members of the firm were Dan Lang, Sr., KC, a marvellous man who must have been in his late sixties and one of the Liberal stalwarts of Ontario; his partner, Roland Michener, KC; Robert Cranston, KC; Dan Lang, Jr., (later Senator Lang); John H.O. Peppler, the real estate and conveyancing wizard; and Jim Jenner, who worked with Cranston.

My pay was a large amount, somewhere in the range of five hundred dollars a month. In those days that wasn't bad. It went a reasonable distance. I helped Roly Michener prepare his court cases and most importantly his Ontario Municipal Board appearances on behalf of trucking companies. There was also a large number of commercial clientele, who came to us largely because of Roly's reputation.

The elegant Michener, a handsome, wavy-haired, mustached, dignified soul, was an outstanding lawyer, both corporate and in litigation. He was also a dedicated politician, having as a Conservative served in the Ontario Legislature. But by the time I joined the firm in its Bank of Montreal offices at King and Bay, Michener had his eye on a federal seat, the St. Paul's riding of Toronto. Roly Michener was a Conservative through and through. So was I, having been introduced to the Conservative party through Walker Whiteside, KC, an arch-Tory if there ever was one, who had strong connections to George Drew. Roly Michener and politics are relevant to my departure from the Royal Canadian Air Force and 411 Squadron.

With Mary-O being pregnant and my law practice becoming established with the Lang, Michener firm, I began to realize it was time for me to stop flying and get out of the military. I really had had enough.

On top of that I was quite disillusioned by what the Liberal government of the day was doing and saying about the military. The Minister of Defence was the Honourable Brooke Claxton.

I never did meet Claxton, but I had had a confrontation with him in the summer of 1952. Not directly with him, but with the captain of the DC3 that was carrying him from Ottawa to Downsview.

It centred around the move of all of the Downsview Vampires of 400 and 411 squadrons down to St. Hubert for the beginning of the summer camps there.

I wanted to take all twelve of the Vampires down to Montreal in a grand squadron formation. But to get all of the aircraft with the limited number of electrical starting machines that we had available, and given the limited range of the Vampire, it meant that I had to carefully coordinate the starting of the aircraft, one after another. I then had to get all of them airborne, formed up, and making tracks for Montreal. Everything had to be done in a very tight sequence. We just had enough fuel to get to St. Hubert, and there could be no delays.

As the leader of the squadrons I, Wing Commander Rohmer, was the first to start up. When the three that were to fly with me in the lead section had started I then began to taxi out to the runway with them following me. The plan was that my section of four would take off, form up, and then circle until the rest of the squadron, the other eight, were also airborne. They would form up on my aircraft and then we would proceed directly to Montreal.

When I was taxiing out I heard the captain of a DC3 coming in — I hadn't been informed about this — calling the control tower at Downsview saying that he had the Honourable Brooke Claxton on board and wanted clearance to land.

I immediately responded before the tower could say anything. I instructed the tower that the DC3 could not land because I had to get my squadron airborne. For me the situation was simple. It was a matter of marginal fuel to get to Montreal. The safety of my squadron was at stake. If we delayed to allow the honourable minister to land I would have to take all my aircraft back to the ramp and order the shutdown of the entire takeoff operation.

The captain of Claxton's DC3 kept insisting that because the minister was on board he was going to land. I had made up my mind. If the minister's captain had prevailed and Claxton had landed and I had had to take my squadron back to the ramp, then I was going to resign my command right then and there and give notice to Claxton face to face.

I finally prevailed. The captain of the DC3 agreed to wait until I had the squadron airborne and underway to Montreal.

That was the closest I came to meeting Claxton.

CHAPTER 32

To Don Mills, North York Council, and the Civitan Club

———◆———

I TENDERED TO THE GROUP captain my written resignation from the Royal Canadian Air Force and as Commanding Officer of 411 Squadron to be effective on March 1, 1953.

By this time I was planning to do a speech in which I would accuse the Liberal government and the Department of National Defence of misleading the public about the strength of the RCAF in Canada's north.

There were no RCAF squadrons in the far north, yet the government was telling the public that there were. Of course the Soviet Union bomber threat at that time was enormous. Indeed, Canada should have had fighter squadrons in place far north in order to intercept any incoming bombers. The public was being told that we had them, and I knew that we did not.

So I tendered my resignation. With Roly Michener's encouragement I wrote my speech attacking the government and laying out what I thought was a deception on its part.

I had the co-operation of a prominent journalist of the day who was going to get the scoop for the *Toronto Telegram*.

The forum for my address was to be the Canadian Progress Club, of which I was a member. It had its meetings at the Royal York Hotel on a weekly basis.

On the assigned date of March 26, 1953, and with Roly Michener at the head table, I delivered my speech. The Canadian Press report from Toronto the next day said this in part:

> A former post-war commander of two R.C.A.F. auxiliary fighter squadrons here said Thursday

the Air Force, with its present resources, "could not stop one Russian bomber attacking over 30,000 feet in broad daylight unless it stumbled into the Quebec area."

Wing Cdr. Richard H. Rohmer, 29, who won the Distinguished Flying Cross in operations in support of the Normandy invasion in 1944, said in an address to the Canadian Progress Club that Canada is defenceless to an air attack.

"After the billions of dollars have been spent, after years of so-called preparation, except for three Sabre jet squadrons under training to go to Europe under N.A.T.O., Canada could not put up a single modern aircraft in its own defence."

"There are no fast-moving R.C.A.F. jet fighter squadrons guarding the north," he said. "The Russians know that, the R.C.A.F. knows that, the government knows that."

Lo and behold, my accusations hit the front page and top headlines of the *Telegram*. And of course the *Star* picked it up as well, doing its editorial best to make me look like a congenital idiot because it didn't like my attack on the Liberal government.

Well, I tell you the furor that followed was enormous, as the press clippings of the day demonstrate. The government even sent in the Royal Canadian Mounted Police to knock on my door in the Lawrence apartments. They wanted to go through the documents I had used in the preparation of my speech, suspecting that I had used something "secret." Of course, the two constables who came by found nothing because there wasn't anything secret. It was a well-known fact inside the Air Force that Canada simply did not have fighter squadrons in large enough number and certainly not in the north. The fighter squadrons of the Royal Canadian Air Force were largely auxiliary, not regular force. And like every other auxiliary commander I knew exactly where those squadrons were. So did the press, for that matter.

That speech burned my bridges behind me insofar as the Canadian military was concerned. I was out of the Royal Canadian Air Force and out of the military loop forever.

There was one incident I have to report on, however. Sometime in May on a Thursday night after my resignation and speech (parade night for 411 squadron at 1107 Avenue Road), I received a telephone call at about ten o'clock in the evening. It was from one of the squadron members at the officers' mess at Avenue Road. They were having a grand time at the bar and some of the men wanted to come to our tiny apartment to celebrate the birth of Catherine Rohmer, our baby daughter, who had arrived on the May 6. "Sure, come on over, I'd love to see you."

Mary-O was still in the hospital, so I was in our two-bedroom apartment by myself. In about half an hour there was great banging on the door and the gang arrived, probably about a dozen of them. I had told them to bring their own booze because I didn't have any. They had that in quantity. There's no question, the uproar was enormous for our neighbours in the two-storey apartment building. But no one complained. Or at least we thought no one did. However, someone in the crowd had hit a construction barrier somewhere en route, causing the police to follow the trail.

About fifteen minutes after the gang arrived there was another big banging on the door. I went to it and there were two hulking young policemen standing there. Instantly they were invited inside. We explained what was going on. I offered them a drink, which was accepted, particularly since they wore wartime service medal ribbons.

Then the phone rang again. It was the one and only Harold McGill, still at the mess, trying to figure out where everyone had gone, and Squadron Leader Chuck Darrow, the new CO of 411 Squadron, a wonderful bon vivant and operational wartime Spitfire pilot. They were obviously (or at least Harold McGill was obviously) much worse for wear. Well, he sounded as if he'd had quite a bit to drink. I told him how to get to our apartment, and he said he and Darrow would be right there. That meant it would take about fifteen minutes going across Eglinton to Bayview and down Bayview to Moore Park Road then a slight cut to the east and there you were.

A cruel plot immediately arose in my mind.

As soon as I hung up, I went to the two police officers and I gave them a scheme, which they accepted with great laughter.

They put their caps on and the two of them were out the door.

About fifteen minutes later there was a knock on the door again. We opened it and there in the custody of the two police officers with handcuffs on were Darrow and McGill, ashen-faced, scared out of their wits.

Our two friendly police officers had intercepted them just as Darrow and McGill pulled up in their car out in front of the apartment building. The arrest took place right there. They were charged with all kinds of serious offences, not the least of which was drunken driving. Then they were marched into the apartment in handcuffs.

That has to be rated as one of the grander practical jokes that I have had a hand in over a long lifetime.

But that was over fifty years ago. The police today wouldn't even think about taking part in such shenanigans!

That was how the first eleven years of my military experience ended; they started in 1942 and finished in 1953, with a slight break in the first two years of my Osgoode Hall career. From that point to the beginning of the 1970s I was out there in the untouchable wilderness so far as the Royal Canadian Air Force was concerned. After 1968 the RCAF disappeared, thanks to Trudeau and his normally eccentric defence minister, Paul Hellyer. The pair made the first move to destroy the Canadian military by amalgamating them together into one force, the Canadian Armed Forces, with a single green uniform — except for the Navy (partly).

The demise of the Canadian military establishment to the point of the near farce that it is today can be traced directly back to those two politicians, for whom the military meant nothing. Trudeau had spent the war avoiding service, while Hellyer-the-brilliant had risen to the rank of corporal. He apparently hated the military structure and in particular the general officer corps. Both men were brilliant in certain spheres, but when it came to the military, its existence, its traditions, its history, and its achievements, their mutual intent was to denigrate the Army, Navy, and Air Force and reduce them to the lowest possible numbers, cost, and status in our democratic society. The two of them were successful in achieving their intent.

As I explained earlier, Catherine Olivia Rohmer arrived safely at the beginning of 1953 when we were in the Lawrence Construction apartments. Catherine was a healthy, beautiful baby, the joy of her mother and father's life. Of course, Mary-O had had to give up her teaching with her new responsibilities, and as I appeared to be settled with the Lang, Michener firm, it was time to consider the next step, which was to buy a house and get out of that apartment.

We had heard about the new development that E.P. Taylor was putting together, a place called Don Mills out at the intersection of Don Mills Road and Eglinton, the Don Mills Road that I used to drive up from our Kingston Road/Firstbrooke rooms to get up to Wilson and across to Downsview airport.

We decided that we should take a look at what was being done in Don Mills. So in our inexpensive tiny English pre-owned car we went out and looked around in the quadrant of houses being built to the northwest of Don Mills Road on Lawrence Avenue. We found a house under construction that we liked. It was 3 Addison Crescent, standing almost finished in a sea of mud. It was a storey and a half structure with a kitchen, a big living room/dining room downstairs, a carport under the second floor, and three bedrooms and a bath upstairs. It was more than enough for us. The purchase price was just a little over fourteen thousand dollars. It required approximately fifteen hundred dollars down and the balance by way of a CMHC first mortgage of somewhere in the range of 3 to 4 percent. We went for it with money once again supplied by Mary-O's mother and father (again, I don't know where they got it from). In the early spring of 1954 the Rohmer family moved into the house.

We started to decorate but ran out of money when we had the downstairs painted.

The Addison Crescent house was just exactly what we needed and could afford at the time, and then only just. Over the years that we were there we filled in the carport to make a room out of it. I did that work myself without a building permit. After I put the windows in the back and front and put the floor down, the chief building inspector of the Township of North York appeared at the front door. He informed me that I had contravened the building by-laws and code by not getting a building permit for what I had done. He then said it was all right because after all he had been one of my ground school instructors at the Elementary Flying Training School in Windsor in 1942. His name was Harold Atyeo, a fine man who later became the Township Engineer and then moved into the City of Toronto in the engineering department.

Eventually we put in a circular driveway, trees along the east side of the boundary of the house (the dreaded fast growing poplar), and a tiny toilet in the closet at the bottom of the stairs on the main floor. As I said, the house was exactly what we needed.

Our next baby, Mark, a marvellous boy, arrived in August of 1955. Once again we were absolutely delighted. We now had a boy and a girl. Couldn't be better. It was during that summer that Olivia and Walker Whiteside decided that in order for our two families to have a good focal point for the summer they should buy a cottage they had found at Bruce Beach on Lake Huron just to the south of Kincardine.

At the appropriate time before a final decision was made, Olivia and Walker, with Deanne, came up from Windsor to the available cottage at Bruce Beach. Mary-O and Catherine (it was just before Mark's birth) and I came across from Toronto to rendezvous to take a look at this attractive place. If we all liked it, then Olivia and Walker would buy it.

We loved it, 8A Bruce Beach, and the deal was done.

We would spend countless happy summers at Bruce Beach, and even though Mary-O, after her parents had died, sold the cottage (it had been willed to her) to her sister, Deanne Wright, Mary-O and I still rent a cottage at Bruce Beach for two or three weeks during the summer so we can be with old friends.

As for the practice of law, I was still with the Lang, Michener firm when we moved to Don Mills in 1954, and I was happy with my association with those wonderful people. There were only six of us in the firm, and I was attached fundamentally to Roly Michener as his junior. Working with him was a wonderful learning experience. Little did any of us know that in the future he would be the Speaker of the House of Commons, Canada's High Commissioner to India, and ultimately the Governor General of Canada. What we did know was that Roly was the consummate patrician gentleman, always dressed formally with striped trousers and a black vest and jacket with a grey tie, virtually a director's suit as we now know it. He was always immaculately groomed, his grey hair wavy, his mustache perfectly trimmed. On top of all that he was a truly considerate, kindly mentor.

It was my role to help in the preparation of cases for presentation in court or to the Ontario Municipal Board, as it was then hearing not only land use and zoning matters but also contests for licences for trucking. The Ontario Highway Transport Board was later formed under its first chairman, Sam Hughes. But in those days in the middle fifties we had to take our applications for trucking licences to the OMB. Usually there was a battle because existing truckers never wanted to allow a new competitor on the road. The test for a new licence was "public necessity and convenience." It was up to the applicant to bring witnesses to tell the board under oath that there was need for this new service. The opposing truckers would bring witnesses to say that there was no need, that the service being provided was more than satisfactory.

A new client from Winnipeg turned up one day, looking for Roly to act for him before the Ontario Municipal Board. It was a Mr. Reimer and his young son, Donald, who wanted to get licences to operate not only from Winnipeg to Toronto but also inside Ontario. We prepared the application, gathered witnesses, and eventually appeared before the Ontario Municipal Board. We were successful. That was the beginning of Reimer Express Lines Limited in Ontario, which over the decades burgeoned into one of the largest and most significant haulers of goods in Canada. And, like everyone else, when young Donald got older he decided to sell out. But the company's trucks still carry the name Reimer proudly in Ontario and throughout Canada.

Roly was always attracted to politics. If my recollection is correct, he had sat in the provincial legislature earlier, and there's a bit of information that helped us get along together — he was a pilot in the Royal Flying Corps at the end of the First World War. So he understood where I had come from, which made things easier between us.

There was a federal election at the end of the 1950s, and Roly decided to run for the Conservatives in the St. Paul's riding in Toronto, containing the area in which he lived, Rosedale. The campaigning started, and Roly would march out of the office in full striped trousers and business director's suit to go to talk to union groups and people of every walk of life. Never would he dress down when he was going to go out and do political things, whether on the street corner or anywhere else. Lo and behold he won the St. Paul's riding and entered the House of Commons as part of the Diefenbaker majority. At the Lang, Michener office we began to receive word that the bilingual Roly was in contention to be elected as Speaker of the House of Commons. Eventually word came that he indeed had been elected to that high post, which was of course a full-time responsibility for him. He was thus required to leave Lang, Michener, which then became a totally Liberal firm except for me.

Just before Roly left the firm, two young Italian men from California wanted to incorporate in Ontario, and they came to Roly. He handed them over to me to take the basic information for the incorporation. They produced a new form of bathtub equipment. I took the particulars, and Bob Cranston prepared the application for federal incorporation. The first formal directors were Cranston, Peppler, and Jenner. The pair from California was from the Jacuzzi family, just getting started. Jacuzzi Universal (Canada) Limited was incorporated on May 31, 1955. Howard Drabinsky, the 2003 managing partner of the huge Lang, Michener firm, was kind enough to dig out the record for me.

The Lang, Michener letter enclosing a copy of the Jacuzzi Universal (Canada) Limited letters patent was dated April 15, 2003. On April 29, 2003, the *Globe and Mail* published the obituary of one of those young Jacuzzis I had met in 1955. Virgilio Jacuzzi was in his eighty-fifth year; he was born in Casara, Italy, with the name that has become synonymous worldwide with his family's water-aerated bathtubs.

One of Roly Michener's friends was Arthur Walwyn, who maintained offices on the same floor right next to the Lang, Michener firm, the better to be able to get at Roly when required. My recollection of Mr. Walwyn's business at that time was that he was an investor for himself and others in the stock market and clearly had done very well. He was a wealthy and influential Bay Street businessman whose brother was in the stock brokerage business. It is his name that is part of the famous and large organization now known as Midland, Walwyn. Both brothers have been gone for several decades now.

In Don Mills, which was still abuilding, I was approached in the fall of 1956 by a group of young residents to ask me if I would consider running for the council of the Township of North York in the ward that encompassed Don Mills, Victoria Park, and the area to the south that would later become Flemingdon Park. With the support both of that vigorous Don Mills gang, which included Jim Crang, an up-and-coming architect, and of Mary-O I decided to go for it. My friend Doug Breithaupt, who had been part of 411 Squadron when we formed it back in 1951, threw in considerable advertising knowledge and experience for campaign slogans and materials, and off my campaign went. I decided that if I were going to be elected, I would have to get out and knock on as many doors as possible, which is exactly what I did. I'd march up to the door, bang on it, have a brochure when the person came to the door, then identify myself: "I'm Richard Rohmer, running for council, hope you'll vote for me." Then leave!

The man I was running against, the incumbent, Don Alcorn, was a friend of mine and a member of the Don Mills Civitan Club, of which I

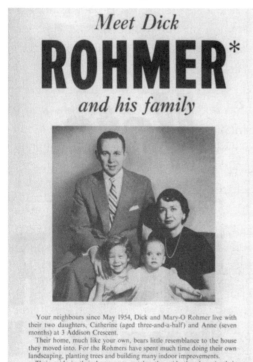

Meet Dick

ROHMER*

and his family

Your neighbours since May 1954, Dick and Mary-O Rohmer live with their two daughters, Catherine (aged three-and-a-half) and Anne (seven months) at 3 Addison Crescent.

Their home, much like your own, bears little resemblance to the house they moved into. For the Rohmers have spent much time doing their own landscaping, planting trees and building many indoor improvements.

Their pride in their home now matches the pride they have in their community . . . *your* community.

That is why Dick Rohmer, at the insistence of a delegation of leading Don Mills' citizens, agreed to contest the council seat and become

✳ **Your delegate for Ward 1 Council** TOWNSHIP OF NORTH YORK

My 1956 election brochure as the successful candidate for Ward 1 in the Township of North York Council.

had been a member from its inception. So it was a friendly campaign, which I won with a reasonable margin.

The new Township Council took office on January 1, 1957. Representing Ward 1, the most easterly in the huge municipality, which was still principally rural, I sat at the southern end of the huge, semi-circular, elevated desk in the council chamber with the six other councillors and the reeve arranged to my left. Directly opposite me was Bill Lyon, a great lawyer, handicapped by polio when he was young, and an elegant person with an extremely sharp mind who later went on the County Court bench and became its chief judge in Ontario. The new reeve (mayor) had been on council, a tall, strapping fellow by the name of Vernon Singer. Norman Goodhead, who was later to become reeve, was there with Dalton Bales, who down the road was to become a minister in the provincial Cabinet. Stanley Honsberger, QC, who in his middle sixties was by far the most senior person by way of age, was also a lawyer. Then there was Irv Paisley, an insurance person, slight and slender with a peculiar paisley opinion on most subjects. Basil Hall, who was later to become reeve, was an affable, highly industrious man who represented the Avenue Road area of the township.

For two years (that was the length of term of our office) this group was to handle all of the political decisions that were forced upon it by the rapidly expanding township. North York was the target of all manner of housing and apartment and commercial proposals brought on by the services of water and sewer, roads, electricity, and everything else being made available through the recent mid-1950s creation of the Municipality of Metropolitan Toronto. The City of Toronto and the Townships of North York and East York and Etobicoke and others were all melded into one but under a metropolitan government that allowed each of the constituent municipalities still to function and make their own decisions. The chairman of Metro Toronto, Fred Gardiner, QC, had been appointed to that post by the Honourable Leslie Frost, the premier of the province, when Frost and legislature created the Metropolitan Act. Big Daddy Fred Gardiner was a huge man, very powerful in the sense of his intellect and his presence. It was said that if old Fred liked you, you were in; if he didn't like you, you were toast. As matters developed he and I got on very well. I think he was rather fatherly when it came to the activities and opinions of the very young lawyer representing Ward 1 in North York.

I had my opening run-in with Vern Singer when I discovered that the surveyors had staked out a new road in my riding without any notice to me. This was at the beginning of 1957. The road was from Eglinton Avenue North up to Lawrence through fairly dense bush. At that intersection it connected to Leslie. The extension of Leslie south to Eglinton would soon become an important metro thoroughfare. My first visit to Reeve Singer made it clear that if anything was going to go on in my ward, I had to be given notice of it and, furthermore, had to approve it. Running things simply through the reeve's office was not good enough. From that point on, there was little or no discord between us.

My most important committee membership was as chairman of the Works Committee responsible for the provision and layout of new services, particularly water and sewer, that would service the new developments that were being brought to council for rezoning, especially residential subdivisions and high-rise apartments, a rather new beast in the development mix.

It did not take the developers long to discover that if they could find a piece of land close to existing services and get it rezoned for one hundred or two hundred apartments the land value would be transformed from next to nothing to perhaps millions of dollars. So the gold rush was on.

At Lang, Michener, I was still practising law. I had become a partner, and without complaint my colleagues were good enough to allow me to attend council and committee meetings and to pursue the business of the township.

Some of the very young developers that come to mind in that period who behaved themselves very well were Al Green, Stan Leibel, and Eph Diamond, to name but a few. All have gone on to much greater things based on their entrepreneurial beginnings in North York.

It was at about this time that my involvement with the Don Mills Civitan Club brought on a new project. When I was on council I led the negotiations between the township and Don Mills Developments Limited through Jim Kelley, who was vice-president there. The negotiations were for the acquisition of a piece of land right in the centre of the Don Mills Shopping Centre. The Civitan Club had been instrumental in sponsoring little league hockey clubs for kids around the Don Mills community and was involved in transporting them to various distant arenas. The decision was made that we should attempt to put together an arena for Don Mills. So the negotiations began, and I had a strong part of the leadership because of my role as a member of council. All things being done, Don Mills Developments gave us the tract of land, the township put in a bundle of money, the Civitan Club raised the rest, and so the Don Mills Civitan Arena was built. It opened with much fanfare in about 1958. Tens of thousands of young Don Mills and area kids and their parents have used that facility over the past four or more decades.

CHAPTER 33
Civitan Visit to President Eisenhower

O UR STAY IN DON MILLS — I called it the Centre of Canada — was a period of growth in my profession of law and in several other areas. All the people moving into E.P. Taylor's new creation were young. By that I mean they were in their late twenties or early thirties. They were creating families, kids. They were into the first houses that they had owned. They were either starting new businesses or making progress in the firms that employed them. Very few — if any — of the women worked outside the home. They were committed to raising their families and looking after their husbands, and normally the husband's income was sufficient.

It was a great disaster, but we lost Mark at Christmastime in 1955 in Windsor. He had had a throat infection, and unfortunately the diagnosis in Windsor was not sufficient to really alert us or the doctors to the seriousness of the situation. So we lost our little man at the age of six months. Believe me, it took a long while to get over that event. But our families and even the people at the law firm stood behind us and helped us through.

The world became much brighter again when little Ann Rohmer was born on March 7, 1956. Our little family in Don Mills was complete. Mary-O, bless her soul, had given up the teaching profession to look after the family, and with Ann's arrival to augment the presence of the beautiful Catherine, as well as looking after me, Mary-O's hands were indeed full, and she carried on.

As Anglicans we became involved in the creation in Don Mills of the Church of the Ascension. The rector, Canon George Thompson, arrived from Nova Scotia at about the same time we moved to Don Mills. Canon Thompson had the task of gathering the flock, performing his

Sunday services in a factory building at the south end of Don Mills on Don Mills Road, then finding the money to build the church, which he ultimately did. It is located on Overland Drive in the centre of the community. The church was completed in the mid-1950s, and we were very much a part of its activities and, as I recall, some of its financing.

At about the same time, a new service club was formed in Don Mills. It was the Civitan Club. The international headquarters was and is based in Birmingham, Alabama. The principal role of the club is to be "builders of good citizenship." Many of my Don Mills friends joined Civitan, and so I was enticed into the club. Dick Groom, John Rice, Bob Scott, Gerry Brown, and Don Alcorn are a few of the names that come to mind. The Civitan Club did an enormous amount of good work in the community. It was the driving force behind the creation of the Civitan hockey arena in the Don Mills Shopping Centre and was a grand fundraiser for many community activities. While I never had the office of president of the Don Mills Civitan Club, I found myself eventually in the position of being elected as regional lieutenant-governor and then governor for Ontario. From that post I was plucked by the international organization and eventually became treasurer, which was the number-two post in Civitan International. That activity in the early 1960s required a great deal of travelling on my part because Civitan was very large in the United States and had (and still has) clubs from the Atlantic to the Pacific. As the number-two person behind the president I was called on to speak at this convention and that. It really was heavy duty. As often as possible Mary-O would travel with me, but on the long trips it was not possible, particularly with the two little ones at home. For me it was an excellent learning period. I gained much experience in speaking and in dealing with people that would stand me in good stead in later years.

The pressure was on in 1963 to have me run for president of Civitan. As the treasurer, my success would have been assured had I elected to run. However, at that period the practice of law was intense and I simply could not afford the time away from the practice that Civitan would have demanded if I had taken the presidency. So I declined, and in a short period of time I really moved away from Civitan altogether. What Civitan did do for me, however, was to give me the opportunity to meet President Eisenhower.

While I was treasurer of Civitan I proposed to the president and the executive body that in keeping with the Civitan principles of good citizenship we should create a special international award. It would be the World Citizenship Award of Civitan in recognition of superlative service to mankind in war and peace, and President Eisenhower and Sir Winston Churchill should be our first recipients.

The proposal was agreed to enthusiastically. In due course an elaborate Civitan plaque was developed, and we were ready for the first presentation, which in our plan was to former President Dwight D. Eisenhower.

Eisenhower was writing his memoirs at his offices at Gettysburg. He had not been at all well and had a heart problem troubling him.

Our Civitan staff at Birmingham made the appropriate arrangements for the attendance of the president of Civitan, Dr. John Pate, the executive director of Civitan, and me. On the chosen date and at the exact time we of the Civitan team appeared at President Eisenhower's offices at Gettysburg. We were shown to a reception room on the second floor and asked to wait.

President Eisenhower soon appeared and warmly shook hands with all of us. He looked pale and gaunt. In the presence of our photographer we gathered in front of the fireplace of this elegant room. With an eloquent statement President John Pate presented the Civitan World Citizenship Award to President Dwight D. Eisenhower, who was at his remote, vague best.

He allowed us to have a brief discussion in which he asked about Civitan. But clearly he was not tuned in to who we really were or what we were doing.

Finally I decided to go for it. I said, "Mr. President, General Eisenhower, I have to tell you that I served under you on D-Day. I was up and down the beaches in my Mustang fighter at five hundred feet when the first landing craft hit the beaches at H-hour. I had the best seat in the house."

Well, I tell you, it was just as if I turned on a light switch in his great brain. I was one of *his* boys in the most successful military operation that had been ever carried out. To the exclusion of my Civitan colleagues, the

General and I had fifteen minutes worth of delightful discussion about D-Day and the Battle of Normandy. His eyes were alive with pleasure as we talked about those incredible moments, hours, and days in Normandy and then on up into Belgium and Holland where Montgomery had executed his ill-fated operation, Market Garden, at Arnhem and Nijmegen, in which I had also taken part in the fall of 1944.

All in all, President Eisenhower was a most gracious recipient, the first one, of Civitan's World Citizenship Award.

For the record I have the photograph with President Eisenhower duly autographed by him.

With President Dwight Eisenhower for
Civitan's World Citizenship Award.

Later that year Mary-O and I travelled to London, England. Churchill was gravely ill and so the best we could do was to attend at his home, where I gave the World Citizenship Award to his lady secretary. A shaky photograph taken by Mary-O records that event.

As it happened, both President Eisenhower and Winston Churchill died shortly after our visits. I am sure the arrival of the Civitan World Citizenship Award did nothing to hasten the respective demises of these two world leaders.

CHAPTER 34

The Reichmanns, Flemingdon Park, and the New Queen's Council

———•———

THE PERIOD IS 1958/59. It was time to leave North York Council. It was also time for me to part company with the Lang, Michener firm. They had treated me as well as possible, and I believe that I carried my weight when I was with the firm. But it was the moment for me to strike out on my own. By this time I had enough trucking clients who were really mine and not the firm's, so I had some assurance of a reasonable amount of income when I started off.

I rented office space, if you can call it that, in the attic of a very ancient residence that was located at the northwest corner of Don Mills Road and Lawrence Avenue in the centre of Don Mills. This site is now populated by apartment buildings and a Tim's. But the place would do for the moment. It was close to our home at 3 Addison Crescent, about half a mile away, and it was at the centre of the developing of Don Mills, which was accelerating.

When I was finished with my council duties, two clients immediately surfaced, both of them in the land development business.

I received a telephone call from a Paul Reichmann at my attic office. He had a piece of land he had acquired and wanted to have it rezoned for apartments. Would I come to see him and his brother, Albert, at their tile wholesale and retail location in the Keele, Wilson area? I said, "Of course I will."

When I arrived at the Olympia Tile warehouse located south of Wilson just to the east of Keele, I was greeted by two young, very orthodox Jewish men, one with a beard, a long face, and an ever-present black fedora. That was Paul Reichmann. His brother, also wearing a black fedora but with a rounder, beardless face, was Albert. My guess was that they were in their late twenties or early thirties.

They took me into their office and showed me the plan of the land that they had purchased and told me that they wanted to rezone it for apartments in high-rise form. This was their first land development. Would I act for them? Of course I would. The site looked to be reasonable, services were there, and it was located on one of the main streets in North York that was open for this kind of use. That entire venture was successful. I got the rezoning through, and off they went buying other pieces of land, embarking on a legendary pattern of success.

The second client who surfaced was Toronto Industrial Leaseholds (TIL), an aggressive real estate development firm headed up by Alex and Harry Rubin. The project they had in mind was backed by New York entrepreneur Bill Zeckendorf. But it wasn't the Rubins who retained me, it was young Bud Andrews, who had been retained by the Rubins to put together a planning and development team for the lands in the southeast quadrant of Don Mills Road and Eglinton, bounded on the east by the Don Valley Parkway and the Don Valley. It was a huge piece of land. The concept was that it would be developed into a comprehensive new town comprised of high-density residential apartment towers based on the kind of development that was going on at that time in Sweden. Bud Andrews asked me if I would be prepared to act for the TIL group and for him as the manager of the planning and development. To convince the planning board and council of the Township of North York that this kind of novel, massive development should be permitted on this type of site would be an enormous challenge. Bud had already retained Macklin Hancock, one of the world's foremost land use planners, and his company, Project Planning Associates, to undertake the basic planning of Flemingdon Park, the plans and details that would be presented ultimately to the North York Planning Board and North York Council. No question, the team that Bud Andrews had put together to bring this whole project from the point of concept to the point of the development was strong in terms of experience and ability. The brilliant Murray Jones, the Metro Toronto planning director, would be one of the people who would have to be dealt with because of Metro's interest; as well, John Curtis, the planning director of North York, had to be consulted at every turn.

With my recent involvement as a councillor in the Township of North York, it was seen as an advantage if I could be retained to assist in developing the presentations and making them to the staff, the planning board, council, and Metro Toronto.

My friend Don Alcorn had again taken over the post of councillor for Ward 1 just as I had taken it over from him earlier on. Norm Goodhead was now the reeve and was open to new ideas. What Bud Andrews proposed was that when Macklin Hancock had the basic concepts and drawings on paper, we would then say to the reeve, "We would like all of you to accompany us on a trip to Stockholm, Sweden, where you can see on the ground and fully developed the kind of new town that we're talking about. Stockholm is the only advanced city where this can be done, and so in order to give you a reasonable perspective, we would like to take all of you to Stockholm." "All of you" included not only the reeve but also the clerk of the municipality, the Chair of the North York Planning Board, Councillor Donald Alcorn, the Chair of the Metro Toronto Planning Board, and Murray Jones. And, of course, Bud Andrews and me. After a lot of discussion, Norm Goodhead and his team agreed that this should be done in order for them to have a far better understanding of what was proposed.

The Stockholm adventure was a great success all around. We had accommodations at the Grand Hotel in the centre of the city. Through associates in Sweden, Macklin Hancock had arranged for tours of the new town areas that were comprehensive and highly instructive. Everyone was impressed by the skill and ingenuity of the Swedish land use planners and architects. Their new towns were austere but beautiful. New high-rise buildings clustered in peaceful geometric forms rose high above manicured and deftly designed gardens and recreational facilities such as tennis courts and swimming pools sitting above hidden underground garages. We had to remind ourselves that we were in a highly socialist state where the government planned, developed, built, and constructed everything that we were seeing, where wages were controlled and life was much ordered by the state. Even so, the accommodation provided for Swedish citizens in these new cities appeared to be attractive and acceptable.

Our delightful and accomplished tour master, Macklin Hancock, with his infinite number of contacts all over Europe and in particular Sweden, had achieved complete success in convincing all of our tour members that a new town comparable to what we had seen in Sweden could indeed be developed on the Flemingdon Park lands. It would be done in accordance with the comprehensive land use layouts that he had prepared with, of course, the odd constructive change that might be proposed by John Curtis, the township's planner, and his staff, with appropriate input from Murray Jones, the Metro Toronto planner.

As a whole, the travelling group got along famously. The splendid meals in fine restaurants and reasonable amounts of wine and other libations encouraged conviviality among the crowd. I must say that Donald Alcorn turned out to be one of the most amusing and funniest people ever. From the time we got in the aircraft in Toronto until we returned many days later he had us all in stitches with gales of laughter from morning until night. Upon our return from Sweden, Bud Andrews had his team working constantly to finalize the preparation of the plans and application for the necessary Official Plan Amendment that would lay the groundwork for the presentation to John Curtis's staff and then on to the North York Planning Board.

It was decided that the northerly land on the south side of Eglinton Avenue between Don Mills Road and the newly built Don Valley Parkway should be designated for office/commercial; the lands to the east of Parkway north of Eglinton would have a similar designation. The remainder of the lands to the south, including parts of lands to the east of the Don Valley Parkway on the edge of the Don River Valley, would be the new town, comprised almost exclusively of high-rise apartment buildings.

Early in the process Alex Rubin and his team came up with a deal with the Canadian Broadcasting Corporation in which the CBC would acquire the large parcel aligned to the east of the Don Valley Parkway and to the north of Eglinton. This transaction was so attractive to everyone involved that I was able to manage one of the fastest Official Plan changes in the history of land use planning in Ontario. As I recall, the time between the filing of the application with the township and the final approval by the Ontario Municipal Board was in the range of thirty days. It follows that no one objected to the land use change and that the appropriate zoning by-laws would follow once the Official Plan was established. However, in the end, the deal with the CBC collapsed. There exists today on that parcel a mixture of highly sophisticated high-rise apartment buildings with a clutch of office towers, including the headquarters of McDonald's, where my energetic friend George Cohon, the man who brought McDonald's to Canada and who took McDonald's to Moscow, is securely ensconced while leading his highly successful corporation's battle against competitive old age.

In the early 1960s, Toronto Industrial Leasehold's original partner, big Bill Zeckendorf, the mercurial New York land developer and promoter, fell into some degree of financial difficulty, which also backed into the Toronto Industrial Leasehold's ability to keep on with the development of Flemingdon Park. By this time some of the first apartment buildings had been built and the development was making good progress. I have no idea of the corporate or financial arrangements that were made. That was not in my terms of reference as municipal counsel for the project.

What did happen was that my first land use clients, Paul and Albert Reichmann, and their Olympia & York Corporation moved in to take over control of all aspects of the project. At that point Bud Andrews and his team went on to other activities elsewhere in the Toronto area. Paul and Albert's project manager, Lloyd Brown, moved into the picture to carry on with the development and in particular the land use aspects in dealing with the Township of North York. I continued to act as counsel to the project for the Reichmanns and to develop my own practice in the land use and zoning field and in trucking licensing.

By this time in the early 1960s I was coming along well with the development of my practice before the newly created Ontario Highway Transport Board. I was representing not only Reimer Express Lines Limited but also many other truckers who had applications before the board or who were opposing applications, as the case might be. In fact, my practice before the board was progressing so well that I was able to write and publish my first book, *Practice and Procedure Before the Ontario Highway Transport Board*.

My little family and I were prospering reasonably well. In fact, things were good enough for us financially at that time that Mary-O and I decided to take a six-week vacation in Europe that summer. We arranged to buy a beautiful little white convertible that we picked up in England, and off we went from London through the British Isles then over to France, Spain, and Italy before heading for the beaches of Normandy, intending to be there for June 6, 1960. We finally arrived in the château country of France, having found potential relatives in Lyons, the family of Marcel Rohmer, whom we visited. We were all certain that Marcel and I looked so much alike that the common genes were certainly there. We kept in touch with Marcel and his son, Jean, for several years but in recent times have lost touch.

We then went on toward Tours, intending to visit the remarkable Château de Chenonceau, which sits like a bridge over the placid Cher River a short distance to the west of the town of Montrichard.

As we drove into Montrichard from the east on our way to Chenonceau on June 3, 1960, it was a very hot day in our top-down car. It was approaching midday, and Mary-O and I decided we should stop and have a cooling beverage. On the main street we saw a sign which said, "L'Hôtel de la Tête Noire, English Spoken." That placed looked inviting, particularly with English spoken. We parked the car at the front door of the hotel, went in, and were greeted by a delightful young woman by the name of Muguette. She was one of three daughters of the owners, Monsieur and Madame Louis Coutant. Muguette had just returned from England, where she was learning to speak English and doing reasonably well. We ordered our drinks from her and sat in the small bar off the hotel's entrance lobby. That done, Muguette proceeded to give us a tour of the hotel, which at that time was about thirty rooms with accommodation next to the Cher River in a separate building.

We were intrigued by the accommodation and by Muguette, whom we found to be utterly charming. She was an innocent twenty-year-old at that time and just a delight to be with.

We left L'Hôtel de la Tête Noire and went on to Chenonceau, where we were absolutely captivated by the magnificent architecture, history, and grounds of that fabulous building. We were the only visitors there! This was 1960, and France was trying to get itself awakened from the onslaught of the Second World War and from the difficulties in Algeria. In effect, tourism did not exist. Today, Chenonceau in season is flooded with busloads of tourists and people from all over the world. But on that first visit we were the only people there. As we walked through the grounds of the château taking photographs and absorbing the beauty that surrounded us, we decided that we should go back to L'Hôtel de la Tête Noire to see if Muguette could accommodate us overnight. She could indeed, and instead of one night we stayed two, still leaving us enough time to get to Normandy and Juno Beach, where the Canadians had come ashore as I watched from my Mustang I, and to Arromanches, where the Mulberry had been located. We would then look for my wartime B8 airfield between Arromanches and Bayeux.

We stayed at the hotel and met all the family: mama and papa Coutant and the other two daughters, Françoise and Nicole. Papa Louis was the master chef of great fame in the region. His son, Jackie, a chef trained by his father, was at that moment serving time in the French Navy. We would meet him some years later.

As of that visit in 1960 we became part of the Coutant family. We have been back to see them many, many times. Muguette came to visit us in Canada and was with us in Barbados in the middle seventies. Muguette, poor soul, developed a brain tumour and was taken in the late 1980s, a crushing blow to that close-knit Coutant family and to us. Nicole lost her long battle with cancer early in 2004, and mama died shortly after.

After Montrichard, we drove to Normandy, visited the beaches on D-Day, and, after a long and arduous effort, found the huge stone farmhouse where 430 Squadron had maintained its pilots' waiting room next to 129 Airfield's airstrip at B8, Magny, just off the main road between Arromanches and Bayeux, perhaps two miles south of Arromanches. Finding the farmhouse was a moment of high nostalgia as the memories of the teeming activity and events that had flowed from that pilots' waiting room on the second floor and from the airstrip there sixteen years before came flooding back.

The farmhouse was then in the possession a group of nuns from Bayeux who were using the place as an orphanage for girls. We met the Mother Superior, established a relationship with her, and for several years thereafter sent contributions annually for the maintenance of the place and the people in it.

It was time to return to our children and to the practice of law. We shipped the little white car home by freighter, and it remained with us until 1962.

In 1961, Mary-O and I decided it was time to look for a bigger residence. With two daughters we needed more than three bedrooms. As simple as that. After much looking around we discovered a house that we thought was perfect and we bought it. It was a magnificent, roomy residence, English Tudor style. It was located on that part of Sandringham Drive just north of the Canadian Forces Staff College on Wilson Avenue off Old Yonge Boulevard. The house was 74 Sandringham and was close to the new Highway 401 that was being built across the top of Metropolitan Toronto. 74 Sandringham was on the very lip of the steep slope of the Don Valley, which was much treed. At the bottom was the municipal golf course that still flourishes there. At the rear of the house and slightly to its east sat a huge two-storey garage that I fancied could be converted someday into a residence (which is what eventually happened). The home had been built by one George Drew, not the famous Ontario politician but a man who had been executive in the mining industry. Drew had recently passed away, and his widow wanted to move on.

Because the house was senior it needed some renovations. We hired an outstanding architect who was famous for his house refurbishing designs to do the necessary work, particularly the kitchen area. In the summer of 1961 we sold 3 Addison Crescent and moved across town to our new digs at 74 Sandringham, complete with a magnificent pool table in the basement family room, something that had been left behind by Mrs. Drew when she sold the place to us.

By this time, with my practice flourishing (I had been made a Queen's Counsel in 1960), the wonderful litigator and superb gentleman Peter de Carteret Cory and I had decided to establish a partnership and a firm and to move into appropriate offices downtown. We decided on a second floor rabbit warren of offices at 728 Bay Street owned by a remarkable old gentleman by the name of Greey who rather reminded me of a film person of those days called Sydney Greenstreet. Peter would continue with his burgeoning litigation practice. I would carry on with my land use and development practice as well as my Ontario Highway Transport Board clients. We would bring in other partners with specialties such as real estate, wills, and corporate expertise. Before long the firm

The new Queen's Counsel, 1960.

became Rohmer, Cory, Hogg, Morris, Haley and Givertz. Stanton Hogg was a criminal law specialist, well regarded in his field, who eventually went to the County Court bench and then on to the Superior Court of Ontario. Donna Haley was our wills and real estate expert. She too went on to the Superior Court bench. Hugh Morris was first a student and then a partner who assisted me mainly in the Ontario Highway Transport Board activity. That field became one of his basic law practice foundations when he went on to form his own firm. Marvin Givertz was also in the litigation end of things, and he too ultimately developed his own successful practice when the Rohmer, Cory firm dissolved in later years. Peter Cory? He went on to be an outstanding judge, a member of the Supreme Court of Canada, a Companion of the Order of Canada, and Chancellor of York University in 2004.

For me the practice of law at that time was a flourishing success. So much so that Mary-O and I decided in 1962 that we would do a repeat of the six-week European tour that we had done in 1960.

There would be one major difference: the automobile that we would buy in order to carry us on this great adventure.

As we had in 1960, we organized Mrs. Ruby Davies (who had been my fraternity mother with Delta Chi back in the late 1940s when I was going to law school) to come to the house and take care of Catherine and Ann. That done, then the next step was the automobile.

I had seen photographs of this particular machine, which was just about to come off the production line in England. It was a coupe with a jump seat and a hard top. It looked like a racing car, and in reality it was. The body was put on a racing car chassis with a huge, beautiful engine. It was one of the original Jaguar XKEs. As I saw it, it was one of the most attractive automobiles being built at the time, and with its gorgeous lines it was totally innovative.

Arriving in England, we stayed, as we had earlier, at the Stafford Hotel on St. James Place just behind the Ritz. Prices then were quite affordable whereas these days, they're right off the clock.

Mary-O and I went to the Jaguar dealership that was then across from the Ritz on Piccadilly. There it was, a gleaming, shining dark blue, my beautiful XKE. I produced my documentation and took delivery on the spot. The price? You won't believe this but I still have the bills — $4,500 Canadian for this gorgeous brand new piece of machinery.

We did our usual tour of England then across to France down to Venice. We went to Quiberon on the Brest Peninsula, then a remote French fishing port and today a bustling commercial resort. Then back to see the Coutant family in Montrichard. A visit to the Normandy beaches and my 430 Squadron farmhouse at Magny, where the nuns were still in operation with their orphanage. Then we headed for Britain, flying our wonderful XKE with us on the same aircraft from Strasbourg across to the south of England.

We shipped the Jaguar on a freighter back to Canada, but I had one major failure with regard to the car. I did not have it undercoated for protection against salt. Perhaps the technology wasn't available at that point, but in any event it went across the ocean without protection. I was to pay the penalty two years later when it started to rust out. If the XKE hadn't had that irreversible contamination of its beautiful body I would probably have the car to this day. What is an XKE of that make and model worth today? Probably in the range of $70,000 to $80,000. As for the date when I got rid of it, it must have been sometime in 1964, because by 1963 I was operating, among other things, as John Robarts's special counsel. I can recall many times after a working breakfast session with him at the Westbury driving him to Queen's Park in the XKE. Because it was so low to the ground and he was of such heft, I would ask him to get his feet out on the ground when he was leaving the car, then I'd give him a heavy push from behind so that he could get up and out.

My Jaguar is gone. And so is John Parmenter Robarts, about whom much more later.

CHAPTER 35
Starting the North York General Hospital

I N THE TIME THAT I was on North York Council, 1957 to 1958, a group of us in Don Mills somehow came together for the purpose of discussing the need for creating a new hospital that would accommodate the growing number of people moving into E.P. Taylor's Macklin Hancock–designed Don Mills. We could see a clear and obvious need for a hospital. We knew it would take a long time to get it organized and off the ground. But we were young and idealistic. I don't have the original letters patent, but if I could find it I could recite the names of the people who were involved in applying for the incorporation of the North York General Hospital. Suffice to say that I prepared the application for incorporation, and it was granted by the provincial government.

What we did know was that none of us in the organizing group had any clout. We would have to go and recruit some wealthy and influential people to populate our board of directors. It took a while, but that is exactly what we did.

The first person I approached was Colonel Clifford Sifton of the family that owned both newspapers and radio stations throughout Canada. The colonel was a hard-nosed First World War veteran who had fought at Vimy Ridge. He was a man of local residence, his large, prestigious home being located on the north side of Lawrence Avenue just as it met Bayview Avenue, where also had a huge arena where he and his family and others played polo. Yes, Colonel Sifton would be interested. A hospital was needed in the rapidly growing area. Did he have any suggestions about other people that we might approach? Yes, he had one or two suggestions. It was Colonel Sifton's agreeing to be on the board that gave us some instant credibility when we approached the likes of

Jim Grand of Grand & Toy, one of the Posluns of the important family that bore that name, and Angus McClaskey, president of E.P. Taylor's Don Mills Developments Limited, all of whom agreed. This was the core group of the new board of the North York General Hospital. In addition, we had with us Murray Jones, the Metro Toronto planner who was now into his own consulting business. All the original board members resigned in order to make room for the incoming team. All, that is, except me. Clifford Sifton became the chairman, and I continued as secretary and counsel.

By the mid-1960s the new board came up with a parcel of land that it wanted to acquire for the building of the hospital. It was in the northeast quadrant of the intersection of Highway 401 and Leslie. Preliminary fundraising had been started and was successful, sufficient for the completion of the first land acquisition. The firm of Rohmer, Cory, Hogg, Morris and Haley had participated in the negotiation of the acquisition and the agreement that gave rise to it. We were proceeding with the searches necessary of the title of the land when I discovered that without any notice to me, Angus McClaskey had given the purchase agreement to the solicitors for Don Mills Developments Limited and unilaterally had asked them to act on behalf of the hospital board in the purchase.

At this point I "blew my stack." This was an entirely inappropriate move on McClaskey's part, himself a lawyer. But instead of attempting to fight it I decided had had enough. I called the chairman, Colonel Sifton, told him what had happened, and promptly resigned from the board of governors of North York General Hospital.

Fortunately, we had created a strong enough board that the departure of an individual such as me did not impede either the acquisition of the land or for that matter the ultimate building of the hospital.

On the other hand, my resignation from the North York General board freed me up to take on the as-yet-unheard-of task of planning, building, and developing Thompson House, a 135-bed charitable home for the aged at the southwest corner of the intersection of the Donway West and Overland in the centre of Don Mills itself. That project started in 1967.

CHAPTER 36

JFK, the Rohmer, Cory firm, and Allan Waters of CHUM

I T WAS THE YEAR THAT Senator John F. Kennedy went after and won the Democratic nomination for the presidency. He was out campaigning everywhere he possibly could, and once in a while he would return to the family compound.

At that point I was still heavily involved with Civitan International as its second-in-command in the post of treasurer. I had to be in Washington to speak to a group at a Civitan club there. Then I was to fly on to West Palm Beach airport, where I would be met by Mary-O, our two children, and my father, who then had a home in Stuart, Florida, on the river there. I got on the aircraft in Washington. It was a twin-engine lunker on a tricycle undercarriage with piston engines and the door sitting in the centre of the airplane. It was a Convair.

The airplane was fairly full. We landed safely at the West Palm airport and taxied in to the ramp. I was sitting right opposite the doorway. As we were waiting for the door to open up and the steps to go down from it, the stewardess said to me, "Have you seen Arthur Kennedy on board? He's down at the back of the airplane."

Arthur Kennedy was a well-known movie actor at the time.

My response was, "No, I haven't seen Arthur Kennedy, and I don't think he's seen me either!" A flip response.

Being close to the door I was one of the first down the steps. There were Mary-O, the kids, and my father, Ernie. Kissing, greetings, and hugs, then we turned to go into the terminal building. Standing there, talking to his father, Joe, who had come to greet him, and his sister-in-law, the blonde and lovely wife of Ted Kennedy, was Senator John Kennedy, the candidate. Obviously, the excitable stewardess had had the names a little screwed up. Then I made one of my life's great mistakes. Instead of marching over to John F. Kennedy to congratulate him on his candidacy and wish him well, I didn't want to bother him. So I walked by, staring, of course, like any normal human being in the presence of a famous person. Big mistake.

I can tell you that ever since I have made it a practice to move smartly when in the presence of any major international or national celebrity to go over to that person to present myself, shake hands, and always thereafter be able to say that I met and talked with so-and-so. There will be an anecdote or two in these memoirs that results from my following that course of action.

It was about this time that my clients Paul and Albert Reichmann were building a high office tower at the northwest corner of Dundas and University Avenue in Toronto. Rohmer, Cory, Hogg, Morris, Haley and Givertz was functioning with great success at the rabbit warren of offices on the second floor at 728 Bay Street. I convinced Peter Cory and my other partners that we should look at some space in the new Reichmann building. After some negotiations with the Reichmanns, the Rohmer, Cory firm negotiated a lease for the penthouse floor with offices facing south toward the lake, east over University Avenue, and west over the adjacent buildings on Dundas. By remarkable good fortune I was able to acquire the large office at the southeast corner of our new suite, from which I could oversee most of the development that was going on to the south into the centre core of the city.

When we finally made the move to University and Dundas, we had new lawyers with us in the firm such as Murray Hardisty, who was skilled in corporate matters and was my right hand in terms of looking after those requirements for my new clients, CHUM Limited, headed by Allan Waters, and the Bramalea group, which was headed by Allan Taylor and Arthur Armstrong.

I had been introduced to Allan Waters by one of my Don Mills and Civitan Club friends, Ernie Towndrow; he and Bill Stevens were partners in the firm that did substantial sales and promotional work for CHUM Limited and others. Allan Waters had only recently acquired the 1050 CHUM Limited Corporation with its powerful AM licence on the frequency of 1050. When he had acquired the shares in the company from a friend of his, Allan had decided to take this radio broadcasting vehicle and expand it into a media powerhouse. That he did. In the year 2003, when he gave corporate control of the CHUM television and radio empire to his two sons and its operational control to Jay Switzer, the CHUM group was formidable in both its value and its influence on Canadian culture and society. With the acquisition of the Craig organization in 2004, CHUM is now truly national.

When I first started to act for Allan, he was the owner of 1050 CHUM Limited with only that single powerful AM station in Toronto. His program manager was a young guy from out west called Allan Slaight. One of the first functions I got involved in was to go to Buffalo with Allan Slaight and negotiate there with a Buffalo broadcaster named Jungle Jay Nelson. One of the Waters kids, Allan's daughter, had heard Jungle Jay on a Buffalo station and recommended to her father that he be hired to come to Toronto. As I recall, Slaight and I met Jungle Jay in a Buffalo motel and went at it tooth and nail, finally convincing him that joining CHUM in Toronto would be the best thing for him. Which, of course, it was. Jungle Jay came to CHUM and was an enormous success as the morning man over a long period of time. He was a very important factor in CHUM 1050's building up its share of the audience, which also meant a good share of the advertising dollars.

Then there was the issue of that highly eloquent, opinionated terror Pierre Berton and his pal Charles Templeton. When Pierre was operating on his own and doing a daily opinion piece for CHUM, probably in the range of two or three minutes, Allan Waters decided that I should listen to Pierre to make sure that he didn't step over the line of defamation or say something that would cause CHUM to be sued or to lose its operating licence. There was only one occasion when I had to step in and recommend that his recorded piece not be used. Pierre reacted with maximum fury, as was fully expected. The piece was not used. It is fair to say that over the years, as a result of that, Pierre and I have always been at arms' length, and I can tell you his arm is much longer than mine. Mind you he narrated the Mid-Canada film that Acres made without my knowledge or permission. But Pierre probably didn't know that the Mid-Canada Development Corridor concept was mine. If he had, he probably wouldn't have agreed to do the narration. But that's another story.

During the time that I had the privilege of acting for Allan he made an acquisition of an AM radio station in Simcoe managed by a young man, Fred Sherratt. Fred became Allan's right hand over the decades since Fred, like Allan, is truly an outstanding gentleman and executive.

Then there was the first really big CHUM purchase. It was of the radio station CFRA in Ottawa. CFRA was owned by the estate of a fine Irish gentleman by the name of Ryan who had put the station together and developed it. We had to deal with his widow. It seemed that she had a lawyer who was not experienced in radio station matters. I had recently met and been impressed by a young corporate lawyer by the name of Trevor Eyton. Through Mrs. Ryan's Ottawa lawyer I recommended Trevor as counsel for the estate, and my recommendation was accepted. Trevor and someone from my team drove with me to Ottawa in the middle of winter on bad roads to close the deal, since aircraft were not flying at the time.

Young Trevor went on, of course, to be a major player in the development and history of Brascan and a host of corporations in Canada where he has been a director. Indeed, he was put in the Senate by the Prime Minister of the day when it was necessary to appoint a majority of senators who would support the installation of the Goods and Services Tax.

When Allan Slaight returned from his sojourn in the United Kingdom, where he operated a "pirate" radio station beamed into the UK market, he wanted me to act for him because he was about to acquire a radio station north of Toronto. As I recall it was Richmond Hill. I told him that I couldn't do so because I was still retained by Allan Waters. The lawyer I recommended, whom he had never heard of, was Trevor Eyton. They met, got along very well, and to my knowledge Trevor has been a strong influence on Allan ever since. Allan has gone on to great success as a broadcaster and has accumulated substantial wealth, much to his credit.

Back to Allan Waters and CHUM. In the early sixties Allan had developed a close relationship with Ralph Snelgrove, who owned CKCB, an AM radio station in Barrie, with a tie-in to Collingwood. Ralph had also applied for and received a television licence and had his new station CKVR (V for Valerie, his wife, and R for Ralph) up and running in Barrie.

The two, Allan and Ralph, had their eye on the Toronto market. This was before the introduction of cable, which has allowed CKVR, the New VR, to access Toronto in any event. What they decided to do was to apply to the Board of Broadcast Governors for permission to move the CKVR broadcasting tower from Barrie to a choice location at Palgrave where the signal could go directly into Toronto and its lucrative market.

With the aid of Allan's team, including his engineer, George Jones, whose evidence was necessary to satisfy the technical requirements in the move, we put together an application and duly filed with the Board of Broadcast Governors.

The hearing date was set and the application was publicized. We then discovered that Standard Broadcasting, the owners of CFRB at the time, had decided to oppose. So here we had a radio station, big, famous, and powerful, just up the street from CHUM, opposing a television matter. We weren't too sure if where they were coming from was good grounds for opposition. Perhaps they wanted to have a television station licence themselves, and if we obtained authority to move our tower then that would interfere with their ability to ultimately get the board's approval for a new facility in the market. As it turned out, that was the thrust of their argument.

To show that they meant business, the CFRB people retained that outstanding lawyer Joseph Sedgewick, QC, a formidable senior counsel, litigator, and orator. He was the man with whom I would have to do battle in arguments before Chairman Stewart and members of the Board of Broadcast Governors on the chosen day.

Allan and Ralph had a partner in this transaction. New capital would, of course, be needed in order to move the tower and create a new one at Palgrave, so the flamboyant entrepreneur and radio station owner Jeff Northcotte was part of the team that went to Ottawa to prepare for the hearing and put in his opinion and advice where the three of them thought it necessary. It was my role to coach the three as to how the hearing would be handled. I would do the talking and put Allan and Ralph in to give evidence as required. In preparation, we went back and forth over what each of them was to say. I did not want to use Jeff as a witness because of his mercurial nature. It was dangerous. In the result I had to convince him in my own way that he shouldn't give evidence and that he should let Allan and Ralph carry that burden.

At the hearing, I made my opening statement, dealing with the rationale of the move of the tower and, of course, with the market numbers in Toronto, all of which we were sure would be sufficient to persuade the board that there was plenty of room for us with our station serving that lucrative area. Allan and Ralph were in the front row of the spectators' area along with Jeff. As we made our case, I was satisfied that we had produced a good, solid, fact-filled proposition that the board would find persuasive. On the other side, Joe Sedgewick had to argue the concept that if we got the tower at Palgrave his client would in fact be cut off from making an application to serve Toronto by television. And after all, his client, CFRB Standard Broadcasting, was the biggest and most powerful radio station in Toronto and by virtue of that had a preeminent position and should have first rights to the next television licence.

The tensions were high, the histrionics were colourful and, as usual, the board reserved its judgment. In the end, the board eventually granted our application, but upon the appeal to the federal Cabinet by CFRB other forces were at work, and lo and behold the BBG's decision was overturned. Hence CKVR and its tower — a huge new one built after an aircraft hit it some years ago — are still in their original positions in Barrie. The signal of Channel 4, which is the allocated number for the New VR (the name used instead of CKVR), is received loud and clear by all cable viewers in the Greater Toronto Area. Their programming, of course, has included for many years my "Generally Speaking" editorial comments and now "Rohmer and Rohmer," a weekend commentary that Ann and I do for the New VR and CP24 in Toronto.

My time as counsel for CHUM slowly came to an end at the end of the 1960s when I became heavily involved in organizing my Mid-Canada Development Corridor Conference. It took so much time I had to leave much of the CHUM corporate work to others in the firm. That was not satisfactory as far as Allan Waters was concerned. So I finished my work for that wonderful gentleman even though he kept me on retainer for more than a year. That spoke to his generosity and loyalty. Allan Waters is one of the finest men and one of the best clients I have had the privilege of knowing and working with. Who knows … if it hadn't been for Mid-Canada I might still have been his counsel.

CHAPTER 37
John Roberts's Leadership Campaign and the Premier's Special Advisor

---

T HE TIME WAS 1961.

I had met John Roberts, MPP, on one or two occasions when he had appeared before the Ontario Highway Transport Board as counsel for the trucking firm Husband Transport, based in London where John lived. This was before he had become the Minister of Education in the Frost government in December of 1959, so he was still free to act as a lawyer because he was merely a backbencher member of the provincial legislature. I had not appeared for anyone in opposition to Husband, but I had been before the Ontario Highway Transport Board at the same time he was there.

I had been highly impressed by this tall, heavy-set, black-haired and mustached, strikingly handsome and robust man.

John had been elected to the provincial legislature in 1951. Premier Leslie Frost, a wise and paternalistic old bird, decided that the impressive young lawyer from London should be his new Minister of Education. John joined the Cabinet in 1959, and that was the last we saw of him in relation to the Ontario Highway Transport Board.

In early 1961, rumours began to circulate that Les Frost was going to retire. When he formally made the announcement, I immediately called John Roberts in London and told him in no uncertain terms that I thought he should run and if he did I would do whatever I could in the Toronto area to help him win the leadership. At that time, I was heavily involved in the Don Mills Progressive Conservative organization. In fact, when I was still on North York Council in 1958 I had attempted to win the Conservative nomination for East York (provincial) in a tightly fought battle with the then Conservative incumbent, Hollis Beckett, a battle I had lost.

I knew that John Robarts's best and closest friend, Ernie Jackson, a London native who had also sat on the legislature with John, would be at his right hand if John decided to run. Jackson was not in the legislature in the time. Ernie was just about as tall as John, round-faced, full head of brown hair, a striking-looking man whose profession was in the general insurance industry. Like Robarts he enjoyed fishing and hunting, and he could stay with Robarts drink for drink when it came to rye, Scotch, or whatever was going. And as it turned out, Jackson was a brilliant political tactician.

When I called Robarts to offer my services he was still undecided about running and rather vague about the whole thing.

I heard nothing back from him or Jackson. Then the announcement came that John Robarts would in fact run for the leadership. That word came from London. I had still not heard anything.

So I got on the phone again and called John once more. My message to him was that he just had to make plans to campaign in Toronto; that I knew or had access to every delegate in the Toronto area; and that if he would plan to come to Toronto I would set up meetings and take him to the home or business of every single one of the people who would be voting.

Which is finally what happened after I kept up the pressure to get him to visit Toronto the Good and its suburbia. I think we did not miss any one of the delegates from the Toronto region. I can tell you that the lady delegates, most of them well past their forties, were absolutely thrilled when John would walk into their homes to pay a small visit and have tea. He was young, virile, with a look sort of like Clark Gable. What a man! With his gravelly voice he was irresistible.

The Robarts Toronto campaign was clearly going to have a great payoff at voting time. As a result I became the Toronto anchor of the campaign team. Robarts was quite comfortable with me, and Ernie Jackson was prepared to see me in a tight role with him and John as the leadership campaign planning got underway well in advance of the convention's opening date, which was October 23, 1961. Jackson enlisted the entire London "mafia" (as we called them), including David Weldon,

John Cronyn, and Dick Dillon. Jackson organized the people, the money, the banners, the entire strategy of the campaign. Delegates had booked rooms in the Park Plaza Hotel, which was just a few steps away from the place where the great event would occur in the ancient Varsity Arena on Bloor Street.

Robarts continued to be based at the Westbury Hotel, where he was living now that he had become a minister, coming up to Toronto on Sunday nights or Monday mornings and going back to London on Friday night or whenever it was possible to get away.

My base of operations was at the Rohmer, Cory, Hogg Morris, Haley and Givertz firm at 728 Bay Street, not far from the legislature and in fact not all that distant from Varsity Arena. Mary-O and I had just moved with our little family to Sandringham Drive in North York.

As the final few weeks before the leadership convention arrived it was time for Robarts to start touring the province. The plan was that I would accompany him as his aide-de-camp, making sure that he was properly greeted, looked after, accommodated, and fed and that in the middle of any local meeting he could be collared by local riding members only for a certain length of time. In other words he was not to be tied up exclusively with anyone. I very quickly became adept at extracting him from one person or little group and getting him on to the next person or group who had to speak with him.

Nora Robarts was not what you would call a political wife. She wanted to stay in London, letting John go and do his political thing and then come back to her in London or at their place in Grand Bend on the weekends.

However, for the leadership campaign she allowed herself to be taken to a few local meetings in the area, not too far away from London. And during the convention, she was right there in Toronto with John, a visible and enthusiastic supporter.

Finally it was time for the convention to start. Excitement was high, rumours were multitudinous, particularly about whom it was that Les Frost was going to support. Jackson had it planned that John would go to the Park Plaza to the various delegates' caucus rooms and be there at specified times. I would accompany, him carrying out my shepherding function. John, bless him, did not get annoyed when I would tug at his sleeve or pull at him to get him away from a particular situation and on to another.

And so it went from the Thursday night at the Park Plaza and other hotels in the area where the delegates had bunked in. We went from place to place and room to room. Of course, John had to be careful of the amount of booze he was putting away. We would catch up at his room back at the Westbury when the night's travelling was over.

It was quite obvious that John was being very well received everywhere he went, particularly by the ladies.

His entire campaign team was quite optimistic.

Mind you, the other Cabinet ministers who were running for the leadership were tough competition. I mean really tough.

The kindly, gray-haired Jim Allan and the hard-nosed lawyer Kelso Roberts were in the fray. Then there was the brilliant, charismatic Robert MacAulay.

MacAulay had been an instructor of mine at Osgoode Hall when I was taking my law school course. I had run across him several times in my practice of law. A most pleasant man. Mercurial. Brilliant. An outstanding counsel in administrative law matters such as the Ontario Municipal Board, the Energy Board, and the like. We were good friends. He was at the time of the campaign a minister in Frost's Cabinet and a leading contender.

MacAulay saw me for the first time with Robarts somewhere in the environs of Varsity Stadium where we had gone to take a look at the place before the convention actually got started. MacAulay was shocked to see me at Robarts's right hand. For seven years thereafter MacAulay would not speak to me. However, after that period of time we had many good sessions together before the Ontario Municipal Board and in other venues. A real character.

As the days passed and we were right up against the convention itself, Jackson had mustered his troops extremely well, particularly the London mafia, the loyal gang from the hometown.

While that was going on, Robarts and I worked on his speech to the convention. It would tell all the delegates why they should vote for him.

The person running the convention, Elmer Bell, QC, from Exeter (dear old Elmer), had decreed that each candidate would have only a certain amount of time to speak. Perhaps it was ten minutes or something of that kind. John and I thought we had his timing pretty well settled into the limited space. But to be on the safe side we decided that I would sit in the front row of the audience and be the timer. I would give him the signal when he was getting close to the expiry moment. Which is exactly what we did. John plowed through his speech to the best of his ability, his gruff, gravelly voice resounding through the Varsity Stadium, ringing with conviction, sincerity, and "you can trust me and believe in me" tones. I gave him the cut-off signal, and John stopped exactly on time. That was the night before the voting was to take place, and all the candidates put in their two cents' worth. What an exciting time.

The button-holing of delegates continued apace, with the London mafia doing their best to persuade to vote for Robarts everyone they could put their hands on that night and through the morning until the voting began at Varsity Arena.

At all times John and I were in touch by radio phone with Ernie Jackson from his command post in Varsity Arena.

Long before the results of the first ballot were announced Jackson had them and had passed them on to us. I had no idea, nor did Robarts, how Ernie got the figures so quickly, but he had a system going and it really worked. There were several ballots held before the winner was finally selected. It was a tough campaign. There were no runaway favourites at all.

The second-to-last ballot was an almost even spread between MacAulay, Kelso Roberts, and John Robarts. MacAulay was the third man in that ballot. What would he do? Would he go to Kelso Roberts or would he go to Robarts or would he go to either of them?

At the crucial moment in the crowd-filled arena Bob MacAulay marched over to his good friend Robarts, took off his own MacAulay pin, and stuck it on Robarts's chest. This signal to the crowd and to MacAulay's delegates was dramatic. I was right beside Robarts (as usual) when that magic event took place. The MacAulay gesture was enough to swing it for Robarts on the last ballot as John and Kelso went down to the wire.

John Parmenter Robarts had won the leadership of the Conservative party and automatically with that he was to become the premier of Ontario. As he walked up to the podium to deliver his acceptance speech, as usual, I was two steps behind him, as the photograph I have from one of the local papers shows.

Robarts and Rohmer, leadership night.

The euphoria was transparent. It was an incredible moment not only for Robarts but also for Jackson, all the London mafia, and those who had joined us from other parts of the province. And, of course, for myself.

Mary-O had taken a substantial part in the convention proceedings. She had stuck with Nora Robarts during all of the days leading up to the balloting. In other words, the Rohmers as a team were totally in support of the Robarts couple. I don't know what time it was that all of us, the Robarts, the Jacksons, and the Rohmers, got back to the Westbury Hotel to have a huge post-victory meal and champagne and whatever else was available. Those two pals, Robarts and Jackson, could drink anybody under the table, and on more than one occasion I, being about two-thirds the size of either one of them, could not keep up. I can clearly recall that at our celebration dinner in John's suite at the Westbury I distinguished myself by knocking over a glass of champagne on the table. I was embarrassed for about two seconds. At least it wasn't red wine. That evening was really the last I saw of Robarts for some time.

The next day John went to attend upon Premier Les Frost. Les gave him a date when he would step down and hand over the leadership to John; on that occasion John would formally become the Prime Minister, or premier, of Ontario and would be so sworn in by the lieutenant-governor of Ontario.

That formality out of the way, John and Nora headed back for London, and I returned to my heavy-duty practice of law in the firm of Rohmer, Cory, Hogg, Morris, Haley and Givertz.

Over the next two years I saw Robarts once, and it was at a party at the then Ports of Call restaurant on Yonge Street just north of the railway overpass south of St. Clair. He was doing extremely well as premier, and my law practice was booming; I was appearing before the Ontario Highway Transport Board and before municipal councils, planning boards, and the Ontario Municipal Board regarding land use.

In 1963, Robarts decided that he should have an elective mandate of his own from the people of Ontario. He called an election. After a hard battle with the Liberal and New Democrat parties, he won the day with a majority.

It was probably a month after Robarts's successful election that I received a telephone call from him inviting me to dinner at the Westbury. John told me he had a proposition he wanted to put to me.

Over dinner John told me that he would like me to consider taking on a special role for him. I would do for Robarts what Alex McKenzie, QC, a senior lawyer, had done for Les Frost during his time as leader and premier. It would be to act as Robarts's total confidant, his organizer on a personal basis, and become involved in everything that the premier was doing as "his man." There would be no pay involved, but Harry Price, the Conservative Party treasurer, would make sure that my expenses were covered. Robarts and I would meet for breakfast two or three times a week at the Westbury to go over the matters that had to be looked after.

When I was doing his business I would operate out of the office next to the premier's own. It was like a dentist's arrangement. From the premier's office, you could walk straight into the second room, which was normally used for meetings. I would have access to his staff for stenographic and research services, that kind of thing.

Needless to say, I was flattered and honoured to be invited and to be so explicitly trusted. I was sure my partners would have no objection to my undertaking that part-time role. There would be no title granted to me. That wasn't necessary, because all the members of John's Cabinet knew me. Once he announced to the Cabinet what I was going to be doing they would certainly all nod their heads knowingly and accept my presence.

So began a three-year association with Robarts as his special advisor and counsel, in which I was to be involved in everything he did. But there was always one line that I did not want to cross, and that was Cabinet. I never at any time attended a Cabinet meeting. Nor was I invited to.

The next morning after our dinner I reported to John in his office, got myself organized in the next door office, and had a long chat with the gentleman who was the deputy minister in the premier's office and had been there some time for Les Frost. His name was Malcolm McIntyre, he was in the range of sixty at the time, and he probably knew that he would not last much longer.

What I found in assessing the premier's office was that fundamentally, except for McIntyre, a fine man by the name of Ray, and a secretary, Robarts had no staff. That's unbelievable when one looks at the size, scope, and scale of the premier's office in the 1970s, 1980s, 1990s, and certainly now where scores of people are employed.

I couldn't believe it!

I immediately hit him with the proposition that he just had to have a civil servant executive assistant to look after his day-to-day administrative affairs to supplement the activities of the deputy minister, old Malcolm McIntyre.

John immediately agreed. After all, one of my jobs was to get him organized and put his office put together properly. He told me that he and Nora were going overseas for two weeks and would I please do whatever had to be done to find the appropriate candidate to do the job.

My first step was to call the chairman of the Civil Service Commission, a man who later became my good friend, Donald Collins.

Donald came to see me in the office next to the premier's. I explained to him what was going on and asked if he would please come up with three candidates to be the executive assistant to the premier. They had to be senior civil servants with excellent backgrounds. When the time came, Donald would have to sit in with me when I interviewed the people he produced. After all, I had no position in the government, and so his presence would be necessary to give my activities some degree of imprimatur.

In due course Donald produced three candidates. After the interviews with each I said, "There's only one man out of that trio." He had an absolutely outstanding war record (RCAF navigator on Mosquitos). He was a Deputy Minister of Lands and Forest, the holder of a PhD. He was courteous, highly intelligent, just the perfect man — if he would accept the offer to move into the premier's office.

Donald did the negotiating with Dr. Keith Reynolds, who somewhat reluctantly agreed that, if the premier approved of his appointment, he would be prepared to leave his senior Natural Resources post to serve as Robarts's executive assistant.

By the time the premier arrived back from the United Kingdom the first major step in reorganizing (or organizing, as the case may be) his office was ready for him to accept or reject.

The rest is history. After meeting Keith Reynolds, Robarts immediately approved of his move. Within a few days Reynolds moved into an office in the premier's complex. So began a close relationship between Robarts and Reynolds, one of loyalty and affection that lasted through the entire life of John Parmenter Robarts.

As my working relationship with Robarts developed, I obtained a long foolscap folder that had no rings but a clamp kind of mechanism, a big black book made in Britain. I filled it with blank lined foolscap notepaper. It was to be my main tool for our working breakfast meetings. In it I would keep a list of the matters that were on the agenda to be done or considered by Robarts. When a matter was completed it would be stroked out. It was not very long until the entire page was filled with items that had to be looked after. A new page would be prepared every week or two weeks. I soon discovered that John was a master procrastinator, particularly when it came to tough matters that had to be decided. If I raised a particular issue he would snort, wave his hand, and say, "We'll deal with that one later." When it came to deciding or not deciding, he had an uncanny ability as to when to put things off, because as the weeks went by the political flavour of the moment would change, and quite often it came to the point where no decision would have to be made.

In any event, that was my organizational job, to keep track of all of the items and matters that Robarts had on his plate, whether it had to do with making policy, making an appointment, or whatever.

I also soon discovered that at breakfast John would often appear still well hungover from the previous night's drinking bout or partying that he had done with his cronies, foremost of whom was the minister from down east in the Kingston area, Jim Auld. Jim was a tall, good-looking, delightful bon vivant, an Army officer during the Second World War, and a very popular man both in his hometown and at Queen's Park.

One of John Robarts's basic problems in those days and right through to the end of his marriage with Nora was that that dear lady would not come to Toronto to live with him during the week. She would stay in London, and John would live at the Westbury. As a result, John, a gregarious, fun-loving, robust man who loved his liquor and a good time, soon found himself out in Toronto with the boys on a regular basis. In fact, all too regular and with far too much booze.

At that time the Toronto press corps protected the premier and did not print stories about his cavorting and partying.

So far as I was concerned I had no idea what he was up to in the evenings, where the parties were, or who was at them. All I knew is that I was regularly confronted with a premier with bloodshot eyes, slightly slurred speech, and hands that twisted each other as he fought off the morning hangover.

Hangover or not, we always got through our business, going down the list item by item, with John giving me instructions as to what he wanted done or not done.

Another problem regarding Nora was that John would go to London for the weekends. In the spring, summer, and fall he and Nora would drive from London on up to their cottage at Grand Bend, where they would spend the weekend drinking and fighting. This activity was to go on for some years during John's premiership until the marriage broke down.

Robarts was always reluctant to be critical of anyone or to confront his Cabinet ministers over some action they had taken or something they had said publicly or anything that did not sit well with Robarts as the premier and the leader of the Progressive Conservative Party in Ontario. So it didn't take very long before one of the functions that I grew into was to be John's messenger. I carried the news to the offending Cabinet minister that the premier was not pleased and would the minister please consider doing so-and-so to rectify the situation or, if worse came to worst, "to keep his goddamn mouth shut!"

The performance of that job was not that difficult. Every Cabinet minister was fully aware of my relationship with Robarts, and so there was never any questioning or challenging of me. The door to every minister was immediately opened at my request. Mind you, there were only a few occasions over a period of three years when I had to do the messenger's job, and I will not provide the names of anyone whom I had to visit in the spirit of communication of the premier's unhappiness with an individual.

I soon discovered the Liberal and NDP opposition members, many of whom I knew from my law practice, were also aware of the nature of my association with Robarts. Vernon Singer, a powerful Liberal member, had been the reeve of North York when I sat on North York Council, so I knew him very well indeed. Jim Renwick of the NDP was a lawyer with whom I had been briefly associated at the law firm of Borden, Elliot when I began my articles back in 1948 and started at Osgoode Hall law school.

On important occasions in the House when the debates were on I would venture in from the government side and sit behind the Speaker's chair just to the right of it where I could see the premier and his Cabinet and all the Conservative members on the east side of the chamber. But even though the opposition members knew that I was in the legislature and knew of my role, not one of them ever raised a challenge to me in the legislature, not for the three years I served Robarts.

Shortly after I joined John Robarts as his special advisor and counsel he suggested that it might be appropriate for me to go to the upcoming federal Conservative conference that was going to be held in Fredericton, New Brunswick.

I travelled to that great city and took part in the entire two-day activities. I have no notes of that event, but one thing sticks out in my mind.

Two Québécois were among the speakers. And when they got up to the microphone they lambasted all those *maudit Anglais* in such a violent way about what the English were doing to their Quebec that everyone was shocked by what we heard. This was a new attitude that none of us had been exposed to before. Frankly, it shook the hell out of us.

The tone of the speeches displayed such animosity, enmity, and belligerence that we really couldn't believe what we were hearing. It was strong stuff. And if it in any way indicated any kind of a general mood and general belief in the province of Quebec, it was a real danger signal for Canada's confederation and for the unity which we had all believed up to that point was solid.

As soon as I got back to Toronto I told Robarts about what had happened. I said that Ontario and the rest of Canada had a real problem with Quebec. There was a complete lack of understanding on the part of English-speaking Canada about what was going on there. He instructed me to put together a plan of action that he and his government could follow in reaching out to the people of Quebec and their premier. About that time John had retained a brilliant young economist, Dr. Ian Macdonald, to be the deputy treasurer of Ontario. With his academic background as a professor, Ian had a broad understanding of national affairs and of politics, including Quebec and what was going on there.

I was quite impressed by young Macdonald. As soon as Robarts gave me the Quebec mandate I collared Ian for lunch at my favourite restaurant, now long gone, the Celebrity Club. I also invited to that luncheon George Hogan of the automobile family, also now long gone. George was a good Conservative political tactician. I thought that among the three of us we could come up with some ideas as to how we might come to grips with this serious new threat out of Quebec; and what we might be able to propose to the premier by way of strategy as well as tactics in reaching out to the people of that province.

At that meeting we decided that we should recommend to the premier that he personally begin a dialogue with the premier of Quebec and with important Progressive Conservative leaders in that province. But Premier Daniel Johnson was to be the principal target. Secondly, we would recommend that there be a formal, high-profile conference organized by the Government of Ontario to which representatives of the Government of Quebec, its premier, and Cabinet ministers would be invited to deal with topics of mutual interest to both sides and, in particular, to have the Quebecers voice their complaints and concerns about their place in the Confederation.

From his new and powerful post as deputy treasurer, Ian Macdonald would lead the organization of such a conference. George and I would be resource persons for Ian.

Robarts accepted our proposal immediately and authorized me and Macdonald to get on with the planning.

The end result was the hugely successful — at least cosmetically — 1967 Confederation for Tomorrow Conference that Robarts convened in Toronto.

CHAPTER 38

Bramalea and Its Beginnings; Kuwait

————◆————

IN OR ABOUT 1964 I was approached by a major British-owned land development company called Bramalea Developments Limited that had acquired massive tracts of land in the rural township of Chinguacousy, which lay to the east of Brampton, straddling Highway 7. The Bramalea group's office was on Dixon Road, south of Number 7, while the offices of the Township of Chinguacousy were located on Highway 10, north of Brampton, in a hamlet called Snelgrove. The Bramalea people wanted to develop a new town on the lands that they had acquired. That was the objective, and ultimately it was fully performed. But in 1964 they had no more than the land itself and the concept.

The corporation was headed by two grand British gentlemen. The head man was Allan Taylor, a huge bear of a man who had been a colonel in the British Army during the Second World War, assertive and a pleasure to work with.

The number two man in the Bramalea organization was Arthur Armstrong, a handsome, mustached person, quite the opposite of Taylor in terms of personality but highly effective, a good negotiator. The two of them complemented each other very well.

Taylor and Armstrong approached me and asked me if I would have lunch with them at the then famous dining room on the main floor of the Royal York, where Louis Janetta held forth as maître d' and emperor. I knew Louis well in his Imperial Room capacity. When Mary-O and I would book for dinner and the show of the celebrity who was performing, such as Ginger Rogers or Peggy Lee, Louis always made sure that we had the best table in the house or, if not the best, then very close to it. Over a lunch well lubricated by martinis, as was the custom in those days, Taylor and Armstrong asked me if I would be prepared to act for them as municipal counsel in the presentation of their plans and proposals for their new town, which they described to me in glowing terms. They had retained one of Canada's foremost land use planners, Norman Pearson, who was at that time also a professor at one of the universities in Ontario. I knew of him and his first-class reputation.

By the time lunch was finished, I agreed to act for them. They were content with a basic retainer that I asked for, and our arrangement was settled.

Over the months and years that I acted for Bramalea I made countless presentations to the council of the township, which was headed by an unusually wily and clever farmer who must have been about sixty at the time by the name of Cyril Clark. I never did any negotiations with him in regard to services, water, sewer, that kind of thing. That was done by either Taylor or Arthur Armstrong. The deputy reeve at the time was a well-known and capable veterinarian by the name of Dr. Williams. There are now roads in the area named for both Clark and Williams.

The presentations made to council were usually in concert with Norman Pearson, as we sought changes in the official plan and zonings and presented subdivision plans for approval while Bramalea started to build in phases. Things went so swimmingly that the Bramalea group decided that it was time to start building their shopping centre. There was a great sod turning event at the site of what is now their enormous commercial centre. The sod turning was actually done with a shovel and then a huge blast of dynamite to get things really moving.

During the long period that I acted for Bramalea, one event stands out in my mind. It was the trip that Allan Taylor and I took to Kuwait to see if we could raise some capital for Bramalea in that tiny Middle East country that was being hugely enriched by its massive oil reserves.

I have to go back in this story to talk about Minister Charlie MacNaughton, a good friend of mine whom I had first encountered during the Robarts leadership campaign in 1961. Charlie MacNaughton was a lad from Exeter, Ontario, a protegé of the great Conservative guru Elmer Bell, QC, of the same place.

When I joined John Robarts as his special counsel in 1963, it was at that same time that Robarts appointed Charlie to be Minister of Transport for Ontario. I spent quite a bit of time with Charlie as he made his transition into the portfolio and, in fact, went with him for his first visit to the Ministry of Transport offices at Keele and Wilson. It was the day that he took possession of the minister's office and had his first session with outstanding, capable Deputy Minister Cam McNab. I later had the privilege of input in solving the question of what to do with the land and building owners on each side of 401 who were regularly raising hell about being damaged by this new highway that was being built. The solution was to offer each of them within a limited range of the highway an option: the government would buy them out at an independent fair market appraisal or they could stay in place. The next idea was to put in sight and sound barriers in those areas where 401 went through residential sectors.

In 1964, Charlie MacNaughton, with others in the Cabinet, did a "world tour." When they arrived in Beirut, a wealthy Lebanese entrepreneur was lying in wait for Charlie at a meeting with him and he proposed the setting up of a bank (I think the name was Intra Bank) in Ontario using emerging Middle Eastern money. Charlie was impressed by the people who had approached him but wanted somehow to check out their credibility and substance. Upon his return to Toronto, he and Robarts (with my concurrence) decided that I should go to Beirut to meet with this gentleman to check out his background. In fact, I was in New York City en route to Beirut when that huge, famous, pregnancy-causing blackout of electricity occurred there. Nevertheless I made it to Beirut, where I met and had many discussions with the man who had approached Charlie. Through him I met a wealthy Kuwaiti by the name of Sheik Abdul Rahman, a handsome, mustached man with jet black hair whose visage reminded me of Roly Michener's.

I reported back to Robarts and MacNaughton that to the best of my investigation the Beirut connection was substantial and credible.

Later, when I had been acting for Bramalea for some time, Allan Taylor decided that Bramalea would like to get some fresh capital into its coffers, the better to finance the substantial costs of putting in its road and water and sewer and other services. Perhaps the gentleman in Kuwait that I had told him about might provide a source for Bramalea.

It was decided by Allan Taylor that he and I should travel to Kuwait to meet with Sheik Rahman. Through my Beirut connection I made an appointment to meet with the sheik. Off Allan Taylor and I went on our great Middle East adventure, stopping first in London, England, where Allan had arranged a suite at the premier Dorchester Hotel, probably the most elegant and expensive in its day. I can recall Allan in the dining room of the Dorchester when the waiter wasn't paying enough attention to him. He simply lifted up his napkin at arm's length above him and waved the napkin until the poor waiter finally appeared. If nothing else, Allan Taylor was a free-spending person who liked and insisted on doing everything first class. It was difficult to keep up with him, since I was about half his size. It was sort of reminiscent of Robarts and Jackson when I got in the middle of one of their drinking sessions. No way I could keep up.

We stopped in Beirut for two days and managed to find the superb casino that was in operation to the north of the city. It had the most elegant, sensational floor show on its stage: elephants, horses, gorgeous girls from Europe dancing, that sort of thing. Then it was reluctantly on to Kuwait, where we met with Sheik Rahman. He received us courteously and introduced us to various of his colleagues who might be interested in investing in land development in that faraway place called Canada. They were interested but would have to do some strong investigation into the financing of Bramalea and the plans we had brought with us for its development.

We left Kuwait with not even a promise but with some expectation of possible success. The flight from Kuwait back to Beirut was the first and only time in my life that I suffered a sensation called claustrophobia. We were in a British Comet jet liner, a relatively small passenger aircraft that eventually wound up having several of them disintegrate in mid-air. Back in Beirut we had to attend the casino once again, at least that was Allan Taylor's mandate. After another stop at London, at the Dorchester, we managed to make our way back to Toronto.

Unfortunately, the trip to Kuwait did not produce any investment money for Bramalea, but that is not to say that the adventure was not worthwhile.

My time with Bramalea, as with my time with CHUM as counsel, began to finish when I began to concentrate almost all my time on the creation, organization, and execution of my Mid-Canada Development Corridor Conference in the late 1960s.

I am pleased to have had some substantial part in the beginning of Bramalea and getting it approved and its construction underway with the plans covering all of the area that was to be developed. As a community, Bramalea is now part of the city of Brampton, made huge with its massive inflow of population over the last four or more decades.

CHAPTER 39
Patents and the MiniStation

———◆———

T HIS IS A STORY ABOUT one of the inventions for which I have received patents.

The most practical and reasonably successful idea was the concept of the MiniStation. It had its beginnings in my roots as a gasoline service station attendant working for my father.

I had worked on his various service stations from the time I was about eleven, almost always in the summer months. By the time we were living in Fort Erie and I was sixteen I had managed his station in Fort Erie, and then he assigned me to manage his service station at Stamford, Ontario.

Suffice to say that with my family background in the service station business I knew how and why service stations existed. In the middle sixties I realized that there were many urban sites where gasoline service stations could be located temporarily while vacant land was being held for later development. This was particularly so in the centre of Toronto.

I reasoned that if one could come up with a concept whereby both the tanks holding the fuel and the building holding the pumps and the office and toilets could be easily removed as well as easily installed, then there would be a market for it. A moveable service station was something that did not exist at the time and for that matter still doesn't. The first thing I put together mentally was a vertical tank, as opposed to the normal horizontal gasoline tank that you see going into the ground.

If I could make a vertical tank then I could use a huge drill to make the hole into which I would then lower the tank. I would then put a plate on it to hold it down to prevent it from rising by the lift of ground water. Lo and behold I would have my tank installed. When it came time to move it, I would uncover the plate, lift it off, then haul the tank straight out of the ground to be moved to its next location.

I had drawings made and filed an application for the tank patent and eventually received it.

The next thing was to design a portable building complete with the gasoline pumps on it and the toilets, storage, the whole bit. I approached the splendid architectural firm of Crang and Boake, then the prominent Canadian architects. Both Jim Crang and George Boake got involved and produced a superb design while I took out another patent, this time on the features of the building and structure that would make the unit liftable and portable.

The MiniStation.

Then I had to get a trademark and corporation to handle this portable service station. The trademark was MiniStation. It can be seen on the photograph of the unit.

Then I did a deal with Roy Dunlop of Shell to install the first unit. This was done at the southeast corner of Thorncliffe Road and Don Mills Road. The unit went in and started operation in the summer of 1964. It was John Wiggins, later president and originator of Creemore Springs Brewery, and a commercial artist and watercolour painter as well, who designed the trademark of MiniStation for me. The second

MiniStation unit was also a Shell installation at the northwest corner of Front and Simcoe Streets in Toronto.

Even though the MiniStation was a success technically, I could never get Shell to build any more, nor could I flog the MiniStation to any other oil company. The rental to Shell of both the units was sufficient over a period of years to pay out the cost of development. But after about ten years of operation both units disappeared, the one at Don Mills and Thorncliffe to a redevelopment into a permanent site, which is still going strong. The one at Front and Simcoe gave way to the creation of a massive office building that now sits on its land.

The MiniStation almost made it, but not quite.

CHAPTER 40
The McMichael Art Gallery

————◆————

T HE STORY OF THE McMICHAEL Art Gallery begins on a TTC subway train in 1965.

I was on a Yonge Street TTC subway train one morning on my way
to my downtown office when a handsome young lawyer whom I had
known for some time came and sat beside me. It was Patrick Hartt, later
Mr. Justice Hartt of the Supreme Court of Ontario, chair of various
Royal Commissions and an outstanding Canadian. At that time he was
just Patrick Hartt, lawyer. Patrick obviously knew that I had an association with Premier Robarts. He told me that he had clients by the name
of Robert and Signe McMichael who had accumulated a large collection
of Canadian art. They had put together an art gallery at their home in
Kleinburg. What they wanted to do was to donate the entire art collection and the art gallery in which it sat to the Government of Ontario,
but there was no mechanism in place for the government to accept such
a gift. Patrick had found that it couldn't be achieved, notwithstanding
the high value of his clients' collection and of their land. Could anything
be done about the situation? Patrick's credibility with me was quite
high. As I recall he was then practising with Arthur Martin, QC, who
was one of the great criminal lawyers of Canada.

Patrick suggested that if I were interested in seeing the McMichaels'
collection, he would make all the necessary arrangements. I told him on
the TTC train that, yes, I would be willing to see what his clients had,
and if I thought it was a worthwhile project, I would then raise it with
Premier John Robarts.

A few days later I went to the McMichaels' residence and gallery at
Kleinburg, met the McMichaels, and viewed their collection of Canadian

art, principally paintings. I was much impressed by what I saw, by the structure of the gallery itself, and by the comfortable residence of the McMichaels, who appeared to be quite wealthy. I told them that I would be prepared to recommend to Premier Robarts that he should come out and see what was there. I acknowledged that there was no existing mechanism for a gift at that point, but the premier was creative, and as a lawyer I felt that something could be constructed if Robarts gave me directions.

I met with the premier the next morning for breakfast. I recommended a visit to the McMichaels, and he agreed.

A few days later the two of us went to Kleinburg with John's driver, Bill, at the wheel of the premier's car, John sitting in the front seat as was his normal practice. John was favourably impressed by the McMichaels themselves and particularly by the huge collection of Canadian art they had put together. Then we drove back to Toronto. John had made his decision, and on the way back, we discussed how the Government of Ontario could do a deal with the McMichaels.

I then asked Deputy Attorney General Rendall Dick, a classmate of mine, to develop an agreement, a form of mechanism whereby the Government of Ontario would accept the McMichaels' gift of paintings and the gallery itself and their home and land at Kleinburg. The intent was that the whole of their holdings at Kleinburg would be in the package, that there should be an independent appraisal of the value. There would be certain stipulations by the McMichaels, conditions as to the type of art that would be acquired by the organization that would be created to receive the gift and maintain and operate it. It followed that the name would be The McMichael Art Gallery at Kleinburg.

Premier Robarts had given the green light. As was his custom, he left it to me to put the entire package together then bring it to him for his final approval.

In the next two or three weeks I talked extensively with the McMichaels to sort out the conditions that they wanted to impose when the gift was put together. Some were acceptable, some were not. Rendall Dick and his people prepared the first draft of the intended agreement. I have that draft, and my amendments in my vertical handwriting are all over the document.

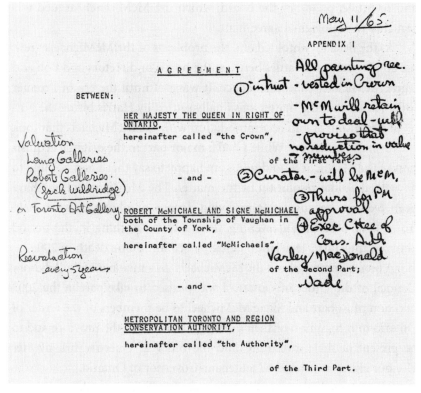

*Draft title page (with my notes) from the 1965 agreement
I organized between the Province of Ontario, Robert and
Signe McMichael, and the Metropolitan Toronto and Region
Conservation Authority whereby the McMichaels gave their land
and collection of Group of Seven paintings to the province.*

In any event, the deal was finally done, and the McMichael Art Gallery became a possession of the Government of Ontario. At that point, all was sweetness and light, and everyone was completely happy with this result.

The section of the agreement that would provide the basis for an enormous amount of controversy had to do with the control of the acquisitions that were being made by the new board of directors and the power of the McMichaels to block decisions made by the new board. The McMichaels later had concerns about loss of control of the board and the artistic direction of the McMichael Art Gallery. There had been what the McMichaels considered to be a complete change of acquisition and retention policy by the board, which the McMichaels argued was contrary to the original agreement.

As the decades unfolded and the problems of the McMichaels grew, the controversy and battles between the board of directors and Bob and Signe McMichael continued apace. It was not until the era of Premier Mike Harris that the matter was finally settled by Harris biting the bullet and working out an accommodation with the McMichaels that took the form of legislation. While I had a major part in the original acquisition of the McMichael holdings, I am happy to say that I had nothing to do with the final resolution of the matter. The McMichaels must have been pleased, because after receiving dozens of phone calls for help from them over the intervening years I heard nothing in the period between the Harris legislation being passed and Bob's death in 2003.

A final comment about the McMichaels. As a member of the Advisory Council of the Order of Ontario I was pleased to take part in the 2002 selection of Robert and Signe McMichael to be members of the Order of Ontario in recognition of their great contribution to the province and to be present at their investiture into the order at Queen's Park by Her Honour Hilary Weston, the Lieutenant-Governor of Ontario.

Also I was privileged to be an honorary pallbearer — along with my distinguished acquaintance Pierre Berton — at the funeral of Robert McMichael when he was buried on the grounds of his and Signe's beloved estate.

CHAPTER 41

Origins of the Ontario Science Centre

———◆———

IT WAS THE THURSDAY EVENING before the August 1965 opening of the Canadian National Exhibition, the everlasting CNE. John Robarts had agreed to open the Ontario building, which had just been renovated and was all dolled up. I agreed to go with him for this wonderful event and then have dinner at the Westbury afterwards.

He was running a Cabinet meeting and had decided that he would leave for the CNE at about five o'clock. I waited in his car with Bill the driver under the porte cochère at the east side of the legislature building.

Eventually Robarts appeared through the huge doors, clumped down the steps, and got into the passenger seat next to Bill.

As soon as he got in, it was clear that he was agitated and angry, judging from the salty, naval expletives that he was emitting.

"What's the problem, John?" I asked.

His answer went something like this: "My problem's Jimmy Auld, goddamnit. I gave the press a firm commitment that I would tell them what the Centennial Project is going to be and I promised them without fail — we've put it off several times now — I promised that I would do that a week from next Monday. Everything was supposed to be ready by today, the location picked, architects selected, drawings underway, the whole nine yards. It's Auld's responsibility and he tells me this afternoon that nothing's ready! Nothing, goddamnit!"

"What's the project supposed to be?"

"A science centre. We've had a whole bunch of sites examined. There's a whole book full of them."

"Has Auld got the book?"

"He has, and that's all he's got. And I have to face the press a week from Monday, and I can't put it off again, I just can't!"

"John, leave it to me. I know what has to be done. I'll get the book from Jimmy's office in the morning and I'll start from there."

"Do it!"

The next morning at nine o'clock I was at Auld's office. We called him Uncle Jimmy. I was given the book, which I immediately took to the office I used beside John's main office.

When I settled in, I went through all the locations researched in the book, such as the CNE and spots to the north, east, and west of Toronto. But there was one location that jumped right out at me. It was a vast tract of land located in the centre of what had been my ward when I sat on North York Council in 1957 and 1958. It was across the road from Flemingdon Park, where I had done all of the municipal zoning work for several years. I knew the whole area very well indeed. The Don Valley Parkway was half a mile to the east. The intersection of Eglinton and Don Mills Road where the property was located at the southwest quadrant would provide perfect traffic access.

In my opinion that was without question the best location.

On the other hand, the site had a couple of major problems. The first was that the land sloped drastically down to the west into the Don Valley where the west branch of the Don River flowed through it. So there was a contour problem with trying to put a building on it. On top of that, the almighty Metro Toronto Conservation Authority, the child of Hurricane Hazel, had put a ban on any construction in the Don Valley. The second problem was ownership of the land. I wasn't certain, but I thought that the land would be owned by Metro Toronto or by the Conservation Authority or by an estate. Somehow the ownership question could be resolved. The main thing was that the land was vacant and not built on except for an old farmhouse on Don Mills Road.

A couple of quick telephone calls to the office of the Metropolitan Toronto chairman, Bill Allan, sorted out the ownership question. It was in the hands of Metro Toronto. I then made an appointment for Monday to attend on Bill Allan to open the door with him on the matter of a conveyance to the provincial government. But first things first. I had to have architects and a land use planner.

It was Friday morning, the day after the new Robarts assignment was hastily born. The deadline was one week from the next Monday when the premier was to give a press conference to announce the province's Centennial Project.

I telephoned Ray Connell, the Minister of Public Works, told him what I was doing, and asked if he could have his deputy minister retain two firms of architects and have them at his office at two in the afternoon that same day. Ray agreed that it could and would be done. I told him that I did not care who the architects were but that the land use planner should be Project Planning Associates headed up by Macklin Hancock, whom I regarded as the best use land use planner in North America. I had worked with him closely in the development of Flemingdon Park.

I arrived at Ray Connell's office shortly before two and went over the project with him and his deputy minister. In his conference room the three of us met the architects. One was Raymond Moriyama. The other was a representative of a well-known and respected Toronto firm.

I explained that I was acting as a special counsel to the premier of Ontario and that the Centennial Project was to be a science centre. By this time I had documentation from the Cabinet office that explained in some detail what the concept of the science centre was to be in terms of its function and scope and scale.

I presented the site to them and the material in the report that I had obtained from Jimmy Auld's office, which fortunately contained some basic topographical drawings that showed the property's dramatic slope down the west side of the Don Valley.

Words of concern were spoken by the architects in relation to the position of the Metro Toronto Conservation Authority. My response was that that was an issue that would have to be left to me. I then told them I wanted schematic drawings of a science centre building that would flow down the slope of the valley from Don Mills Road and Eglinton, and that the architects would work with a representative of Project Planning. By this time I knew that it would be Walter Mayer, who would be coming to be briefed after the architects were finished.

I then said the drawings had to be in my hands in seven days, one week from that morning. I had to have them by that day at the latest so that I could then prepare, write, and produce the text and drawings for the premier's press conference, which would take place on Monday at ten o'clock at Queen's Park.

The response of the architects was that there was no way that they could do that in such a short time, at which point I told them in no uncertain terms that if they wanted to do this project they would have to have something to me by Friday or I would have no alternative but to find architects that day who would do it. That settled the matter. With great reluctance they agreed to undertake the project.

Then they were out the door. There was no time to waste.

The next appointment for the three of us was with Walter Mayer of Project Planning Associates. I went through a similar routine with Walter, told him who the architects were, and then told him of the time frame of drawings by the following Friday. Walter's response was the same as the architects. It couldn't be done, there was too much studying to be undertaken. Not possible. By the time our meeting with Walter was finished he had agreed.

On Monday my meeting with Bill Allan was successful. Bill said that the province could have the land. Not a problem as far as he was concerned, but I would have to deal with the Metro Toronto Conservation Authority, and that would be a tough nut to crack. They would have to give permission for whatever we wanted to do on the land. And with Hurricane Hazel still looming large in everyone's mind, Bill predicted that I would have a tough time.

I was immediately on the telephone to my North York friend Ross Lord, the chairman of the Metro Toronto Conservation Authority. I told him what was on and asked him if I could have an emergency meeting with the full Conservation Authority as soon as possible. Ross immediately obliged and structured the meeting for ten o'clock on the Wednesday. It would take place at the then headquarters of the Conservation Authority in an old house in Hogg's Hollow on the street just to the east of the Jolly Miller. On the Wednesday before I left for Hogg's Hollow, Robarts and I had our usual breakfast at the Westbury. I told him exactly what was going on. We then went to his office at Queen's Park. As I left him to go to this important meeting he said, "You know what to tell them if they give you a hard time." I replied, "I sure do." By that he meant, "Tell them that if they don't grant permission the government will enact legislation taking the land out of their control."

At the Conservation Authority's office I was met by Ross Lord. Had a brief chat with him and then was shown into the conference room, where it appeared to me all the members of the authority were present, including staff. Ross introduced me. I then made my pitch, asking them to keep in total confidence the material I was going to place before them. The only person who gave me a hard time was Charles Sirois, a dedicated, senior ultra-conservationist. But when the matter finally came to a vote it was unanimous to grant permission for the project, provided it was undertaken in complete co-operation with the Conservation Authority and that there would be no structures on the floor of the Don Valley.

So now I had the land and the Conservation Authority's blessing. All during that week there were pressing telephone calls made by me to the architects and to Project Planning. It was apparent that the architects had decided that Moriyama would be the lead person in the conceptual phase. I did not know it then, but Moriyama was on the threshold of becoming one of the world's foremost architects, a truly brilliant designer.

On the Friday, as required, Raymond Moriyama and Project Planning delivered their drawings to the Minister of Public Works at his office, where I was waiting to gather them up and begin to go to work.

I can tell you I was delighted with what I saw from both. They had obviously collaborated and worked well together. And Moriyama's design of linked pods on the side of the valley was just superb.

I spent the weekend writing the press release and having the drawings copied and set up on briefing boards. They were also reduced so that they would fit into the press package.

By the time John Robarts arrived in his office on the Monday morning, the entire presentation was ready. At ten o'clock he strode into the press briefing room and made his detailed announcement, with text and drawings, as to the Government of Ontario's Centennial Project, the Ontario Science Centre at Eglinton and Don Mills Road in the Town of North York. I have to add that when the Ontario Science

Centre was built it was almost an exact duplicate in design of the draw-ings that Moriyama had produced. It was a brilliant achievement by the young architect.

I did not attend the press conference, nor was I invited to attend at the opening of the Ontario Science Centre.

CHAPTER 42
The Start of GO Transit

———◆———

THERE HAVE BEEN SEVERAL VERSIONS as to how GO Transit got started. None of them tell the story of its true origins.

GO Transit was developed from a concept created by John Robarts and Minister of Highways Charlie MacNaughton, with a little bit of my own ideas thrown into the discussions. The concept was developed from a recognized need to create a system whereby we could get as many cars as possible off the Queen Elizabeth Way, which by 1964 was already becoming congested. We could see the possibility of using for public transit the rail system from Hamilton across to Oshawa. It parallelled the Queen Elizabeth Way on the west side of Toronto and what was developing into the 401 Highway proceeding easterly.

The question was, how could we create a system that utilized the existing rail structure? The CNR would be the best organization to approach to look at the feasibility of such a service and, of course, its cost. The decision to talk to the CNR was made by Robarts and MacNaughton.

The next step was to find an expert to advise us in approaching the railway people. My suggestion was Frank Turville, a former football player and a practising lawyer retired from either the CNR or the CPR. He had spent a career handling rail legal matters. I called Frank Turville and set up a luncheon meeting with him at his club, the National Club on Bay Street.

Charlie MacNaughton and I had that opening meeting with Frank. We outlined the concept of the rail transit system, which would start in Hamilton and make frequent stops all the way into Union Station, doing the same thing between Oshawa and Union.

Turville thought that the idea had a lot of merit and that the CNR, which owned the tracks, would respond positively. It would take a lot of time and negotiations to work out the details.

There was no need for me to participate in the negotiations with the CNR. Frank Turville and Charlie MacNaughton and his team sorted that out very well. Months later, in May 1967, Robarts, MacNaughton, and I ceremonially rode on the first GO Transit train. The service was truly inaugurated. As in today's time, the main east-west GO Transit rail system is operated by the CNR under agreements with the Government of Ontario, with other spurs in deals with the CPR.

From the modest beginnings the GO system has grown into a network of trains and buses that brings commuters from the west, the northeast, the northwest, and the east into the centre of Toronto and keeps cars off Ontario's highways by the tens of thousands.

CHAPTER 43
John George Diefenbaker

———◆———

I HAD NEVER MET JOHN GEORGE Diefenbaker, but in the early 1960s, as a member of the Don Mills Progressive Conservative Association, I had been one of those who had vocally and loudly taken the position that it was time to dump Dief. Believe me, I wasn't alone in that line of thinking. Whether my public opinions reached the attention of the old boy I'll never know, but I'm quite sure that they were known by his immediate staff. That factor is relevant in the upcoming story of the Great Train Ride of the National Election Campaign of 1965. When that event got underway I had no connection whatever with the campaign. I was running my large law practice at 728 Bay Street and was treasurer of Civitan International. At the same time, I was functioning as John Robarts's éminence grise. Each of these activities took up an enormous amount of time.

It was no surprise that a particular power-hungry Toronto lawyer was the central figure in the campaign organization of John George Diefenbaker in 1965. He knew that Robarts really didn't like Diefenbaker. As the campaign wore on, Robarts was clearly sitting on his hands in terms of saying anything positive about the federal Conservative leader. How to get Robarts on side? That was the question for Diefenbaker's organizer.

The answer was that if he could get me involved in the Diefenbaker campaign, I could then persuade Robarts to publicly get behind the old boy, perhaps even appear on the speech platform with him. The master plotter made his move, and I fell for it hook, line, and sinker.

I was somewhere in the United States on Civitan business when I got call from Robarts's secretary at Queen's Park saying that a telegram had arrived for me from Diefenbaker. The gist of the message was that

Diefenbaker invited me to join his campaign train for the purpose of writing policy suggestions that he could use in his speeches. I was in those days a policy buff, my greatest success being the development of the paper known as "Design for Development," which Robarts adopted and put forward in the legislature. It became the basis for regional planning and government from that point forward.

Let me tell you, I looked on that invitation as a wonderful challenge. I thought I could join the Diefenbaker train and churn out all kinds of policy ideas that Diefenbaker could use that would turn the campaign around and absolutely ensure his success and return as the Prime Minister of Canada. What delusion! As soon as I arrived back in Toronto, I went to Robarts to talk about the Diefenbaker invitation. John's reaction was simple: "You're out of your goddamn mind. But if you want to do it, go ahead!" I was out of my mind. I went for it.

Diefenbaker's campaign train was in Toronto. It would head east into the Maritimes, return to Ontario, then go up through to the Owen Sound area and back down to London. It looked like about a ten-day haul. Mary-O and I were living in our Sandringham Drive house in Toronto at the time. She drove me down to the train to see me off and to meet Olive and John Diefenbaker. Quite an experience.

Arriving at the train, which was in the yard near Union Station, we were ushered into the presence of Mr. and Mrs. Diefenbaker in the comfortable dining area of their special car with its "wave to the crowd" and speaking platform. The Diefenbakers received us courteously, but he was quite stiff, his body language and attitude clearly indicating that he really didn't know why I was getting on the train. I was an intruder, but the advice from his manipulator/organizer clearly must have been that Diefenbaker had to tolerate me. It was soon obvious I was not going to be part of his inner circle, which was led by Tom Van Dusen and a commanding major-domo secretary, Marjorie Le Breton.

After that audience, Mary-O departed. I was shown to a compartment that would be my residence and workroom for the next ten days. It was on another car in the train because John and Olive Diefenbaker had to have their own car all to themselves. Fortunately for me, the car in which I was lodged was filled with young journalists, including the highly talented Martin Goodman of the *Star*, Ron Collister, and others.

As the train rolled eastward it soon became evident that I was an unwelcome commodity so far as Diefenbaker's staff were concerned. This was particularly so when it came to Marjorie Le Breton, who regarded me as some sort of Toronto interloper. Le Breton took an instant dislike to me, a quality that has lasted to this day. It was mutual. She was particularly effective against me during her time as appointments person for Prime Minister Brian Mulroney before he appointed her to the Senate, an example of why the Senate should be abolished.

As the train moved east, I very quickly started to work manufacturing policy suggestions, one per sheet of paper, which were then typed out and (as I believed) eventually given to Diefenbaker for consideration and potential use in the next speech.

As to speeches, the old boy had a particular mode of action. He would take a sheaf of papers with him to the platform. Ostensibly these were the notes for his speech. He would put them under his chair as he sat through the preliminaries. When he was introduced, he would pick up the pile of papers, go to the podium, and start to speak with the papers on the lectern in front of him. Watching him perform at gatherings as we moved toward the Maritimes, it became apparent that, even though he had the top journalists of the country captured in his audience and on his train, Diefenbaker never said anything new. He announced no new policies, no new ideas, no new suggestions as to how to run or improve the country. It was the same stuff day after day and night after night. As for my productions, there was no reference to anything, no discussion with me about them. I was becoming frustrated to say the least.

By the time we got to Charlottetown, I decided I would buy some pink notepaper. I would have my policy pieces typed on that bright stuff. In that way I would know whether I had anything in the pile of papers that he was taking to the platform. Never once did I spot a sheet of pink paper in his collection.

By this time I was testing my ideas on Martin Goodman, Collister, and others and getting good responses from them as to the substance and credibility of what I was giving to Diefenbaker. But would he use any of it? No way.

Finally, from some remote railway platform in the Maritimes, I called Senator David Walker, Diefenbaker's closest Ontario ally. I vent-ed my anger and frustration and told him I really had to get off the train. My being there was a terrible waste of time. But the senator persuaded me to stay and keep trying.

It was at this stage of the game that I first met a young, slim Maritime newspaper journalist who was later to become a close pal of mine and a national television fixture, Mike Duffy.

Eventually the train headed west back into Ontario. Mary-O joined me at Toronto as we swung north into the Owen Sound area and then back south to London.

I had talked to Robarts several times during the course of the tour. He was fully aware of what I was going through. He could have said "I told you so," but, kind soul that he was, he refrained from doing that. It had been arranged that he and Charlie MacNaughton would meet the train when it arrived in the late evening at London. I can clearly remember getting off the train, standing on the gravel well outside the station, watching Robarts and MacNaughton walking toward me, and my words of greeting: "God, am I ever glad to see you guys!"

Robarts and MacNaughton had a cordial but cool meeting with Diefenbaker and wished him well. Then all of us, including Mary-O, left the train. John Robarts could never bring himself to support Diefenbaker, and I made absolutely no effort to persuade him to do so.

The one highlight for me of that ten-day tour of agony was an event in Ottawa where I accompanied Diefenbaker to an interview at one of the local television stations. We were driven in the automobile of one of Diefenbaker's supporters. In the back seat the old boy decided he would tell me about his confrontation with John F. Kennedy in which Diefenbaker found something that Kennedy had written on a piece of paper and discarded. What had been written on the piece of paper was totally derogatory toward Diefenbaker. The old boy was still upset about that one. By the time we arrived at the television station he was showing signs of fatigue, literally drooping. But as soon as he got into interview mode and the questions were being put to him he straightened up, eyes flashing, jowls shaking. The old trial lawyer was doing what he did best. He was performing for an audience.

John Diefenbaker knew that I was a most unhappy camper. Some years later he was on an airplane and sitting next to Tom Smith, then an

Imperial Oil executive, who had been associated with me in the naval reserve as the senior naval reserve advisor when I was Chief of Reserves. Somehow Smith and Diefenbaker started talking, and eventually Smith got around to mentioning my name and our association. At that point Diefenbaker wanted to know if I was still mad at him. I'm not sure what Tom Smith's answer was, but it should have been "yes."

CHAPTER 44
The Creation of the Ontario Flag

———◆———

I T WAS THE TIME OF the furor over the creation of the new Canadian flag.

John George Diefenbaker stood for the Red Ensign being adapted in some way or another to be the Canadian flag. He fulminated, of course, against the ultimate design put forward by the Liberals. Robarts was very much aware of all the flag activity going on in Ottawa.

On top of that, as a wartime Royal Canadian Navy officer, Robarts had his own attraction to the Red Ensign, which flew on the stern of all Royal Canadian Navy and Royal Navy ships. It was over dinner one evening at the Westbury, just the two of us, that we began to kick around the concept of Ontario having its own official flag. Why not? And why not use the Red Ensign as the basic flag and put some sort of an Ontario crest on the fly? Why not? We would meet in John's office again in the morning and see what we could do with the idea.

As agreed, we met in John's office with Malcolm MacIntyre, still his deputy minister, present. As requested, MacIntyre had a Red Ensign in hand. He also had large copies of the several available Ontario coats of arms that were in use at the time, such as those with moose and deer standing rampant, with beavers, maple leaves, and all that sort of thing.

After much discussion, John Robarts made up his mind. It would be that one that looked like a shield with maple leaves and the red cross on white and the crown on top.

It was settled. He instructed MacIntyre to consult with the necessary authorities to make sure that what was going on was legal and to have the design properly prepared, applications made to wherever they had to be made (possibly to some herald in England), arrangements made to have the appropriate proclamations created, and a date set up for a grand ceremony.

All of which was done in due course. The declaration was duly made by the lieutenant-governor. The Ontario flag was officially promulgated, and it flies everywhere throughout Ontario today thanks to John Parmenter Robarts. I had in my possession for many years, and I may still have, what is considered to be the first Ontario flag to be flown over Queen's Park.

CHAPTER 45
The Police Bill

———◆———

T HE EMERGENCE AND THE HANDLING of the so-called Police Bill was the most difficult time of my period with John Robarts as his special advisor.

It was a Thursday in March 1964. At Cabinet the day before Attorney General Fred Cass, hard-driving, determined, and, yes, opinionated, from a wonderful eastern Ontario riding, had put a police bill before Cabinet which no one really paid attention to in terms of vetting what it actually said. Cass then went public, criticizing his own bill as giving too much power to the police.

What it did was to give the police forces of Ontario enormous and intrusive new powers. The press picked up the Police Bill on the Thursday, and their front pages and editorials were unanimous. They mounted a horrendous attack against the government, accusing the Conservatives of taking the province into a police state.

By Friday morning the crisis was on. It was an enormous political blunder that seemed to come out of nowhere.

From that Friday morning until the next Tuesday I was with John the whole time except for my return in the middle of the night to my home at Sandringham Drive and the comfort of Mary-O and my daughters.

The decision was ultimately made over the weekend to meet the situation head-on. John would make an exculpatory statement in the legislature. A sort of *mea culpa*, "I am responsible" statement. He would withdraw the bill as being totally unacceptable in our democratic society. When the legislature met on the Monday, the House was packed, as were the galleries. I took my usual seat behind the Speaker's chair to the right so I could see the entire Progressive Conservative benches with Robarts front and centre flanked by his Cabinet ministers.

The debate on the Police Services bill opened with Robarts making an extensive statement. As soon as he was finished, he was immediately under attack by the NDP and the Liberal front-benchers. Then to everyone's, and certainly my, astonishment, a Conservative backbencher directly behind the premier in the back row stood up and began an attack on his own government and on the premier. It was unbelievable that Allan Lawrence, QC, would do such a thing, but he did — to John Robarts's great disappointment and hurt.

Finally, the Cass Police Bill was disposed of by its withdrawal by Robarts.

So closely was I emotionally associated with this event that I developed what I thought was a stomach ulcer. Certainly I had pains for quite a period of time that I directly attributed to the stress of that event.

I felt so bad about what had happened to Robarts that I sat down and wrote a history of the event and what was in effect an apology to him for not having performed better on his behalf.

Let me say this about Fred Cass. He was a highly principled and most honourable gentleman. He had a good war record. He was valiant, and obviously he had great faith in the police, both the OPP and municipal who served our communities in those days. Somehow the consequences of his proposed legislation drafted by whoever seemed to have totally avoided him and his premier and the entire Cabinet. Fred Cass resigned over this fiasco.

As for Allan Lawrence, Robarts was a remarkably forgiving soul, soft-hearted in the extreme. Later down the road, Robarts was to make Allan Lawrence a minister. At that point, all was forgiven but not necessarily forgotten.

When the Police Bill crisis broke on the Friday, Robarts did what he often did. He needed advice. The instruction to me was to "find Les," his predecessor, the distinguished Les Frost, whose experience and wisdom Robarts could rely upon. Les immediately came to Toronto and was there for John and consulted with him during the whole of the Police Bill matter.

Les was also available during the British Trust Corporation collapse when the great fear of Robarts and his team was that the financial status of the British Trust would cause a run not only on that trust company but also on other financial institutions.

After Robarts handed over the premiership to Bill Davis, it was one of John's ongoing disappointments that in the event of a crisis, no matter what, Bill Davis would never call on him for advice or counsel. So far as Robarts could see, Davis had put out the word that he was now the premier and his team was in place and he didn't want any interference from Robarts or his old boys' network. That hurt Robarts very much.

On the other hand, when it came time in the mid-seventies to create a new Royal Commission to examine Metropolitan Toronto, Davis accepted the strong recommendation of his then treasurer, D'Arcy McKeough, to appoint Robarts as the one-man commission (I was counsel to Robarts's commission). That happened in about 1974. But beyond that move, Bill Davis's position so long as he was premier was that Robarts would not be asked for advice. Bill Davis may quarrel with these words, but that's the way it was from Robarts's perspective.

CHAPTER 46

Design for Development, Donald Fleming, and My Federal Candidacy

A T THE TIME I JOINED Robarts in 1963 I was heavily involved in land use and land development for many clients and also in matters before the Ontario Highway Transport Board. Having served on the council of the Township of North York and having been active in the Progressive Conservative party both provincially and federally out of the Don Mills sector, I was aware of how municipalities that abutted each other dealt with each other always at arm's length and usually confrontationally. That was particularly so when it came to the matter of providing one another with the basic services such as water and sewage disposal, particularly in the booming areas around Toronto. Having experience in all those matters, I was concerned that the Ontario government did not have a philosophy or policy statement that would give guidance to both municipalities and land developers as to the coordinated handling of the growth that was going on.

After extensive discussions with the Honourable Stan Randall, who was then the Minister of Economics, and Deputy Treasurer Ian Macdonald, I set about writing a policy paper that I named "Design for Development."

When it was ready and both Randall and Macdonald had given it their basic approval, I gave the paper to John Robarts with the recommendation that if he thought it suitable, it could be promulgated by him in the House as the basic philosophy of the government for the future orderly development of Ontario.

I'm not sure that John really comprehended the substance of the paper or what its consequences might be, but nevertheless he did it. On Tuesday April 6, 1966, (I was sitting in my usual place behind the

Speaker's chair) John presented "Design for Development" to the House and tabled the report as government policy.

A brief summary of "Design for Development" is given in Appendix I.

The principles set out in "Design for Development" are the genesis of what are now known as regional governments in Ontario. It was also the conceptual beginning of a comprehensive regional development plan including greenbelts for virtually the whole of southwestern Ontario. An economist from the United States was later retained to prepare such a plan. In the end that plan destroyed the ambitious creation of a new town in the Uxbridge area that I had proposed to my client, Revenue Properties Limited, and that they had acted upon by beginning to assemble lands.

1966. It was time for me to leave my association with Premier Robarts. I was receiving intelligence that certain members of the Liberal opposition were thinking about "going after" me in the Legislature. I had escaped that sort of treatment for over three years. I really was concerned about the harm that could be done to me and my reputation with no chance to defend myself.

I proposed to John that he should officially retain me as his counsel. That would give me "solicitor and client" protection. But somehow John couldn't come to grips with that idea. So I respectfully withdrew from his activities as premier, although not from our continuing close friendship.

And so I departed, I think to John's regret. The great constructive ship of Robarts's state sailed on for another five years of his stewardship, including another general election, which he won.

I then took leave of my better judgment and decided that I would like to get the nomination for a federal seat for the Progressive Conservative Party. A new riding called York North had just been established, lying to the northeast of Toronto, centred on Markham and Unionville and that area. With my Don Mills background I thought I could have a pretty good shot at getting the nomination and immediately decided to go for it. Everyone knew of my connection with Robarts. It was my assessment that that would work to my advantage in attempting to win the nomination.

So I made contact with the riding executive, the people who were going to put the new riding together. After many meetings and canvassing of the people who were to make the decision, when nomination meeting night arrived I had one opponent, a lawyer by the name of John Gamble, who was a resident of York North riding, whereas I was not. I won the nomination and started my work to become notorious enough in the riding that my name would be recognizable so that when the next election arrived, whenever that might be, I would have a good chance of attracting voters.

But having won the nomination, something happened that would in effect turn me off down the road. That something was the Progressive Conservative leadership convention of 1966.

Early that summer I had been approached by the Honourable Donald Fleming, who asked me if I would support him as a candidate for the leadership. He was one of the first people out of the gate. I knew the very formal, small of stature, tough-minded Donald Fleming. He was an interesting person, a former member of Dief's Cabinet. I thought he had a good chance, provided that if someone far more attractive entered the field he, Fleming, would give up and go on to other things.

So I said I would work for him from an organizational point of view. It was understood that Sidney Hermant, the splendid man who was the principal of Imperial Optical, would raise the necessary funds.

I was on a trip in Europe when I found out that another candidate had thrown his hat in the ring. It was the highly popular premier of Nova Scotia, Bob Stanfield. When I arrived back from my trip I expected a call from Donald Fleming saying that with Stanfield running that he would back off. But that was not in Fleming's makeup. He thought he was good enough to take on Stanfield or anyone else who might appear. With his background in the Diefenbaker Cabinet and as a loyal Conservative he must have thought that he could take Stanfield hands down.

With my doubts about Fleming I was quite concerned about the eventual outcome. Nevertheless, having made a commitment to him to organize his campaign, I stayed with it with the help of my great partner, Mary-O, who had become deeply involved, as had her mother, Olivia Whiteside, when we came to preparing for and taking part in the final convention night.

However, in the run-up to the convention I had witnessed and experienced political infighting and activities that turned me totally off of wanting to run for office. In short, I became disillusioned, a condition that was capped on the night of the voting, which took place at Maple Leaf Gardens.

The entire Fleming team, which I had had a major hand in pulling together, was on hand. We did our marches, had our banners, the whole thing. The candidates gave their speeches and then the balloting started. It was not very long until Donald Fleming was knocked out of the race. Without consulting with him I went straight to Stanfield and gave him my personal support, which did not mean by any means that the rest of the Fleming group would follow me. Be that as it may, Donald Fleming was extremely incensed that I would do such a thing.

That fine gentleman, Bob Stanfield, became the leader.

As for myself, I had had it. I decided I would give up the nomination but that I would give a good reason for so doing so. I explained that as a result of the Police Bill debacle in which I had been deeply involved I had developed an uncomfortable stomach condition, which was true. As a result, I could not carry on as the standard-bearer for the Progressive Conservative Party in York North.

Without realizing it, that was one of the better decisions that made in my lifetime. Soon after I vacated the scene the Liberals had their own convention. A young man called Pierre Trudeau took over the leadership of the Liberal party and became the Prime Minister. That was quickly followed by the general election in which I would have run. The reality was that Trudeau swept the Toronto area clean. As I recall, the Conservative candidate who took my place lost the riding by at least ten thousand votes.

The person who won it has become one of my close friends over a long period of time. He is the Honourable Barney Danson, who later became Minister of Defence. He was in that post when, with his approval and that of the Prime Minister, I was promoted to the rank of major-general and Chief of Reserves in 1978.

CHAPTER 47
Building Thompson House and
E.P. Taylor Place; E.P.'s Biography

———————◆———————

IN 1967, CANON GEORGE THOMPSON, the rector of the Anglican Church of the Ascension in Don Mills (where we had continued to worship even though we had moved to Sandringham Drive some miles away) asked me if I would take on the post of rector's warden. After consulting with Mary-O, I agreed to take on the task, which would last for a year, perhaps two at the outside. The people's warden, the person elected by the vestry, was Claude Uzielli, a church stalwart who was always ready to pitch in, no matter what the project was, for the benefit of the church.

Canon Thompson had come to Don Mills from the Maritimes at the beginning of the development of Don Mills and had put together his first congregation using rental office space in an industrial building at the south end of Don Mills. From that beginning he raised the money and built the church and with it its parish hall. He was a truly dedicated man of high principle, an excellent, caring parish priest. We were good friends with him all his life as well as with his wife, Ellen, now into her one hundredth year as this is written and with whom we keep in constant touch.

When I settled into my job as rector's warden I began to take a new look at the piece of property that had been given to the Anglican Church to the east of the church and parish hall. It was a large tract, probably about three-quarters of an acre, big enough to accommodate a good-sized structure. The Don Mills Development Company, in its donation of the land, which was part of the overall subdivision plan, had a covenant on the land that it would only be used for church purposes. To take that piece of land and sell it for apartments or some other use would have required the Don Mills firm to lift the covenant and also to get a rezoning by the Township of North York.

At that point I reasoned that there might be some use for the land that would be in keeping with the actions and Christian beliefs of our Anglican faith. I was aware of an Ontario government program designed to encourage the construction and operation of charitable homes for the aged. When seniors were so old that they could not work and only had their pensions, be they government or otherwise, to live on, then the government, through the "charitable homes for the aged" legislation, would provide accommodation.

I undertook some basic research and discovered that the provincial government would provide a $5,000-per-bed grant for the construction and operation of a charitable home for the aged. I then consulted one of our parishioners, Murray Legge, a highly regarded architect, who looked at the tract of land. He prepared some basic sketches of a three-storey building that would accommodate approximately 135 residents with all of the appropriate support facilities and basic living and medical assistance. That number of beds would provide financing by a grant of $675,000. The church already owned the land, subject to the covenant. Where would we get the rest of the money? Central Mortgage and Housing Corporation and bridge financing from the Royal Bank of Canada. All the basic pieces were coming together. As the concept developed, I worked closely with Canon Thompson and Claude Uzielli, keeping them informed and getting their concurrence every step of the way. I knew that eventually we would have to have a vestry meeting in order to approve the transaction once we had it finally structured.

The Don Mills Developments Limited executive was quite happy to waive the covenant, or at least say that what we were doing met the spirit of it.

The next thing I did was to incorporate Ascension Charitable Foundation Inc., a non-profit corporation with a majority of its members of the board of directors to be members of the Church of the Ascension, with provision for other independent board members. It would be the foundation that would buy the land from the church, obtain the grants, and build the charitable home for the aged.

Through my friend Bud Andrews, I obtained an appraisal of the subject parcel, which came in at $140,000, a relatively generous sum for 1967/68.

Through the bridge financing that I had arranged with the Royal Bank against the commitment of the Ontario government to provide the $5,000–per-bed grant, the Ascension Charitable Foundation bought the parcel from the Church of the Ascension for $140,000, which conveniently wiped out any indebtedness that the parish had at that moment. Central Mortgage and Housing Corporation gave us a commitment for a mortgage somewhere in the range of $1 million. The plans had been completed. The vestry approved of the transaction, especially since the building of the home for the aged cleared the church of its mortgage indebtedness of $140,000, the result of building the church and the parish hall.

The architect, Murray Legge, obtained the building permits. At the ground breaking ceremony, Canon Thompson put the shovel in the ground to commence the construction of this new institution, which as its principal organizer, I decreed would be called Thompson House in honour of Canon George Thompson. As I saw it, our clergy were always underpaid, overworked, and not properly recognized. And since Canon Thompson had been a part of the trio who had developed the entire project it was only fair that this place be named for him. There was only one drawback to the lifestyle that seniors could enjoy at Thompson House: in order to meet the requirements of the provincial government in terms of the grant financing it was necessary that residents would have to be two to a room. There would be no single-room accommodation.

Eventually the cornerstone was laid with great ceremony, Canon Thompson officiating. Then finally the day came for the hiring of the appropriate staff. Applications came flooding in, and Thompson House was up and running as a charitable home for the aged. With various later changes of an administrative kind, such as the change of the foundation's name to Don Mills Foundation for Senior Citizens, Thompson House has been a major achievement of the Anglican Church and the community of Don Mills.

Some five years after the doors of Thompson House were opened, the board of directors, under the leadership of my good friend James B. Milner, and others decided that they wanted to raise a big parcel of money in order to build a recreation centre next to Thompson House. The new structure would provide recreational facilities for all the senior citizens of Don Mills — arts, crafts, dancing, bridge and other card games, the whole range of appropriate activities. The budget was somewhere in the range of three-quarters of a million dollars. Would Richard Rohmer be good enough to approach the most prominent Canadian entrepreneur of his day, the man who had put Don Mills together in the first place, E.P. Taylor? It might well be that Mr. Taylor would be prepared to make a sizeable donation to the project. I agreed to do that.

After some negotiating with Mr. Taylor's guard-the-gate secretary I had my first of several meetings with him at his huge estate house on Bayview Avenue on its east side just south of York Mills Road. I met him at his office, which was (and still is) in a small bungalow at the north entrance to the Taylor estate, which he and his wife, Winnie, had chosen to call Windfields Farm when they'd bought it many years before.

At our first meeting I found E.P. Taylor sitting at ease in his office surrounded by pictures of his horses, particularly Northern Dancer, and trophies and ribbons of all kinds. Sitting at his desk he was able to look east out a huge window across his vast farmlands, which were in the process of being developed for housing.

E.P. Taylor wanted to know all about this project that was proposed and, of course, the details of the success of Thompson House. What were the plans for this recreation centre? What would it do for his beloved Don Mills? I had three or four meetings with Taylor in my attempt to convince him to support the creation of the recreation centre for Thompson House. He was not an easy sell.

On the other hand, I am convinced that he had made up his mind from the time of my first visit that he would make a contribution.

At the end of the final meeting, he asked me if I had a pledge form from Ascension Charitable Foundation. Of course I had one with me. He took it and wrote out his pledge. It was to be paid over a short period of time, but it was the capital amount that was exciting. It was for $250,000, a princely sum in those days. It was that donation that was the go-ahead for the building of this splendid new recreation centre locked in as part of Thompson House.

However, once again I did my decree of a name. I said it would be called Taylor Place, much to the objection of the donor. But I would have none of it. It was originally called Taylor Place, and then I prevailed upon the board of directors in the 1990s to change it to E.P. Taylor Place. To my knowledge it is the only structure named for this wonderful gentleman who contributed so much to Canada and to the world of horse racing during his long, productive lifetime.

The Taylor Place cornerstone was laid by E.P. Taylor. His recreation centre opened for the senior citizens of Don Mills in the late 1970s. It has flourished ever since.

Immediately after Taylor had given me the pledge he turned to me and said in effect, "Richard, my family has wanted to have a biography done of me for quite some time. They retained the services of a gentleman at one of the local universities to begin the process to do the research and the writing, but that hasn't worked out. We have all his material, which would be available. So I'm wondering if you might be interested in taking on the project of doing my biography?"

Well, what could I say in the circumstances? I was by this time an experienced author, among other things, having published my first novel in 1973 as well as two previous works of non-fiction (more on these later). The man was famous and had enjoyed a productive lifetime and much success. He was enormously colourful in everything he touched, including the raising and racing of horses and his leadership in the enormous Woodbine Racetrack. After discussions that involved E.P. and his son, Charles, a prominent journalist, I agreed to do the biography and to arrange for its publication, which was ultimately done by McClelland & Stewart.

After an enormous amount of work and many months of research and writing, which included trips to the Bahamas, where E.P. Taylor had developed Lyford Cay, the biography was finished. It was apparently to the satisfaction of E.P. Taylor and his family. It was a popular publication, and many copies were sold across the country, the book eventually going from hardcover to quality paperback and then to a mass market paperback.

When we celebrated the publication of his biography I said to Taylor, "Eddie, I'll never do another goddamn biography as long as I live!" He appeared hurt. "Why not?" My reply was to the point: "It's too much work!" As with many other things in life I failed to live up to that pledge to myself: I was to write yet another biography with the same result.

With E.P. Taylor in the Bahamas researching and writing his biography.

My final time with E.P. Taylor was when the National Film Board did a film largely based on my life. Eddie was kind enough to allow shots of the two of us to be taken at the Windfields Farms stables at Oshawa. His life was finished shortly after that event.

CHAPTER 48

The Official Plan for CN and CP's Metro Centre Lands Around Union Station

———◆———

Wth Flemingdon Park underway Bud Andrews, young, vigorous, and enormously talented as a negotiator and manager of development, was ready for a new challenge. It came in the form of an engagement by a joint venture of Canadian National and Canadian Pacific railways. They had jointly decided to come to grips with the vast acreage of lands that they owned in the vicinity of Union Station in Toronto, which were crisscrossed by all manner of railway tracks and railway facilities.

The CN and CP were to call these lands Metro Centre. In basic terms, Metro Centre is bounded on the north by Front Street, on the south by the Gardiner Expressway, on the west by Bathurst Street, and on the east by Jarvis Street.

The CN/CP people recognized that their lands in the Metro Centre core were of enormous future value in terms of their potential development for residential, commercial, and transportation value, sitting as they did at the southern base of the office tower building occurring immediately to the north up Yonge and Bay Streets.

The Metro Centre lands were valueless simply as railway holdings. What was required was the preparation of long-range policies and plans for the future development of all the Metro Centre lands.

The preparation of such policies and plans required of the coordinated study and input of a complete range of skills and expertise: engineering; land use planning; rail operations involving the readjustment and realignment of the rail tracks into and around Union Station including railway yards; soil testing; the laying out of roads interconnecting with Bathurst, York, Bay, and Yonge Streets; the coordination of water, sewer, and hydro services; and the development of agreements between CN and CP in regard to their working arrangements, particularly in regards to the fact that they would each maintain ownership of their separate parcels of land while continuing their joint relationship in regard to Union Station and passenger handling.

In order to coordinate and oversee the efforts of all of the different professions that would be involved in the preparation and development of the required plans, CN and CP decided to retain the services of the experienced and skilled Bud Andrews and his company, S.M. Andrews & Associates.

Bud eagerly accepted the appointment and immediately invited me to become counsel and to be involved from the outset in the entire process, participating and advising from a legal and municipal law point of view. It was clearly understood that our ultimate goal was to prepare a massive document called an official plan amendment, have it approved by the council of the City of Toronto, and, if challenged, take it to the Ontario Municipal Board for a hearing for approval.

Bud was the leader, assisted by his colleague John Barden, his "back room" man. Part of the team was Michael Davies, a most capable lawyer designated by CN/CP in relation to the preparation of agreements and other documents required between the parties and also with the municipality as requirements arose.

After months of preparation, it was time for a huge press conference. Plans for land use and for moving the railway tracks and eliminating as many as possible had been created; a massive model that demonstrated the type of structure that could be accommodated on the various parcels of land as being delineated by residential or commercial had been built; and elaborate brochures, containing photographs of the model and text and drawings, had been prepared. It was an event attended by the mayor, members of council, and the planning board of the City of Toronto and its officials — plus, of course, the appropriate executives of CN and CP, largely headed by one Stuart Eagles, who was the main point man for the consortium and who had worked closely with Bud Andrews in the development of the entire project to that point.

A photograph of the Metro Centre model that was exhibited for the first time discloses not only the concept of the residential and office buildings but also the location of a dominant feature tower that is now the landmark symbol of Toronto. Nevertheless the tower concept was part of the plan right from the very beginning. The Metro Centre lands received a positive response from the public and the press and from the City of Toronto politicians and planners.

Metro Centre board meeting where Bud Andrews explains the plan for Metro Centre lands. Also in attendance were (left to right) Donald Anderson, Norman MacMillan, Buck Crump, Leslie Smith, Duff Robbin, Stuart Sales, Michael Monk, Maurice Anchor, and Paul Blanchet.

In due course, as counsel, I had a leading role in the presentation to City Planning Board and Council of the Metro Centre plans and official plan amendments that would be required so that the appropriate zoning by-laws could later be enacted.

The ever-calm, totally organized, highly intelligent Bud Andrews was the leader of this entire enterprise, subject, of course, to direction from the CN/CP owners. Bud produced a planning and development masterpiece. There is nothing in Canada that can compare to his achievement for the Metro Centre lands. Even as this is written enormous structures are in place that match the proposals that he made. The CN Tower has long been built with substantial input from him in terms of its design and construction. The Sky Dome has been in location for many years and is dominant, with the CN Tower, in the central utilization of the lands flanked in the distance to the east by the Air Canada Centre and to the northeast by the enormous and popular Metro Convention Centre building. Huge apartment towers are emerging out of the ground. The railway corridors have been changed in accordance with the overall Metro Centre plan that was put together decades ago, with the result that the Metro Centre lands are becoming what they were planned to be: central to the core of the City of Toronto.

However, all was not cut and dried even though we moved the proposals through the City of Toronto Planning Board and the City Council.

A citizen's group headed by a capable and highly motivated left wing former mayor of Toronto, John Sewell, and supported by other socially conscious members of Toronto society appeared at the Planning Board hearing and then at the hearing of City Council to object to the Metro Centre plan. They raised issues such as the lack of provisions for such things as low-cost housing, the needy citizens of Toronto, and recreation facilities, as well as a whole list of things along the same lines. The question for us was whether at the end of the day Sewell and his associates would appeal Toronto Council's decision to approve the Metro Centre plan all the way to the Ontario Municipal Board.

In the end they did appeal. That triggered a hearing before the Ontario Municipal Board that lasted longer than any other previous session, more than six weeks. I was privileged to act as counsel for the CN/CP group for the preparation and conduct of this significant OMB hearing.

The chairman of the OMB deemed the matter to be of such importance that he, Joseph Kennedy, QC, originally a lawyer out of Windsor, conducted the hearing himself. Mind you, Joe Kennedy was a tough bird, knew his role, and was never afraid of making a decision or ruling that was equitable and fair.

Sewell and his colleagues retained as counsel a young lawyer by the name of Ian Binnie. Binnie was a most capable counsel. He conducted his clients' case before the OMB with integrity, recognizing from the outset that the chance of defeating the powerful CN/CP organization would have to be categorized slim indeed.

It was the same Ian Binnie who at the end of the 1990s was appointed by Jean Chrétien to be a judge of the Supreme Court of Canada, even though Binnie had not been on any bench prior to that time. As matters now stand, Binnie is touted as one of the most capable of the crop of current Supreme Court judges.

When the case was finished, Chairman Kennedy reserved judgment. Within a few days he gave his decision in favour of CN/CP Metro Centre official plan amendment proposal — to Bud Andrews's, CN/CP's, and my satisfaction.

That decision by Chairman Kennedy approving the amendment to Toronto's official plan, which would allow Metro Centre to go forward, is the foundation for all the development that has occurred on those lands: the CN Tower, Sky Dome, the Air Canada Centre, and countless major building projects for the future.

I am privileged to have been part of the Metro Centre process, thanks to my old friend Bud Andrews.

CHAPTER 49
The Mid-Canada Development
Corridor and Conference

———◆———

M Y FOCUS FOR SOME TIME during the Robarts years was the invention, if you will, of policies that could be utilized by governments either provincial or federal.

In addition to that and my law practice I was immersed in land use activities, acting as counsel for major developers such as Bramalea, the Reichmanns, and the Canadian National and Canadian Pacific railways and their lands in the Union Station sector.

At that time, in the late 1960s, Mary-O and I and our girls were resident at 74 Sandringham Drive in North York, a large home on the edge of the Don Valley ravine. It was beautifully situated, close to the new 401 Highway as it crossed Metropolitan Toronto. At Sandringham Drive, I used the library at the south end of the house on the main floor as my principal workspace. In that room, I would do my legal work for clients and write my speeches. I was doing quite a bit of speech making in those days.

One evening I had a map of Canada spread out that showed, among other things, the location and shape of the vast boreal forest that stretches from the Pacific Ocean, northern British Columbia, and the Yukon in an arc across Canada through the Northwest Territories and all of the provinces by James Bay, across Quebec, and into Labrador and Newfoundland.

As I looked at this map, the great green boreal forest jumped right out at me, and a concept emerged in my mind. Here was a stretch of Canada that was habitable and extremely sparsely populated, mostly by Native and Métis bands. There were two urban areas in various sectors, but by and large there was little population in comparison to Canada south, where it was said that 90 percent of the population lived within two hundred miles of the American border.

To the north of the boreal forest was treeless, barren tundra where very few people lived. They were the Inuit, who had been in that barren sector while the Native peoples and the Métis were in the boreal forest.

I reasoned that surely policies and plans could be created that would look at the future population of the boreal forest by people who wanted to come to Canada from all over the world. What transportation could be provided across the boreal forest? Could there be new highways and new railways? The bush aircraft and regional airlines already provided the basic infrastructure. And pipelines could carry oil and natural gas. Could there be new ocean ports, and where would they be?

Where were the natural resources, the iron and copper and gold that could be mined? They could be centres of new population and urbanization, new cities.

What about the social impact on the Native people if urbanization and industrialization was to occur? And the environmental issues, what would they be and how would they be coped with?

As the concept came together in my mind, I could see that the potential for a long-range land use and development plan could be real and practical. It could point the way to the future of Canada in that nearly uninhabited sector of forest.

How could I test the concept? To whom could I put the question of whether this was something that would be of value for the future of Canada? Was it a concept that could be translated into physical plans? Was it a concept worthy of investing time and effort into exploring its potential?

In my law practice I had had occasion to deal with some engineers from H.G. Acres Ltd., the prominent firm that had had its origins in the Niagara Peninsula. Their top people were aware of me because of my law practice and my association with Robarts and the Government of Ontario. I had some credibility, and so did they.

I made an appointment and went to see the president of Acres at the time, Norman Simpson, a blond-haired engineering entrepreneur who had vision and much experience.

I explained the concept to Norman. He immediately thought it was worth some preliminary research. He convened a meeting of himself and his senior planners and engineers, during which I went over the written proposal that I had cobbled together setting out the basics of the potential development and use of the boreal forest. At this point I named the forest Canada North, and the first study produced for me by Acres used that title, "The Canada North Development Corridor." I used the word *corridor* because the arc shape of the boreal forest did in fact resemble a corridor that could be filled with transportation, urbanization, industrialization, and population.

The principal person at Acres who seized the concept and undertook its research was Peter Van Es.

Working with me over a period of months, Van Es and the Acres team produced the first Canada North Development Corridor study book, which comprised a series of brilliant maps covering all of the ingredients and characteristics found in the boreal forest. It was a superb production that Acres put together for me against my one-dollar retainer.

The inscription and foreword in the Canada North Development Corridor book follows.

FOREWORD

The anomaly presented by Canada's vast areas of potentially rich northern resources and undeveloped space in relation to the highly developed 200 mile southern band concerns all interested in our optimum economic development. There is a constant search for the vehicle to support intensive investigations and development of northern resources.

Richard Rohmer has, in retaining the professional services of Acres for this study of Canada North Development Corridor provided us with an opportunity of applying our resource and planning skills to a challenging task. Northern development is among the most inspiring Canadian opportunities which lie ahead. There is little doubt that the next decade will bring great progress in this field.

This document presents the results of a preliminary study and should form the basis for an intensive research and planning programme to achieve fullest possible benefit from our northern resources.

C.N. Simpson
President, Acres Limited

There was absolutely no question in anyone's mind that the Canada North Development Corridor concept was the intellectual property and creation of Richard Rohmer, although later there was some attempt to encroach on my authorship. It was an attempt that was most disappointing to me although I squelched it firmly and with finality — but that story is down the road.

When I saw the first prototype of the Canada North Development Corridor study book I realized that I was onto something of great potential. I wondered if I could use that study book as the core of a nationwide conference that I could put together to examine the feasibility and practicality of the corridor as a bridge into Canada's future growth.

After discussion with the Acres people and a host of others I decided that, yes, a national conference could be developed, but in order to do so I would have to sit down and chart a business plan for the creation of the conference.

This I would have to do fundamentally as a one-man project. It would become my personal Centennial Project. I would have to use my limited financial resources to take the Canada North study and go out and sell the conference concept to the most influential people and corporations that I could find. I would have to entice them into investing money and personnel. But first I would have to change the name of the corridor to something more descriptive and precise. The words *Canada North* could be interpreted to include all of the north, including the high Arctic, and that certainly was not what I had in mind (except to the extent that the corridor would go up the treed valley of the MacKenzie River to Inuvik and Tuktoyaktuk).

So I decided to change the name to the Mid-Canada Development Corridor. Mid-Canada was the boreal forest, and it lay between the highly populated southern Canada and the barren high Arctic.

Acres arranged for the printing of a smaller study book, at which time the name change was implemented. I could easily mail the new edition and carry it with me while I went to visit potential participants in the Mid-Canada Conference. Make no mistake, without that splendid Acres study book there would have been no Mid-Canada Development Corridor Conference.

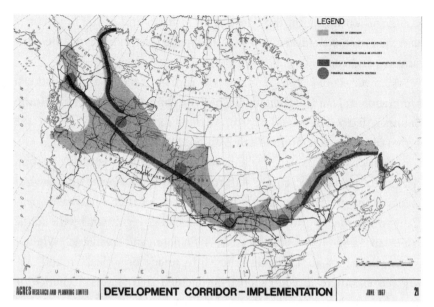

*Map prepared by Acres in 1967 detailing the Canada
North Development Corridor implementation.*

By the same token, if it had not been for my original concept and my ability to sell it to Acres as something worthwhile and viable, and if it had not been for my dedication to the proposition of creating a conference and being able to spend countless days in getting out there across Canada to sell it, there would have been no national coming together to look at Mid-Canada and the boreal forest.

The first major businessman to whom I took the proposition of the Mid-Canada Conference was a wonderful, gruff old bird who was the chairman of Canadian Pacific Railways. His name was Buck Crump. Well, I tell you, I got the appointment with him, went to Montreal, talked with him, took him through the study book, and had an immediate enthusiast for the Mid-Canada Development Corridor Conference. Not only did Buck sign up the CPR for the five-thousand-dollar, fee but he immediately started to talk up the conference among his powerful friends.

Having Buck Crump on board was a tremendous selling tool as I made my way around Montreal, Toronto, and the West. Old Buck gave me and the Mid-Canada Conference credibility.

If you look at the list of people (see Appendix II) who were part of the conference, some 150, it will be seen that my individual effort in going and knocking on the doors of all of them and of the universities and the provincial government was, to say the least, extensive, time-consuming, and costly.

I never could get Minister of Indian Affairs and Northern Development Jean Chrétien to take part, but one of his top people, André Saumier, decided he would pay some federal money and join in. As to the provinces, every one of them came on board without difficulty.

As the participants enrolled, and their money came in, it soon became important to acquire staff to assist with all aspects of organization and the myriad details that had to be looked after. I had met a brilliant young man working with the provincial government by the name of Brian Hay. He was impressive, articulate, and available. When I approached him about joining the Mid-Canada organization and taking the executive director's post he decided that it was a chance he would be prepared to take. Brian Hay became the executive director of the Mid-Canada Development Corridor Conference and of the Mid-Canada Development Corridor Foundation, which I had incorporated to receive funds and "run the business."

With Brian on board I was able to step up the recruitment of new members, while he moved into the law office of Rohmer, Cory, Hogg, Morris and Haley to take up temporary space to begin the process of putting the conference together.

There were two major elements for the conference.

The first was the "people side," which meant recruiting not only members but also honorary participants whose reputations would enhance the credibility of what we were doing. Then there was the matter of hiring and recruiting university students who would form part of the team organizing and running the first session of the conference.

The second element was organizing and administering the first session. The decision had been made that the conference would have its opening session at a university in an appropriate place. Following that first session there would be tours of the Mid-Canada Corridor region by air. Then there would be a final closing session somewhere in Canada. In between the opening and closing sessions, which would be approximately two years apart, there would be meetings of the working committees, such as environment, industry, urbanization, transportation, and whatever other committees were to be established. The decision was soon made that we should have the first session at Lakehead University. I approached the president of that institution, Dr. William Tamblyn, who immediately signalled that Lakehead would indeed be prepared to play host. There was then the question of timing. The conference would have to be in the summer during the non-academic part of the year so that all the accommodation would be available to us to house and feed some 150 people.

After negotiations with President Tamblyn, the date was set. It would be from to August 18 to 22, 1969.

It was then necessary to decide the range of topics that the conference would discuss. Having established that curriculum, the next step was to find, approach, and engage the best possible experts in their particular fields who would be invited to present their papers and lead the discussions.

I took the liberty of approaching my former senior partner, now Governor General, the Right Honourable Roland Michener, to be a patron of the conference. Through him I invited his good friend the Prime Minister, the Right Honourable Lester B. Pearson, to be a patron with him. Both men accepted the invitation, thereby lending a great deal of credibility to our endeavour. Then, for provincial balance, I invited the Honourable Leslie Frost to be the third patron, and he accepted.

As for the nitty-gritty details, those were the fiefdom of Brian Hay, who performed admirably dealing with everything: designing the symbolic letterhead; getting an Arctic bibliography put together; arranging for speakers; dealing with Lakehead University with regard to meeting space, food, accommodation, and transportation; and recruiting our university student staff. It went swimmingly.

Strangely, and without consulting me, Norman Simpson of Acres decided that the Mid-Canada Development Corridor concept was really his. To my surprise and astonishment I discovered that Acres had created a Mid-Canada film in which they had the venerable Pierre Berton do the narration. Pierre wasn't venerable then. He was just his usual sandpaper self. Out of the blue, Mary-O and I were invited to the showing of this film at one of the theatres in downtown Toronto.

I had been fortunate enough to assemble an independent board of directors of the Mid-Canada Development Corridor Conference before

I was alerted to the Acres attempt to take possession of and credit for the Mid-Canada concept and conference. I was able to rally my board behind me, and an ultimatum was given to Acres to back off. Acres ultimately agreed to do so when Simpson and I agreed that the copyright in the study book that Acres had originally prepared for me should be transferred to Lakehead University.

That was the only disappointing glitch in the entire Mid-Canada Conference episode. But I stress that the Acres team that put together the study book based on my Mid-Canada Development Corridor concept did a superb job. Clearly, however, from the original introductory statement in the Canada North study book, there was no doubt that Acres recognized from whom all this had come. They had overstepped the mark.

The conference was a huge success, thanks largely to the organizational and administrative skills of Brian Hay.

The young students he had assembled carried out the various tasks he assigned them, such as meeting the delegates when they arrived at Lakehead, showing them to their accommodation, acting as ushers during the conference sessions, guiding participants, and generally just doing every job that Brian Hay thought had to be done. Many of the students went on to great individual successes. John Honderich became the publisher of the *Toronto Star*, John Campion went on to study law and became one of the foremost litigation counsels in Ontario with the firm with which I had an early start, Fasken and Calvin, and Tim Taylor became a distinguished hotelier, to name just a few. The importance of the work of the conference was underscored by the attendance and participation as a speaker of Governor General Roland Michener. There was no expectation that the Prime Minister would be there, but Roly Michener brought Lester B. Pearson's greetings.

In the lists of presenters and participants shown in the program of the first session (Appendix II), there are many famous names, such as Dalton Camp, the Honourable Keiller McKay, Buck Crump of the CPR, and J.J. MacMillan, chair and president of the CNR.

At the conclusion of the session, it was reported by the members of the conference that the entire idea of Mid-Canada as a development corridor was practical, exciting, and had given each and every one of them an opportunity to take part in a grand-scale examination of the future and potential of Canada. But there was more work to be done; the Lakehead Conference was planned as the opening of the overall conference, which, as I noted earlier, was scheduled to last for approximately two years. The planning included an air tour of a major part of the Mid-Canada Corridor across the northern sectors of Ontario, Manitoba, Saskatchewan, Alberta, British Columbia, and the Northwest Territories, where the treed segment of the corridor ran north up the MacKenzie River to the MacKenzie Delta and Inuvik and Tuktoyaktuk.

When all arrangements for the airlift and accommodations, including meeting places, had been organized by Brian Hay and his team, the travelling members of the conference flew to Winnipeg, where the chartered DC4 aircraft awaited us. The air tour took us through Manitoba from the oil sands of Thompson to Churchill to Winnipeg and as far north as Norman Wells on the MacKenzie River. Our first stop was Thompson, where we were greeted by the mayor and various officials. We had come to see the tar sands operation, the mining of sands embedded in heavy oil. Of particular interest were the huge trucks and the massive machines that dug up the black material in an open pit operation. Then there was the equipment that took the oil out of the sand. This was major Mid-Canada stuff and still is, since billions of dollars have been poured into the extraction of crude oil from the one of the largest oil deposits in the world.

Then it was on to Churchill, where we inspected the harbour facilities of this unusual northern port, which is open for only a certain length of time during the year because of the ice. We talked about its potential for the future, the annual presence of the polar bears (still a tourist attraction there), and the beautiful white beluga whales that make their seasonal visits to Churchill. I had two later visits to Churchill when I was the honorary lieutenant-colonel of 411 Squadron. In 1972, the airport facilities there would be the launching pad for 411 Squadron's operation Flight North of the Ancient Bird, in which we flew two single-engine Otters up to Ellesmere Island.

With the so-called global warming going on at this time, Churchill appears able to enjoy a much longer shipping season, although the insurance underwriters in London, England, appear not to have been made aware of this fact. The result is that while the port might be ice-free for longer periods, the barriers in place by the underwriters may keep the shipping season at the same length it was before.

The capital of the Northwest Territories, Yellowknife, was our next stop. There we were warmly greeted by the commissioner of the Northwest Territories, the tall, mustached, gregarious Stuart Hodgson. He and his deputy, John Parker, were delighted to have such a distinguished group coming to look at their vast territory — at least the part of it that was treed and green. They had a big dinner for us at the local hotel, held briefings for us on the treasures of the Northwest Territories, and generally impressed us with what was going on in their land, particularly the oil exploration in the MacKenzie Delta and, of course, the oil production that had been going on for some time at Norman Wells.

Pacific Western Airlines (PWA) was the licensed carrier out of Edmonton to Hay River, Yellowknife, Norman Wells, and Inuvik. To make the several trips that I, as chairman of the Mid-Canada Conference, was to make, particularly to Yellowknife and Inuvik over the eighteen-month period that we were working on the Mid-Canada Project and also on the licensing and installation of a radio station at Inuvik, Pacific Western generously provided me with an ongoing pass on their new Boeing jet aircraft. Daily it made the run north and south between Edmonton and Inuvik. Rhys Eyton, president of PWA and cousin of Trevor Eyton, was good enough to make that arrangement for me.

The citizens of Inuvik, particularly Dick Hill, who was the mayor at the time, and the local Native organization, the Committee for Original Peoples Entitlement (COPE) headed up by Agnes Semmler and Nelly Cournoyea (later to become premier of the Northwest Territories), greeted us with dinner in the local gymnasium featuring caribou meat, a delicious meal that I had for the first time and that made me unhappily ill for a moment. We toured Inuvik and saw all the sights, particularly the way the houses were built on the permafrost and the fact that the services of sewer and water were installed with modern techniques. Since it was summer, we were particularly impressed with the masses of mosquitoes that dwell and thrive in that territory.

One of the people I met at Inuvik was Freddy Carmichael, a young Native pilot who had put together a charter service of small aircraft operating out of Inuvik. Later he was to fly me to Tuktoyaktuk and then out east of that village to Atkinson's Point, where the first find of oil and gas had occurred to the credit of an Esso, Imperial Oil Limited drilling team. I can recall that at the time we went the entire terrain was still frozen over and white. There in the distance was a little black dot that, as we approached, took the form of a drilling rig and the attendant steaming buildings around it. The find at Atkinson's Point was the harbinger of the spending of hundreds of millions of dollars by corporations looking for oil or natural gas or both (because if you found oil you would also get natural gas coming out of the hole).

CHAPTER 50
Presentation of the Mid-Canada Report

———◆———

INUVIK HAD A FULL-SIZED runway large enough to take the PWA Boeings as well as the CF5 fighters and the Hercules aircraft that were being flown by the Canadian Armed Forces. This was the period before the end of the Cold War, so the great Russian Bear bomber and recce aircraft would sometimes appear from their bases in Siberia, lurking close enough to our soil to put the Canadian Air Force to the test.

This Mid-Canada Conference tour was the first time that any of the participants had been into the Northwest Territories, let alone as far as Inuvik. It was a whole new world for them, the mix of the Inuit whose land we were on and the white people with the European faces. It was also an interesting discovery for us that at Tuktoyaktuk many of the Natives bore American (usually Texan) names. The reason was that in the nineteenth century, the great gray whales that would come up from the Pacific and through the Bering Strait to summer in the Northwest Passage were fair game for the great whaling ships that would come up to kill them and take their blubber and oil and other marketable parts back to market. So it was that the sailors would come ashore at Tuk and other places along the Arctic coast, where they found the women attractive. Children would be born as a result, and the names survived. One of the leaders was named Steen, and the name Carpenter was famous. But the blood of the original generation of fathers was so diluted that no traces of European contours could be seen in their faces or bodies.

Also at Tuk was a Distant Early Warning (DEW) line radar station that had been in place for many years but was becoming obsolete. It had provided much employment for the people of the area. To the south of the community was the airstrip, which ran east and west. It was rough but serviceable and was used by the transport aircraft moving in drilling equipment and bringing in supplies to the people of Tuk from time to time. At this time in 1969, no one in the region of Inuvik or Tuk really had any comprehension of the upcoming impact of the hundreds of millions of dollars that would be spent in the pursuit of exploration for oil and gas. The search ultimately became reasonably successful, even though a pipeline for the natural gas has not yet been built to bring that valuable energy commodity down to market. By the same token, no attempt has been made to move crude oil by either pipeline or ship from that area. Plans are now emerging for the building and financing of a pipeline, and the same Freddy Carmichael is heading up the participation in the project of the Inuit and other Native peoples!

Today, there is also much discussion about moving natural gas from the Alaskan Beaufort Sea oil fields of the United States down through the Yukon and Alberta into the American market. An alternative plan would allow Mackenzie Valley gas to be coupled with the Beaufort Sea gas and then moved to markets in Canada and the United States. Yet another alternative, which seems to have the best chance for early success, is a gas pipeline from the MacKenzie Delta south to markets in Canada and the U.S.

After three days of intense discussion with the people of Inuvik and investigation of how they had built their town (because Mid-Canada also looked at the question of the feasibility of building new cities within its regions), the Mid-Canada Conference tour members then flew on to Whitehorse, the capital of the Yukon Territory.

Whitehorse appeared to us to be a more urbanized place than Inuvik, much more comparable to Yellowknife.

After public meetings with the local government people in Whitehorse, the Mid-Canada Conference tour finished its travelling in the Yukon and Northwest Territories, and its members returned to their various home bases across Canada. Their work was not finished — it was really just beginning. It had been decided that the members would be broken up into committees, each assigned a specific topic. As the Mid-Canada Conference report shows, the membership was divided into these committee units that functioned for a period of months under active supervision of their designated chairpersons, the goal being to work toward a final report. The committees were Environment; Transportation; Urbanization; Industrialization; Social Impact on the Native People; Science and Technology; Research, Education, and Information; Culture and Social Purpose; and Political, Legal, and Legislative Aspects.

Ultimately it was decided that there was no need for an organized tour of the Mid-Canada sections of Ontario, northern Quebec, Labrador, Newfoundland, or Prince Edward Island. There was enough known by the particular members of the various committees about those regions without having to go to the expense of yet another air tour.

There had to be a final session of the Mid-Canada Conference. That meeting would examine the preliminary reports of each one of the committees. The draft reports would be wide open to debate by constituent members or anyone else who was involved in the Mid-Canada Conference.

That final session was held in Montreal at a hotel next to the Dorval airport.

As I recall, the session became an environmental battleground, a graphic signal of the ecosystem wars that have carried on in Canada, North America, and around the world since those early days of 1969 and 1970.

What the environmentally concerned participants in the Mid-Canada Conference really wanted to say was that Mid-Canada should not be subject to any development (that is, urban development as we know it in the Western world) at all. The place should remain pristine, untouched, undeveloped. That was an extremely difficult position for the majority of non-environmentalist program members to swallow. Finally, after much heated discussion and theatrics, compromises were made all around.

After much post-meeting work by Brian Hay and his team, with some input from me you can be assured, there began to emerge the form of a draft report of the Mid-Canada Development Corridor Conference. It was understood from the outset that once the final draft was put together and approved in English it would be translated into French. The document would be in both official languages.

So far as I know, the Mid-Canada Conference was the first and only national conference on any issue that was not subsidized or participated in by the federal government of Canada. Furthermore, the Minister of Indian Affairs and National Development of the day, the Honourable Jean Chrétien, would have nothing to do with the conference because at the time he thought Richard Rohmer was a Tory and part of the Establishment. That was probably the same attitude reflected in Trudeau's mind when he deigned to attend a luncheon at the Governor General's residence to receive the final report. If I had been a raving Liberal, the Mid-Canada region would have long been in existence with supporting bureaucracies. Yes, I was a Conservative at the time I put the Mid-Canada Development Corridor concept together and at the time the conference was held. But I have never been part of the Establishment, whatever that is. For the record, I resigned formally from the Conservative Party of Canada in 1985.

On the specified date, February 16, 1971, Brian Hay, Bob Fleming (Mid-Canada's ever-present photographer/journalist), my vice-chairman, Brigadier Bill Ziegler, and I arrived at Rideau Hall at ten-thirty in the morning for a scheduled presentation to the Governor General and Trudeau at eleven, to be followed by lunch.

It was planned that the Mid-Canada conference people would be asking the Prime Minister to positively consider the recommendations of the conference, which in essence said that it was in the public interest that long-range policies and plans be developed for the future orderly development of the Mid-Canada region and that the federal government take a lead in bringing the provinces and territories together to create a planning organization.

The Governor General received us in the foyer of Rideau Hall, then the Prime Minister arrived, full of his usual stuff and vinegar. I presented to them the voluminous Mid-Canada Conference Report. An appropriate photo was taken by Robert Fleming.

We then went into the library, where a projector and screen had been set up so that I could use our prepared slides to brief the Prime Minister.

We all settled down, a glass of sherry was poured in a very civilized way, and I began the briefing to explain the entire background of the Mid-Canada Conference and its findings.

To my unhappy surprise I discovered very quickly from the questions that he was asking that the Prime Minister hadn't looked at the material and really didn't know what it was we were talking about. It was

*With Governor General Roland Michener and
Prime Minister Pierre Trudeau presenting the Mid-
Canada Report. (Photo courtesy Robert Fleming.)*

a matter of enormous indifference to him, even though the Mid-Canada region had a major sector in the province of Quebec and, indeed, had national implications. I was not happy about Trudeau's reaction, his blasé attitude and apparent indifference.

After the briefing, we went into the dining room for lunch. The Governor General was at the head of the table. The Prime Minister was on his right, and I was on his left. The Prime Minister's people with him were down the table, as were Bill Ziegler, Brian Hay, and Bob Fleming. During the luncheon I made it clear by my words and my body movement that I was not happy with Trudeau's attitude toward the extensive work we had done. I pressed him to give us a commitment that we at least would be able to make a presentation to those members of his Cabinet who had a piece of the action in the north — Indian Affairs and Northern Development, Transport, and so forth. Well, there was no way that Trudeau was going to succumb to my arguments. We got somewhat heated in our discussions in front of the Governor General, who was clearly becoming more uncomfortable as the two of us went at it.

Finally, just before the luncheon was finished, Trudeau decided that as a compromise he would arrange it that we could take the findings to a committee of deputy ministers of the departments that had an involvement in the north. When he said that, I knew that the Mid-Canada initiative was doomed.

Trudeau was still testy and agitated when he left Rideau Hall to go to question period in the House of Commons. When he took his front bench seat in the House he was immediately confronted by the Conservative MP, Lincoln Alexander, with a tough question.

In his answer it was the first time that he used the word *fuddle-duddle*. I therefore claim much of the responsibility for the creation of the phrase that has become part of the Canadian parliamentary legend and Pierre Elliot Trudeau's legacy.

A personal comment about Trudeau. In my opinion he was one of the truly great Canadian leaders of the twentieth century, a man of powerful intellect and powerful eccentricities, a man for all seasons, including fathering a child when Trudeau had entered the winter of his remarkable life.

The meeting with the appropriate deputy ministers was duly arranged. Deputy Minister Gerry Stone and Tommy Shoyama, the deputy minister of everything, were the key players in the meeting. Stone was very understanding and sympathetic to the proposition we put forward, but I could sense that the others, including Shoyama, were thinking, "Who the hell are these peculiar civilians coming forward with a concept of this kind, the sort of thing that is the sole purview of the civil service? On top of that, the chairman of the Mid-Canada conference has distinct Conservative connections, and we serve Liberal masters." The meeting with the deputy ministers produced no conclusion. They would be in touch. Stone was indeed in touch, but in the end I knew that nothing would come of what we had proposed.

On the other hand, there was no question that the Mid-Canada Conference raised the awareness of all manner of Canadians about the potential of the Mid-Canada region and of the high Arctic. It was a worthwhile effort on the part of everyone who participated.

I suppose the real ending of it all for me came at a luncheon meeting of the Canadian Club at the Royal York Hotel in 1972, when the commissioner of the Northwest Territories was scheduled to speak. Stuart Hodgson and I had always gotten on very well and he was sympathetic to what we were doing. By this time the radio station at Tuk was in full swing, and I had also taken the initiative of attempting to create the University of Canada North, which is another story.

I was invited to be at the head table for the commissioner's speech. To my great astonishment, when he was on his feet delivering his words he announced that the annual Commissioner's Award for Public Service to the Northwest Territories, his own personal award, was going to go to Richard Rohmer. To say that I was delighted and surprised is an understatement. A few weeks later, Mary-O and I were taken as guests to Yellowknife, where, at a huge formal dinner, the magnificent Commissioner's Award, a large circular brass plaque embellished with northern symbols and figures and mounted on a small wooden table stand, was presented to me.

From Yellowknife, Mary-O and I went on up to Inuvik and Tuk so she could see the terrain where the Mid-Canada team and I had been operating for such a long time.

Because I was doing various things on a legal basis in the Northwest Territories, I decided it would be appropriate to receive a call to that bar. That was accomplished in 1971 in court at Yellowknife. As I recall, I had a matter before the court on behalf of Freddy Carpenter. But that was the only time that I made a judicial appearance there. Ultimately I let my membership of that bar slip away.

There was another initiative I had taken in the Northwest Territories that the commissioner recognized. It was apparent to me that there were educational opportunities for the people of the Northwest Territories that were not being taken advantage of. The young Native people were going to the schools at Inuvik and Tuk and also at Whitehorse. But there was no opportunity to achieve any kind of post-secondary education without going south at enormous expense.

I thought that it would be beneficial to form a university that might provide the post-secondary education that I thought was clearly needed. When I advanced this idea at Inuvik to people such as Mayor

Dick Hill and others it seemed that there was a good deal of potential support, including from the Native people.

I decided that the best way to proceed would be to incorporate the University of Canada North, which I did using the federal jurisdiction in Ottawa. The letters patent actually allowed the university to grant degrees, much to the horror of the Association of Universities located in southern Canada. I was able to pull together meetings at Inuvik and Whitehorse to further the concept and principles of the university. But there was no government support, either federally or territorially. Eventually the university concept subsided, but fragments of it carried on. In fact, a university student in southern Canada wrote a relatively comprehensive thesis titled "The University That Never Was." Of course, in the early 1970s I had no idea that I would subsequently be invited to be Chancellor of the University of Windsor some eight years later and would actually be able to enter the mainstream of the university structures.

But the Mid-Canada Concept had not died. In early 2001, Member of Parliament Rick Laliberte, from Churchill River in Saskatchewan, telephoned me in Collingwood from his office in Ottawa. He had come across the Mid-Canada Concept and had been told by Prime Minister Chrétien that if he wanted to know about Mid-Canada that he should find Richard Rohmer, which he did. The story of the temporary resurrection of the Mid-Canada concept will come later.

CHAPTER 51

Manhattan, *the Icebreaker Tanker,* and the Northwest Passage

———◆———

IMMEDIATELY AFTER THE MID-CANADA Conference wound up, but before the final report was delivered to the Governor General and Prime Minister, Brian Hay raised the possibility of the Mid-Canada organization conducting a tour of Siberia, an area of the world that also contained part of the great boreal forest that encircles the middle Arctic.

I decided that it would be appropriate for Brian, Bob Fleming, and me to take an investigatory trip to the Soviet Union in which we would attempt to meet with the proper officials in order to determine whether we would have co-operation for a tour to places such as Irkutsk and other important Arctic communities in the Soviet Union.

With his usual adeptness at putting things together, Robert Fleming found an acquaintance in Helsinki by the name of Heikki Lampela who had Scandinavian origins and was well connected in that part of the world. He knew what to do in Finland and the Soviet Union. Heikki worked with Fleming and Hay to organize our adventure and accompanied us throughout. We were off to Finland and the Soviet Union at the end of May 1970.

At this period of time there was enormous controversy in Canada over the *Manhattan,* the ice-strengthened oil tanker of U.S. oil giant Humble Oil and Refining Company.

Humble and others had made a huge find of crude oil at Prudhoe Bay on the north coast of Alaska. The company had to have a transportation system to get the black gold to market in the U.S. It could build a pipeline to Valdez (which it ultimately did). Or it could move the crude oil by ice breaking tanker either through the Bering Strait to California or through the Northwest Passage, waters claimed by Canada, to the east coast of America.

The *Manhattan* had made its first experimental trip through the Northwest Passage and was embarked on its second voyage when the three of us left Canada for Helsinki. The Government of Canada under Prime Minister Trudeau had reacted to the *Manhattan* intrusion into Canada's waters (the U.S. government saw — and still sees — the Northwest Passage as high seas with no Canadian jurisdiction) by enacting the Arctic Waters Pollution Protection Act to assert Canada's domain. But Canada had no way to enforce its claim of territorial possession.

If Humble was to decide to go for a big ice breaking tanker fleet to carry the two million barrels per day of Prudhoe Bay crude oil through the Northwest Passage to the U.S. east coast, what could Canada do about it? Canada had but two relatively small icebreakers, *John A. Macdonald* and *Louis St. Laurent*, which had assisted *Manhattan* to get through the McLure Strait (it couldn't get through the thick ice) during its first voyage when the U.S. icebreaker *Northwind* failed to perform.

During the *Manhattan's* first trip through the Northwest Passage I was privileged to be among Nordair's guests to be flown out of Montreal straight north to have a view of the monster tanker transiting the ice-covered waters. It was quite an impressive sight. My photo of *Manhattan* taken on that flight is on the back cover of my second book, *The Arctic Imperative* (1973), in which I covered the issues then of concern in the Canadian Arctic.

The *Manhattan* matter was on everyone's mind and certainly on ours when the three of us arrived in Helsinki in late May. What we were to discover there was directly related to the *Manhattan* and the building of a huge icebreaker that could shepherd ice-strengthened tankers through the Norwest Passage during all seasons.

Heikki Lampela met us at the Helsinki airport. He advised us that the foreign minister would be hosting a lunch and that afterwards we would visit the shipyards of Oy Wartsila Ab, the world's premier manufacturer of polar icebreakers.

Following an elegant luncheon, Lampela took us to the Wartsila works, where we were met by Christian Landtman, Wartsila's managing director, and two vice-presidents, one for sales and the other engineering. After a brief welcoming discussion, the vice-president for engineering took us on a tour of the yards. During the tour our host decided to risk everything and take us on board one of the polar icebreakers Wartsila had produced for the Soviet Union. The *Leningrad*, which was in for a refit with its entire crew, is 122.1 metres long and has a displacement of 15,300 tons with three screws and diesel electric power.

After being issued and donning ill-fitting hardhats and screwing up our courage, we ascended the gangplank with our host and began our tour of this superb ship. The *Leningrad* is one of eight polar icebreakers built by Wartsila for the Soviet Union. Of these eight, the *Murmansk*, the *Vladivostok*, the *Moskva*, and the *Kief* are all of the same type, 22,000-shaft horsepower ships. These vessels are used off the shores of Siberia, where they keep the northern sea route open. The *Leningrad* was most impressive, both as a feat of technological achievement by Wartsila and as a textbook model of how to maintain a tight ship. We were impressed.

Then we were taken back to the managing director's office, where we continued our discussion with him and his two senior people. As the talk went on, Landtman disclosed that Wartsila had been working as consultants for Humble for quite some time. This was news. My interest quickened. Wartsila had been advising Humble on the *Manhattan* project, it appeared, but the important news was that Humble had retained Wartsila to do some preliminary research for Humble's account (not for the Government of the United States) on what would be the largest polar icebreaker ever constructed. It was to be a ship of 140,000 horsepower and 50,000 tons dead weight. This information, almost casually delivered, was astonishing.

No inkling of this activity had been leaked or even intimated by Humble — and for good reason, because the implications for Canada's sovereignty, even in the presence of the sovereignty legislation passed by Canada the month before, were staggering. Earlier that year, it had been announced that Humble had placed design contracts with Newport News Ship Building Company in Virginia for a fleet of 250,000-ton tankers, each about twice the size of the *Manhattan*. But no mention had ever been made of a super icebreaker.

In the storm over the *Manhattan* and the ensuing legislation, not one mention had been made of the polar ice breaking shortage, but here for the first time was evidence that Humble, with its high-powered

American efficiency, had not overlooked this serious vacuum and that having perceived the problem had gone in unerring fashion straight to the world's expert polar icebreaker firm. The terms of reference for Wartsila would probably have looked like this: "Here is the data we have obtained from the first *Manhattan* voyage. Here is what we found in the McClure Strait. Can you design and produce a generation of ice-breakers to assist our 250,000- to 300,000-ton supertankers? The ship should be about the size of the *Manhattan* with engines of about 140,000 horsepower. It should be able to cut through the McClure Strait ice, which would then allow us to operate beyond the three- or even twelve-mile territorial limit of the Canadian government and out of its regulatory clutches."

Just think of it — a fleet of twenty to thirty 250,000- to 300,000-ton ice-strengthened tankers carrying a total of about two million barrels per day of Alaskan crude through the Northwest Passage escorted through ice-covered Canadian waters between the Canadian Arctic Islands (or "high seas," if the United States has its way) by at least two massive Humble polar icebreakers designed and built by Wartsila.

Where would Canada's sovereignty be if these gargantuan icebreakers appeared in the Northwest Passage? This was not the government of a sovereign country beginning the preparatory steps for a polar icebreaker but an oil company so powerful, so strong, so rich, so under pressure to move its newfound commodity to the U.S. market that it was prepared to construct its own ice-strengthened supertanker fleet. Furthermore, these ships would provide the ice breaking, ship-saving facility that would ensure that the system could operate in the most difficult of polar ice, even through the previously impassable McClure Strait, thereby removing the fleet from those three-mile jurisdictional clutches that Canada unquestionably had, or from the twelve-mile limits that Canada now claimed under its new legislation. Implicit in this action was a total disregard for the hundred-mile scope of the Arctic Waters Pollution Prevention Act.

It was apparent to me that Wartsila had given us information that had not been reported publicly in Canada. It was also apparent that if information of this nature had not been reported publicly it was likely the Canadian government did not know about it either. And yet the implications for Canada's sovereignty were both obvious and alarming.

Landtman gave me brochures and drawings of polar icebreakers they had built and of a vessel they then had on the drawing board with a shaft horsepower of 36,000 and main diesel-electric screws of 41,400 horsepower. He wanted us to know that even if Wartsila did not get a contract to build for Humble, they were interested in giving technical and consulting assistance to the Canadian government.

That evening I gave the Canadian ambassador to Finland our new-found information in the hope that he would pass it on to Ottawa.

Immediately upon my return to Canada I made contact with the office of the Minister of Transport and outlined the information I had obtained. The minister, Don Jamieson, asked me to speak with Dr. Camu, the head of the marine branch of the Department of Transport.

Early in June I met with Dr. Camu and Rear Admiral A.H.G. Storrs, then director of marine operations for the department. I told them all that I had learned during our visit to Wartsila. Admiral Storrs was highly skeptical of my claim that Humble was taking such steps with Wartsila. What he was really skeptical about was that the U.S. government would permit Humble to embark on an independent polar icebreaker program. After about fifteen minutes of hard discussion, the Admiral conceded that indeed it might well be possible that the U.S. government would readily be prepared to let Humble bear the brunt of smashing through the Northwest Passage with its own polar super icebreakers leading the vanguard.

My information was obviously the first knowledge the ministry had of Humble's intention to acquire its own polar icebreakers to support its Northwest Passage system. It was sufficient to trigger a short-term interest on the part of the government on the question of whether or not it was advisable for Canada to build new giant polar icebreakers, a question that was a matter of concern during hearings of the Standing Committee (House of Commons) on Indian Affairs and Northern Development during 1971, to which a representative of Wartsila was invited to give evidence.

The decision of whether Canada should build such a class of icebreaker or take steps to prevent Humble for acquiring or operating the Finnish super icebreakers in the Northwest Passage lost its urgency and priority when, on October 21, 1970, Humble announced that it had decided to suspend its studies on ice breaking oil tankers in order to concentrate on the pipeline alternatives. The company said that tanker transport appeared to be commercially feasible but that pipelines had the economic edge.

The *Manhattan* project was dead. Any initiative that the Government of Canada had to have Wartsila build a huge icebreaker died with it. Canada's assertion of sovereignty over the waters of the Northwest Passage may someday again be challenged by the Americans should it be in the national interest of the United States in the opinion of its president or its congress.

In any event, we three of the Mid-Canada Development Corridor Conference decided that we had performed a small service for Canada by visiting the Wartsila shipyards in May of 1970.

From Helsinki we went by train across to what was then Leningrad. When we reached the Soviet border it was fascinating to watch the heavily armed soldiers comb the train from one end to the other, underneath and through the corridors. We were scrupulously examined, as were our baggage and our passports. No question that we were entering another world with values entirely different from our own. Our stay in Leningrad was brief. Then it was on, again by train, to Moscow. There we were booked into a massive ancient hotel very close to Red Square, where we knew all the rooms were bugged. In any event we had nothing by way of any secret or other information that could be of value to the Soviets. Arrangements had been made for our meetings with the appropriate Intourist Agency, which would be in charge of any tour that we might arrange for willing Canadians to go under the Mid-Canada banner into Siberia. Vodka, of course, was on the table during the meetings, an element that appears in any of my novels that deal with Russia or the Soviet Union, including *John A.'s Crusade*, in which Sir John A. is in Russia and eats a loaf of bread before a meeting with the Russian foreign minister, Gorchakov.

At the hotel restaurant one day we were approached by a peculiar-looking man, about fifty years of age, who could speak enough English to communicate to us that he wished to come to Canada and get out of the Soviet Union, that sort of thing. Clearly he was a KGB agent of a nondescript sort. We saw him two or three times, and he would appear without warning when we were taking a meal. I can only say that we played the game and provided him with all sorts of false information about Canada and the United States.

After appropriate photographs in Red Square we flew back to Toronto, apparently none the worse for wear, but our experience had convinced me of one thing. There was no way that I or the Mid-Canada organization was going to get involved in babysitting a group of twenty, thirty, or forty innocent Canadians on a trip to the Soviet Union and Siberia. End of the matter. But it was a marvellous learning experience.

CHAPTER 52

Back to 411 Squadron as
Honorary Lieutenant-Colonel

I HAD RESIGNED COMMAND OF 411 Squadron back in 1953, and shortly thereafter I had made my big speech to the Canadian Progress Club at the Royal York criticizing the government of Canada for misleading the public regarding squadrons of fighters in the north. From the publicity given to what I said by all of the major newspapers, particularly in Toronto, I was sure that the military establishment would never allow me back inside an Air Force or military uniform ever again. I had really blotted my copybook by telling the truth.

As it happened, one of the people Rod Smith and I had taken on as a member of our newly formed 411 Squadron in 1951 was a wartime Spitfire pilot with the Distinguished Flying Cross and Bar. By 1951 he was also a graduate engineer. While we didn't have room for another pilot in our establishment, there was certainly an opportunity for him as an engineering officer. His name was Bill Draper.

After I left the squadron, Bill started to fly again, and after a period of time flying the Vampire jets, he became Commanding Officer of the unit with the rank of wing commander. Draper continued his association with the auxiliary squadrons in Toronto, eventually becoming Group Captain Draper (equivalent rank colonel). Then came the infamous integration of Canada's military by Trudeau and Hellyer at the end of the 1960s. With integration came the introduction of the common green uniform to be worn by all of the services, with some exceptions for the Navy. Gone was the Air Force blue, Army khaki, and Navy blue. Gone were the RCAF and its rank designations, in favour of Army ranks. The Navy was able to keep its ranks.

I won't get into all the calamities that followed from the act of integration.

One thing that happened, however, was that the Royal Canadian Air Force disappeared. There was no structure known as the Air Force until the mid-1970s. It was a time of mass military confusion in Canada.

However, one small but significant (for me) change occurred as a result of integration. A reserve Air Force unit could for the first time do what its Army reserve counterparts could do, that is, appoint honorary lieutenant-colonels to support and participate in the work and morale of the unit.

By 1971, Billy Draper had achieved the exalted rank of brigadier-general in the newly created capacity of senior air advisor to the Chief of the Defence Staff. My old friend General Draper decided that I would be the ideal candidate to be honorary lieutenant-colonel of 411 Squadron for all the historic reasons that have already been recorded. I can recall his coming to my office at the Lang, Michener firm that I had rejoined for a short period. I thought that being the honorary lieutenant-colonel would be a challenging thing to do. On top of that, I had really missed my Air Force connections and flying with a squadron. This after eighteen years of no association whatever.

I was apprehensive about someone at National Defence Headquarters in Ottawa remembering that I had made the Big Speech. But nothing seemed to have arisen when my name was in fact put up by the Commanding Officer of 411 Squadron for the appointment. It went to Chief of the Defence Staff General Fred Sharp, DFC, an acquaintance of mine. In due course the appointment was confirmed. I was once again a member of 411 Air Reserve Squadron, no longer Auxiliary but Air Reserve. The squadron commander was a lieutenant-colonel, and my rank on an honorary basis was equivalent to his.

So I have to thank Billy Draper for his enthusiastic efforts in getting me recycled back into the Air Reserve, even on an honorary basis.

I was soon fully outfitted with my new green, not blue, uniform with three gold bands around the cuff of the sleeve to signify my rank of lieutenant-colonel and a bit of braid on the peak of my flat hat.

The squadron commander, Lieutenant-Colonel Ron Richardson, and all members went out of their way to welcome me to the unit again.

None of the people who had been on 411 Squadron when I left in 1953 were still part of the organization. Perhaps one or two of the senior ground crew had remained, but otherwise everything had changed, including the type of aircraft and the colour of the uniforms.

The aircraft that the squadron was flying in 1971 was the light transport machine the De Havilland Otter, manufactured right there at the De Havilland plant at Downsview, the airport from which 411 Squadron had operated in the 1950s and was still operating from in the massive hangars at the northern side of the airport.

The De Havilland Otter is a single-engine, short takeoff and landing, tail-dragger aircraft with high lift wings at the top of the fuselage, a large cockpit for two pilots, and an ample cabin behind the cockpit for passengers and freight. In addition, the machine can be equipped with amphibious floats, straight floats, or skis to go with the wheels. It is truly a Canadian bush aircraft, rugged and reliable with a huge piston-driven engine and a three-bladed propeller. It was also a flying challenge with nothing easy about its handling characteristics during its takeoff and landing. I very much wanted to fly the Otter, get checked out on it completely, and become a line pilot with my squadron. But being only an honorary it was probably out of the question.

I should add at this point that I was the first honorary lieutenant-colonel in Canada's Air Force. After integration, only the reserve squadrons were permitted to appoint honoraries, although after a lot of lobbying years later the privilege was also taken on by regular force squadrons, to their great benefit. In due course I was also the first honorary full colonel in the Canadian Air Force — which at that point had no name but was soon to become Air Command. More on that later.

After my appointment was confirmed I was equipped not only with my complete new uniform but a mess kit as well. The mess kit is the black-tie uniform that officers wear on formal military functions such as mess dinners. The Conference of Defence Associations (CDA), an organization representing all elements of the reserve force in Canada, had its annual meeting in Ottawa. This would have been in January of 1972. Bill Draper persuaded me to go to Ottawa to attend the meetings, meet as many people as possible, and go to the mess dinner that was going to be held at the Rockcliffe mess. So I had to buy my mess kit.

I went to Ottawa with Draper, found the speeches given at the conference at the Château Laurier Hotel to be interesting, and met all manner of CDA people and regular force senior officers, most of them of the brigadier-general rank and above. There I met for the first time a wartime contemporary of mine from bomber command, the great Lieutenant-General Chester Hull, DFC, who was the Deputy Chief of the Defence Staff at that point. Another was Air Force Major-General Dave Adamson (later a lieutenant-general). He had had a hand at National Defence Headquarters in processing my appointment and seemed well pleased to have me on board. He was the same general who within a week had sent a signal from National Defence Headquarters to 411 Squadron authorizing Honorary Lieutenant-Colonel Richard Rohmer, DFC, to participate in flying activities with the squadron. In effect, he gave me authority to be fully checked out as a captain on the single Otter and to fly with the squadron as a line pilot. In reality there was nothing on the books to allow the General to give that authority. But since the signal came from a high level at National Defence Headquarters in Ottawa, who was to challenge it?

Major James Foy of 411 Squadron became my mentor. Week after week he instructed me on flying the beautiful machine to the point where I was achieving a reasonable degree of competence in handling the big aircraft.

One of the first functions I was to be involved in on behalf of the squadron was in 1971 in a formal parade at Downsview Airport in which the Queen's Colours, a specially created and embroidered flag with the squadron's crest on it that had been approved by Her Majesty, were to be presented to the squadron.

It must be understood that a parade for presentation of the colours is probably the most formal and auspicious parade that occurs during the lifetime of a squadron or regiment. In the United Kingdom it is customary to have royalty present the colours. Who better, I thought, than a former Royal Flying Corps pilot to present the colours to us, namely my one-time senior partner and my supporter in the Mid-Canada Conference, His Excellency the Governor General, The Right Honourable Roland Michener, PC, CC? My Commanding Officer agreed, and in short order I had made the arrangements with His Excellency and with the Chief of the Defence Staff, General Fred Sharp, DFC, for their attendance.

On the chosen summer date the parade was formed up in the sunlight on the Downsview Tarmac. The squadron's pipe band was ready; everything was in place. The Honorary Lieutenant-Colonel and the Commanding Officer of the squadron greeted first the Chief of the Defence Staff and escorted him to the dais. The next to be formally greeted was His Excellency the Governor General, who was similarly escorted to his place on the dais, whereupon the parade commander called for a general salute and the band played; the Governor General returned the salute that was given to him. The parade was underway, complete with drums being played, prayers said, and the standard being formally presented by His Excellency. The whole affair was an outstanding success.

Then the next flying weekend for me it was back to more training on the Otter.

411 Squadron flew every second weekend using the flying facilities at Downsview, while 400 Squadron, of which I had been a member and commanded in the 1950s, flew on the opposite weekends.

The one thing that I had to do before I could win my official captaincy on the Otter was to pass the most difficult instrument flying test. However, after a lot of studying and flying training I was able to achieve this goal and to win my Green Ticket, my instrument rating. From that point I was a fully qualified captain on the Otter.

CHAPTER 53
Flight North by Otter (the Ancient Bird) to Ellesmere Island

A S A RESULT OF ONCE again flying with 411 Squadron, my experience in the High Arctic was by no means finished. I successfully pushed the Commanding Officer to take the squadron for summer camp to operate for two weeks out of Churchill, Manitoba, to give our people some experience in operating in the Mid-Canada region and the High Arctic. We went to the Churchill airport in the summer of 1971 and became acquainted with rough northern flying.

I next proposed that as part of the summer camp for 1972 we again go to Churchill. 411 Squadron would undertake an operation that would see us fly two single-engine Otters all the way from Churchill north to Resolute Bay on the Northwest Passage and beyond that further north to a place called Eureka, which was in the area on Ellesmere Island where a great deal of exploration drilling was going on for oil and natural gas. This seemed to have the potential for a great adventure.

The Commanding Officer, Lieutenant-Colonel Ron Richardson, agreed. I then went to my friend General Fred Sharp and sold him on the idea of the Arctic adventure. I had to have Freddy's approval because it was necessary for him to authorize putting in a supply of gasoline for us at the appropriate airstrips along the way. Freddy liked the idea and agreed to support the operation.

I then went to the appropriate people at the Canadian Broadcasting Corporation in the *This Land* series to see if they might be interested in filming this great adventure, which we soon began to call Operation Flight North of the Ancient Bird. As it happens there were two ancient birds. One was the airplane and the other was the honorary lieutenant-colonel. The

CBC soon signed on, as did my friend Ben Wicks, the superb cartoonist and inimitable journalist and author.

As soon as the squadron arrived at Churchill with its eight airplanes, the air and ground crews of each of the two aircraft designated to fly north to Eureka began their preparations in earnest. Supplies were collected — emergency tents and equipment of all sorts required for survival in the event that some mishap occurred. The Otter was a single-engine aircraft, and if that quit somewhere in the middle of frozen nowhere it was essential that we have everything on board to allow us to stay alive until we were rescued. The leader of the Flight North of the Ancient Bird was quite properly the Commanding Officer of the squadron, Lieutenant-Colonel Ron Richardson. With him was Captain Bill Purdy (who left this world in the 1990s, as did Major Jim Foy). Captain Serge Holoduke and I were the pilots in the second aircraft. Each airplane would have its own mechanic on board, and we would alternate carrying Ben Wicks and the CBC crew of two.

We were ready to go. With an appropriate loud send-off from the rest of the squadron, we launched the first leg of the Ancient Bird.

The first stop for our two Otters was Baker Lake, straight north up the west coast of Hudson Bay to the north-south airstrip of the fairly large Inuit village. I had been into Baker Lake in the few days that led up to the launch of the Ancient Bird, so I had a good handle on what the strip looked like and what its facilities were: zero, except that there was gasoline available. As we flew north from Churchill we never really got above two or three thousand feet, and we watched the flat terrain roll along under us: rock, no trees, lots of ponds and pools of water. This was the Canadian Shield at its most naked, and it would be the Canadian Shield for us as we flew hundreds of miles to the north parallelling the coast of Hudson Bay. I would later use my experience on that trip and eyeballing the terrain and Hudson Bay in concepts later examined by the Great Plains Project.

We arrived at Baker Lake without incident. We bunked in with a couple of Inuit families in their recently constructed Canada South–type houses. Then in the morning we were off for a place called Sheppard's Bay, a DEW radar station at the south end of the Boothia Peninsula. The station had been there for some time and was still in operation, complete with its living quarters, manager, and staff. No problem getting there, no difficulties whatever.

I flew that leg out of Baker Lake, and I must say I did a beautiful landing at Sheppard's Bay that was recorded in the CBC film. It was one of those "are we really on the ground?" touchdowns.

As soon as we shut down our two machines and were out of the Otters, the manager came to meet us. My first question to him was, "Where's the fuel that the Hercules was supposed to bring?" The Hercules was a transport aircraft based at Trenton that was supposed to bring in the forty-five-gallon drums of gasoline as ordered by the Chief of the Defence Staff.

"What Hercules? What fuel?" was the blank-faced response of the manager. The fuel had not arrived. So what were we going to do? I asked the manager, "How about some of your fuel, can we buy some from you?"

"Christ, we haven't got any fuel. Sorry."

"Okay, I have to get to a telephone. Where do I do that?"

The manager took the four pilots to his office, whereupon I got on the blower to the Chief of the Defence Staff. Finally, I got him on the line and put the question to him, "Freddy, where the hell is my fuel?"

Poor Freddy was embarrassed. He was sorry, but the Hercules hadn't been able to get it up there. There were other tasking priorities that had come into play just at the last minute, so we would have to wait for a couple of days, maybe even longer. That was it. I couldn't get mad at Freddy. That wouldn't do any good.

He told me, "We'll let you know when the Hercules leaves Trenton. Sorry about that."

Well, we didn't have to wait a couple of days or longer because the manager saw that we had some cases of beer on board (for survival purposes, of course). He immediately negotiated. "As a matter of fact I do have some aviation gas around the back of the hangar over there, it's in a bag. I'll give you the fuel you'll need in exchange for two cases of beer." Ron Richardson and I huddled for maybe five long seconds. Ron announced, "You've got a deal!"

We had a splendid beer-filled evening with the manager and his team. There are pictures of us at the bar. The next morning refueling was completed. I was in the right seat, as Serge Holoduke was going to fly this leg up to Resolute Bay on the north side of the Northwest Passage. With all the procedures out of the way, Serge started our aircraft. The engine chugged to life, belched out some blue smoke, and we were all set to go except that when he moved the throttle forward the engine was going all right but didn't go any faster. Something was drastically wrong. He shut the engine down, and our worthy young mechanics went to work pulling the panels off around the engine. Serge got out, and I worked the throttle from the cockpit when the mechanics told me to do so. It took a little while, but the problem was found. The throttle cable had become disconnected from the carburetor, a rare event but a major one. If it had become disconnected in flight, especially on takeoff, we would have been in serious trouble.

The problem was quickly rectified. The connection was made secure, and off we went for the run from Sheppard's Bay to Resolute Bay, with Ron Richardson in the lead.

We had a somewhat scary patch when about an hour into our flight we ran into clouds that created some ice on our windscreen and our wings. Otters don't fly well with ice on wings. However, we drove through that and burst out into clear weather. Flying low over the ice-covered Northwest Passage waters we enjoyed watching enormous seals sunning themselves, nonchalantly looking at us as we flew by. The odd one had enough energy to slide into its hole. It was an absolutely spectacular flight, particularly when we flew by a peak on our starboard side. It was some three hundred feet high, sitting all by itself in the middle of an open stretch of the water on the south side of the Northwest Passage. From its high top flowed a never-ending plume of cloud created as the winds from the west swept by. It was a rare sight. Then we were into the airfield at Resolute Bay, with its hotel, warm beds, and a comfortable evening.

The next day, having refueled, we were again off. We flew straight up the Sound at the west side of Ellesmere Island, a beautiful grouping of fjords, until we reached the airstrip at Eureka, a remote weather station about six hundred miles south of the true north pole (not the magnetic north). Eureka was the planned terminus of our flight and therefore cause for a beer celebration, this time in the dining quarters of the crew that manned the weather station.

They told us about an airstrip that had been built about twenty miles to the east in support of an oil drilling rig that had been there that spring. The drilling was finished, so everything had been taken out.

After some discussion we decided that Holoduke and I would take our Otter with the film crew and Ben Wicks on board and go take a look at this airstrip and the terrain where the drilling had been done.

Off we went on this side adventure. There was the strip. Serge was in the left-hand seat at the controls. The landing was straightforward except that we could see sort of dark brown patches in the lighter brown colouring of most of the airstrip. There weren't very many of those dark brown patches, so we decided we would avoid them if we possibly could. Which we did, up to the last few feet of the landing rollout, when the right wheel went into one of them.

This was the middle of the summer. What happens in the Arctic is that where areas have been cleared off, for example for an airstrip, the permafrost in the presence of the sun will melt in patches, and what was rock-hard material suddenly becomes goo. This is what our right wheel had settled in.

We all took a look around the area of the airstrip, then it was time to fly out. The decision was made. Serge would be at the controls, and the rest of us would be outside pushing the Otter as Serge poured the coal to the engine. With luck we would get the Otter out of the piece of bog that had caught us. Then, after all of us were on board, we'd take off.

As it happened, from the moment we had taken off out of Churchill, Ben Wicks had been making notes in his precious little flip notebook. He had made a deal with the *Globe & Mail* that they would run his article on this marvellous trip. That would provide a prestigious entry in his resumé and also provide him with a few welcome dollars.

I don't know what pocket Ben had put his notebook in, but when we were all out on the airstrip ready to push, as soon as Serge opened the throttle and the engine and propeller really went to work, the slipstream became an immediate hurricane vigorously whipping our clothes, hats, everything. Unfortunately, the massive propeller blast somehow caught Ben's notebook, wherever he had put it, and off it went. In fact it went off into the distance, and undoubtedly it and its pages are still floating around somewhere in the High Arctic. Poor Ben had to make a complete set of new notes using his agile memory. The CBC cameraman took great shots of us pushing, Ben being hammered by the wind, and the aircraft fortunately moving out of the entrapping bog. And, yes, we did get out of there all right and safely back to our Eureka position.

As contracted for, Ben Wicks published his article on the Flight North of the Ancient Bird, and the CBC photographers made a documentary that was in due course shown on the *This Land* series. In 1999, after the technicians' strike was settled at the CBC, I was able to obtain (at great expense) a copy of the documentary of Flight North of the Ancient Bird, a flight that ended uneventfully on our safe return to Churchill and into the welcoming clutches of our squadron mates. In due course 411 Squadron's summer camp was over and we flew our aircraft and crews back to Toronto.

There is one image that remains strongly with me from that trip. It was the sight of a long-abandoned U.S. Army Air Corps landing strip complete with metal Nissen huts still standing with flapping doors that had been built during the Second World War for military aircraft moving toward Alaska. This location was on our leg north out of Baker Lake for Sheppard's Bay. It was reminiscent of an old wartime movie. Each side of the runway was lined with forty-five-gallon drums. The place had been abandoned probably since 1945. Of course, the Americans had not been back to clean up the mess. It was so far from anywhere. No one lived near it for hundreds of miles. So why bother cleaning it up? What that memory tells me is that somewhere in that great Canadian Shield sector where absolutely no one lives for hundreds of miles, in that solid, rock-laden permafrost, a vast disposal area for high-level nuclear waste could be constructed that could take material from Russia, the United States, France, the United Kingdom, and elsewhere in the world. A huge all-weather airfield could be easily built. The railway could be run up from Churchill, and a port could be constructed on the west coast of Hudson Bay and called Northport, a concept we examined as a group in the Great Plains Project in 1975, which I will deal with a little later. That concept is the cornerstone of my as yet unpublished novel *Ultimatum 2*.

Two stories flow from the Flight North of the Ancient Bird. One is my involvement with the Great Plains Project. The other is my escalating involvement with the Canadian military, which ultimately moved me from an honorary post to a post as brigadier-general in command of the Air Reserve Group and finally to that of major-general and Chief of Reserves.

CHAPTER 54

The Great Plains Project, Northport, and Boeing's Resources Carrier Aircraft

———————◆———————

IN 1973, I WAS APPROACHED by Dr. Verne Attrill, a distinguished university professor and robust pipe-smoker, balding, mustached, probably about sixty years old at the time. An economist, Attrill had an active interest in the potential for development in the Arctic, and he wanted to put together an organization that could look at the resources of the entire Arctic area.

He had found a willing supporter in Dr. Ivan Head, a brilliant academic who was in the Prime Minister's office at the time and very much in sync with the remarkable Pierre Elliot. Through Ivan, Attrill's concept found support, sponsorship, and funding.

The organization would be called the Great Plains Project. It was funded through the Prime Minister's office. Attrill was chair of the project. The invitation to me was to be vice-chair, which I accepted.

There were two conferences staged by the Great Plains Project, and two major studies in which I had a direct involvement.

The first was the concept of developing a major new ocean port on the west side of Hudson Bay north of Churchill at Chesterfield Inlet. It would be called Northport, and, like Churchill, it would be accessible from the south by road and rail through Churchill and by a major new airport.

The economic rationale was underpinned by the need for large iron ore carriers to deliver their cargoes into port facilities that could handle the vessels — Churchill could not. There were (and still are) huge, untouched iron ore deposits in the northeast sector around Hudson Bay that would provide the resource.

In addition, at Chesterfield Inlet there was a good depth of water, and the port could be ice-free and open for a much longer season than was historically available at Churchill.

I needed someone with credibility to develop the Northport concept, and so I approached Canada's then leading Arctic seaman, Captain Tom Pullen, who had retired from the Canadian Navy but was the Arctic navigation expert of his time. I explained the concept to Tom, and between us we developed the positioning, the concept, and the fundamental principles of Northport.

I approached my good friend Macklin Hancock, one of the world's great land use planners, to ask if he and his team could come up with a conceptual plan for the development of Northport. In his usual way, Macklin agreed to do it pro bono (as was my own Great Plains participation).

And so it was that the Great Plains Project conducted its first conference. Its purpose was to examine the feasibility of Northport. I have the full Northport research paper upon which the conference was based. The meeting was held in Winnipeg with a select group of invitees who had expertise that could be brought to bear on the question. I had to prevail upon my friend Fred Mannix, Jr., who had been part of the Mid-Canada Conference, to do an estimate of the cost of running a railway north from Churchill. Fred's estimates were included in the report.

During the conference, Tom Pullen and I got raked over the coals by supporters of the port of Churchill. They felt that Northport would be too competitive and would take away from the economic viability of Churchill. The reality is that the approaches to Churchill would not allow sufficient draught for major ore carriers or any other big ships to approach the dock facilities. That did not deflect the opponents. However, in the end the first conference was a success, and the concept of Northport survived. It would be reviewed again at the main Great Plains conference that was held in Churchill later on.

The second potential development that caught my and Vern Attrill's attention was the fact that on some of the major islands in the High Arctic discoveries of huge quantities of natural gas had been made. Vern and I flew to Ellef Rignes Island, the location of a major natural gas find. We inspected the island and were satisfied that a major airstrip could be built there.

The next thing we did was descend upon Boeing Aircraft, asking them for the design of an aircraft that could carry liquid natural gas from the islands to the head of a pipeline that might be built to the south. The pipeline we were thinking about was the one that could possibly start in the MacKenzie Delta, run down the MacKenzie Valley, and then flow on into Canada South. That pipeline has not yet been built, but as the price of natural gas increases it is likely that both the Mackenzie Valley and the U.S. pipeline from the Beaufort Sea will be constructed before the end of the second decade of the twenty-first century.

With the imprimatur of the Prime Minister's office, Dr. Attrill and I arranged to go to Seattle to meet with Boeing's aircraft designers. We laid out the objective, namely that the natural gas on the islands would be liquefied, cooled to a temperature of about 650 percent below zero Fahrenheit. The liquefied material could then be put in to tanks on board the aircraft and flown from the island to the pipe head destination in the MacKenzie Delta. There it would be unloaded, gasified, and put into the pipeline for transit south to market.

The Boeing designers were intrigued with the concept. For the airborne pipeline (let's call it that), they produced the design of an enormous aircraft with a huge payload capacity. The drawings and specifications of this massive airplane are in Appendix III, as is Macklin Hancock's plan for Northport.

The alternative to an airlift is a liquid natural gas tanker. But it would also have to be an icebreaker of the *Manhattan* type. You will not be surprised that the Great Plains Project also looked at the feasibility of a huge icebreaker LNG tanker.

Of course, as an airman, my interest in the Boeing aircraft was enormous because its potential was not limited to carrying liquid natural gas. There was also the possibility that you could put hundreds of people in that aircraft, not only in the fuselage but also in the wings. While it was designed to be subsonic, and its wings were not swept back in the way that those of virtually all modern jet aircraft are, it did have a highly satisfactory airspeed of three to four hundred miles an hour.

The main Great Plains conference was held in Churchill, Manitoba. Captain Tom Pullen again got hammered by the Churchill supporters, who opposed Northport. But he survived, and for that matter so did I.

As for the tanker aircraft, the Boeing people were there with their drawings and a model of the aircraft. Everyone thought their big machine was marvellous. I should remind Fred Carpenter about the Boeing air tanker — which the current generation of Boeing people knows nothing about.

Like the Mid-Canada Development Corridor, neither Northport nor the big tanker aircraft ever came to reality. The natural gas still sits tightly confined in the Arctic islands. Captain Tom Pullen, Dr. Vern Attrill, and the iron ore man, Murray Watts, have all gone to their just rewards, and Murray's iron ore on Baffin Island has never been touched.

On the other hand, the new novel that I am working on brings Northport back to life. *Ultimatum 2* involves a confrontation between on the one hand a partnership of the United States, Russia, the United Kingdom, and France, who together are looking for an international high-level nuclear waste dumping site, and on the other hand Canada, which is reluctant to deal with even its own nuclear waste. The international partnership recognizes that Canada doesn't know what it's doing and will probably say no. So they have come up with a comprehensive plan whereby nuclear waste can be taken by air, by sea, by rail, or by road into the Canadian Shield well north of the Mid-Canada Region (or boreal forest), well away from any place where any human being lives. The nuclear waste will then be put underground in massive caves and shafts that are built to receive it. The harbour that would receive such nuclear waste would be Northport. What else?

CHAPTER 55
The Radio Station for Tuktoyaktuk

D URING MY TIME AT TUKTOYAKTUK and Inuvik, it became apparent to me that apart from the CBC, which had its bureaucratic
restrictions, there was no Inuit radio station that could allow the
Native people in their various settlements and locations around the
MacKenzie Delta to communicate with one another. I thought that it
would be a great Mid-Canada project to find a sponsor to build a
radio station and hand it over to the Native people to operate. The
obvious location would be Tuktoyaktuk. The men to give leadership
in its establishment would be Father LeMeur, a strong oblate priest,
and the Indian Affairs and Northern Development representative
based at Tuk.

As it had happened, I was still acting as counsel for the man who is
now the patriarch of Canadian broadcasters, both radio and television,
Allan Waters of CHUM. I told Allan about the scene at Tuk and the need
for a radio station and asked if CHUM would put up the money for the
creation of a station. I would look after the Board of Broadcast
Governors approval application. To my great pleasure, Allan agreed. The
cost would be somewhere in the range of forty to fifty thousand dollars
for the tower and the broadcasting equipment. Under the Income Tax
Act, the municipality at Tuk could give a tax-deductible receipt for whatever was spent. That was wonderful news. The next step was to try it on
for size with the people at Tuk.

So I went back up to Tuk, thanks to PWA. I asked the federal government representative and Father LeMeur to arrange a "town hall"
meeting for me with all of the people at Tuk. They all came into this
huge wooden building with its earthen floor. I sat on a stool in the mid-

dle, and all of the people were around the outside walls. These were Native people, all of them Inuit.

This was one of the most unusual meetings I have ever experienced. I was introduced by the government representative, but they all knew who I was and why I was there anyway. I then outlined what I was proposing and asked for any comments on it. (This was all done in English; everybody at Tuk spoke English, as they were educated by the Roman Catholic and Anglican schools in Tuk and in Inuvik.)

Well, a good ten minutes went by before the first person spoke up. I quickly discovered that a question left to the crowd took between five or ten minutes for the first person to get up enough gumption to really come to grips with it and respond. It was a slow process that night, but we covered all the bases. The consensus was that, yes, the people of Tuk would like to have their own radio station. On that commitment I went on to complete the arrangements with CHUM, to file an application with the Board of Broadcast Governors in Ottawa, and to attend the hearing (whenever that might be) when the application was heard by the BBG.

Wes Armstrong (right), vice-president of CHUM Toronto, and I (second left) at the send-off ceremony for the tower initiating the Tuktoyaktuk radio station.

Back in Toronto, Allan Waters gave his final approval and a budget of about $40,000 to purchase the tower and equipment and to get it up to Tuk. For my part, I prepared and filed with the Board of Broadcast Governors the application for an AM licence at a power that would give the station a reasonably good range out over the flat terrain of the MacKenzie Delta. A non-profit corporation was formed to make the application, with Father LeMeur and other Tuk people as directors.

After several weeks of processing, the Board of Broadcast Governors heard the application for the licence in Calgary. Father LeMeur came down from Tuk, courtesy PWA, and I went out as counsel to conduct the hearing. It went extremely well. After reserving the decision, the BBG granted the application.

Then it was a matter of getting down to the business of actually putting the station together. With Wes Armstrong of the CHUM organization and CHUM's engineer, George Jones, we made the appropriate equipment purchases for delivery. Radio Tuk was in operation within the year. Historically, it was the first AM radio station to be operated as well as owned by the Inuit people.

CHAPTER 56
The Royal Commission on Book Publishing

——◆——

I N THE LATE 1960S AND early 1970s I was appointed to the Board of Directors of the Ontario Development Corporation (ODC) and, at the same time, the Northern Ontario Development Corporation (NODC).

I attended countless board meetings in Toronto and elsewhere in Ontario, particularly in the north, when it came time to consider applications for funding for new enterprises of various kinds that the Ontario government found appropriate. The funding was usually in the form of forgivable loans, and each application was purportedly based on credible facts upon which the members of the board, about ten or twelve people, could make a good decision.

Many of the large recreational facilities in middle Ontario (such as Collingwood) and the northern parts of the province would not be there if it had not been for the funding by taxpayers' money and the credit of their start-up loans. One of the Robarts's London mafia, the Honourable John White, was the minister that put most of us together on the boards. In those days the young Ralph Barford, who was clawing his way up the corporate mountain heading up GSW, a steelware manufacturing company, was on the ODC board, as was Gino Francolini, also climbing his way up the financing ladder. Gino has had enormous success in corporate financing as founder, owner, and president of Xenon Capital Corporation, purportedly of London, Ontario, but in actual fact based at Gino's home in Tillsonburg. I think Gino is on every major national board of both commercial and pro bono organizations, while Ralph has gritted his teeth and turned over his now vast and substantial corporation to his offspring while he himself has "retired," so to speak. In recent decades, Barford, Francolini, and Rohmer have had a splendid annual reunion dinner together at someone's club. The exceptional John Cronyn, a man of substance, a distinguished wartime soldier, and part of Robarts's original mafia, was a welcome part of that team, as was the comfortable Donald Early, a Toronto financial mover who was chairman of ODC when we were there those many years ago. It is this kind of continuing association of good friends with ancient roots together that affords one a bright spot to look forward to every year. With the exception of John Cronyn, who departed in February 2004, we're all going to live forever.

My experiences on the ODC and NODC boards were to be of assistance in formulating policies and recommendations that would be required in carrying out the work of a Royal Commission that was about to be created.

As the year 1970 began, my Mid-Canada team and I were working hard on the preparation of the Mid-Canada Conference report when two events occurred.

The first thing was that I was approached by my friend Brigadier-General Bill Draper, then the senior Air Reserve advisor to the Chief of the Defence Staff, to ask if I would fill the newly created post of honorary lieutenant-colonel of 411 Squadron.

The second thing was that Premier John Robarts decided to create a Royal Commission on Book Publishing to deal with the commotion going on in the book publishing industry in Canada. The Americans were threatening to take over ownership of English language publishing, which was mainly concentrated in Toronto. When I offered my services to be part of the commission to John, I did so through his executive assistant, Dr. Keith Reynolds. John offered me the post of chairman of that Royal Commission to work with its two members, Dr. Marsh Jeanneret and the famous Dalton K. Camp. It was an offer I could not refuse.

The terms of reference with the Royal Commission on Book Publishing are found in Appendix IV, Orders in Council.

Marsh Jeanneret was one of Canada's most learned literary academics and was highly knowledgeable in all aspects of Canadian book publishing. Adding credibility and prestige to the Commission was Dalton K. Camp. He had been highly successful in the advertising field with his firm of Camp and Associates. Camp was a skilled creator of words, phrases, images, and concepts; his frequent columns would in later years appear regularly in the pages of the *Toronto Star*.

As chairman I had in my hands two highly intelligent and experienced Canadians. At the time of my appointment to the Royal Commission I had but two publications to my credit, *Practice and Procedure Before the Ontario Highway Transport Board* and *The Green North: Mid-Canada*. Not much. However, as a lawyer I had lived my adult life in a sea of words, both written and spoken. I had developed certain skills in dealing with people, organizing material and activities, and handling or running meetings. On top of that, I had the experience of having been the sometime special counsel or éminence grise (or noire, as some might have described my work) for the premier of Ontario, John Parmenter Robarts.

The members of the Royal Commission immediately met several times to get to know one another and at the same time to plan and develop a working strategy that involved defining the main problems facing the Canadian book industry. Coupled with the escalating takeover of Canadian-owned book publishing houses, there was the matter of financing for most of the Canadian publishers. Our job was to examine virtually every aspect of the operation of that industry that was and is so important in terms of the Canada's national identity and its separateness from the United States of America.

A main concern was that if all Canadian book publishing firms were bought by Americans, then the decision as to whether or not a Canadian-authored book would be published would be made in New York or Chicago or wherever in that vast country, and given the ignorance and indifference of most Americans in those locations, it is highly likely that 98 percent of the works authored by Canadians would never see the light of a reader's day.

After our initial meetings my colleagues and I soon decided that we should set up a dinner gathering of the owners of significant Canadian-owned book publishing houses so that they might have a look at us and get some idea of where we were coming from. We in turn would be able to get some preliminary attitudes from them as to the nature of our work and what their expectations were. This was done early in the game at the University Club in Toronto with such Canadian publishing luminaries as the one and only Jack McClelland of McClelland & Stewart and Dr. Bill Clarke of Clarke, Irwin. It was a gathering of some twelve prominent book publishing Canadians.

We explained what we considered to be the terms of reference, how we would approach the matter of the inquiry, and then asked for input. Marsh Jeanneret outlined the list of topics where we thought there should be research and investigation papers prepared by knowledgeable experts. We told them that we expected to have public hearings in the normal course of events and that they, as well as the foreign-owned book publishers, would be invited to make presentations. They were informed that if any urgent matter came up that might be appropriate for consideration by the Commission and recommendation to the government that they should feel free to be in touch with us directly or through our staff.

One of the things that had to be done as soon as the Commission was appointed was to bring together a competent staff to look after all of the myriad administrative details on a day-to-day basis. I recommended my fellow commissioners accept my proposal that we retain the learned Robert Fleming, an excellent writer and photographer who had been part of the Mid-Canada Conference. As it turned out, Robert was an amazingly competent choice who served us well from start to finish. It was rather like inventing the wheel, because generally speaking, Royal Commissions have no rulebook or standard operating procedures to be followed. The Commission had to hire an executive secretary and secretarial staff, obtain and lease appropriate office space, organize public meetings, record appropriate events, and "guard the gates." Robert Fleming did all of those things extremely well.

As the Royal Commission settled into its preliminary organizational work we heard more and more rumours about McClelland & Stewart being in financial difficulty and suggestions that Jack McClelland was looking at selling the company to a foreign buyer. This, of course, was exactly what we had been put in place to prevent. The sale of Ryerson Press to Americans had moved John Robarts to say "enough already" and to appoint a Royal Commission. If McClelland had negotiated a sale to a foreign buyer, the Commission would have been put immediately in the position of having to recommend that government legislation be enacted to prevent it.

However, that isn't what happened.

I was at some function at the Inn On The Park at which McClelland was present. He took that informal occasion to tell me that unless the government gave him some special financing he was either going to go bankrupt or sell to an American firm. I asked him how much money he needed. The response was immediate and somewhat shattering. One million dollars, and soon. Having recovered from my initial shock, I advised Jack that before we could consider what he had just told me we would have to have a formal application, a letter from him, with financial statements to back up his position.

Jack's material arrived at the Royal Commission offices shortly after our discussion. It was painfully obvious that we had to do something and that Jack was neither joking nor exaggerating. He really did need that million dollars.

We knew full well that if money were given to Jack McClelland there would have to be provision for money to go to other Canadian book publishers in similar circumstances. In other words, a comprehensive program would have to be developed quickly with a formula that would anticipate approaches by other Canadian publishers and a mechanism though which the money, if provided by the Ontario government, could be handled and disbursed. The Ontario Development Corporation, of which I had been a member, would be the appropriate vehicle.

Acting with considerable speed because of Jack McClelland's threat, and because of the public sensitivity to American takeovers in the book publishing industry, the Commission came up with a rational set of reasons that said that it was in the public interest that Canadian-owned and -controlled book publishing companies should remain Canadian controlled, and in order to support this proposed policy the Ontario government should provide favourable loans to Ontario-based Canadian-owned book publishers.

Finally we had the policy statements that we wanted formulated in the form of the first interim report of the Royal Commission on Book Publishing. (See Appendix IV.)

I took our first interim report to Premier Robarts, who had already told me that in principle he would accept it, and if he accepted it his Cabinet would as well.

In the end result our interim report was accepted quickly by the Robarts government, and McClelland & Stewart, with Jack McClelland firmly at its rudder, received the money it needed to stay alive and stay Canadian.

It followed that a long list of Canadian book publishing companies lined up to receive support. While all this interim report business was going on, the Commission was busy preparing for the public hearings that it had promised. In due course we began those sessions using the auditorium of the Ontario Institute for Studies in Education (OISE) building on the north side of Bloor Street adjacent to Bedford Avenue, where we had conveniently obtained office space.

The format of the hearings was simple. The three commissioners sat at a table at the east end of the OISE auditorium stage while the witnesses who appeared sat at a table at the west end, where they could comfortably deliver their remarks, which were dutifully recorded by the Commission staff.

In due course all of the Canadian-owned book publishing firms sent representatives to appear and give their views as to what was wrong with the industry, what could be done to protect it from total consumption by foreign ownership, and any special problems they thought might be worthy of consideration.

For example, there was the matter that plagued the industry then and still does today: the custom of returns. Retailers have the right to return any unsold books to the publisher for full credit value against the original billing. In other words, the publisher would have to take the hit for any and all unsold books. The Commission attempted to deal with that particular problem, but we could find no fundamental solution. We might have recommended to the government that it pass legislation requiring the retailers to pay the publishers at least fifty percent of the value of the returned books or for that matter terminating the ability of retailers to return the books at all. But the Commission could not bring itself to suggest that kind of interference in the book retailing marketplace. It is doubtful that the government of the day would have accepted that recommendation in any event.

The failure to find a solution for the return question led in recent years to the debacle involving Chapters and other major retailers returning to the publishers millions of dollars worth of books, a situation that ultimately led to the bankruptcy and destruction of Jack Stoddart's General Publishing, its chain of subsidiary titles and imprints, and his vast distribution company that delivered books, be they Canadian or foreign, across the country. That bankruptcy had an unexpected benefit for me. It returned to me ownership of the copyright of many of my novels and non-fiction works that Stoddart and General had published over the years. Those books are now for sale on the internet as e-books!

The most memorable hearing day for the Commission occurred when the authors appeared to state their cases. At some event where many authors were present I had been confronted with the celebrated, ever belligerent Farley Mowat, for whom I have the greatest respect as one of Canada's leading authors of fiction and non-fiction and as a highly intelligent man who is never without an opinion. Farley complained bitterly that no provision had been made for the authors to speak to the Commission and vent their ideas. My response was that no author had asked for such an opportunity, but we were wide open to an approach. All that had to be done was to make a request. Whereupon Mowat vowed that he would do so. And he did.

On the highly anticipated authors' day we had set up at the west end of the OISE auditorium stage a two-tiered seating structure rather like the bleachers at a sporting game. There was enough room to accommodate perhaps a dozen of the scribes who wanted to come and address us. For those allocated to the front row, such as Farley Mowat and Margaret Atwood and other famous literary denizens, there was a table placed so that they could put their working materials in front of them.

My Commission colleagues and I took up our positions at the east end of the stage, and I then invited the authors to come up from the audience to take their reserved positions.

They all stood up and trooped up the steps, carrying their required gear.

When they finally seated themselves, the kilted Farley Mowat, who was front centre at the table and the key organizer and spokesman, put down not only his papers but also produced a bottle of what appeared to me to be either gin or vodka and a glass, into which he poured a sizeable shot.

As chairman, it was clear to me that Farley's histrionics were designed to show his contempt for the Commission. At the same time he was looking for a theatrical, emotional response from me showing outrage and fury that he would so blatantly attempt to stick his finger into the dignified eye of the Commission. It was a pure, delightful Farley Mowat moment in which he relished the opportunity to be outrageous.

Without conferring with Marsh Jeanneret or Dalton Camp, who flanked me, I chose to ignore Farley's move with the booze. I asked who would be speaking to lead off for the authors' group. He announced that he would speak first. I asked him to proceed without making any comment on his production of the bottle.

What a disappointment for Farley Mowat that must have been, that not one of us rose like a trout to catch his elusive booze fly on the calm waters of the Commission's hearing.

Off he went with his learned discourse on how Canadian authors ought to be treated. All the authors ultimately had their say, which of course decried the concept of American publishers taking over the Canadian-owned firms and explained what it would mean to them if the decision to publish their books was to be made in New York or Chicago or anywhere else in the bowels of the United States.

We listened to their respective views, putting questions to them as they seemed appropriate. All in all it was a peaceful and productive hearing, at the conclusion of which I'm not sure what Farley's condition was. But we all dispersed without fisticuffs even being considered.

The work of the Royal Commission on Book Publishing suddenly shifted to consider a problem that hadn't yet arisen when the Commission was formed. During its weeks of operation we began to hear rumblings about what was going on in the mass market paperback and magazine distribution industry in Ontario. What we were being told alarmed the Commission. For a given region, such as Metropolitan Toronto or London, or Windsor, the producers of weekly or monthly magazines such as *Time*, *Newsweek*, or *Maclean's* — there were scores of them, if not hundreds — gave the magazines to one single distributor. In effect that distributor had a monopoly. The same distributor would also be selected for mass market paperbacks.

In the Toronto area the firm that had this monopoly was Metro Toronto News. A comparable corporation had the distribution rights in Windsor, another in London, and yet another in Kingston. And so it went throughout Ontario.

What the Commission was hearing, and it turned out to be exactly correct, was that a family called Molaski from St. Louis, Missouri, was moving into Ontario and beginning to buy up Ontario regional distributors, including Metro Toronto News. The apparent intent was that the Molaskis would acquire all of the mass market paperback and magazine distributors in Ontario. If our information was correct, then to have an American family, which brought with it rumours of ties to inappropriate groups in society, come in and buy Metro Toronto News was one thing. It probably would have escaped attention as being contrary to the public interest. But coming in to buy up *all* of the various distributors in Ontario with individual monopolies was quite another; it would in fact give the Molaski family a complete Ontario monopoly of the distribution of mass market paperbacks and magazines. This was unacceptable.

Faced with this information, and with the approval of my fellow commissioners, I approached the government and asked for a broadened mandate that would require us to investigate, examine, and, if necessary, hold public hearings on what the Molaskis were doing, and if it was deemed to be contrary to the public interest to so report to the government and recommend action to be taken.

With this new mandate and the power to subpoena witnesses, the Commission immediately prepared for public hearings on the mass market paperback and magazine question. At this point it was obvious to me that in order to effectively undertake these hearings it would be necessary for the Commission to appoint its own counsel to assist in the preparation for the hearings and to conduct the questioning of witnesses on behalf of the Commission in keeping with our new mandate.

I had been much impressed by the ability to think on his feet of a young counsel with the Basil, Sullivan firm by the name of Richard

(Dick) Holland, QC. I had seen him in operation at various court matters. With the consent of my fellow commissioners I put a call in to him and asked if he would consider being counsel for us in this totally unexpected set of hearings we would be conducting in relation to the activities of the Molaski family. Dick very quickly agreed. From that moment on he was a part of our team, advising and doing all things necessary, including issuing subpoenas to the various members of the Molaski family and to the companies and corporations to whom they had purportedly made offers.

When Dick Holland advised us that the case was ready to be heard by the Commission, we set an appropriate date, issued the subpoenas, and set the stage.

The auditorium stage was literally set. It was the usual forum in the auditorium of the OISE building. Marsh Jeanneret, Dalton Camp, and I were still in our usual position at the east end of the stage. But instead of counsel and the witnesses being on the stage with us they were to operate on the level immediately below between the front row of seats and the stage. A lectern for counsel was placed in the middle. Dick Holland's table was to the left from our vantage point, and to the right was a table for the Molaskis and their counsel, should they retain one, which, of course, they did.

At the opening of the hearing, I was pleasantly surprised to see sitting at the Molaski counsel table a man for whom I had great respect and whom I knew would present all manner of challenges to the Commission and its counsel. It was the unique Joseph Sedgewick, QC, with whom I had been confronted at the Board of Broadcast Governors hearing on the move of the CHUM CKVR tower from Barrie to Palgrave. I knew immediately what the eloquent Joe would try to do and immediately prepared for his onslaught.

What I expected Sedgewick to do was to attempt to take over the conduct and operation of the hearing, he being so much older. Actually, I would have been disappointed if he hadn't. He went for it exactly as I expected.

I listened politely to Joe and all of his arguments as to his wonderful clients and how the Commission should treat them, how it was such a terrible insult to bring them before this panel, how the panel should actually be complimenting them on their efforts to consolidate the mass market paperback and magazine distribution in Ontario, how the Commission had no right to require his clients to be testify, and so on and so forth. Joe went at it, utilizing his full and persuasive oratory to tell us how we should handle the Molaski process, which included exonerating them without even hearing any witnesses.

When Joe finished I think he fully expected the three-member Commission to wither and fall under the table, or at least apologize for existing, then retreat in order to allow the great Mr. Sedgewick to have his own way in the conduct of the hearing. That is not what happened. I simply responded by saying that the panel had carefully listened to every argument that Mr. Sedgewick had made, that we understood the difficult position that his clients from St. Louis were in, that we had a strong mandate from the government to inquire into the circumstances of the Molaski attempts to acquire all of the significant mass market paperback and magazine distribution companies across Ontario, and that we, the Commission, were going to run the hearing as we saw fit, not as Mr. Sedgewick saw fit. With that I called upon Mr. Holland to present his first witness, who, as I recall, gave evidence as to the attempted Molaski acquisition of Metro Toronto News and others.

Sedgewick had no choice but to sit down, and we proceeded.

During the course of the hearing everything went relatively smoothly, notwithstanding the frequent interventions by Sedgewick, which were handled with respect and firmness.

A younger member of the Molaski family was present through all of the hearings but declined to give evidence, and we were not inclined to force him to so to do.

The Commission was convinced that the Molaskis were indeed attempting to acquire all of the monopolistic distribution firms of mass market paperbacks and magazines in Ontario with the clear intent of having complete control in the entire province. It was also our opinion that this activity was contrary to the public interest; whether it was conducted by Canadians or Americans was not the issue, although it was a factor in our judgment.

What was the Commission to do? It was to put together another interim report. As I had with the McMichael Gallery, I worked with Deputy Attorney General Rendall Dick, QC, and his best drafter of legislation. Together we quickly constructed a piece of legislation called The Mass Market Paperback and Magazine Distributors Act, which became part of the interim report. I took the report and the proposed legislation to Premier Bill Davis, who had recently taken over as premier from John Robarts. Within a few days the legislation was introduced in the Ontario Legislature and quickly passed into law. It was designed to make illegal the activities of the Molaski group from St. Louis and to prevent any corporation, whether Canadian or American, from owning and operating either directly or indirectly more than one mass market paperback and magazine distributor in Ontario.

During the Molaski hearings I proposed a particular course of action in relation to the hearing that Richard Holland approved of as our counsel. When we announced it — I've forgotten at this moment what exactly it was — the *Globe and Mail* editorial board decided that they didn't like it and that it was trampling on the rights of individuals, that sort of thing. So the editorial board of Canada's then leading national newspaper wrote a lead editorial severely criticizing the Commission chair and Holland for their unacceptable actions. I did not know it, but Holland was at that period negotiating and hoping for an appointment to the bench of the Supreme Court of Ontario. He was certain that this editorial would ruin any chance that he might have for such a distinguished post. It did not. A short time after his services to the Commission were completed, my good friend Richard Holland, QC, was appointed to the Supreme Court of Ontario, Trial Division, where he served as a remarkably outstanding judge for the full term of his career, adjudicating in some of the most important corporate cases in the history of Ontario with judgments that withstood the scrutiny of the Court of Appeal of Ontario and the Supreme Court of Canada. Upon his retirement from the bench, Richard Holland became one of the most successful and respected mediators and arbitrators in Ontario, serving with many distinguished former judicial and other colleagues with a firm he had assisted in putting together, ADR Chambers Inc. of Toronto.

After the mass market paperback and magazine hearings the Commission got on with its work of examining all aspects of the Canadian book publishing industry. The papers it had requisitioned from various experts came in, and it was time to write the Commission's report. The bulk of the writing, which all three of us signed off on, was done by the learned Dr. Marsh Jeanneret with Dalton Camp and myself adding input every step of the way.

On December 1, 1972, under my signature as chairman with the signatures of Dalton Camp and Marsh Jeanneret, the Commission delivered its massive two-volume report to the Government of Ontario. The Commission hoped that its findings and recommendations, which were extensive, would assist the government in developing programs that would both protect and enhance the Canadian book publishing industry, at least that part of it that was based in Ontario. If nothing else, with our interim reports concerning financial assistance to the book publishing industry and the creation of the mass market paperback and magazine legislation, we believed that we had directly and positively influenced the course of events.

The members of the Commission then waited for a response from the Ontario government. Our report was turned over to a senior bureaucrat who knew nothing about the book publishing industry, and he responded accordingly. After months of waiting, Jeanneret, Camp, and I were convinced beyond a shadow of a doubt that it was beyond the ability of the government of the day or its bureaucrats to come to grips with one, let alone all, of the recommendations.

Thus it was that the recommendations of the Royal Commission on Book Publishing, except for its interim reports, went the way that Royal Commission reports are usually received by government: they were filed, never to be heard from again.

On the other hand, the Government of Canada was paying attention to what we had recommended. Without admitting its interest, it began to evolve national programs for the assistance of Canadian book publishing houses and Canada's authors. So in the long haul Jeanneret, Camp, and Rohmer were comforted in the belief that our work had indeed led to the strengthening and the survival of Canada's book publishing industry, a most important part of Canada's unique culture and society.

As for my good friends Marsh Jeanneret, Dalton Camp, and Richard Holland, like many of my friends and acquaintances around whom the anecdotes of these memoirs are built, they are gone but well remembered.

CHAPTER 57

Commander of the Air Reserve Group and Chief of Reserves of the Canadian Armed Forces

———————◆———————

BACK TO THE MILITARY.

In 1973, after a lot of massaging and encouragement to those in power, I was appointed by the Chief of the Defence Staff to be a full honorary colonel, the first in the Canadian Air Force. I was much honoured as well as pleased by this promotion and distinction.

In those days I was often in Ottawa. I decided it would be a good thing if from time to time in full uniform I would visit the Chief of the Defence Staff in his office at National Defence Headquarters (NDHQ). In 1973, Fred Sharp's successor, General Jacques Dextraze, a wonderful Second World War Army hero, became CDS. The two of us had met earlier, and we got on well with each other.

So it was that I would visit Jaydex, which was his nickname, in his offices in the new NDHQ building, always in my full colonel's uniform.

As it turned out, Jaydex was always delighted to see me, for a reason that I very quickly began to understand. The Chief of the Defence Staff is at the top of the pile with his vice-chief and deputy chief under him and a host of generals and admirals. But he rarely has anyone to whom he can unload his major problems in total confidence knowing that nothing would ever be repeated by that party — me. Also, I was never reluctant to give an opinion. He had all kinds of things going on that were causing him day-to-day problems, not the least of which was his tough relationship with a fellow French-Canadian by the name of Pierre Elliot Trudeau, the Prime Minister. Be that as it may, I would spend an hour, perhaps two hours, with him and then we would both go about our business. I would usually wind up with some senior Air Force general at

NDHQ asking for some boon for the Air Reserve and in particular my 411 Squadron. I would also visit the vice-chief and deputy chief and their staffs wherever possible. In the end I became a relatively familiar face, a harmless, benign one, in full colonel's uniform and replete with my Distinguished Flying Cross and other ribbons, which gave me some degree of authenticity.

By this time the senior Air Reserve advisor was another Toronto airman, this time from 400 Squadron, Brigadier-General Barry Howard. Barry and I had known each other reasonably well over a long period of time, but there was always some distance between us. By 1975, Barry had served out his term as senior Air Reserve advisor, and it was time for the CDS to pick his successor. By some leap of faith, Jaydex decided, in consultation with his senior Air Force officers, that it would be appropriate if Honorary Colonel Richard Rohmer might be promoted to brigadier-general and become the senior air advisor to the Chief of the Defence Staff. With no reluctance whatever I was privileged and honoured to receive the appointment and immediately and proudly put on my sleeve the wide general's gold band and on my shoulders the general's epaulette with one maple leaf, or star, as the Americans call their ranks. I was a one-star. And my flat hat had to be replaced with a new one with the ample gold braid of a general on the peak of my cap.

This was to be a new, virtually unpaid career, but it was an exciting one that allowed me to continue to fly while doing my work, which was in effect to oversee the Air Reserve squadrons in Montreal, Toronto, Winnipeg, the West, and the Maritimes.

An office was set up for me at Canadian Forces Base Downsview so I had the resources of both 400 and 411 squadrons available to me for support and flying transport. The duties of the senior Air Reserve advisor to the Chief of the Defence Staff were vague indeed. For example: go and see the CDS when he needs special advice in relation to matters that relate to the Air Reserve; keep in contact with the Conference of Defence Associations; visit your squadrons to see what their particular problems are so that you can approach the regular force, hoping that they would rectify those problems. In all it was a vague "as you make it yourself" situation. I was enormously assisted by the fact that as the carrier of the post I was of brigadier-general rank with all its door-opening potential even in the domain of the regular force, who mostly (but not all) have an ongoing tendency to look down their noses at their reserve force colleagues. However, for myself I have never had that treatment personally, probably because I had been around so long and had a few recognizable achievements both large and small.

In 1975, things were about to change for me in my advisory position.

At National Defence Headquarters, the decision had been made that the air component of the military, the former Royal Canadian Air Force, should be reconstituted under the name Air Command, with its headquarters to be located at Canadian Forces Base Winnipeg. That was exciting news indeed for all of us in Canada's Air Force, be it regular or reserve.

The first Commander of Air Command was to be Lieutenant-General Bill Carr, DFC, a wartime fighter pilot who had served with distinction in the post-war period. We were contemporaries, much of the same age and certainly from similar air backgrounds. From the outset I was much impressed with the abilities of Bill Carr as a leader, an organizer, and a pilot as he put together his headquarters staff in Winnipeg, where I went to visit him. I wanted to put forward my proposition with regard to the Air Reserve.

It was Bill Carr's plan to divide Air Command into various groups according to their roles. There would be the Transport Group, the Fighter Group, the Tactical Air Group, and the Maritime Air Group. My proposition to him went this way: there are Air Reserve squadrons in the Maritimes, Montreal, Toronto, Winnipeg, and Edmonton. Maritime units should go with the Maritime Air Group, the Otter squadrons at Montreal and Toronto should stay in Tactical Air Group, and Winnipeg and Edmonton should go with Transport Group, all for operational purposes, command, and direction. On the other hand, I proposed that there be a fifth group known as the Air Reserve Group, commanded by an Air Reserve brigadier-general who would have administrative and logistical control over the group, whereas the operational aspect of each unit would be in the command and control of its appropriate group commander. In this way the Air Reserve Group and its wings and squadrons would finally have a strong identity. The input of the Air

Reserve at meetings of the group commanders could be of enormous value in terms of having information and understanding and appreciation of the position of the Air Reserve, which often was quite different from that of the regular force.

General Carr bought my proposition, as did the CDS.

The result was that on April 4, 1975, at a huge parade at Air Command Headquarters in Winnipeg, I was installed by Lieutenant-General William Carr, DFC, as the first commander of the Air Reserve Group, under Minister of National Defence Jim Richardson. I finally had a job in the military into which I could sink my teeth, which by this time were somewhere in the range of fifty-one years old.

I had asked Bill Carr to appoint as my deputy commander a young lieutenant-colonel by whom I had been impressed when I had seen him in operation

The new brigadier-general, 1975.

in Toronto. I was granted my request even though it meant that the young lieutenant-colonel would also be promoted to the rank of full colonel, as the establishment of my staff required.

To his credit, Colonel Val Patty was absolutely ideal for the handling of the details of the formation of the Air Reserve Group. It must be kept in mind that I was still practising law heavily in Toronto and accordingly trying to earn a living. In addition my new book writing career was demanding a lot of time, and my family was more important than anything. I was doing a lot of professional public speaking, usually on Mid-Canada. The MiniStation business was still in operation in North York and Toronto. For the military side of things, I had responsibilities virtually from one end of the country to the other, with regular visits to my squadrons and to my headquarters at National Defence Headquarters in Winnipeg as circumstances required. It was a busy, busy time in my life, and I must confess that I thrived on it. As for my book career (which I will expand upon later), in 1973 I had published my first novel, *Ultimatum*, with Bill Clarke of Clarke, Irwin. Because of his active promotion activity and my cross-country book tour, *Ultimatum* received an enormous amount of attention. It went to the top of the Canadian best-sellers list. So I was established as a novelist and began the process of turning out a novel a year, such as *Exxoneration* in 1974 and *Exodus UK*, which was in process in 1975. Yes, and there was the Royal Commission on Book Publishing thrown into the mix, to be followed shortly thereafter in 1975 by my selection to be his counsel by John Robarts in his capacity as the Royal Commissioner on Metropolitan Toronto.

I acted as Premier John Robarts's counsel during
the Royal Commission on Metro Toronto.

During my period as commander of the Air Reserve Group, not only did I visit my headquarters at Winnipeg three, four, probably five times a month, but I also regularly spent time with my squadrons and flew with them whether they were on the Tracker aircraft of the Maritime Air Group, the Otters of Montreal and Toronto, or the DC3s and twin Otters of the Western squadrons. I was at the head of a flying organization, and it was important for them to meet me and see me. And it was exceedingly important that they could fly with me.

I must say that Bill Carr and his regular force group commanders treated me as one of their own in every respect and in particular at the regular conferences Bill Carr had with his group commanders. All of them were highly capable, proficient officers of the first quality. They had all risen to general rank solely because of their ability and dedication. And the fact that I was a reservist meant nothing to them. I was part of the team. Mind you, like Bill Carr, I had wings and a flying decoration that they respected.

During my stint as commander of the Air Reserve Group, I maintained my captaincy on the Otter aircraft and frequently flew with the Toronto and Montreal squadrons. It was my practice to have an experienced, qualified young captain in the right seat when I was flying. My instructions were always the same to the man in the right seat: "When I am flying this aircraft, particularly at landing or takeoff, although you may be signed out as captain, if you become apprehensive about my ability, which you should not in any event, do not under any circumstances grab for the controls. I will break your arms if you do so." That injunction was only violated once, when an over-eager, forgetful young captain attempted to reach for the controls when I was about to touch down at Ottawa International Airport.

In 1978, the Air Reserve Group was flourishing, and my military career (long though it was from 1942 but short though it was from 1971, a mere seven years from the time I had relaunched as an honorary lieutenant-colonel) took a substantial upward turn. The post of Major-General Reserves, then held by Major-General Bruce Legge, a militia member, was about to become vacant with the expiry of Bruce's term. I and my visible supporters in the military, particularly at National Defence Headquarters, got behind the proposition that the first Air Reserve officer should be appointed to that post, which had always been filled before with militia (Army) major-generals.

I am not aware of the process that existed at that time, but I believe it was the singular choice of my friend Jaydex that caused him to promote me to major-general and to fill the post of Major-General Reserves.

The new major-general, 1978.

Whatever the process, Minister of National Defence Barney Danson approved and announced that upon promotion to major-general I would become the Major-General Reserves. You can be assured that I was delighted and thrilled with the promotion and appointment. Much later there would be other Air Reserve appointees to the post of the top reservist, but as the first one I was specially privileged.

The Chief of the Defence Staff who succeeded Jaydex was a man I had known since the middle of the Second World War, when he was then Lieutenant Robert Falls of the Royal Canadian Navy. He was now Admiral Falls, CDS, having been appointed by the Minister of Defence, the Honourable Barney Danson, who is a good friend of mine.

I have already told the story about Bob Falls and his letting me fly the Fairey Swordfish at Dartmouth in 1947.

When I was appointed Major-General Reserves, I already knew that my predecessor had had no office or staff and that fundamentally he had worked out of his prestigious law office of Legge & Legge in the centre of Toronto. On my first trip to Ottawa in my new post I had time with Admiral Falls. I suggested that if I was going to be an effective Major-General Reserves I should have an office and staff at NDHQ so that I would be in a better position to advise him and the CDS and to work with the regular force staff who were responsible for the administration of the militia, the air and naval reserves, and the cadet organizations spread across the country. He immediately agreed, and within a short time I was allocated an office two storeys above his at National Defence Headquarters. In addition, a regular force lieutenant-colonel (Army) was seconded to me as my staff person; he would function for me when I was not in attendance at NDHQ, although I tried to be there one day a week.

The next step was to persuade the CDS that since I had an office within NDHQ I should be permitted to attend "morning prayers" whenever I was in Ottawa.

Morning prayers was the traditional 0800 hours briefing of the CDS, the deputy minister, the vice-chief, deputy chief, and other senior generals as to the current military and other events around the world and in Canada. It was also an opportunity to present various policy proposals that had to be considered by the Chief of the Defence Staff.

With an appropriate security clearance in hand the CDS allowed that this would be a good idea, and I attended my first meeting, much to the astonishment of the various generals and colonels assembled in the morning prayers briefing room. I was allocated a seat at the far end of the long table, away from the CDS. I was the first reserve general ever to attend morning prayers. I maintained my attendance and privilege during the entire term that I was Chief of Reserves.

Another change that I asked of the CDS was that since I was the first Air Force Major-General Reserves, and since it was likely that someone from the Navy would succeed me at some time with the equivalent rank of rear admiral, the name "Major-General Reserves" was not appropriate. What was? I had noticed in the regular force staffing of things there were many chiefs of this and chiefs of that. For example, the current head of the Canadian Air Force is once again called the chief of the air staff. In any event, I proposed that my post be changed so that I would be Chief of Reserves. Granted. And so the name changed.

Indeed, one of my successors was a man I had recruited in Windsor in 1946 into the University Naval Training Division (UNTD). His name was Tom Smith, and he rose through the naval reserve ranks and was senior naval reserve advisor with the rank of commodore during my term of office. He was the second successor after me. He then held the rank of rear admiral.

As the senior reserve officer of the Canadian Armed Forces responsible to the Chief of the Defence Staff for advice in relation to Army, Navy, Air Force, and communication reservists, it was more essential than ever that I visit units across the country on a regular basis so that I could report to the CDS and his staff with regard to the state of the reserve forces and any important problems.

Travelling and visiting Army, Navy, Air Force, and communications units was what I did for the three years of my tenure. And I must say that all of the admiral's staff at NDHQ were very supportive of what I was doing. On the other hand, I was totally frustrated by the fact that at NDHQ day-to-day reserve affairs were in fact being administered by regular force personnel headed by a brigadier-general and by the fact that in reality I had only a nominal input into what was going on out there. I was quite satisfied that my predecessor, without an office at NDHQ or access to morning prayers and the CDS on a regular basis, had enjoyed even less of an opportunity to influence the course of events.

There are two events that I recall from my tenure as Chief of Reserves, neither of which is particularly serious.

In 1979, the admiral in command of Maritime Command decided that he would have a mess/wardroom dinner at HMCS *Carleton*, the naval reserve land ship at Ottawa. He would host it with the then senior naval advisor.

Commodore Tom Smith was to attend, with the up-and-coming Captain (N) Wally Fox-Decent, who was destined to later succeed Tom Smith. Fox-Decent was a brilliant academic from Winnipeg who, like Tom Smith, carried a lot of weight in his community.

I had discovered a technicality in the integration of the Armed Forces that provided an interesting approach to this dinner. In the scheme of things, an officer who had served in another service, such as the Navy, was entitled to wear the mess kit of that service, even though he was now serving in another element, such as the Air Force. I decided that I would use that technicality, since I had served in the naval reserve in the late 1940s, and attend the mess dinner in the full old-style naval mess kit of a rear admiral, which was my equivalent rank.

I immediately shopped around in Toronto to see if I could find a naval mess kit that I could borrow or rent — I wasn't about to buy one. Nothing could be found. I did the same thing in London, England. Nothing. One day I happened to mention to Admiral Falls that I was looking for a mess kit and told him the reason. He immediately informed me that he had such a mess kit and, believe it or not, it had his old rank of rear admiral still on it. He had not worn the old naval gear for some time, using instead his modern integrated force mess kit. I proposed immediately that if he would let me have it for use at this grand affair that I would return it to him with his full admiral's rank newly and properly emblazoned on the sleeves. The deal was sealed. The next week when I was in my office at NDHQ there was the complete mess kit hanging on my coat rack. The only change that had to be made was to temporarily shorten the trousers by a couple of inches. Otherwise, the fit was perfect.

On the evening of the gala dinner at HMCS *Carlton* I appeared in my rear admiral's mess kit resplendent with miniatures. Up my left sleeve was of, course, the traditional Royal Navy handkerchief. I can tell you that my appearance caused quite an amusing sensation that night. It was great fun and all perfectly legal.

A few weeks later I was able to return the mess kit to Admiral Falls with his proper rank on it, which had unexpectedly cost me a small fortune to have done. In any event, I was quite properly a rear admiral, a major-general, and, in technical terms, I could still be called air vice-marshal.

The second event occurred in the summer months. When visiting militia units in the field, it was my practice to wear appropriate Army work clothes complete with boots and beret. There was no way I was going to appear among an Army crowd as their leader dressed in an Air Force uniform. As Chief of Reserves I was entitled to wear the gear of any one of the services (Army, Navy, Air Force) that I was to visit. Being primarily based in Toronto with my law practice and residence, I continued to use the Otter resources of 400 and 411 squadrons, always on the condition that I would fly the airplane and some young captain or major signed out as captain on the aircraft would sit in the right-hand seat. In the summer of 1980 I had flown from Downsview to St. Hubert, the then headquarters of the Army, that is to say the land forces. I had business to do with the general in command of Canada's Army. Then I was to proceed to Canadian Forces Base Petawawa, where several of the militia regiments of the central region Ontario were in place for their annual summer camp training period of two weeks.

I flew down to St. Hubert in a Toronto Otter then sent it back, having requisitioned an Otter from 401 Squadron in Montreal (St. Hubert) to take me up to Petawawa for my visit there, then I would fly it back to Toronto. When I was ready to depart St. Hubert a staff car took me from the headquarters building down to the airfield. There was my Otter sitting ready to go and a fairly young captain in appropriate Air Force flying gear standing beside the aircraft waiting for me. He and I had never flown together.

When I got out of the staff car dressed in my Army major-general's gear the response I got from the Air Force pilot was, "Sir, you can't fly dressed like that!" He was deadly serious. I laughed, saying, "I can and I will. Don't let the Army rig fool you. Get in. Sit in the right seat and we'll go." I also gave him my usual injunction that he was not to touch the controls under any circumstances. Off we went. We were highly successful in reaching Petawawa on time, and I carried out my happy visit with the militia units — properly dressed, of course.

In 1978, I received a totally unexpected honour, right out of the blue. In the published list of recipients of the Order of Military Merit, Canada's highest military decoration, it was announced that I had been made a Commander of the Order of Military Merit, the highest rank. It allows me to use the initials CMM after my name.

There was a splendid investiture ceremony later on at Rideau Hall when Governor General Ed Schreyer invested all of the new recipients of the order. For me the highlight was the Governor General hanging my beautiful CMM decoration with its red and white ribbon around my neck: a few words of congratulations from His Excellency, shaking of hands, and it was done. I knew this Governor General from a visit I had paid him in Winnipeg when he was premier of that province and I was promoting membership in the Mid-Canada Development Corridor Conference. He remembered me from that occasion. He was to pay me a special salute later on the occasion of my retirement as Chief of Reserves.

During my six-year tenure first as commander of the Air Reserve Group and then as Chief of Reserves I made several trips across the Atlantic, particularly into Germany to visit air and Army reserve personnel working at Canada's major military base at Baden Soelingen. Those trips to Germany also involved exciting rides in the back seat of Canada's ancient CF104 fighters. There was a special trip to Egypt, where I visited our troops and airmen located at a strategic place on the Suez Canal. My host on that occasion was Colonel Don McNaughton, who later rose to the rank of lieutenant-general and was destined to be second-in-command at the North American Air Defence Command (NORAD) mountain fortress at Colorado Springs. A fine host, the young colonel was able to find time to take me to the pyramids, ride on a camel, and have a fulsome vision of a superb belly dancer at one of Cairo's top hotels.

Many years later, when he was deputy commander of NORAD, the young general invited me to Colorado Springs to be the guest of honour at a major mess dinner the Canadians held to pay tribute to their American counterparts at that massive headquarters. I do not remember the substance of my brilliant speech on that occasion. Suffice it to say that I did not cause any ripples in the calm water between the cooperating American and Canadian generals present at that festive occasion. General McNaughton has long retired from the Canadian Armed Forces, as have all of the people I mention in this significant military sector of my life. For that matter, many of them are gone from this earth.

Just before he retired as CDS, Jaydex told me confidentially that he was interested in a job that was open. It was chairman of the Canadian National Railway. He had no idea how to go about trying to get the post. We talked about Trudeau, who clearly would have a strong hand in saying either yes or no to the appointment. It was my opinion that Bob Bandeen, the president of the CNR, whom I knew, having met him during the Mid-Canada days, would have the main say on who was to be the new chairman.

I told Jaydex I would call Bandeen and arrange an appointment with him at his Montreal office for both Jaydex and me. I would fly down to St. Hubert from Toronto in an Otter and Jaydex would fly down from Ottawa and meet me at St. Hubert. We would go in to see Bob Bandeen from there.

Bandeen said he would be pleased to talk with us, and we set a time and date.

Jaydex and I rendezvoused at St. Hubert, then changed out of our military clothing into our best civilian dress. A car was waiting for us, and in short order we were in Bandeen's office, where I introduced the two of them. The meeting was most cordial. After things were underway and the ice was broken, I left them together and went out into the executive waiting room. In due course the pair emerged from Bandeen's office, both smiling.

As events later unfolded, Jaydex retired from the Canadian Armed Forces and became chairman of the Canadian National Railway.

Jaydex's stay in that post was not very long. As I heard the situation, Bob Bandeen quite properly wanted to keep executive command and control of the CNR. What he wanted the chairman to do was to take the company's special entertainment railway car and go to visit executives of CNR's major customers. I remember visiting Jaydex in his CNR offices in Montreal when he first told me that he was really not happy about his role. This was probably within a year after his appointment. It was not long thereafter that General Jacques Dextraze resigned from the CNR to pursue other interests.

Early in 1980, Admiral Falls told me that he was going to go to Norway to visit his good friend General Hamre, the commander of the Norwegian Forces. He would travel to Oslo, meet General Hamre there, then Falls would proceed independently by Canadian Forces Twin Otter up to Tromsø in the far north sector of Norway, relatively close to the Soviet Union border. A NATO exercise was being held near there with Canadian, American, Norwegian, Italian, and British forces taking part. Would I like to go? Of course. After a long haul across to Canadian Forces Base Lahr in Germany and then by Twin Otter up to Oslo we were finally greeted by the diminutive General Hamre.

Obviously he and Bob Falls were fond of each other and mutually supportive. Hamre's people gave Bob Falls and me a tour of their main Oslo establishment, and then we all headed to lunch, where General Hamre was waiting for us in the officers' mess of the base. We all enjoyed a convivial time until the very end when the cheese tray was passed. I thought that I would like to have something from the selection, so I picked up the triangular device that was accompanying the tray. It had a slot across the middle. I used that device to cut the cheese vertically like an ordinary knife. Well, you should have heard the jovial commotion and noise that happened immediately. General Hamre and his people shouted their instructions at me that that was not the way I should use the cheese carver, if I can call it that. What you have to do is lay the blade flat on the top of the cheese with the cutting device ready to be inserted into the cheese, then you pull the cutter's long blade toward you. It then slices into the cheese and delivers up a slim, sophisticated portion for you.

It may well be that that was the first time I had ever used such a cheese cutter. The ribbing that I got from it was worth the effort.

Two days later we arrived in Tromsø. Bob Falls was flying around in a British helicopter and soon convinced the captain of it that he, Falls, was a skilled helicopter pilot and could he fly the machine? The young pilot agreed. From that point on Falls flew the helicopter, and I must say he did so with great skill. Frankly, I was impressed.

This was mountainous country we were in, although the hotel at Tromsø was quite satisfactory. The next morning Bob Falls and I were with an Italian artillery regiment high up in the snow-covered mountains when a huge Norwegian helicopter came clattering in to stop close to where Falls and I were standing. When it was landed the door opened and there in the entrance was General Hamre waving at me to come toward the machine. Being an obedient major-general I did not hesitate. When I reached the door he handed me a package with a big smile and a salute. Then his helicopter was off again. We would see him back at the hotel.

I couldn't figure what in heaven's name he had given me, but when I immediately opened the package I discovered that it was a beautifully crafted Norwegian cheese slicer, a permanent souvenir of my first visit to Norway. General Hamre's cheese slicer is one of my prized possessions.

An addition to that 1980 story of General Hamre. In the fall of that year I received a call from a protocol colonel at National Defence Headquarters, who advised me that Admiral Falls had invited General Hamre and his wife for a courtesy visit to Canada. Admiral Falls and his wife and the Hamres would be in Toronto on such and such a date, and was there a restaurant that I could recommend to Admiral Falls for dinner? That was easy. It was Winston's, where Robarts and I, John Turner, and countless people whom I knew regularly had lunch back in those days. The marvellous John Arena was the owner and undoubtedly the best restaurateur in Toronto. I made the final arrangements with John. He was highly impressed by the prestige and quality of the guests who would be at his restaurant.

Mary-O and I were at Winston's a bit early, just before Bob and his charming wife, Belle, and the Hamres arrived. General Hamre was delighted to see the cheesy general again. We were all in our civilian clothes, of course.

The dinner went splendidly, with sumptuous food and flowing wine. John Arena, originally an Italian, could speak several languages as a result of his having been a waiter in many cities in Europe. John could handle the Swedish language, which was good enough for General Hamre. Furthermore, it was John himself who waited on our table, taking the orders and serving the food with great expertise and actually backing away from the table when he had served each course.

The whole occasion was a great success, and, as usual at Winston's, I walked out without looking at or signing the bill. No problem so far as John Arena was concerned.

About a month later I received a plaintive call from Ottawa from the same protocol colonel who had called me in the first place. He said, "General, have you seen the Winston's bill?" There was clear shock in his voice. I replied, "Colonel, I haven't seen it and I can advise you that no matter what it is just pay it!" That was the end of the matter, and believe me I have never seen the bill.

By the end of 1980 my tour as Chief of Reserves was coming to an end. It had been decided that Brigadier-General John Dunn of Montreal, the militia senior advisor to the Chief of the Defence Staff, would succeed me. I was pleased with his nomination and promotion and had supported it.

In recognition of my departure, the CDS arranged for a private dinner at the Château Laurier, to which all the senior advisors, including the commander of the Air Reserve Group, were invited, in civilian clothes of course. There was an extra special guest who honoured me greatly by attending. It was Governor General Ed Schreyer. Needless to say I was much flattered by his presence.

My service as Chief of Reserves and as a member of the Primary Reserve of the Canadian Armed Forces ended on January 24, 1981, which was my fifty-seventh birthday.

On that day Mary-O and I were at our farm southwest of Creemore in the Mulmur Hills some twenty miles south of Collingwood for the weekend. An Otter from the Toronto wing was flown up to Collingwood airport, where I was waiting in full flying regalia, including my beautiful white flying helmet. I climbed into the captain's left seat and with a quaking young major in the right seat I flew the magnificent Otter for the last time. It was a wonderful way to leave.

I had earlier made arrangements to spend a week of intensive flying training on the Kiowa helicopter at CFB Portage La Prairie. I was going to do that to at least be able to say that I was a "qualified" helicopter pilot. But I begged off that session, believing, quite correctly, that it would be a waste of government money for me to do that and then walk out the door.

One of the reasons that I had wanted to do the Kiowa training was that I had been instrumental in a major change in the Air Reserve squadrons in Montreal and Toronto. That change was being implemented just as I left in January 1981.

As commander of the Air Reserve Group and as Chief of Reserves I had been concerned that the Montreal and Ottawa Air Reserve units were flying the single-engine Otter, an aircraft that was not part of the regular force fleet. As I reasoned, the reserve should be an organization able to augment the regular force in the event of an emergency or other urgent requirement. I believed that the aircraft that Montreal and Toronto were flying should be the same aircraft that the regular force was using. The designated aircraft was the Kiowa, a single-engine, four-placed helicopter.

But there was no money in the military budget for the purchase of a fleet of perhaps twenty brand new Kiowas for the Air Reserve units.

Finally, in about 1979, I had a breakthrough at National Defence Headquarters. I negotiated with the appropriate Air Force procurement people a deal that General Carr, the Commander of Air Command, approved. The deal went this way. The Air Reserve would turn over to the regular force for sale through Crown Assets Disposal all of the single-engine Otters, which would then enter the commercial aircraft stream in Canada. My recollection is that we had about twenty Otters in inventory, some with amphibious floats and skis and, of course, a host of spare parts. It was reckoned that each Otter would bring in about $150,000. The proceeds would then go into the military budget for whatever use, including the purchase of new aircraft for the regular force squadrons that were using the Kiowa.

In return, each of the Toronto and Montreal wings (two squadrons in each) would receive eight well-used but still serviceable and flyable Kiowa helicopters from the regular force squadrons.

The out-with-the-Otter-and-in-with-the-Kiowa plan was already being implemented by the end of 1980. It was fully executed after I left as Chief of Reserves, and the surviving units in Montreal and Toronto have been flying helicopters ever since.

So it was that on January 24, 1981, as Chief of Reserves I flew my last sortie with Air Command and the Toronto squadrons in a single-engine Otter and not a Kiowa helicopter, ending my long on-again, off-again association with the Canadian Armed Forces, which had begun on January 24, 1942.

A pension from the government for my military service? In the United States, yes, big time. In Canada, well, we don't do that sort of thing. Can't afford it, eh?

CHAPTER 58

Ambulance for Tortola from the Queen, and Princess Di at Green Park, June 1994

———◆———

GOING BACK A FEW YEARS, the time was early 1977. I was still commander of the Air Reserve Group, with my headquarters in Winnipeg. It was the year of Her Majesty Queen Elizabeth II's Jubilee, twenty-five years on the throne. It was to be a busy year. Nothing new.

Early in the year I received a telephone call from my old friend Brigadier-General Bill Draper, by that time a resident of Tortola in the British Virgin Islands. A professional engineer by trade, Bill had somehow been attracted to Tortola, where he was running a bare-bottom rental boat business for an entrepreneur. He and his wife, Sandy, a nurse who had been with 411 Squadron, were living in a house high up on the side of a mountain on the island of Tortola, where one could see forever.

Bill's request was straightforward: Her Majesty was coming to visit Tortola, and the people of Tortola needed a new ambulance. Through my connections with St. John Ambulance (I was on the board of the Ontario Council at the time) and in the name of St. John, Bill asked, "Please raise the money to buy the ambulance and get it down here to Tortola in time for Her Majesty to present the keys to the Chief Minister during her visit."

What could I say to this challenge? I said, "I'll do my best."

I then set about raising the necessary money. I obtained a major donation from Harry Jackman, a wonderful capitalist entrepreneur whom I had befriended much earlier. Harry was a great deal older than I. He was the father of Hal Jackman, later Lieutenant-Governor of Ontario and Chancellor of the University of Toronto, and of Frederick Jackman, later to succeed me as Chancellor of the University of Windsor. Father Harry had an ongoing love of statues and monuments, which he brought at great expense from as far away as India to populate Queen's Park and other niches in Toronto. Harry was also instrumental (and I with him as part of his operating committee, as was his good friend Roly Michener) in funding, obtaining municipal approvals for, acquiring, and erecting the Air Force monument at the southern mid-section of University and Dundas in Toronto. After Harry's demise, Hal kept the project going. It was eventually unveiled by Queen Elizabeth, accompanied by Prince Philip.

Harry came up with a very substantial part of the money that was required. I found an ambulance fabricator in Ontario and placed the order for the much-needed vehicle. The next step was to have transportation for the ambulance down to Tortola. Time before the delivery date promised and the Queen's arrival in Tortola was getting short.

In Winnipeg I approached my Air Force boss, the Commander of Air Command, Lieutenant-General Bill Carr, and told him what was happening with the ambulance. Bill ordered that two days in advance of the Queen's arrival a Hercules transport aircraft out of Canadian Forces Base Trenton would perform a training mission to Tortola and that it would carry the ambulance.

On the evening before our departure Mary-O and I went to the Trenton airbase. In the darkness as we passed the Hercules hangar area there was the huge transport aircraft, back end down, but with the gleaming white ambulance clearly visible in it. That was the first sight that I had had of this gift of St. John to the people of Tortola.

We spent the night in the appropriate suite at the officers' mess. In the morning we were on the Hercules aircraft, where we carefully inspected the inside and outside of the beautiful ambulance. It was emblazoned on each side door with the crest of the Order of St. John, of which Her Majesty is sovereign head. I was, of course, in my brigadier-general's uniform, still green at that time. Off we went.

Some hours later we were over the airport at Tortola. We could see a huge crowd around the terminal building, and to our surprise we could see another Hercules sitting on the ground on the arrival ramp. As it turned out this was a Royal Air Force transport on its yearly colonial visit to the island with the RAF regional commander, an air commodore, on board. The people were waiting for us and the ambulance, not for the British.

Evidently when the RAF Hercules landed all the people thought it was from Canada and expected to see the ambulance on it. When the tail ramp of the aircraft was lowered and there was no ambulance the crowd was quite disappointed and thought that the whole scheme was false. But then we appeared, and the beautiful white ambulance emerged to great cheers.

The tall British air commodore and I had a quick opportunity to exchange a few words about the coincidence of his Hercules and ours being there together.

Waiting for us as soon as we got off the aircraft were Bill and Sandy Draper, accompanied by Deputy Chief Minister of Tortola Lavety Stoutt, who by this time was a close friend of Bill Draper. Lavety was also Minister of Health, so this ambulance was a great treasure for him.

A much pleased and by now white-bearded Bill Draper eventually led Mary-O and me to his vehicle; in the back he had a cache of piña coladas, which in celebration he immediately shared with us and with two of the local policemen, who, when they finished their libations, got into the ambulance and drove it off to I know not where.

Draper then drove us to his huge nest high on the side of the local mountain. His handling of his car up the approach roads, which had breathtaking vertical drops within two or three feet of the edge of the road, was thrilling to say the least.

Two days later the fabled royal ship *Britannia* arrived in Tortola. Her Majesty was doing a tour of the various islands that were still members of the British Commonwealth, and Tortola was, of course, en route. Before we left Toronto I had attempted through the offices of the Honourable Paul Martin (he was Canada's high commissioner in London) to obtain an invitation to *Britannia* for a reception that Her Majesty and Prince Philip were to give on the evening of her visit to Tortola, just before *Britannia*'s departure. However, we had received word that the reception was for local residents only. Understandable, but disappointing. I then made contact with Sir Philip Moore, the Queen's private secretary.

With Bill Draper and Sandy, Mary-O and I attended the opening of the legislature by Her Majesty. The legislature was an open-windowed square building of one storey, probably one hundred by one hundred square feet in size. It was sweltering. We listened as Her Majesty read the Speech from the Throne. When she and Philip left the building, Lavety

Stoutt hustled us into his automobile and drove us directly to the hospital. From the main road up to the hospital was a ramp leading to the front door, which was under a porte cochère. There, sitting to the left of the entrance on this ramp, was the beautiful white ambulance, the gift of St. John Ambulance of Toronto. Its snout was facing down ramp and was just to the west of the main door to the building. The distance between the British driver's side of the ambulance to the edge of the ramp was perhaps two feet maximum, with a drop-off of some ten feet if one were to fall off the ramp.

Mary-O and I were in position, standing in front of the ambulance waiting for Her Majesty. I was in uniform and had my medals on my left chest, the DFC as usual at the front of the row. The royal party walked up the ramp from the road toward the hospital entrance, led by Her Majesty.

When she reached the entrance I could see officials speaking with her and motioning toward us and the ambulance. By this time she had been presented with a bouquet of flowers. Finally, she was brought to us by the Chief Minister. I could see her reading my medals as she approached. I think she was briefed for this event at the door of the hospital rather than well in advance. As she stopped in front of me, I said, "Your Majesty, this ambulance is a gift to the people of Tortola made by St. John Ambulance of Toronto. Here are the keys to the ambulance." I handed them to her saying, "Would you please be good enough in your capacity as the sovereign head of the Order of St. John to give these keys to the Chief Minister?" The Queen took the keys, handed them to the Chief Minister, and then said to me, "General, you may know that I drove an ambulance during the war, and so I would be obliged if I might see the inside of this beautiful vehicle."

I said, "Of course, Your Majesty, please follow me." That she did, as I was saying, "Be very careful, Your Majesty. The ramp is extremely narrow here."

As the two photographs show she did indeed follow me, still with the flowers in her arms. When I reached the front door of the vehicle I pushed the opening button under the handle only to discover that someone had locked the doors. And where were the keys? Way back there with the Chief Minister. I turned and said, "Your Majesty, somebody has locked the doors. Sorry."

The Queen receives St. John Ambulance keys in 1975
for a new ambulance for the people of Tortola.

She smiled, saying, "It's all right, General," then turned and made her way back to the Chief Minister and the group under the porte cochère. Thus the St. John Ambulance ambulance was delivered by Her Majesty to the Chief Minister of Tortola and its people.

Among the group standing in front of the hospital door was a gentleman with whom I had corresponded in relation to one or two matters concerning this presentation. It was Sir Philip Moore. Sir Philip and I had, through our correspondence, become friends. When he later moved on from the post of private secretary he became Lord Moore.

Through my negotiations with Sir Philip, at the last minute, Mary-O and I, with the Drapers, had received an invitation to attend the Queen's reception on board the *Britannia* that night. Bill Draper and I were in our brigadier-general mess kits with miniatures, and Sandy and Mary-O were formally and beautifully dressed. Somehow we got to *Britannia* in time to be the last ones through the reception line. Her Majesty, with Prince Philip, greeted us warmly and we had more discussion about the ambulance and its locked door. Prince Philip went off. Her Majesty then wanted to talk with us about the time that she had spent in Ottawa during this Jubilee tour. I can only tell you that she was very unhappy with the way Prime Minister Trudeau had kept her confined to Ottawa. "Tudeau," as she called him.

It was an extremely elegant evening capped off by *Britannia* departing from the Tortola harbour close to midnight after the Royal Marines Band had performed magnificently on the jetty. It was a true royal spectacle. Wonderful. We watched as *Britannia*, emblazoned with lights, with Her Majesty and Prince Philip standing at the rail amidships waving to the crowd, moved slowly out of the Tortola harbour and on to the next Jubilee tour destination.

Seventeen years later, in 1994, I had an unexpected opportunity to remind Her Majesty of the locked ambulance door incident at Tortola. And she remembered.

To properly tell that story I must begin by describing the events that led up to my being in the presence of the Queen on June 3, 1994, in Green Park, across from Buckingham Palace.

Around three years before, probably in 1991, a retired Canadian major-general named Desmond Smith, a man who had served in the Second World War, formulated the idea that somewhere in London, England, there should be a monument to the Canadians who had served in the United Kingdom in the First and Second World Wars, nine hundred thousand of them by count.

Desmond had been a resident in London, England, for many years and was married to a prominent member of British society. Desmond's efforts began to build support for his proposal. There was no monument or other edifice in London marking the presence of Canadians in the wars, whereas the place was "littered" with British monuments to themselves and American self-tributes, particularly at Grosvenor Square, where the American Embassy was located. Desmond decided that something should be done about it.

Eventually he came to Canada to see what he could get for support for his proposal. The wonderful Joan Sutton, the brilliant columnist and author and now a full-time resident of New York City, knew Desmond. Joan was firmly taken by his idea and began to solicit support for him. Through Joan I met Desmond and said that I would be prepared to be part of a team that would put a Canadian monument in the right place in London. Desmond was also able to get my friend Conrad Black (now Lord Black of Crossharbour) keenly interested. Conrad was then living in Canada and was intensively involved in Canadian matters, including the several corporations that he owned and controlled. It was expected that by nature he would take control of putting an organization together that would raise the funds, negotiate a location in London, and see to the design and building of the monument.

I told Conrad that I would be happy to participate. Then the line went blank for some months, at which point I let Conrad know that since nothing was happening I would withdraw my willingness to get involved.

That provoked an immediate response from Conrad, who vowed that he was going ahead with the project and who insisted that I stay with him on it. Of course, I agreed. He then had serious discussions with Galen Weston about participating financially and as a member of the board of directors of the corporation that Conrad proposed we create in order to do all necessary things, including issuing tax receipts. The

Canada Memorial Foundation Inc. was incorporated with Conrad Black, Galen Weston, and Richard Rohmer as its first and only directors.

An intense fundraising campaign was launched and was successful, the budget being somewhere in the range of C$2 million. For my part I visited my friend Paul Reichmann for a contribution. Paul's Canary Wharf connection was exceedingly obvious. Conrad was to move his *Daily Telegraph* headquarters to Canary Wharf.

In London, Conrad was negotiating with the appropriate British authorities to secure a location for the Canada Monument and was having all manner of difficulties. However, with determined effort and using his considerable persuasive skills he ultimately secured a site in Green Park close to the Canada Gates, immediately across from Buckingham Palace. A superb location. A competition was held for the design of the monument and was won by a Quebec artist. He produced a splendid structure: large, flat granite with maple leaves artfully engraved in its surface with running water flowing down its face. Near it was a large circular cast-bronze plaque laid in the ground describing the nature of the commemoration of the monument. Conrad's and Galen's names are on its surface for perpetuity. I'm still looking for mine.

The date was set for the unveiling by Her Majesty Queen Elizabeth. It was June 3, 1994, three days before the fiftieth anniversary of D-Day.

With Conrad at the helm and Fred Eaton in place as high commissioner to the Court of St. James, all arrangements were in readiness.

On June 3, Mary-O and I were staying at the Royal Air Force Club on Piccadilly, as we often do, just across the street from Green Park. The Queen was to arrive at eleven o'clock. By ten-thirty we were in the lobby of the RAF Club. I was in my major-general's uniform, by this time blue thank goodness, and with all my decorations and medals in place. I had forgotten to bring my St. John Knight's Cross with me and had spent the previous day arranging to obtain a new one from the Order of St. John in London. It was in place on my left chest below my medal bar and would figure in an event at the end of the unveiling.

We had our seats designated and reserved. In the RAF Club lobby I met for the first time a distinguished gentleman in his full regalia as marshal of the Royal Air Force, Sir Michael Beetham. Sir Michael had retired from the Royal Air Force but was also in full uniform, as we ancient airmen (he was a wartime contemporary) are wont to do if our uniforms still fit and it is appropriate to wear them. As it happened, we were seated together in the front row, next to the monument. Sir Michael's wife, Patricia, was in the row immediately behind him, and next to her, behind me, was Mary-O at the ready with an umbrella because there were showers skittering across the sky. The front row start to finish was populated with Second World War veterans, with their wives and caregivers immediately behind them. This was appropriate for the Queen's walkabout.

With great fanfare Her Majesty arrived and was greeted by Fred Eaton and Conrad. She mounted the covered platform adjacent to the monument. When the speeches were over and she was ready she pulled the rope that unveiled the monument with a great clatter that startled her. That was followed by her walkabout. In the twenty minutes before her arrival at Green Park, Sir Michael and I had talked incessantly and had found out a great deal about each other. So he was in the position to be able to introduce me to Her Majesty when she arrived in front of us, followed by all of the appropriate dignitaries: Conrad, Fred, and even Prime Minister Jean Chrétien.

When she stopped, Sir Michael said, "This is General Rohmer from Canada, a D-Day veteran," all that sort of thing. I then said, "Your Majesty, I met you in Tortola in 1975 on your Jubilee tour. It was a St. John's ambulance in front of the hospital. I

June 3, 1994. Talking with the Queen at the unveiling of the Canadian Memorial monument in Green Park opposite Buckingham Palace.

asked you to present the keys to the Chief Minister. Then you wanted to see inside because you had driven an ambulance during the war. We went up to the ambulance and someone had locked the doors." Astonishingly she remembered, and the expression on her face is seen in the photograph of Sir Michael introducing me, followed by her laugh as she recalled the event. Then on she went.

In another two minutes this gorgeous creature arrived in front of me, tall, beautiful, wearing a large hat set well back from her unforgettable face. It was Princess Di. Sir Michael began the introduction of General Rohmer, but she had something else in mind. She looked down at my St. John Knight's Cross and said, "General, you're losing your decoration." With that she reached down and pulled it off my jacket, then held it up to me saying, "General, I'd like to keep this." I replied, "You can't, Your Royal Highness, it's mine!" A joke. With apparent

Princess Diana speaks with me and fondles my decoration as she follows the Queen in the walkabout.

reluctance she gave it back to me, then moved on. Therefore I've always been able to say that Princess Di fondled my decoration.

CHAPTER 59
With Rosemary Clooney, Donald O'Connor, and Senator Tommy Banks

I N MAY OF 2003 THAT wonderful Canadian orchestra leader and enter-
tainer out of Edmonton, Alberta, Tommy Banks (now a senator), was
good enough to send me a tape of his show that took place October 14,
1974, with Donald O'Connor, Rosemary Clooney (trim and attractive),
and I — doing a book tour for my novel *Exxoneration* — as the guests.
After the show Tommy took us to his favourite watering hole for dinner.
I sat on Rosie's left, Donald on her right, and she was engaged across the
table in heavy-duty conversation with Tommy Banks. Donald and I over
many drinks had great conversations behind Rosie's back. Don't ask me
about what, but there was never a moment of silence.

Appearing on the Tommy Banks Show *with
Rosemary Clooney and Donald O'Connor in 1974.*

I have to tell you that seeing oneself being interviewed thirty years after the actual event is somewhat traumatic, because the face and body of today are different than the features of 1974. However, there was one part of Tommy's perceptive interview of me, with jocular interjections by O'Connor, that struck me. It was that my opinions about Canada's relationship with the United States, the knowledge of Americans about Canada, and what we should be doing with our armed forces really hasn't changed one iota over that whole period.

I thank Senator Tommy Banks profusely for digging into his colourful past and producing that marvellous video jewel of one of the fun evenings of my life.

Some years ago, when Toronto's premier hotelier, Hans Gerhardt, was in charge of the Sutton Place Hotel, he had Rosemary Clooney and her man as guests. Hans invited Mary-O and me to have dinner with him and the two of them. By this time, Rosie had been transformed from her slim to her huge self. Even so, she was performing her lusty, lovely singing routine to sold-out audiences every evening. She was doing her thing at the O'Keefe Centre, as it was then called. After the show, which we enjoyed immensely, we had a most pleasant dinner at the Sutton Place. Rosie remembered that Donald O'Connor/Tommy Banks affair, and we had a lot of laughs at dear Donald's absent expense.

Donald and Rosie were among the world's top and best-loved entertainers. Both departed this world in 2003. For myself, I was a most fortunate soul to have drunk, eaten, laughed, and had a short period of good friendship with each of them.

CHAPTER 60

The Sir John A. Macdonald Grave Caper at Kingston

———————◆———————

I<small>T WAS IN THE MID</small>-1970s, after John Robarts had retired from the premier's job in Ontario, that I was to get both John and Charlie MacNaughton involved in my Kingston project. John was at that time conducting his Royal Commission on Metro Toronto, and I was acting as his counsel.

John was a great Confederation buff and much admired Sir John A. Macdonald and Sir George-Étienne Cartier. In fact, he had named Highway 401 the Macdonald-Cartier Freeway. I had been in on the discussions over dinner at the Westbury back in the mid-1960s, when he had decided to give the new highway system that name.

On one of my trips down past Kingston on the 401 I had noticed that there was no marking on the highway that indicated that the burial place of Sir John A. Macdonald was just off the 401 on Sydenham Road. And this was the founder of our Confederation, equal, in my opinion, to George Washington or Abraham Lincoln in the United States. But here we were in modest, self-deprecating Canada. Furthermore, with a little exploration I went to his gravesite in the churchyard and found it to be rather dilapidated, with nothing special about it. To the north of the graveyard and the church was an open section of land abutting the cemetery.

What about a project that would involve acquiring that piece of land and then building a Sir John A. Macdonald museum and library there with direct access to the gravesite? It would take a great deal of organizational effort and fundraising, but surely the public would support such a project — even the Liberals and the New Democrats, for that matter.

I reasoned that if we formed the Sir John A. Macdonald Memorial Foundation Inc. it would be the corporate body that could put all this together. Who better to have as its directors than Robarts, MacNaughton, and me?

Those two Macdonald admirers thought it was a great idea.

I visited the site two or three times, taking photographs and working out in my mind's eye how the museum/library might be located, how it could be connected directly to the gravesite, and what had to be done to tidy up and enhance Sir John A.'s burial plot. In addition, I secured the interest of some Kingston leaders who seemed to be supportive of the concept. Progress was being made.

In a speech (I was doing a lot of speaking at that point) I went public with the concept. The press reported it without editorial comment.

However, the great *Globe & Mail* printed on its marvellous op-ed page a scathing, critical article that shredded the idea. I do not recall who authored the article, but the *Globe & Mail* editorial board saw fit to print it. As a result Robarts, MacNaughton, and Rohmer decided immediately that we had enough problems as it was and if that was the kind of reaction we were going to get from an undertaking that we thought was a highly worthwhile national project, then forget it!

So as I write this little anecdote some decades later, Sir John A.'s gravesite is the same as it was. There is no special marking on Sydenham Road, nor is there any sign on the Macdonald-Cartier Freeway that tells travellers of this most significant of all Canadian burial locations, that of Canada's first Prime Minister, who was knighted by Her Majesty Queen Victoria on the birthday of Canada, July 1, 1867.

In 1995, General Publishing published my novel *John A.'s Crusade*. It is the only fictional treatment of the negotiations that John A. and the Fathers of Confederation undertook with the British government. They started in December 1866 and finished in early 1867 with the passing of the British North America Act. John A. Macdonald is at the centre of the book from start to finish. It is certainly available on my e-book website!

CHAPTER 61
Trooping the Colour

———•———

URING THE PREPARATION FOR THE 1977 trip to Tortola in which Mary-O and I took the ambulance down by Hercules, I had taken the liberty of corresponding with Her Majesty's private secretary, Sir Philip Moore, and we had struck up a reasonably strong acquaintance.

Later, when I had become Chief of Reserves, I was scheduled to go across to the UK and then to the Canadian Forces base at Lahr in Germany to visit the Canadian Reservists. The timing of the proposed trip, in June 1980, coincided with the magnificent event staged at Horse Guards Parade, down the Mall from Buckingham Palace, when Her Majesty, in celebration of her birthday, reviewed the magnificent marching troops in a spectacular celebratory parade known as "Trooping the Colour." In those days, it began with her riding her favourite horse all the way from Buckingham Palace to the Horse Guards Parade followed by her husband, sons, and daughter, all mounted and wearing their military uniforms with their enormous bearskin hats, swords, and decorations.

On the off chance that Sir Philip might be able to obtain tickets for Mary-O and me, I wrote to him.

To my enormous delight his response was favourable; he had shown my letter to Her Majesty, who had ordered that we should have tickets from her own personal group. Furthermore, I had told Sir Philip when we would be arriving at Gatwick on the morning of the designated date. He advised that one of Her Majesty's limousines would be there waiting for us to take us into Buckingham Palace, where we would have lunch with him. Such a kind invitation!

We made our bookings with the Stafford Hotel through Trevor Moore, then the managing director (still there in 2004 and now an honorary major-general). The Stafford, our favourite hotel, is on St. James Place, close to St. James Palace and not far from Buckingham Palace. You can walk through from St. James Place to Green Park, then head across the park to Buckingham Palace. At the Canada Gate is located the Canada Memorial Monument that Conrad Black, Galen Weston, and I (a spear-carrier) developed.

As it happened, the Canadian Forces transport aircraft carrying us out of Ottawa to Gatwick was two hours late leaving Ottawa, which meant that we were at least two hours late arriving at Gatwick, which put us beyond the luncheon opportunity with Sir Philip. Nevertheless, when we arrived Her Majesty's Rolls Royce limousine was waiting for us. With great ease and dignity we travelled into London and straight to Buckingham Palace.

As the grand limousine entered the gates at Buckingham Palace, Mary-O looked around at the crowd outside the gates saying, "I hope there's somebody here who knows us!" Of course, there wasn't.

I went in to Sir Philip's office. He wasn't there, but the tickets were.

Then it was on to the Stafford Hotel, where we were greeted effusively by the managing director and taken to a suite that he had reserved for us. We had a wonderful homecoming at the bar and got ready for the parade the next day. Well in advance of the appropriate hour for Her Majesty's arrival, Mary-O and I walked to the Horse Guards Parade to find our seats, which were front and centre. Of course I was in full uniform (with decorations and medals), still that peculiar green colour that had been decreed by Messrs. Trudeau and Hellyer. I am sure that most of the Brits there thought I was from some banana republic with that peculiar shade. Finally, Her Majesty and her family came into view behind glorious marching bands, and the parade began. Her Majesty was under a reasonable degree of stress but performed superbly even though she was under constant threat of someone taking a shot at her. She remains to this day a shining, brave example for all Britons and even for those of us in the colonies, or should I say the Commonwealth. It was a grand spectacle that Mary-O and I, in our privileged seats enjoyed to the maximum thanks to Her Majesty and Sir Philip (now Lord) Moore.

CHAPTER 62
Chancellor of the University of Windsor

———◆———

FOR SOME UNKNOWN REASON (AT the instigation of my esteemed brother-in-law, Professor John Walker Whiteside), the senate of the University of Windsor decided that at its 1975 spring convocation Brigadier-General Richard Rohmer should be given an honorary doctorate of laws, LLD. I was both honoured and flattered. Assumption College, perpetually an institution of the Basilian fathers, from which I had graduated in 1948, was now one of the colleges in the ecumenical university structure. So I had my ties to the university. By this time I had embarked on what appeared to be a reasonably successful literary career with the publication of my books *Arctic Imperative*, *Ultimatum*, *Exoneration*, and *Exodus UK*, running up from 1973. The convocation, under the Chancellor, former Speaker of the House of Commons Lucien Lamoreux, took place outside one of the beautifully designed old campus buildings on a pleasant June day. I had been invited to address convocation and did so after the honorary doctorate had been bestowed by the Chancellor. The president of the University of Windsor was then Dr. John Francis Leddy, who had come from a university in the west to place his irrevocable imprint on the university as its first president.

Roughly three years later, on a weekend that Mary-O and I were enjoying at our newly built farmhouse in the Mulmur Hills southwest of Creemore, the telephone rang. It was a member of the board of governors of the University of Windsor, a man I knew well, the Venerable Ron Matthewman, an Anglican priest. After the salutations were out of the way, Ron got to the essence of his call. Would I be prepared to take on the role of Chancellor of the University of Windsor? It took a split second for me to find the appropriate answer, which was, of course,

Hugh McLennan and I receive honorary degrees
at the University of Windsor, 1975.

"yes." I had just become Chief of Reserves Major-General Rohmer. Even so, I was sure that I could fit in the Chancellor's tasks, which consisted primarily of presiding over convocations in the spring and fall of each year and attending major ceremonies and celebratory occasions at the university. It was not appropriate to ask Ron Matthewman why I had been invited. Mary-O and I were thrilled and delighted to have such an honour, particularly in Windsor, the city where she had been born and had grown up, and where her distinguished family of legal practitioners — her late grandfather, John Rodd, KC, her father, Walker Whiteside, QC, and her brother, John Whiteside, QC, LSM, DCL — practised law.

On September 30, 1978, in the same location where I had been given my honorary doctorate, I was installed as the third chancellor of Windsor, having been preceded by my friend the Honourable Mr. Justice Keillor McKay, a former lieutenant-governor of Ontario, as the first chancellor and Lucien Lamoreux as the second.

The symbol of the Chancellor's power, the mace of the University of Windsor, was a special gift to the university in memory of Mary-O's father, T. Walker Whiteside, QC. Mary-O's wonderful mother,

*Being installed as Chancellor of the
University of Windsor, September 1978.*

Olivia, and brother, John Whiteside, went to elaborate lengths to have the mace designed and constructed in England. It is a gorgeous device with a rough stone embedded in the base of the length and a polished stone in the head, with the coat of arms and crest of the university at the head. The mace was presented to the university by Olivia and John at the June convocation in 1965 and was received by then Chancellor Keiller McKay. At convocation the mace is carried by the gowned beedle, immediately in front of the Chancellor. The two lead the academic profession into the building where the convocation is being held, proceed up to the platform, and ascend it. The Chancellor walks to his high-backed carved wood and red leather chair, where he waits for the honorary doctorate recipients, the appropriate officials, and academicians to be seated. The beedle is still standing just in front of the Chancellor with his back to him, the mace still on his shoulder. "O Canada" is sung by all participating, and the orchestra plays it. When that is done the beedle places the mace on its blue velvet covered cradle.

With that symbolic gesture, convocation is underway.

At the University of Windsor after the invocation is recited the Chancellor and the assembly listen to the citations being delivered about the respective candidates for honorary degrees. The Chancellor then confers those degrees on the recipients after which he asks one of the honorees to address convocation. When that learned address is concluded it is time for the Chancellor and Vice-Chancellor (the president of the university) to shake hands with each of the robed graduates from the multitude of courses that the university offers. Roughly half are directed to the Vice-Chancellor and half to the Chancellor, who shakes the graduates' hands, asks what that person is going to be doing next, and gets a short answer. Then it's on to the next one, until the entire group of perhaps two thousand have crossed the stage and picked up their degrees, beautifully printed on parchment paper ready for framing.

The Chancellor then walks to the front of the stage close to the mace of his power and delivers the following conferral: "In virtue of the authority vested in me by the laws of the Province of Ontario and in accordance with the direction of the Senate of the University of Windsor I confer upon these candidates the degrees, diplomas and certificates to which they are entitled." The big crowd of graduates immediately erupts into great cheering and shouting. They have officially obtained their degrees in the presence of their families and loved ones.

During my first eleven years at Windsor as chancellor I estimate that I granted over fifty thousand degrees and somewhere in the range of sixty honorary doctorates to people famous and not so famous, but all great achievers. People such as Peter Gzowski, Richard Pound (of International Olympic Committee fame), and Maurice Strong come to mind but are in fact merely the tip of the iceberg. A list of my honorary graduates is in Appendix V.

At my installation as chancellor in 1978 I was blessed by having two good friends of mine come all the way from Toronto to attend. I was particularly flattered that they had done so. It was Adrienne Clarkson, the marvellous CBC television personality, and her new friend John Ralston Saul, who has now become Canada's most outstanding commentator on matters social and philosophical, a best-selling author, and Adrienne's husband. Adrienne and I were good friends, would have lunch from time to time, and enjoyed each other's company. I did not keep in touch with Adrienne for perhaps a decade but have watched her ascendancy to the post of Governor General with great pleasure. She and John have done an amazingly effective, deeply committed job for Canada during her term of office. Are there some controversies? Of course. When you have two such articulate and brilliant people at Rideau Hall who are out front and centre on a daily basis there cannot help but be some issues. But apart from that the two of them have been exemplary.

As soon as I was installed, my first duty was to install the new president and vice-chancellor, Dr. Mervyn Franklin, a learned microbiologist of great repute. Mervyn and I became the best of friends over the time that he was president. His equally learned wife, Dr. Maxine Holder-Franklin, is also a world-class microbiologist.

It must be confirmed that the chancellor has no administrative or other duties to perform at the university of Windsor. He or she is not an ex officio member of any committee. Accordingly, the chancellor is there to advise the president should the president seek advice.

The chancellor is there for the purpose of conducting convocation. As my registrar used to say when I was starting off on the academic parade, "It's show time Mr. Chancellor." Which, indeed, it was.

I conducted convocation at the University of Windsor
from 1978 to 1989 and from 1995 to 1996.

My first term at the University of Windsor was for four years. That was renewed without too much of a battle by the board of governors, and in fact I stayed on until 1989, a good eleven years. My successor was Charles Clark, QC, a Windsor lawyer who had been of enormous support to the university from its inception, both financially and otherwise. I was absolutely delighted with his appointment and was deeply upset when poor Charles died of cancer in 1996 in the middle of his second term as chancellor.

The board of governors decided that they would invite me back. So I served again as chancellor in 1996 and 1997 until I was succeeded by an outstanding choice, Frederic Jackman, of the distinguished Toronto family of Harry Jackman, my old friend.

My long tenure as chancellor was marked by no real upheavals at the university. At the conclusion of his six-year term of his office, Dr. Mervyn Franklin was succeeded by Dr. Ron Ianni, QC, a brilliant member of the law faculty. He and his wife, Mina, a CBC executive, also became our good friends. We often stayed with them at the president's residence in Windsor when we came for convocation or any other purpose. Ron was an exceedingly popular president and vice-chancellor. He initiated building programs, calmed troubled waters when workers became upset, and handled the senate at the university with skill.

To everyone's shock and grief, Ron Ianni contracted the Lou Gehrig's disease. Evidence of it began to show in his speech. On the telephone one would have thought that he had been drinking, which, of course, he had not. I presided at the last convocation he was able to attend. It was for the law faculty, and Ron's great pal and roommate from their Osgoode Law School days, Patrick LeSage, the chief justice of the trial division of the Superior Court of Ontario (the man who presided over the wretched Bernardo trial), was given an honorary doctorate. Ron's voice was virtually gone by this time. As I recall, I delivered his address for him to the law class graduates. Soon after that Ron was reduced to speaking through a computer voice because his own had been totally lost. Finally, Dr. Ron Ianni, the much-loved president of the University of Windsor, was gone. As chancellor I took a major part in the ceremonies marking his death.

Being the chancellor of a university in Ontario or Canada is an enormous honour, a privilege that is conferred upon few. Serving the University of Windsor in that capacity was one of the major events of my life.

Mind you, I had served so long at the University of Windsor that when I did depart they decided to let me have the chancellor's gown and cap. The gown hangs in my closet with my several uniforms. Once in a while I get it out to wear when I officially represent the University of Windsor, for example when the chancellor or the president/vice-chancellor cannot attend at a function where the university should be represented.

Such an occasion is the installation of a new chancellor at another university in Ontario or Quebec.

I had the privilege of representing the University of Windsor at the installation of Richard Pound, OC, QC, as Chancellor of McGill University. I had given Richard an honorary doctorate at Windsor a relatively short time before. He and I became good friends instantly. So when the time came for his ascendancy at McGill, where he had been on the board of governors for some time, I asked for and received the privilege of attending his installation convocation. John Eaton, who had become Chancellor of Ryerson University, and I were able to support each other during the ceremonies and travel back to Toronto together.

On another recent occasion Mary-O and I attended the installation of Raymond Moriyama, the great Canadian architect (remember him from the Ontario Science Centre story?), as Chancellor of Brock University, where he was well known for the architectural delights that he created over many years. On such occasions my chancellor's cap and gown come out of the closet and I very proudly wear them, representing my excellent University of Windsor.

CHAPTER 63
Prince Charles

———◆———

I N 1978, PRINCE CHARLES, THE Prince of Wales, decided that he would pay one of his rare visits to Canada. His interest in this country is clearly minimal, if his track record of visits is evidence. Be that as it may, an official visit had been organized for him starting with Winnipeg, where he was honorary colonel or colonel-in-chief of an Army unit. He would then proceed to Toronto, where he would, among other things, attend a mess dinner of the Royal Regiment of Canada, a reserve unit under the command of Lieutenant-Colonel Gary Thompson (later Brigadier-General). The regiment's honorary colonel was that fine gentleman Colonel Sydney Frost, QC, a hero of the Italian campaign in the Second World War, where he was severely injured. I had a brief association with Colonel Frost about that time using space in the law firm of Frost and Redway in the Bank of Nova Scotia building at King and Bay.

I had just become Chief of Reserves Major-General Rohmer, which produced some degree of clout. When I heard the news that Prince Charles was going to be at their mess dinner I spoke to Sydney Frost and said, "My dear colonel, I'm quite confident that it would be highly appropriate if the Chief of Reserves of the Canadian Armed Forces might be invited to the mess dinner." Colonel Frost and the Commanding Officer were in complete accord. The mess dinner went exceedingly well. I had the privilege of spending quite a bit of time with the young prince. By this time he had developed a bit of a twitch in one of his cheeks and was quite uptight and filled with his sense of duty to Queen Elizabeth, whom he then never referred to as "Mother."

The next evening was a grand ball at the Royal York Hotel with the prince as guest of honour. Mary-O and I were appropriately at Prince

Charles's table, so he and I were able to continue discussions of the topics of the day. He at that time apparently had no intention of marriage to Princess Diana or anyone else for that matter.

His Royal Highness Prince Charles at the Royal Regiment of Canada dinner with me, Colonel Sydney Frost, and Lieutenant-Colonel Gary Thompson, 1978.

I have not had the privilege of being in the presence of Prince Charles since that period in 1978 although I have had the opportunity to be presented to Her Majesty three times and, of course, to the beautiful Princess Di.

CHAPTER 64
The Funeral of John Parmenter Robarts

———◆———

MARY-O AND I WERE returning from a trip to Europe when we heard the news that John Robarts had suffered a stroke on an Air Canada aircraft going from Toronto to Houston, Texas. Both of us made the immediate decision that as soon as we arrived back in Toronto I would make arrangements to go down to Houston to see him and to assess the situation.

When I arrived at the hospital and found his room, not surprisingly, his wife, Catherine Sikafuse Robarts, was there. John was flat on his back. He looked to be his usual self, but his left side had some evident paralysis. We had a long chat about how he was feeling, and I got him to use his left hand to squeeze my left hand just to see what kind of strength he had. It seemed to be not too bad at all.

The purpose of my visit was very simple. It was to let him know that Mary-O and I were there for him, whatever it was that we could do. Both he and Catherine expressed their appreciation for my visit and all of that good stuff. I flew back to Toronto the next day.

In a few days John was able to travel back to Toronto, where he attempted to resume his life as best he could with the signs of paralysis on the left side. Over the months he had two more strokes, which seriously affected his body and his personality. The once robust man now became a shell of his former self, thin, wasted and hugely enfeebled by his physical condition. He was still able to get to his office at the Stikeman, Elliott firm, and I would meet him there from time to time and get him out to lunch. He could barely get around using a cane. His voice was slurred. It was really very distressing to see this huge man become such a human wreck.

About six months before he died, Mary-O and I were at our farm in the Mulmur Hills when John telephoned. He had a question to put to me: "Richard, you're the only person I know who can handle Catherine. Would you consider being my executor along with Catherine?"

I wasn't quite sure what he meant by "handle." She was certainly a strong-willed person, but I had never had any difficulty in getting along with her. Perhaps what John had in mind was that his London cronies did not like Catherine because they saw her as the cause for the divorce from Nora. Whatever he meant, I said of course, I would be privileged. I had no idea whatever that I would be called upon to perform the function of executor in just a few months.

Fortuitously I was in Toronto on the day John died, October 18, 1982. He died by his own hand using a shotgun that had been out for repair and had somehow arrived back in the house. Evidently, from the beginning of his illness, the relationship between John and Catherine had dissolved in many respects. There was considerable animosity. And, of course, John was quite a different person physically and mentally from what he had been before his strokes.

John got into the shower in the upstairs bathroom, took the shotgun with him, and pulled the trigger just as his unfortunate son had done during the time John was doing the Royal Commission on Metro Toronto, at which I was with him as counsel. That event had been a terrible shock for John, who had been obliged to go to the morgue and identify his son.

As soon as I received word of John's death I went directly to their Rosedale house. The place was already filled with people. A Metro Toronto Police homicide team was there, headed by a silver-haired inspector by the name of William McCormack with two of his sergeants, one of whom was a lad called David Boothby, a huge bear of a man. The inspector explained to me what had happened, saying that in any case of suicide the homicide people had to be called in to examine the evidence and declare that it was in fact a suicide.

Bill McCormack went on to be chief of police for Metropolitan Toronto, and David Boothby succeeded him.

The Robarts funeral and all of the ceremonial events inside it were rather traumatic for those of us at the centre of things.

Two people were outstanding in terms of support. The first was John's right-hand man, who had become a deputy minister, Dr. Keith Reynolds. The other was Don Martyn, who in earlier years had served John as a public relations advisor. Don had somehow appeared out of the blue to be there.

There were an enormous number of details to be looked after.

The first was the church service. It would have to be held at St. Paul's on Bloor Street. No question about that. John Parmenter Robarts was an Anglican through and through. But there was the touchy subject of the fact that he had done away with his own life. The Anglican archbishop of the day, whom I knew well, was a rigid stickler for conformity.

Keith Reynolds, a stalwart in the Anglican church, was the man to deal with the archbishop in terms of the upcoming service, at which we expected the Prime Minister of Canada and his entire Cabinet, among other luminaries.

Through Keith word came back that Archbishop Garnsworthy was not about to lead a burial ceremony for a man who had taken his own life. It was my view then and has always been that a man who has had three strokes, whose brain and personality had been severely damaged as a result thereof, was a man who was not the same person we had known, that he was suffering from a form of dementia and therefore could not be held accountable for taking his own life. This was the proposition that I asked Keith Reynolds to take back to the archbishop.

The result was a compromise.

Garnsworthy would take the service if it were called a memorial service and not a funeral per se. That proposition was acceptable, and so the planning began.

Before the memorial service at St. Paul's there would be a lying-in-state sequence to be held in the lobby of the Ontario legislature building so that politicians and civil servants who had served Ontario with Robarts might come to pay their respects.

So it was that in his coffin John Robarts was placed at the foot of the steps in the foyer of the legislature building. With Catherine Robarts, I was sequestered in a room close by off the corridor waiting for the appropriate moment for her to proceed to the coffin to publicly pay her last respects.

When, with black hat, veil, and dress, Catherine was prepared, she and I left that room and walked out to the coffin, where she touched it and said her tearful goodbye. From the photograph of that event you can see that I was doing what John Robarts had asked me to do, "handling" Catherine. For me, working with her and dealing with her at that excruciating moment was not a difficulty (although if I had been a London, Ontario, person it might have been different). She was John Robarts's widow, and I had pledged to him that I would assist her.

The memorial service at St. Paul's was attended by Pierre Elliott Trudeau and virtually all of his Cabinet, as well as by the premier of Ontario, Bill Davis, and his Cabinet. The huge church was absolutely jammed.

Archbishop Garnsworthy did himself proud. He gave an absolutely outstanding homily, or whatever it should be called, extolling the virtues of Robarts and his enormous accomplishments as premier of Ontario and as a human being.

When that memorial service was finished, Catherine and a handful of us escorted the coffin eastward along Bloor Street to its final resting place in the cemetery at Bloor and Parliament. I have not been back there since.

As one might expect, it took many months to settle the estate of John Robarts. As co-executors, Catherine and I had no confrontations, no difficulties whatsoever.

Catherine Sikafuse Robarts was, and I assume still is, a strong, intelligent woman, a no-nonsense person, a quality that John Parmenter Robarts had known, admired, and respected.

CHAPTER 65
Dundurn Hall, Collingwood, and Robert Fenn

━━━━◆━━━━

I N EARLY 1983, MARY-O and I still had our wonderful farm, then a twenty-five-acre spread on Sideroad 25 of the Township of Mulmur just to the west of the Centre Line. We had bought a fifty-acre parcel of rolling land in 1973, built a huge pond, stocked it, constructed a modest house with a superb view to the east and north, and used it for our weekends away from Toronto. Eventually I developed an east-west airstrip on the northern part of the property, which I used in the summer for flying my own aircraft, a short takeoff and landing (STOL) Helio Courier, or for the use of aircraft that I had rented for the season. And when I was commander of the Air Reserve Group or Chief of Reserves and flying the single-engine Otter, then from time to time one of those huge aircraft would drop in — in the summer, of course.

Mary-O and I used the farm as our base of skiing operations in the winter months. But once I started back into the heavy-duty military operations as commander of the Air Reserve Group and later Chief of Reserves I gave up the skiing because my duties were consuming practically every weekend.

Sideroad 25 was east-west. It was also on the side of a relatively steep hill, with the result that whenever it snowed during the winter — and snow was frequent — the road would fill up with the white stuff very quickly, making impassable the half-mile stretch in from the Centre Line. Eventually Mary-O and I decided that what we should do was to buy as small as possible a house in Collingwood and use it as our skiing base for our weekends at the Craigleith Ski Club, which we had joined many years before. In January 1983, instead of a small house, we found a dilapidated wreck of a place, some seven thousand square feet in size, that had been built in 1882, had been used in recent years as a nursing home, had been abandoned three years before with all its equipment, beds, and everything else in it, and was fundamentally a wreck. It was called Dundurn Hall.

We bought it at a good price and then figuratively stood at the doorway and threw money in to restore it to a liveable dwelling. It once again had its original grandeur, with eleven-foot ceilings, a superb huge stained glass window in the main landing going up the wide stairway, a huge centre entrance hall, and fireplaces everywhere. It turned out to be an elegant residence that we enjoyed for many years. In the early construction process we severed the northern tail of the building and made it into a duplex. We eventually sold it to our long-time family friend James B. Milner, who had retired in Collingwood. He has lived there ever since, recently with his new-found wife, Nancy.

We sold the farm during the summer of 1983, and since that time Collingwood has been our residential town. Dundurn Hall was sold in 2000, and we now live in a house in a new development in the center of Collingwood called (appropriately) Olde Towne. But we have maintained a rental pad in Toronto during the whole period. We use it four or five times a month. Originally we were at the Colonnade at 131 Bloor Street West, and then we moved to a tiny unit at 20 Prince Arthur, where my law firm, Rohmer & Fenn, operated for some years. The firm is now located on Number 7 Highway at the 404 at the bottom end of Richmond Hill, close to the Toronto-Buttonville Airport.

In the early 1990s I was fortunate enough to join as counsel with the firm of DuVernet, Stewart, located then at an office tower at Bloor Street and Avenue Road. I joined them because of my connection with Robert Fenn, a young lawyer and pilot whom I had assisted in joining the Air Reserve when I was commander of the Air Reserve Group. Fenn had later become a lawyer (I gave him his law degree when I was Chancellor of the University of Windsor). I had used his legal services when I was at Armadale/Toronto Airways (more on this later). By this time in the 1990s, Bob Fenn was also an Air Canada captain. When DuVernet, Stewart, Fenn eventually broke up, Bob and I formed the new firm of

Rohmer & Fenn and moved to offices in the ground floor of 20 Prince Arthur Avenue, just behind what was then the Park Plaza Hotel.

I have continued my law practice with Bob over the years and watched him grow his aviation insurance litigation practice into one of the most successful in Canada. He holds every flying licence issued in Canada (and many in the U.S.), including aerobatics and instructing. As an Air Canada captain he has been part of management for many years.

His knowledge of aviation law and aviation regulations is encyclopaedic. He is a superb preparer of litigation cases and drawer of documents and reports for clients that are remarkable examples of craftsmanship. When he is in court, and I have appeared many times with him, he is an excellent presenter and arguer. To sum up, he is one of the best courtroom lawyers practising in Ontario and Canada today. In addition to Ontario, he conducts cases in any jurisdiction in Canada where his aviation clients expect him to perform — and supervises cases in the United States.

My role in the Rohmer & Fenn firm is that of "elder statesman," attending at the offices to assist Bob in preparing cases, drawing documents, and editing those that have been prepared. At the age of just over fifty, he is the son I do not have. Our relationship is that close.

In addition to the professional side of his life, Bob Fenn has a large and vigorous family of four kids, three boys and a beautiful girl, all of whom provide Bob and his wife, Jill, with family challenges and achievements on an ongoing basis.

CHAPTER 66
"The Man Called Intrepid":
Sir William Stephenson

———◆———

T HE YEAR WAS 1985. I was working on a novel that was ultimately entitled *Rommel and Patton*, a story about the Battle of Normandy. As is seen at the opening of these memoirs, I had met General Patton before D-Day and was a great admirer of his. And I met Field Marshal Rommel on July 17, 1944, when I caught him in his staff car southeast of Caen and reported the presence of his vehicle (I didn't know who it was) to Kenway, our Group Control Centre, which then sent in the Spitfires that shot him up and injured him within an inch of his life.

Montreal and Toronto entrepreneur Ben Webster had a magnificent house in Bermuda. Through his wife, whom Mary-O had met at a cocktail party, we received an invitation to use their Bermuda house, or at least the guest wing, and to spend two or three weeks there while I was writing *Rommel and Patton*. We accepted with all polite speed and in due course arrived at their historic Bermuda spread.

Welcomed by the housekeeper and her husband, we soon settled in, and I began my writing.

I was aware that Bill Stevenson, the author who had written the wildly successful book *The Man Called Intrepid*, was living in Bermuda — or at least I thought he was. I found a telephone number and called Bill Stevenson to find his wife at the other end; she informed me that she and Bill had separated and that he wasn't on the island. "But," she said, "Sir William Stephenson is here, and he would want to know that you are in Bermuda."

The next day I received a telephone call from Sir William's nurse, a lovely British lady called Elizabeth, inviting us to go to Sir William's residence for champagne at eleven o'clock the next morning. His chauffeur would pick us up at twenty to eleven.

At the appointed hour the next morning, Mary-O and I were delivered to the residence to be greeted by Nurse Elizabeth in full British nurse's garb, a white uniform with magnificent red cape. All very formal. She ushered us into the spacious living room, and there, in the far corner in a huge leather chair next to the unlit fireplace and against a book-filled wall, sat the diminutive figure of the man called Intrepid, Sir William Stephenson, legendary in his own time.

Diminutive is the best description I can think of for him. He was short when he was young and healthy. "Little Bill," his friends called him. But by this time he was well into his eighties. He had had a stroke and was partly paralyzed. His speech was somewhat slurred, but that brilliant mind was functioning fully, with no impediment whatever.

He greeted us with his sharp, shrill voice as we went to him to shake his hand and begin our acquaintance.

Through Bill Stevenson's book, which Intrepid eventually told us was exaggerated

"Intrepid," Sir William Stephenson.

to a large extent, Mary-O and I knew a great deal about this famous man: fighter pilot, inventor, boxer, and supreme intelligence master for Sir Winston Churchill in North America and in Bermuda during the war. But let me tell you, he knew all about us, all the details, good and bad, through whatever enormous intelligence gathering system he still had at his fingertips — by telephone, telefax, mail, and other means that we were never to find out about. That was the beginning of a long and close relationship that lasted until Sir William's death.

Champagne that morning? A beautiful bottle was opened by Nurse Elizabeth, who looked after Intrepid hand and foot, assisting him with walking and up and down stairs. He was not able to function without her. Elizabeth was then a divorced lady with a very young son called Rhys who had in effect been adopted by Sir William. Little Bill's wife had died a few years before, and so he was on his own.

One thing became very clear from the beginning, and that was that Sir William was an admirer of good-looking women and made no bones about it. As a result he took an immediate liking to Mary-O.

Sir William was a person who enlisted people, usually men, in his ongoing endeavours. He needed people to help him carry out the objectives he thought were worthwhile. I'll give you an example. He had an enormous interest in the future of Air Canada, which was then owned by the Government of Canada. He thought it was in the best interests of the Canadian nation and the people who made up Air Canada that it should be privatized and sold to the public. A favourite of his was a young man named Claude Taylor, then president of Air Canada. He was constantly badgering Claude to persuade the government to take the company private, and indeed his wish came true when the government finally decided that privatization was the best thing (at least it appeared that way then) for the future of Air Canada.

Another of his Sir William's pet projects was how to harness the enormous wasted power that was created by the perpetual moving tides of the Bay of Fundy. That brilliant, imaginative mind believed that the Fundy tides could be harnessed and turned into massive quantities of electricity. I never became involved in that project, but it wasn't long before I was getting frequent directives from Sir William to be in touch with so-and-so or such-and-such a person to communicate Little Bill's wishes on whatever project he had in mind.

One of the world-famous people whom Sir William co-opted to assist him in opening doors and influencing the powers-that-be around the world was the magnificent Canadian singer Jon Vickers, then resident at Random Rocks, Bermuda, when he wasn't off in New York or London or some other place in the world singing his heart out.

During Mary-O and my many visits to Sir William over the years, he always put us up at his favourite Bermuda hotel, The Hamilton

Princess. He would always meet us at the Bermuda Airport with Nurse Elizabeth at the wheel. We had the privilege of meeting Jon and working with him in pursuit of whatever Sir William's project was at the moment. We would be briefed at lunches at the Hamilton Yacht Club or at one of Sir William's favourite restaurants.

Mary-O had met Jon Vickers some years earlier when he was performing in London, England, and she and I were visiting that city. She had gone with a couple of her lady friends who knew Jon to have tea with him in his London suite. But this was the first time I had met him, although I had known his brother, Ab Vickers, very well. Ab had served as a Vampire jet fighter pilot on 400 Squadron when I was on it in 1950 and then became its commander in 1952. But that was another story.

I received a fax from Sir William (he rarely spoke on the phone because of his speech impediment) in which he said he was considering adopting Nurse Elizabeth as his daughter. He wanted her to come to Toronto to talk with me, so I could be satisfied that Elizabeth was creditable, of a proper background, and worthy of being adopted by the man she had nursed for a long time and who was a world figure. He wanted to make sure that the Stephenson name would not be blemished by some undisclosed fact about Elizabeth.

In a few days Elizabeth came to Toronto. We had a long chat in my law office. Elizabeth was a highly professional, appropriately proper woman, honourable in all aspects and in my opinion quite worthy of being Sir William Stephenson's daughter, he being a childless man who wanted to have her and her son, Rhys, as part of his family. Marriage was, of course, totally out of the question.

I notified Sir William of my approval, at which point he asked me to take on the task of making an application to a Canadian court for an order for her adoption. Although he had not lived in Canada for decades, Sir William was indeed a Canadian citizen and therefore subject to Canada's courts.

I took a look at the Adoption Act of Ontario and decided that what I next needed was a family court judge who would be sympathetic to the request. I found such a judge. Along the way I had helped Judge Jim Fuller when he had made his approach to the provincial government for appointment to the bench. In addition, we had had a much earlier association in the practice of law. As I recall, Jim was then sitting at Milton, Ontario. I made an appointment and paid him a visit in his chambers. I explained the situation, my relationship to Sir William, and his wish to adopt Elizabeth — all the background that was available to me at that moment. Judge Fuller said that if the documentation was adequate and satisfactory, the necessary affidavit by Sir William and all of that sort of thing, then he could see no reason why he could not sign a formal Order of Adoption in the matter. Both he and I were satisfied that the order would be recognized not only in Ontario but in Bermuda as well.

I communicated all of that to Sir William by telephone. He was delighted. I told him that it would be necessary for him to swear an affidavit, which I would prepare and send down to him for signing. There were some questions that he had to answer before I could prepare the affidavit. I went through all of those with him and in due course had the affidavit drafted in final form and sent down to Bermuda for execution. There was also a comparable affidavit to be signed by Elizabeth.

In due course all the material arrived back to me in Toronto, properly signed, sworn, and witnessed. The adoption order was engrossed and everything set to go.

I made another appointment with Jim Fuller. He looked at the documents and, being satisfied, signed the order, whereby Sir William Stephenson adopted Elizabeth. With the stroke of Judge Fuller's pen, Elizabeth became Elizabeth Stephenson, the daughter and only relative of the man called Intrepid.

From that date, Mary-O and I paid three more visits to Bermuda and Sir William and his daughter, enjoying their company and many good meals at his favourite clubs and restaurants.

The inevitable came with a telephone call from Elizabeth saying that Sir William had died, but that on his instructions to her I was to be contacted only after the funeral had been completed and he had been put to rest.

We have not been back to the lovely island of Bermuda since, but we hear from Elizabeth Stephenson regularly and hear the news of her son, Rhys, who is now a medical doctor practising and living in England.

The entrance to Sir William's house has a brick edifice around it in the shape of a full moon. Somehow during our visits there we began to call Elizabeth by the name "Moon Girl," a signal of our affection and friendship. To this day all of her letters and cards to us bear that simple signature, "Moon Girl."

One of the more public exchanges Sir William and I had was to write the foreword for each other's books. Bill Stevenson was putting the final touches to his book *Intrepid's Last Case*, which was to be published by Villard Books in New York. With Bill Stevenson's assent, the publisher and Intrepid invited me to write the foreword to the book, which I was honoured to do. My participation was so recognized on the jacket.

I have no idea whether my participation assisted in marketing the book or gave it any extra credibility, but I was pleased, privileged, and honoured to do it for my dear father figure and fellow fighter pilot, Little Bill Stephenson.

When I finished writing the novel *Rommel and Patton* in 1986, I asked Sir William if he would reciprocate and write the foreword for it. Of course he would. In due course a fax arrived at my law office from Sir William. His introduction was sharp, precise, and typical of the splendid use he was able to make of the English language. The dust jacket of *Rommel and Patton* bears the notice, "Foreword by Sir William Stephenson, CC, Croix de Guerre." Later, and in relation to the publishing rights of *Rommel and Patton* being sold to a Romanian publisher, I was able to entice my friend King Michael of Romania to write yet another introduction, but in his language.

There is a curious link between Intrepid and Sir John Colville, Churchill's private secretary, with whom I learned to fly the Mustang I fighter aircraft during the summer of 1943. As the world knows, Sir William was chosen and authorized by Winston Churchill to head up Britain's intelligence operations in the United States, and for that matter North America, which is what he did with remarkable efficiency and results during the whole course of the war. Strangely enough, Jock Colville, Churchill's private secretary, took the position that William Stephenson had no such relationship with Churchill.

It is clear that Sir William did in fact have all of the Churchill imprimatur that was necessary. His operations were funded by the

British government, from which he had full support and from which he took directions during his entire period of service during the war. And then there was the fact of his knighthood, granted on the recommendation of Churchill.

Both men have gone to their respective rewards, so I can't pursue the personal question with either of them. What I will eventually do is research into the nomination for knighthood of Sir William. The British are marvellous packrats. I'm confident that the citation for Sir William, and for that matter for Sir John Colville, are somewhere in the bowels of the Public Record Office in Kew, Richmond, London, where I have spent many hours with my good friend George Cooley, researching the life and times of HMS *Raleigh* in preparation for writing the book *HMS Raleigh On The Rocks*, which was published in 2003.

CHAPTER 67
Colonel Michael Sifton and Toronto-Buttonville Airport

———◆———

I N THE MIDDLE 1980S, I was approached by Michael Sifton, whom I had known from the days of the organization of the North York General Hospital and who was aware of my activities in the military, both as commander of the Air Reserve Group and as Chief of Reserves. Michael wanted to know if I might be interested in joining his family company, Armadale Limited. My role would be to direct the affairs of Toronto Airways Limited, which owned the Toronto-Buttonville Airport and was a subsidiary of the Sifton family corporation. Toronto Airways operated a flight training school of some thirty aircraft, mostly the single-engine Cessna, but with some twin-engine aircraft used for charter. It also operated a passenger service from Toronto to Kingston and Brockville, where for decades the Sifton family had owned a large summer retreat on an island in the St. Lawrence. In addition to the Toronto Airways operation, I could well be involved in the legal side of some of the company's other operations, namely newspapers and radio stations, which came to Mike Sifton when his father, Colonel Clifford Sifton, passed away.

By this time Mary-O and I were living in Collingwood in Dundurn Hall, the huge 1882 residence that we had recently restored from an abandoned nursing home to an upscale building reflecting the grandeur it had had when it was built by one of Collingwood's original entrepreneurs.

To take up Mike Sifton's offer would mean leaving the practice of law while I was with him. But it was an attractive challenge, which I decided to take.

For the next four and a half years, the General, as I was called by Mike and his entire team, ran the affairs of Toronto Airways, subject, of course, to the constant input of Mike and his wife, Heather, both avid and capa-

ble pilots. Heather was and continues to be the driving force in the operation of the Toronto-Buttonville Airport and of her successful aviation
retail outlet called The Prop Shop, located in the terminal building.

Within a short time after I arrived at Toronto-Buttonville I had overseen the expansion of Toronto Airways into the use of a single large aircraft to operate the same route into Brockville with better facilities at
Kingston. But this was not to be a profitable undertaking, and eventually it was abandoned. The flight training school kept in operation, churn-
ing out dozens of students and putting many of them into the cockpits
of commercial operators and eventually the airlines. We researched and
introduced at Toronto-Buttonville Airport the Millionaire Fixed Base
Operator (FBO) franchise service to give special treatment and attention
to aircraft arriving as visitors to Toronto-Buttonville from any place in
Canada and the United States.

I oversaw the creation of a plan of subdivision put on at the southwest sector of the airport, which allowed some industrial buildings to be
constructed there. The land was eventually sold by the Sifton company.

The overall objective was to make the operation of the airport profitable, but in my time of involvement that goal was never achieved, no
matter how hard we tried.

One bright spot in my tenure at Toronto-Buttonville Airport was
the acquisition of an exceedingly brilliant young chartered accountant
who was an absolutely superb flying nut and capable aviator, Peter
Allen, CA, now FCA. I found him and, with Mike's approval, brought
him on board as the financial officer of Toronto Airways. Peter went on
from there to serve as treasurer and an executive officer of two charter
airlines, then moved on to Ottawa as senior vice-president and chief
financial officer of the huge and prestigious Export Development
Corporation, where he continues to make a significant contribution to
those Canadian industries that export major products to the United
States and elsewhere in the world.

My stay with Mike Sifton, Armadale, and Toronto Airways lasted for
some five years, until it was time for me to return to the practice of law.
My period with the Siftons was instructive and productive for me and,
I hope, for them as well. Through influences that I was able to exert,
Mike Sifton became honorary colonel of 411 Air Reserve Squadron,

received his military wings, and spent many years fighting the regular force for the betterment of the Air Reserve Group.

I found a suitable piece of land in Collingwood that I thought would be appropriate for residential development. Mike's son, Cliff, and I developed a partnership where Armadale would do the financing and I would purchase the land, develop it, and provide the engineering, planning, and all other services. The development, which I named The Forest, came into being with fifty-three lots at the west end of Collingwood, with boundaries at Osler Bluff Road on the west and the old railway line on the south. The Forest has turned out to be an exemplary and beautiful development. The houses in this entirely treed area are of substance and beauty. I am quite proud of The Forest, which I consider to be an outstanding land development project, although I can tell you at this stage that the people who know that I put it together or had anything to do with it at all are few and far between. Not that it matters.

CHAPTER 68
Part-Time TV and Print Journalist

———◆———

T HIS ANECDOTE SHOULD BE ENTITLED "How I Became and Still Am a Journalist," mostly in newsprint, plus I also have a bit of past radio experience with CFRB thrown in and an ongoing award-winning television commentary for CHUM's New VR, now functioning under the name of "Rohmer and Rohmer," a program that Ann and I do together.

The story begins with Paul Godfrey, at one time chairman of Metro Toronto Council and a friend whom I admire very much. When I was on North York Council, between 1957 and 1958, Paul's mother was much involved in Conservative and municipal politics, so I knew her from her various activities. Through her I met the very young Paul in the North York area. At that time he was beginning to court his dear girlfriend, Gina, whom we met with him. Legend has it that Mary-O and I actually chaperoned the two of them on one or more occasions. Fast forward to the time when Paul, now a highly successful politician, was attempting to decide what to do when he left the political arena. I had talked with him several times in his Metro Toronto office about that very question, trying to put on a fatherly mantle. I wasn't of any assistance, but I did know that it was time for him to leave. Much to my surprise, and I think to his as well, Doug Creighton, a founder of the *Toronto Sun* and then its head honcho and publisher, decided that Paul would be a perfect fit as Creighton's right-hand man. The two of them negotiated at Winston's Restaurant at Creighton's special table in the southeast corner. A deal was struck, and Paul Godfrey left the Metro Toronto chairman's post to become president of the *Toronto Sun*.

About a year later I was in the Bayview Shopping Centre in Toronto and ran across Paul. We had a brief and friendly chat, at which point I told him I would be much interested in writing a column for the *Sun*. He thought that was a great idea, and so it was decreed, not from the editorial office but from Paul Godfrey, that I would be retained as a columnist. This news was received with much anguish by the editor of the *Toronto Sun* and all associated with him. I mean, after all, this interloper, Rohmer, had written a lot of books, true, but what he did he know about what was going on in the tried-and-true realm of the professional journalist? However, Paul Godfrey prevailed, and I began to write my columns on matters of general interest. So far as I could tell, my columns were being well received by the public, if not by the editor. This general approach went on for several months. Then Doug Creighton had a great idea. He decided that because of my military background I should become the military editor. Being a person ever prepared to please, I said that would be fine, and so I became the military editor of the *Toronto Sun,* writing with skill and determination on all manner of matters having to do with the struggling Canadian military, its relationship with the government, and its relationship with the world, in particular with NATO, NORAD, and the United States.

Also in this time frame, I think it was in the 1980s, the CKCO television station in Kitchener decided they'd like to have my two-minute commentaries twice a month. And so those pieces began and lasted for several years. I also had a relatively brief shot at commentaries for CFRB. That was long before the advent of the Allan Slaight dynasty there.

Things began to change at the *Sun* with the departure of Doug Creighton. To the great relief of the editor of the *Sun* I also departed. I must say the relief was mutual.

From my Collingwood base I then developed a relationship with the New VR, the CHUM television station based in Barrie, where I began to do two two-minute commentaries each week. I then took the scripts and eventually was able to market them to newspapers in various regions of Ontario.

The opportunity to do the television thing at the New VR came through a chance meeting in London, England, with my old friend, one of the fine young people who had obtained from me the film option for *Ultimatum*, the one and only television wizard Moses Znaimer.

Through Tom D'Aquino of the Canadian Council of Chief Executive Officers, I had been invited to the opening, or should I say re-opening, of Canada House at Trafalgar Square in London, England. It was a grand affair, officiated by Queen Elizabeth and Prince Philip. The chief Canadian potentate was Prime Minister Jean Chrétien. Among the invited Canadian guests at the opening and the following dinner, where the Prime Minister spoke, were Chrétien's then policy advisor, my friend Chaviva Hosek, and Moses Znaimer, then executive producer of everything at City TV and of course at the Barrie station, CKVR.

While we were all waiting for the Queen to arrive in the afternoon, Moses said to me, "You know, I think you could do some sort of commentary on whatever you want for us as soon as we get the kind of technology that will work." The technology had arrived, and it did work. It is the video phone. As long as you have a telephone line you can plug into it with your camera and your microphone you can broadcast over your home station from wherever you are. That would allow me to do my commentary programs from my home in Collingwood — or, as matters turned out, from Tobago in the first year.

My scripts for the New VR commentaries were called "Generally Speaking." I was able ultimately to market the scripts in the form of columns to several newspapers. To prepare the commentary for the New VR usually, on Mondays, no matter where I was in the world, I wrote my script, concluding with my "Generally Speaking" paragraph at the end, in which I came to the point I wanted to make. I faxed it to my trusted and always reliable Palma McMartin in Collingwood — she has done all of my books and typing in the last ten years or so — who then puts the column on the e-mail and off it went to my newspapers.

By the summer of 2002 the new program director at the New VR, Bob McLaughlin, decided that he had had enough of my commentaries and that it would be much better if we had a new format. He proposed that it should be "Rohmer and Rohmer," with my wonderful daughter, Ann, the principal host and interviewer at CP24, the cable pulse news arm of CHUM in Toronto. We would very likely be the only daughter-father team on television. Ann would do the questions and I would (in my own way) produce the answers. It would be a four-minute show covering current events. The show is used by CP24 on the weekend and by the New VR on its Saturday (formerly Sunday) night at six-thirty wrap-up of the news of the week. I am happy to report that "Rohmer and Rohmer" has been getting good reviews, but we would like to see it go further out across Canada. Who knows?

In 2003 I was retained as special counsel by the Town of Collingwood for the purpose of attempting to entice major corporate jet owners based at highly expensive Toronto Pearson International Airport to move to Collingwood with its five-thousand-foot runway. After a great deal of effort I was able to conclude without any question that it would not be possible to get any of them to move, even though at Pearson some of them pay as much as $180,000 a year in rent plus premium prices for fuel per aircraft. We could do it for a fraction of that in Collingwood as a satellite of Pearson International. But our airport does not have an instrument landing system (ILS) that would allow bad weather approaches to low level at Collingwood. Without an ILS ($1 million to install), the airport is just too much out of the way. Perhaps that will change in the future.

Also, I have been chasing Air Canada to get them to have one of their flights that overfly Collingwood from Sault Ste. Marie, Sudbury, North Bay, and Timmins into Pearson to stop and drop in to Collingwood to pick up whatever passengers are there. The infusion of new construction by IntraWest at the Blue Mountains ski hills, a short distance to the west of Collingwood, has generated a demand for service to and from Pearson. But, alas, Air Canada is wrapped around its financial axle with its bankruptcy. Getting anyone there to make any positive decision about such a small operation is at this point impossible. However, the Town of Collingwood made the effort, and I gave it my best shot.

The volunteer airport commission, which involves municipalities from around Collingwood, might have better luck than I. But it was an interesting exercise to say the least.

A few months ago I suggested to Mike Sifton of the Osprey Media Group (they now own about fifty newspapers in Ontario) that he should create an Osprey Writers Group. He would get the involvement of eight or ten well-known Canadian personalities and invite them to write an editorial piece, say once a month or once every six weeks, which would be carried by the participating publishers in the Osprey Group. In early 2003 I worked with President Mike Sifton and his editorial vice-president, Lou Clancy, on this one. By September, and with some assistance from me, Lou had retained his distinguished panel of columnists, and the Osprey Writers Group was established and being published.

So in this busy time of 2004, I'll give you an example of how my days go. It's a Thursday shortly after noon in early April 2004. This morning I attended at the law offices of Rohmer & Fenn in Richmond Hill and worked with my partner, Bob Fenn, on the preparation of documents in a major set of litigation files. Now I am on the road on the 400 north to the New VR to tape the program with Ann at one-thirty. I will be on camera at the New VR, and Ann will be on camera split-screen at City TV. The topics today will be, "How should people respond to the expected West Nile mosquito epidemic?", and "Should Canada participate in the American national missile defence system? I sure hope so." All this in four minutes.

At ten o'clock in the morning yesterday I visited Lou Clancy at the Osprey offices at the Armadale Corporation's location at Toronto-Buttonville Airport. Then yesterday afternoon at four o'clock I had an appointment with the Minister of Transportation of Ontario to give him in confidence three concepts that could be used in the upcoming election. The first was to announce a study that would cure the Don Valley Parkway, namely by tunneling under it from Finch in Toronto down to the waterfront and using the 407 fare system to ultimately finance the cost. The second was a proposition to be studied for Toronto garbage, going back to my original proposal to Dennis Flynn, namely that the garbage be taken not to Kirkland Lake, where people are, but to where people are not, namely north, between Cochrane and Moosonee. It would be necessary to deal with the Native people, of course, but the garbage could go there, not necessarily in a mine but on top, as they do in Florida and other places in the States, where they build mountains, provided there is appropriate fill available. The minister received both of those propositions positively, but did nothing, of course. The third thing was my concept of barrier safety signs. These signs would be attached to the concrete barriers that divide the 400 system of highways throughout Ontario. They would be small in size and would be located at each kilometre, marking the kilometre number. They would have on them the Ontario logo and the emergency number to call for the Ontario Provincial Police. At the bottom would be the logo of an advertiser who would pay for the privilege of having his logo on the sign. The logo, without any distracting text, could be any one of the automotive companies, MacDonald's, Loblaws, whoever would want to advertise. They would be safety signs because in the event of emergency a driver would be able to identify his or her exact location. And cat's eyes would be on the edge of the signs facing oncoming drivers, useful in fog, of course. The minister seemed interested in that proposition as well, but did nothing. Then it was off to the law offices of Rohmer & Fenn at West Creek and #7 Highway, Richmond Hill — it's really Toronto!

From the television station at Barrie today I will head for Collingwood and continue getting ready for my trip to London and Paris this weekend. That trip is yet another story, the 60th Anniversary of D-Day Advisory Committee to the Minister of Veterans Affairs. I am its chair and its originator. The story of the 60th Anniversary Advisory Committee is really only getting underway. It will be finished on June 6, 2004, before these memoirs are published, but it's appropriate to mention the sixtieth anniversary at this point.

CHAPTER 69

President Reagan and Conrad Black; Advisory Council of the Order of Ontario

———◆———

I HAD FIRST MET CONRAD BLACK back in the days when he had just published his magnificent tome, the biography of the late premier of Quebec, Maurice Duplessis. I was on a book tour at the time and in Montreal. I had no idea who he was except that his name was Conrad Black and he had published this particular book. Probably no one else at that time knew who Conrad Black was either, but ultimately they would find out, as even the Prime Minister of Canada, Jean Chrétien, did during his legal bout with Conrad at the turn of the century.

Be that as it may, Conrad soon became a public corporate force through his fortuitous acquisition of E.P. Taylor's Argus Corporation and other interests.

When I became Chancellor of the University of Windsor, I was aware of Conrad's Duplessis book and also knew that Conrad had a huge stash of original Duplessis papers that he had managed to negotiate from Duplessis's executors, to whom he somehow had special access.

I was having lunch at Winston's when I spotted Conrad having a meal with another person. My good friend John Turner was at his usual spot at the southwest corner of the room, and the usual cast of now forgotten celebrities was in place in this special watering hole.

On the way out I stopped to speak with Conrad and said, in effect, "Conrad, I know you have all of those marvellous, valuable papers of Maurice Duplessis. I've just become the Chancellor of the University of Windsor. Windsor has a large francophone component historically through Assumption College and French Canadians who have lived in the Windsor sector. I would like you to consider giving the papers to the University of Windsor."

His response was, "You know, I'm on the board of governors of York University. I would find it difficult to give the papers to you and not to York."

My response was, "You could have a copy made for York."

I then made a proposal that he ultimately did not refuse.

At my first convocation after my installation Conrad Black received his first honorary doctorate, and it was from me at the University of Windsor. The Duplessis papers, the originals, had safely arrived at my institution. A copy (I'm not sure) may have gone to York University.

In the 1980s Conrad had control of Northern and Central Gas and was good enough to invite me to sit on the board of directors, which I was pleased to do.

Next came the board of directors of Standard Broadcasting, which he had acquired along the way. I was also pleased to accept that post. By this time he and his group had moved into E.P. Taylor's magnificent old postal building, which is an architectural treasure at 10 Toronto Street. All the board meetings of Standard Broadcasting and other interests in which Conrad had me involved occurred in E.P. Taylor's elegant board-room. His portrait is in the place of honour over the fireplace. Portraits of Bud McDougall, Eric Phillips, Senator McCutcheon, and Nelson Davis are on the walls. George M. Black, Conrad's father and a major business associate of E.P. Taylor, is discreetly in the foyer of the boardroom.

Conrad struck a deal with Allan Slaight (remember him?) whereby Allan would acquire Standard Broadcasting, which meant, of course, the wonderful radio station CFRB. It was necessary for the vendor to strike a committee of the independent members of the board of Standard Broadcasting for evaluation purposes, as the vendor was a publicly trad-ed company. I was chairman of the independent committee that had to do a lot of serious and time-consuming work with financial advisors and the like before we came up with a confirmation of the established sale price. My account to Conrad's corporation was such that Conrad accused me of using the committee chairmanship to set up a "cottage industry." Well, I had to do a good job, and my fees are always reason-able. The cottage industry thing was a joke, not a serious accusation. The sale to Allan Slaight went through, and, using Standard Broadcasting as one of his bases, Allan has gone on to acquire many other broadcasting interests to repay his banker hundreds of millions of dollars. I am happy to report that Slaight the magician has become one of the wealthiest men in Canada.

Standard Broadcasting was gone, and so was my association with Conrad as a director. Notwithstanding that severance, Conrad continued to invite me to his annual spectacular black-tie Hollinger dinners at the Toronto Club. In those days Conrad would invite some 135 special guests to this extravagant affair. An invitation was to die for. He always had as a special guest a world figure, somewhat approachable only because of Conrad's increasingly vast power and influence in international affairs, which became substantially enhanced when he acquired control of the *Daily Telegraph* in London, England.

At these dinners I had the privilege of meeting the likes of Margaret Thatcher before she became Prime Minister. I had the temerity then to send her a copy of my novel *Exodus UK*, which imagines that the economy of the United Kingdom has collapsed, the same thesis that I was developing when I met with Roy Thomson. I have her gracious letter of reply. Other guests included Henry Kissinger, who gave me a blank stare when I met him and said, "Mr. Secretary, the General is here so you're safe." I think that most people could say anything to Kissinger and get the same blank stare.

Then there was President Nixon, who spoke eloquently in his after-dinner speech about his many foreign affairs successes both under Eisenhower when he was vice-president and then in his own time, particularly with his opening the door to China using Kissinger as his emissary. As was my practice at these dinners, before the head table arrived to be seated in the vast dining room on the second floor I would approach Conrad and the guest of honour, standing together, to receive a brief introduction, which Conrad always graciously gave. So it was with President Nixon.

Then came the year that was for me the pièce de résistance.

President Ronald Reagan was the guest speaker at the splendid Hollinger Inc. dinner staged in June 1989. Conrad again invited me to that function, where 130 powerful Canadians (I was an asterisk) assembled to have cocktails on the main floor, then marched upstairs to the dining room. Unfortunately, the American Secret Service team did not allow Reagan to mingle with the crowd before the dinner, so none of us had a chance to speak to him.

The dinner went on uneventfully. Then Conrad made his usual brilliant introduction of the guest speaker. President Reagan took the podium and spoke about world affairs as he saw them. As he was drawing to a close, my bladder was in critical condition. I couldn't leave during his speech (that would have been rude), but I was sitting strategically next to the doorway leading downstairs to the washroom.

As soon as Reagan finished, I was out the door and downstairs. My problem resolved, I wasn't sure if I should go back up to the dining room or wait for the crowd to come downstairs. I decided to wait. I ordered a glass of wine and stood alone in the reception room. I soon heard the crowd coming downstairs.

The first person through the door was none other than President Reagan. I immediately went to him and shook his hand. Within minutes he was telling me about his hero and mine, Old Blood and Guts, General Patton. I was about to tell him about my meeting Patton when Conrad appeared and took the president by the arm to have him photographed with someone important. So ended my discussion with President Reagan. Even so, I managed to be in a photograph with him. This picture is removed from a coffee mug given to me by that now famous singer John McDermott, who made his debut that evening doing Irish songs for Reagan and Mulroney.

From the coffee mug, this photo shows me with President Ronald Reagan and John McDermott at Conrad Black's 1989 dinner.

Not to be outdone, the next day I called Conrad's secretary and was given Reagan's address in Los Angeles. I wrote him a letter and enclosed a copy of *Patton's Gap*. I marked the place where I described meeting General Patton.

Two weeks later, a letter arrived at our home in Collingwood. The envelope had scratchy, vertical writing on it. Up in the right-hand corner, instead of a stamp, was the name "Reagan."

President Ronald Reagan had sent me a handwritten response on his stationery with the presidential seal. This letter and its envelope are personal treasures.

RONALD REAGAN

Letter from President Ronald Reagan.

It was 1999. Mary-O and I were visiting her mother figure, Elspeth Gormley, in England at her home in Chichester on the south coast, about five miles west of Thorney Island, where I had made my fuel-less landing in my Mustang on D-Day morning. The telephone did its peculiar British ring. It was Conrad Black's secretary tracking me down because Mr. Black wanted to speak with me.

In short order he himself called. The reason? As I knew, he had acquired control of Southam, the massive newspaper and general publishing company that had historically been at the forefront of the Canadian newspaper industry. He needed, for technical reasons, three new independent members of the board. Would I consider serving? Of course I would.

Through a myriad of interwoven companies, such as Argus, Ravelston, Hollinger Inc., and other Hollinger associated companies, Conrad was in operational control of newspapers throughout Canada and the United States. As well, he had acquired the *Daily Telegraph* in London, England, and a newspaper in Israel. So it was that the Honourable Charles Dubin, former chief justice of Ontario, Harry Steele, a senior Maritime entrepreneur who had acquired a Halifax newspaper and sold it to Conrad, and I also came on board. The three of us became new independent members of the board of Southam, a most exciting time.

It became apparent through discussions in the board meetings and elsewhere that Conrad was intent upon creating a new national newspaper to challenge the *Globe & Mail* and, for that matter, the local *Toronto Star*. Earlier, Conrad had gathered the publishing resources available to him in the Southam net with a view to having them create a proposal as to how a new national newspaper could be created, how it could be established, and the costs. It was a complete business plan that was produced at a board meeting by Ken Whyte and all of the Southam people responsible for each segment of producing a newspaper and selling its advertising. Led by Whyte, who was ultimately to become the editor-in-chief, the presentation was made. Conrad was sitting at his usual position at the east end of the boardroom table. I was not at my usual place at the west end because the presenting people took up most of that space; I had moved up and put my chair close to, if not next to, Conrad. At that time he was colonel-in-chief of the Governor General's Foot Guards in Ottawa, and so I regularly referred to him as "Colonel," whereas he always refers to me as "General."

When the presentation was finished there was no prompting from Conrad, but I decided it would be appropriate to move that a new national newspaper be created by Southam Inc. based on the presentation that had been made to us that day. Conrad was delighted to have the motion, and it was quickly seconded and carried. That meeting was in the spring, I believe it was May, of 1999.

A few days later I sent a note to Gordon Fisher, the head executive at Southam based in their vast building in Don Mills, Ontario, where I had been the councillor for the area a lifetime before. The same note went to Conrad by fax. In it I proposed a name for the new newspaper. It was the *National Post*.

I heard nothing back from Conrad, but I did hear from Gordon Fisher, a fine gentleman whose calm hand and enormous expertise was felt in every aspect of the Southam organization. Gordon replied that his team had any number of names available that were much better than the *National Post*, but my input was much appreciated. A very polite response that in effect pooh-poohed my humble suggestion.

In midsummer Conrad called a board meeting by telephone, which frequently happened. The gist of Conrad's reason was this: he wanted to report that management had just completed a deal to purchase the *Financial Post*. He wanted approval of that transaction, and then said that with the acquisition of the *Financial Post*, General Rohmer's proposal of the *National Post* was perfect as the name of the new national newspaper.

Within a few months after that event the corporate decision was made at Southam to spin off many of the publishing assets of Southam into a limited partnership structure. This was done by the creation of Hollinger Canadian Newspapers (LP) Inc. and Hollinger Canadian Newspapers (GP) Inc., the general partner. At that point Charlie Dubin, Harry Steele, and I left the Southam board and moved to be the independent members of the general partner.

The last board meeting of the general partner where Conrad was in attendance occurred on September 11, 2001, on that famous morning that has changed the face of the world. Conrad had told us that just the day before that Queen Elizabeth had appointed him to the House of Lords. He was quite subdued during that meeting even though his appointment as Lord Black of Crossharbour must have given him great pleasure. It was certainly a goal of his to acquire that honour. It will be remembered that Prime Minister Chrétien personally blocked Conrad's appointment in the first instance. Conrad brought an action in the Canadian courts against Chrétien but ultimately did not succeed. In the end Conrad gave up his Canadian citizenship, thus clearing the way for his appointment by Her Majesty without interference from Chrétien.

As I see it, it was also the incident that triggered Conrad's decision to sell off as much as he could of the Hollinger Group's Canadian assets, with the majority, including the *National Post*, which went to Izzy Asper, whom I had known since my CHUM days. I had advised Conrad that what he should consider doing was giving up his Canadian citizenship, seizing his elevation to being a lord, then applying for Canadian citizenship when Chrétien was to leave office. At first Conrad said that that was something he would not do — give up his Canadian citizenship and then reapply for it. With Conrad now living in London and spending much time in New York City, but still having his magnificent home in the Don Mills area that his father built probably in the 1950s, my guess is that Conrad is still a Canadian first, as was my old friend Roy Thomson, and that he will retrieve his Canadian citizenship as soon as his turmoil between Hollinger Inc. and Hollinger International Inc. is finished.

I have to go back to 1990 at this point just to tell a little story that comes to mind about Conrad Black, Galen Weston, me, and Bob White, then president of the Canadian Auto Workers Union, a man probably as far to the left in things Canadian as Black and Weston, each a tycoon his own right, are to the right.

In the New Year's Day 1990 list of appointments, all of us mentioned above were made Officers of the Order of Canada.

At the investiture, conducted at Rideau Hall by Governor General Ray Hnatyshn, we were shown to our respective places, which were sorted out alphabetically but in reverse order. That meant that under the B's

Conrad was in a row way toward the rear, whereas as an R, I was in the third row from the front, and Weston and White were in the row immediately in front of me. In the first row were the recipients of the highest level of the Order, Companion of the Order of Canada, which included my friend Youssef Karsh, who by that time had photographed me in four different situations: in my regalia as Chancellor of the University of Windsor; in my uniform as an Armed Forces major-general; as an author with one of my books, *Rommel and Patton*, in my hand; and in the early seventies just as my slim self.

The investiture as usual went with great smoothness. But the remarkable thing was that sitting right in front of me was Galen Weston, shoulder to tight shoulder with Bob White. Both were friendly and courteous to one another, but as symbols of Canadian society you could never find two men with poles that were so far apart.

Later in the 1990s, Galen Weston, as then president of the Royal Winter Fair, invited Mary-O and me to a special formal dinner, an opening that occurred because Mary-O and I were to be prize presenters at the fair. It was at this dinner that we first met Galen's beautiful wife, Hilary, with whom we were to come in contact quite often when she was lieutenant-governor. Also at the dinner were the remarkable Steve Stavro and his wife. He was the owner and operator and the original founder of the huge food retail/wholesale chain Knob Hill Farms. As a result of that dinner Steve, a most generous and considerate man, and I got together. He retained me to act for him in zoning and official plan matters in regard to his vast land holdings. My time was usually spent objecting to some activity by a competitor, but it was an interesting association for a period of years. Steve closed down his Knob Hill Farms operations a few years ago; he continued his interest in the Air Canada Centre, although his involvement has now disappeared from that scene.

Midway through Hilary Weston's spectacularly successful career as lieutenant-governor of Ontario I received an out-of-the-blue appointment to the advisory council of the prestigious Order of Ontario, a body of six or seven members. In 1997 I had been honoured by an appointment to the Order of Ontario and had been invested by Lieutenant-Governor Hilary Weston in the fall of that year. So my qualifications to sit on the advisory council were apparently adequate.

The advisory council is chaired by the chief justice of Ontario, the Honourable Roy McMurtry. My good friend Douglas Bassett of the great Bassett publishing and television family is a member. As members we would be with Her Honour at events prior to the investiture, at the investiture itself, at the reception immediately after, and at the celebratory dinner held only for the recipients and their families in an appropriate downtown hotel.

The investiture is held in the entrance lobby of the Ontario Legislature and a reception is held in the lieutenant-governor's suite immediately thereafter. That accounted for Mary-O and my time with Hilary Weston, including her own investiture in the Order of Ontario, which the advisory council decreed just before she left office. It is now automatic that the lieutenant-governor will become the chancellor of the Order of Ontario, which is what has happened with the new lieutenant-governor, James Bartleman.

CHAPTER 70
Dame Vera Lynn

———◆———

This is my Dame Vera Lynn story, which took place in the early 1990s when Mary-O and I had a rental apartment at the Colonnade at 131 Bloor Street West in Toronto. We were living in Collingwood at Dundurn Hall at the time.

I had been to the opening of the Colonnade many, many years before when my then client Alec Rubin, of Toronto Industrial Leaseholds, had put the building together and opened it with much pomp and circumstance. At the ground level in a conspicuous location there was a drugstore named Kingsway Drugs. At the time the principal pharmacist and owner was a man called Harry, a man of my height, a most affable fellow and just a nice guy. When I would go to the drugstore I would exchange "rude" remarks with Harry. We got along famously.

I had a request to be the master of ceremonies, along with Jacqui Perrin, the lovely CBC-TV television personality, of a Red Cross fundraising show to be held at the Royal York Hotel. It would be a black-tie affair featuring the marvellous British singer and famous wartime vocalist Dame Vera Lynn, of "There will be bluebirds over the white cliffs of Dover" fame. There were two attractions to doing it. The first was the beautiful Jacqui Perrin, a skilled aviator and a wonderful person, and the second was Dame Vera Lynn. There was no way I could refuse the opportunity to be with both of these lovely ladies.

The organizers advised that there would be a rehearsal the same evening as the production itself so that Jacqui and I could coordinate our activities and follow the script properly.

Off Mary-O and I went from Collingwood to the Colonnade, where we got organized around 5:45 in the evening. I went to get out my black-tie gear: the tie itself, the appropriate white shirt, the suit, and the black socks — but I had forgotten the required pair of black shoes. The shoes I had on were brown, believe it or not. And there were no black shoes at the apartment.

By this time it was close to six o'clock, all the shoe stores were closed, I had no idea what to do. For one thing, I considered putting black socks over the brown shoes and wearing those. That really wouldn't work. What to do? A name and face and figure came to mind. Harry in the drugstore downstairs.

I rushed down to Harry's store. There he was behind the pharmacy counter at the rear. I went to him and said, "Harry, what kind of shoes are you wearing, what colour are they?"

"They're black," Harry quickly responded, not knowing why I was asking.

"Harry, what size do you take?"

"Size eight."

"Great. Harry, I need your shoes, I really do."

I then explained what was going on and asked could I please on bended knee have his black shoes even though they were sponge soled. Without missing a beat Harry and I traded shoes, and my black-tie kit was complete.

The evening at the Royal York was a great success. Dame Vera Lynn sang as if she were eighteen. Her little black-haired husband was backstage looking after her every wish. And as for the lovely aviator and CBC personality Jacqui Perrin, with the retired Air Force general in disguise who had actually watched for and had seen the white cliffs of Dover frequently on his way back from France before D-Day, she and I performed admirably.

There were two privileged treasures during that performance. The first was meeting Dame Vera Lynn, and the second, of course, was having Harry's shoes, which were back to him the next morning with words of profound gratitude.

Harry and his Kingsway Drugs later moved from 131 Bloor Street West to the north side of Cumberland, just to the east of the Four Seasons Hotel where in the lower level the business has flourished. Harry has fully retired, still wearing our mutual black shoes.

CHAPTER 71

Return to Venlo and Meeting Prince Bernhard of the Netherlands

———————◆———————

THE STORY OF MY CONDUCT of the artillery shoot at the Bridges at Venlo, told much earlier in these memoirs, was first printed (with illustrations) in the Air Force Association's magazine, *Air Force*, in the fall issue of 1995. In February 2000, a copy of that article somehow arrived in the hands of a journalist on the newspaper at Venlo in the Netherlands. It was a story that no one there had ever heard of. Literally generations had passed since the event on November 19, 1944.

The journalist did two things. He telephoned me to have an extensive interview about the shoot, and at the same time he gave a copy of the article to the mayor of Venlo.

In short order a full-page feature piece with illustrations appeared in the Venlo newspaper. At three o'clock in the morning soon after I received a phone call from the secretary of Mayor Schrijen of Venlo. She spoke excellent English and was shocked when I told her it was three in the morning. She opened the question of an invitation by the mayor and council of the town to come and visit Venlo and be their honoured guest for a few days. It was immediately agreed that we would be happy to come and that the best time would be in May, a few months away. That timing would allow preparations to take place. It was Desirée, the mayor's secretary, who made all the arrangements; she is a highly efficient young woman, a native of Venlo.

It was decided that we should come during the first week of May. At the end of that week there would be the annual May 5 celebration and parade at Wageningen, an hour or so to the north near Arnhem, where the Germans had signed the surrender documents on May 5, 1945, in the presence of Prince Bernhard of the Netherlands.

Mary-O and I left Toronto and arrived at the Brussels airport on Monday morning, April 31, 2000. I had not been at that airport since the day after the liberation of Brussels in September of 1944. The transformation was beyond all recognition.

Our assigned driver found us without difficulty and gathered up our baggage, and we were off for Venlo in a black Mercedes limousine, the first sign of the high quality of the reception that we were about to be given.

As we approached the Maas River and Venlo from the west we came to the bridge that had replaced the ones I had knocked down in 1944, and I had my first taste of the terrain as it appeared from the ground. Some fifty-six years had elapsed since those massive artillery shells had crashed to the ground in the centre of Venlo at Römer Strasse and on the western approaches to the bridges and then on the bridges themselves. There was, of course, no sign of the extensive damage that I had seen, and caused, on that long-ago day.

First we were delivered to our hotel, where Desirée was waiting for us to make sure that we were satisfied with the accommodations, which were excellent. The hotel was on the east side of the Maas River about three-quarters of a mile north of the bridge. From our room and balcony overlooking the river we could see the bridge and we could watch the continual parade of barges working their way up and down the river.

The first event occurred that day, when we were taken to the town hall, a magnificent four-hundred-year-old structure on the town square, which had only barely escaped my first shell. There was Mayor Schrijen standing at the top of the steps, his chain of office proudly around his neck, a large, robust, and friendly man. After warm greetings he ushered us into the boardroom, where several members of the town council were seated around the table waiting for us. The mayor opened with a most pleasant speech of welcome, to which I responded. We then had several minutes of general discussion (everyone spoke English). At that point I decided that it would be opportune to present to them with an original painting that I had commissioned and brought with us to Venlo. It was a splendid work by distinguished Canadian aviation artist Don Connolly, entitled *Shoot at the Bridges of Venlo*. It is in two parts on a single canvas. One part portrays my Mustang in the distance to the east of Venlo with an artillery shell landing in the centre of the Maas River next to the bridges. The second portion is a close-up of the bridges and the first shell landing right beside them. Fortunately, the painting had survived the trip across. I had been very careful to have it professionally wrapped to make sure its three-foot by two-foot frame and the painting itself would be well protected.

The shoot at the bridges of Venlo dramatically brought to life by artist Don Connolly.

Shoot at the Bridges at Venlo was received with surprise and with great pleasure on the part of all in the room. It is my hope that it is on display somewhere in the beautiful town hall of Venlo.

The week was taken up with dinners, luncheons, meetings with various bodies, and then finally on the Thursday the annual parade commemorating the Venlo dead was conducted. It was traditional that the mayor would speak to the gathering of citizens in the town square. Followed by the crowd, he would then march solemnly down and through several streets to a large park where even more people were gathered, including a choir and orchestra. There speeches were made. The mayor requested me to be in uniform and to accompany him at the head of the procession. And once we arrived at the park, I was to speak when he was finished.

As the mayor and I left the town square at the head of the procession, his usual jovial demeanor disappeared. He became intensely serious and quiet as we moved along through the streets. After all, this was a ceremony to honour and remember the dead. There was no doubt in my mind that many innocent Venlo citizens must have perished in the onslaught against the bridge on November 19, 1944.

At the park site everything proceeded as planned. The mayor made his speech, and then I followed using the English language, the only one I have. In any event, everyone in the audience could speak English and understand it well.

Our visit to the remarkable town of Venlo was yet another signal of the esteem which the Dutch people hold for Canadians who took part in liberating their nation. We Canadian veterans hold a special place in the open hearts and minds of the Dutch people, and most certainly in the memories of the people of Venlo.

During the week, we had heard from Desirée about the annual huge parade that was going to be held in Wageningen on May 5 to celebrate the 1945 signing of surrender documents there by the German generals in the presence of Montgomery and Prince Bernhard of the Netherlands. Desirée was able to talk to the Canadian Embassy in the Hague and obtain two special tickets for us.

On the morning of May 5, Mary-O and I proceeded in the Mercedes with our driver to a hotel on the outskirts of Wageningen where the Canadian military attaché, a colonel, was staying with a group of people from the Canadian band that was going to take part in the parade. When I met the colonel, who had our tickets, I was not dressed in my uniform, although I had on my uniform trousers, shirt, and tie and with a sweater. Before we left the hotel I did put on my uniform, with decorations, medals, and all on my general's jacket. The colonel was somewhat shocked by what he saw on the chest of my uniform. Vic Johnson, the editor of *Air Force*, was there and insisted on taking a photograph of me that is one of the better ones. He used it in the article in *Air Force* that he subsequently wrote, saying (by my request) that I wore the uniform with permission of the Chief of the Defence Staff. One always has to be careful with protocol.

Then it was off to the town square of Wageningen, where we attended the splendid ceremonial service in a large, fully packed, ornate church.

We could see in the distance at the front of the church Prince Bernhard, not in uniform, and other members of the Netherlands royal family.

After the service everyone moved out to positions around the square. Mary-O and I had shaded tree seats in a bleacher-type structure immediately behind the reviewing stand. We were in a perfect position to watch the proceedings.

Prince Bernhard appeared with a retinue of men behind him, some in uniform. For a full hour we watched the prince take the salute from marching groups who paraded by, including some Canadian veterans led by the remarkable Cliff Chadderton, CC, who had lost a leg in Holland during the intense fighting there. Except for the lead band, which was Canadian, and a handful of our veterans such as Cliff Chadderton, the parade was composed of Dutch veterans by the hundreds.

Prince Bernhard, then eighty-nine years of age, stood in the sun and responded to every salute that was given, including that of Cliff Chadderton, who was a significant original member of the Advisory Committee to the Minister of Veterans Affairs on the 60th Anniversary of D-Day, which I am privileged to be chairing from October 2002 to June 6, 2004.

When the parade was finished, Prince Bernhard and his entourage walked to a huge, several-storey building about a hundred yards away from the saluting base. It was where the reception was held for all participants in and spectators of the parade.

Mary-O and I, still on our own, went into the reception, where we were fortunate enough to meet and talk with Canada's then Deputy Minister of Veterans Affairs, Vice-Admiral (Retired) Larry Murray. I explained to him the Venlo reason for our presence.

As we moved through the reception crowd I saw through a set of glass doors a room full of people with glasses in their hands, many wearing the uniforms of senior officers. I said to Mary-O, "Prince Bernhard is in there. Let's go and see if we can get in." We walked up two steps to the entrance platform, where a gentleman was guarding the door. He looked at my uniform and all of the decorations and medals I was wearing (and at my gray hair) and immediately opened the door. When we entered we could see Prince Bernhard sitting to our left against the wall with two large senior ladies, one on each side. He had a glass of refreshment in his hand and was relaxing after his strenuous saluting effort. We were standing there for a few seconds when a young man in an Air Force uniform (the same colour used by the Royal Air Force) and wearing an aiglette on his left shoulder came up to us. He said to me, "General, you and I wear the same wings." He had received his pilot training in Canada in the early 1970s. It was Lieutenant-General Berljin, commander-in-chief of the Royal Netherlands Air Force. What a pleasant surprise and reception. We chatted briefly. Then Mary-O said to the General, "Do you think we could have a word with Prince Bernhard?" The General was acting as aide to Prince Bernhard that day, hence the aiglette. In a few moments he approached Prince Bernhard, who stood up and then greeted us.

I explained to the prince the Venlo connection and the reason for being in attendance. He was keenly interested, being an ancient pilot himself. It was the first time he had heard about the shoot at the bridges at Venlo. As we talked he spoke about the first time he went to Canada during the war to visit his family, saying that he had been surprised and disappointed when his children didn't recognize him, didn't know who he was. We chatted for quite some time, and a pair of senior Netherlands officers joined our little group.

Just before it was time to break up I saw a video photographer moving around from our right. He was taking pictures of us with the prince. When the prince left I gave the photographer my card and asked if he would send me a copy of what he had shot.

Some six weeks later the video arrived. It was of the full parade, including the shot of Cliff Chadderton doing his salute to Prince Bernhard. At the end of the video was our meeting with Prince Bernhard. The result was a great surprise for me because I did not remember the scene that was taken first from behind the prince and myself. He has my left arm firmly in his grasp and I have my left arm around his back at the waist. It was a sign of mutual and instant respect as well as affection. There were several frames of this with Mary-O standing immediately to my right taking full part in the conversation. The appropriate glasses of wine are also in hand. That was a great treat, first to meet Prince Bernhard and to immediately establish a relationship with him, and then to have the video. From it Mary-O and I have taken several stills, which we have added to our lifetime of special photographs.

On each following May 5 I have sent a fax to Prince Bernhard reminding him of our meeting and wishing him well on the anniversary of the German surrender so long ago when he had such an important part to play. Without fail I receive a warm fax signed by him in reply.

With Prince Bernhard, May 5, 2000.

It was my hope that, if the 60th Anniversary of D-Day Committee agreed, Prince Bernhard would be an honoured guest at our ceremonies at Juno Beach on June 6, 2004. I raised this possibility to him in my May 5, 2003, fax. His response was that he did not think he would be able to make the journey because of his advancing years. He did not.

CHAPTER 72

Colin Powell, Magna International, and President Bill Clinton

———————◆———————

T he first time I was in the presence of General Colin Powell was when he was chairman of the Joint Chiefs of Staff. The occasion was a major gathering of American generals and admirals for a celebratory dinner on board USS *Intrepid*, named after my wonderful friend Sir William Stephenson. I was the special guest of the beautiful author and columnist Joan Sutton, formerly of Toronto but now strong in the New York scene, and her husband, Oscar Strauss. For a time Joan was the Ontario Agent General in New York, a prestigious posting for that woman of such talent, intelligence, warmth, and connections.

The dinner was an outstanding success. General Powell spoke with eloquent skill, which is par for the course for him. I met a clutch of famous American admirals and generals, mostly from the Vietnam era. Enjoyed Powell's speech. Was briefly presented to him, and that was the end of the matter. Very impressive young man.

Flash forward to November 2, 2000, the heart of the American presidential election campaign, Magna International Inc., and Belinda Stronach.

In the early part of the first decade of the twentieth century, one of my more important clients was Magna International Inc. Magna is among the largest and most progressive auto parts and automobile manufacturers, the creation of the brilliant Frank Stronach, who arrived in Canada from Austria in the middle 1950s with small change in his pocket and one of the most imaginative brains and intellects ever to immigrate. He was a skilled Austrian tool and die maker. That was his main work asset.

During my association with Magna, which began in 1998, I watched Frank's exceptional daughter, Belinda, being groomed by him to take over the reins of the corporations. It was a wise move on his part.

With President Bill Clinton.

Belinda had established an annual innovative program for university and college students called The Magna For Canada Scholarship Program. It had been in operation for two years before my arrival on the scene, when I was invited to write a paper that would be included in the book that would flow from the competition that year. The competition is structured so that university and college students across the country are invited to write a twenty-five-hundred word essay on the topic "If I Were Prime Minister I Would ...," discussing what would be appropriate to provide better government, increase the standard of living, that sort of thing. It is designed to allow each competitor to give full rein to his or her innovative ideas.

From the several hundred essays received, a preliminary judging system brings the number down to fifty. Those fifty are brought to Toronto in August, where, in one of the better hotels, the judging takes place by a panel of usually six people. In recent years the judges have been my old friend and television guru Mike Duffy, Joan Crockatt, the pre-eminent journalist from Calgary, Jean Charpentier, Trudeau's principal media advisor, and Mike Harris, the Ottawa/East Coast author and journalist and media commentator.

Ontario Premier Mike Harris (not the judge Mike) was very aware of the highly successful Magna for Canada program that Belinda had developed. He had invited her to be a member of the committee to establish Ontario's Promise, a plan to help children based on the highly successful American Promise program that Colin Powell had put together and to which he was devoting virtually all his time.

The date had been set for Mike Harris's launch of Ontario's Promise, to be held at eleven o'clock on a Friday morning at Toronto's Metro Convention Centre. Belinda would be front row centre. However, the problem was how to get Colin Powell from Washington to Toronto in time for the launch. Powell was at that time campaigning hard with George W. Bush. The American presidential election was just around the corner. Powell, being one of the most prestigious and popular of Americans, had to be on the platform with Bush in Indianapolis that Friday afternoon as well as elsewhere on the weekend.

The request came from Mike Harris's office that Belinda consider going down to Washington Thursday afternoon with one of Magna's jet aircraft, based at Toronto-Buttonville, to pick up Powell first thing in the morning and fly him up to Pearson International Airport, where he would be met by the premier's staff. As it happened, Belinda's then husband, Johann Koss, the famous Norwegian Olympic gold medal speed skater and every Norwegian's hero, was already in Washington on business. So Belinda readily agreed to pick up Colin Powell. She also invited me to go along with her to Washington. There we would have dinner at the Cosmo Club with Johann and a prominent Washington lawyer, John

Zentay, and his wife, Diana. John was with the Vernor, Lippert firm that acts for Magna in various matters in the U.S.

By six-thirty in the morning Belinda, Johann, and I were in the lounge of the Signature fixed base operator at Washington Dulles Airport. We were preparing to leave the lounge and board our aircraft, which we could see down the ramp a couple hundred yards away, when a huge black limousine drove by and headed straight for our machine. It had to be Colin Powell.

By the time the three of us walked to the aircraft he was already in place. I went in first. There was Colin Powell, sitting in the middle seat on the right side of the aircraft facing the front, his tie off, in his shirtsleeves, his briefcase open and papers already on his lap. He was wasting no time. He knew the identity of his fellow passengers. As I stepped into the passenger compartment he extended his hand saying, "Good morning, General." I responded, "Good morning, General." Belinda and Johann did their greetings and got into their seats across from the General who was facing forward. I sat opposite him and eventually caught him in this grumpy photo with the now politically famous Belinda.

My informal photograph of Colin Powell and Belinda Stronach (now an MP) en route from Washington to Toronto on November 2, 2001.

For the first half-hour of the flight Powell elected to concentrate on reading his papers and documents, obviously not willing to be engaged in conversation if it could be avoided. Eventually the three of us pried him away from his papers and engaged him with questions and comments about the campaign.

As the aircraft was letting down for its approach into Pearson International it was time for me to make my move. I reached into my briefcase and took out the mint copy of *Patton's Gap: Mustangs Over Normandy.* I had already inscribed it to him with appropriate words of praise and recognition.

He accepted it graciously, with some surprise. It was the move that opened the door between us, one general to the other. He seemed really pleased it with it.

At the ramp at Pearson, the Canadian Customs and Immigration people came on board. They were properly wowed by General Powell's presence. We cleared Customs and off he went in the limousine provided by Mike Harris's staff.

I went to the Metro Convention Centre to listen to the proceedings, particularly Colin Powell's speech. He delivered without notes and was articulately brilliant. I thought, "He speaks so well he would have to be careful when he's on stage with George W. Bush that he does not upstage his presidential candidate." Watching Colin operate when he's on the same platform as George W., it is evident that he understands that very well.

I have Colin Powell's fax and telephone numbers in his office as Secretary of State, to which position he was immediately appointed, as expected, by President George W. Bush when the Supreme Court gave its verdict in his favour. I use that direct fax access from time to time to express a gratuitous opinion that is worth what Colin pays for it. Just a few days before September 11, 2001, *Time* magazine had Colin's picture on the front page and had written a very negative article about him, the gist of which was "Colin Powell, our great expectation, where have you gone, where are you?"

I didn't like that article one bit, and so I wrote a letter of encouragement to Colin and faxed it to him. He did reply.

Since then we have exchanged brief correspondence, usually a one-way fax from me making comments and saying, "Please do not reply."

SECRETARY OF STATE *16 Sep*

Dear Richard,

Thanks for flying top cover. Never fear, I'm in good shape.

All the best,
C.

A note from Colin Powell.

In my opinion Colin is the bright star of stability and intelligence and wisdom in the Bush Cabinet. He is a man of enormous intellectual prowess, a gold mine of life experience and prestige with credibility that is unequalled in the United States, notwithstanding the often controversial actions that Bush and his other Cabinet appointees manage to carry out.

It will be interesting to know some time in the future whether I can be, as he puts it, "of service" to Colin Powell in some way.

CHAPTER 73

The Temporary Resurrection of the Mid-Canada Concept

———————◆———————

SINCE 1972, I HAD CONSIDERED the Mid-Canada Development Corridor and anything to do with it to be dead and buried, of no interest to the government of Canada or anyone else for that matter. However, the Mid-Canada Conference had been a long (more than two years) and constructive exercise. The final report had been superbly done by Brian Hay and all the members of the conference who had input, including master photographer/writer Robert Fleming. And there was all the documentation that had been produced: books, bibliographies, everything. Even so, as I believed, all of that had been consigned to oblivion and history.

Not so. Early in 2001 I received a telephone call out of the blue. It was from the member of parliament for Churchill River up in northern Saskatchewan, Rick Laliberte, a distinguished member of the Métis community. He had discovered some Mid-Canada material that disclosed to him the basic concept. Rick thought the idea might be of value to the people in his riding, which was part of Mid-Canada, and, in particular, to the more than six hundred Native bands that populate the Mid-Canada region. For some reason he had spoken with the Prime Minister about it. Chrétien said to him, "Find Rohmer. It was his concept and his conference." Jean Chrétien was the Minister of Indian Affairs and Northern Development at the time we held the conference. While he refused to take part, there was no question that he tracked what we were doing with interest.

Laliberte found me in Collingwood. In a few weeks there was another call from him. He had driven up from Pearson International to Collingwood expecting to find me and had done so. We met and had breakfast at the town's big hotel, the Cranberry Inn. That was the beginning of the resurrection of the Mid-Canada Development Corridor Concept, now simply called the Mid-Canada Corridor (used by Chrétien later on) or the Mid-Canada Region.

Rick was highly enthusiastic about the potential of the Mid-Canada Region and the principles that we had developed in the conference that had taken place so long ago. I agreed to support him in any way I could, provided that I should stay in the background and let him march on as the public standard-bearer of Mid-Canada.

Laliberte has a remarkably efficient executive assistant, Pauline DeHaan, who has been central to his organizational efforts in bringing together staff, ministers, ministers' assistants, policy advisors, and Chrétien's staff and in drumming up support for his vision of the Mid-Canada Region. By the beginning of 2002, Rick and Pauline had arranged a meeting with the Prime Minister himself to present Rick's new approach to the Mid-Canada concept. Rick and I met Chrétien in his office on February 4, armed with Rick's newly developed materials and the two basic documents of long ago: the Mid-Canada Development Corridor Study that had been done for me by Acres and the report of the Mid-Canada Conference.

I had not talked with Chrétien for perhaps years, since I attended the reopening of Canada House at Trafalgar Square in London, England, in the late 1990s. Chrétien was the leading Canadian person there and made a great speech at dinner. I had words with him in the park at Lincolns-In-Fields, where there was a commemorative parade of old RCAF veterans in front of the building that had been used as the London headquarters of the Royal Canadian Air Force during the Second World War.

In we went to the great man's office. He greeted both of us warmly, then sat at his bare desk, his back to the windows, which faced out over the vast Parliament Buildings lawn. Rick and I sat opposite him, Rick on my right. Chrétien opened by looking at Laliberte and pointing at me, saying in an accusatory tone, "He's a Tory and he's Establishment!" Then he turned to me and said with a smile, "I'm only kidding." I don't think so. I had resigned as a member of the Conservative Party in 1985, and I do not know of any establishment to which I could belong except that the word is used in the title of a book by a Canadian author in which I am described as "Richard Rohmer — Renaissance man."

Rick and I had an excellent meeting with Chrétien. The old boy and I had great fun taking shots at each other. The outcome of our discussion was that he asked us to attend upon his assistant, Eddie Goldenberg, whom he tried and failed to find by telephone when we were still in his office. Before the meeting finished, Chrétien insisted we show him that the Mid-Canada Region does in fact embrace and include without question his beloved Shawinigan.

Our subsequent meeting with Goldenberg a few weeks later was courteous, and he promised to look at the material. But nothing ever came of that situation.

Rick's work went on, with the wonderful Pauline at the centre of it. Rick's team prepared comprehensive studies and proposals and had many meetings with policy advisors and staff of any and all of the ministries that have a piece of the action in the Mid-Canada Region.

A turning point occurred when Dr. David Malcolm of the University of Alberta and its Circumpolar Institute became keenly interested in the possibility of Mid-Canada Region and became a driving force, assisting Rick in setting up the goals and objectives that should be achieved.

One of the main goals that came from the recommendations of the Mid-Canada Conference report was that a research institute should be created. It would coordinate and monitor all kinds research that was being done by all federal and provincial departments and ministries within and for the Mid-Canada Region and its people. It was to be called the Mid-Canada Research Institute (MCRI). I obtained clearance of the name from a legal point of view so that incorporation could take place. Dr. Malcolm was able to move in that direction when Minister Allan Rock came through with preliminary funding, and the MCRI was launched in 2003.

There was another meeting with the Prime Minister late in 2002. This time he called in as senior policy advisor Dr. Paul Genest, the son of the late, highly regarded litigation counsel in Toronto Pierre Genest, QC, whom I had known. By telephone, Chrétien called Genest to join us during the middle of our meeting. The Prime Minister was able to give him instructions in our presence while we explained the basics of the Mid-Canada concept and the Mid-Canada Research Institute. The request that we made during the last meeting with the Prime Minister has never gelled. We asked him to declare the Canadian boreal forest the Mid-Canada Region and to promise that the government would support and fund the establishment of the Mid-Canada Research Institute. Upon my advice to Rick Laliberte, he had quietly attended upon the Honourable Paul Martin, a good friend of mine and then in my opinion the only person to lead the Liberal Party on Chrétien's retirement. Rick had a good meeting with Paul. I expected he would be supportive of establishing the Mid-Canada Region and the MCRI. But that has not turned out to be the case. The Martin government is not supportive of the MCRI initiative. So once again the resurrected Mid-Canada concept is dead, and Laliberte is no longer a member of Parliament.

CHAPTER 74

D-Day 1994 and the 60th Anniversary of D-Day Advisory Committee to the Minister of Veterans Affairs

———◆———

I HAVE A SPECIAL PARTICIPATION connection to D-Day, June 6, 1944, which I have already explained.

By the same token I have a direct connection with what happened on the D-Day anniversary in 1994 and particularly with what happened for Canada's D-Day anniversary on June 6, 2004, both at Juno Beach and across Canada.

In 1994, I discovered that Veterans Affairs Canada made no provision whatever for access by D-Day veterans to the beaches of Normandy on D-Day's anniversary. As it turned out, Veterans Affairs decided that they could take forty-five veterans as a "pilgrimage" crew to Juno Beach for that day, plus about an equal number of staff. As I understand it, what Veterans Affairs did was canvas regimental associations and other bodies asking for nominations of people who could represent their particular organizations. There is no certainty that having any association at all with D-Day as participants or anything of that kind was part of the criteria. So far as Veterans Affairs was concerned, only those forty-five would be at the ceremonies at Canada's Juno Beach. They were the Official Party.

As to any D-Day veterans or veterans of the Battle of Normandy outside that Official Party, there was no provision whatever made with the French authorities or anyone else for them to gain access to Juno Beach on June 6, 1994.

I had agreed to be the Air Force resource person for a tour operator in Toronto that arranged for accommodation on the Holland American liner *Statendam* on a twelve-day cruise out of Dover, England, that would eventually wind up at the port of Honfleur near Deauville on the English Channel coast of France, a few miles to the east of the Orne River, the eastern boundary of the D-Day attacks (save for the Canadian and British paratroopers who jumped in east of the Orne just after midnight). The other resource people included Brigadier-General Denis Whitaker, one of the great heroes of Dieppe and of the Battle of Normandy, with his wife, Shelagh, both of them dedicated authors in relation to the Canadian participation in battles in Europe during the Second World War, as well as Rear Admiral Desmond Piers and his wife, Janet. Desmond was the designated naval resource authority, having been involved in the D-Day landings.

The promotional pitches by the tour company revolved around the presence of the proposed resource people, and eventually the tour company had recruited a large body of people who wanted to take part and be in Normandy at the beaches on D-Day.

Whitaker, Piers, and Rohmer performed with lectures during the cruise in anticipation of arriving at the Normandy Beaches on D-Day. As we approached Honfleur, it was quite apparent that the tour had been unable to make any arrangements whatever for access to the beach. As we discovered later, they were not alone. The only provision was for a mid-afternoon service and ceremony to be held at the Canadian cemetery at Beny-sur-Mer, several miles inland from Juno Beach. That was the best they could do. We in the resource group were highly embarrassed by the inability to have access to the beach for us and our fellow passengers. I vowed then that if I had anything to do with it, the same situation would not occur again in 2004. Of course, the Americans flooded their beaches with enormous ceremonies involving the President of France, Queen Elizabeth, the President of the United States, and our Governor General and Prime Minister, along with great potentates from all over Europe.

Then for the British at Arromanches, where the remains of Churchill's great Mulberry Port is still in place, there was a magnificent parade in the presence of Queen Elizabeth, the parade taking place on the beach itself at the appropriate timed moment.

For Canadian veterans in Normandy there was next to nothing.

But, oh joy, we were permitted to attend the ceremony at the cemetery in the presence of the President of France, the Prime Minister of Canada, and many ministers of the Canadian crown. There were several hundred Canadians at that beautiful cemetery. That was the closest they could get to the beaches over which they had flown in support of the Army or onto which their landing craft had disgorged them, Juno Beach.

As a D-Day veteran, I can tell you I was totally ticked off by what the totally inept and uncaring Canadian government did to our non-official party D-Day and Battle of Normandy veterans on of June 6, 1994.

Mind you, I had a special piece of treatment that day from 430 Squadron, my wartime unit, which is still alive and well and flying helicopters out of Valcartier, Quebec.

I had kept in contact with 430 Squadron over the years and had taken part in change of command ceremonies there in the early 1990s. The squadron had honoured me by naming their new high-class briefing room, rather like a theatre, for me: La Salle Rohmer. Some months before the D-Day anniversary in 1994 I became aware that the squadron had been asked to provide three of its helicopters, the Kiowas, to be deployed in Normandy to transport VIPs around the region of the Normandy beaches. It seemed to me that if they were going to be there and I was going to be present at the same time, possibly I could impose upon the Commanding Officer to have my squadron fly me — with me at the controls when airborne, of course — in one of its aircraft up and down Juno, the Canadian beach, and Gold and Sword, the British beaches, at close to 7:00 a.m. on June 6, fifty years to the day and minute after I had flown up and down those same beaches at five hundred feet watching the first landing craft come in and flying through a hail of heavy shells from the battleships offshore and from anti-aircraft weaponry on the ground.

All the arrangements were made for us to be picked up at the airport at Deauville on D-Day morning. Mary-O and I would arrive at 6:00 a.m. and be airborne and over the Beaches at about 6:45 a.m.

There was only one snag. The then Commander of Air Command and I had had a run-in over a speech I had made at a mess dinner at his base when he decided to do away with the Air Reserve Group that I founded. When he heard about this plan to fly with 430 Squadron on D-Day, the Commander of Air Command did everything he could to stop it. He almost succeeded. However, at the reception that Fred Eaton had at the High Commission in London immediately after the unveiling by Her Majesty Queen Elizabeth of the Canada Memorial Monument, I found my old friend David Collenette, then Minister of Defence. I told him what was happening and that the Commander of Air Command was not in favour of my proposed D-Day flight. To his great credit, David immediately instructed that 430 Squadron should carry out its D-Day plans for flying General Rohmer over the invasion beaches.

On the evening of June 5, 1994, *Statendam* was in dock at Honfleur. At 5:45 a.m. the next day Mary-O and I, in heavy rain, were into the chauffeur-driven vehicle that we had ordered and were on our way to the airport at Deauville, some twenty minutes to the west.

When we arrived there, still in darkness, I was surprised to see that the Americans had, in effect, taken over the operation of the airport, including its security. Even though I was in full uniform there was some reluctance about letting Mary-O and me in to the terminal building. There was also similar reluctance about letting in my good friend Tayler Parnaby, the senior reporter of CFRB, who appeared out of nowhere. I was delighted to see Tayler and noticed that he was having difficulty getting through until I called him "Colonel Parnaby" in the presence of the American soldiers. The doors were opened to him immediately.

The Commanding Officer of 430 Squadron greeted us warmly, as did his entire contingent of some twenty-five personnel. But he had bad news. The weather was so difficult that there was no way he would be able to fly us until later in the day. Since I had done two trips on D-Day in 1944, a repeat of the second one would suffice for our purposes, to be sure.

The Commanding Officer had a wonderful surprise for us, and for me in particular. The aircraft that was assigned to fly me had been painted by the squadron to be as close a replica of the Mustang I had flown on D-Day 1944 as possible. There was a roundel, the black-and-white D-Day stripes, and the letters and numbers of my D-Day aircraft and the 430 Squadron crest. What a thrill to see this beautiful machine and the effort that my squadron had put into making this an absolutely unique occasion for us. After all, fifty years to the day, the hour, and the minute with the same squadron, same place was quite remarkable.

While we couldn't fly in the morning, we were able to do so at about one o'clock. We flew across to the Juno Beach sector, landed there, and then flew to a place to land close to the cemetery. Mary-O and I walked the last four hundred yards across a field and entered the cemetery. There

D-Day 1994 flight over Juno Beach with
430 Squadron fifty years later.

was the huge crowd assembled waiting for the ceremonies to begin. Prime Minister Chrétien officiated with President Mitterand of France. The designated Veterans Affairs Official Party was there, and so were scores of other people who had actually fought on the beaches and in the air above and the sea beside fifty years before. Also present were the Commander of Air Command and Minister of Defence David Collenette. I did not advise the commander about our day of flying with my squadron, about the thrill, the privilege, and the honour, and about the magnanimous good-will of David Collenette in allowing it to happen.

Now to the creation of the 60th Anniversary of D-Day Advisory Committee to the Minister of Veterans Affairs.

In February 2001 I had participated in a forty-five-minute meeting with Prime Minister Jean Chrétien in regard to the Mid-Canada concept. Being old antagonists we hit it off very well with lots of good humour.

A few weeks after the events of June 6, 1994, I wrote to him, with a copy to the deputy Minister of Veterans Affairs, whom I knew, Vice-Admiral Larry Murray (Retired). I had seen Larry in Holland at Wageningen on May 5, 2000. We veterans who understood the situation in Ottawa were much pleased when he became Deputy Minister of Veterans Affairs after he retired from the military. He is a truly able and compassionate individual.

In my letter to the Prime Minister I laid out the basic problems that had occurred in Normandy, complaining not bitterly but with as much acid as I could throw on the paper.

I laid out a proposal that a committee should be formed to advise the Minister of Veterans Affairs on how the celebrations for the sixti-eth anniversary of D-Day should be conducted. My proposal cited three objectives: this time Canada should take "possession" of Juno Beach, we should ensure that Queen Elizabeth was with us, and any veteran of D-Day, or for that matter the Battle of Normandy, should be guaranteed access to Juno Beach, accompanied by family or a care-giver or both.

To my amazement, the Prime Minister referred the matter over to Dr. Ray Pagtakhan, the Minister of Veterans Affairs. And to my further amazement, the minister, through his deputy minister, Larry Murray, responded positively to my proposal. After considerable negotiation the terms of reference were approved. They are Appendix VI.

Larry Murray and his team selected the members of the Committee, all of whom were highly experienced former military people. Three of the six were D-Day veterans: Garth Webb, MSC, the creator of the Juno Beach Centre; Cliff Chadderton, CC, O.Ont., chairman of the National Council of Veterans Associations; and me. Chadderton was later suc-ceeded by a distinguished paratrooper, Jan de Vries, also a D-Day veteran. The other members of the Committee are Lieutenant-General (Retired) Charles Belzile, CM, CMM, CD, Grand President of the Royal Canadian Legion and president of the Canadian Battle Foundation, and Colonel Jack Arsenault, dominion secretary-treasurer of the Army, Navy and Air Force Veterans Association. The deputy minister was ex officio on the Committee, as were the appointees of the Chief of the Defence Staff, Major-General Jan Arp and Ian McLean, former Canadian ambassador plenipotentiary to France. Secretary of the Committee was Doug Clorey, who is the Director General of Canada Remembers, a section of Veterans Affairs. Clorey and the project director, Louise Wallis, are based at Veterans Affairs headquarters in Charlottetown, Prince Edward Island, while the deputy minister is traditionally based both in Ottawa and in Charlottetown. The Veterans Affairs department numbers approximately three thousand staff.

At the first meeting of the Committee, held in Ottawa in October of 2002, I was elected chair, probably because of the fact that I had initiated its existence through my correspondence with the Prime Minister and my dealings with Deputy Minister of Veterans Affairs Larry Murray.

No list of D-Day veterans existed. We knew what units had participated from all three services, but there was no list of people. As chairman, in March 2003 I drafted a press release and an article that could be used by magazines such as *The Legion* and *Air Force*. The key element in the press release and the article was the request that any D-Day veteran should register with Veterans Affairs in Charlottetown by calling a given telephone number or faxing or e-mailing and giving their names, ranks, periods of service in D-Day and/or the Battle of Normandy, and all of the information that would be necessary for us to be able to confirm who they were. Many of the regiments have associations, and the Royal Canadian Air Force has the Air Force Association. The organizations represented by Cliff Chadderton and Jack Arsenault embrace a broad sweep of all aspects of all three services. I also prepared an advertising program that could be offered to all of the newspapers across Canada, asking them to advertise for D-Day and Battle of Normandy veterans. I put that proposition forward in March as well, but it wasn't until August 2003 that there was some movement at Veterans Affairs headquarters to create such a campaign. The campaign was finally launched in

November when I sent the VAC ad package to the publishers of the *Globe & Mail*, the *National Post*, and the *Toronto Star*. The *Globe* and the *Star* graciously published the ad. It was hoped that over the months between that early time and April 2004, we would have a relatively complete dossier of survivors. In that way we could do our best to ensure that any veteran of D-Day and the Battle of Normandy who could get there with caregivers could have access to Juno Beach and the ceremonies that were planned.

In the interim, the remarkable Juno Beach Centre was under construction at Courseulles-sur-Mer. It was the dream and creation of one of our Committee members, Garth Webb, an artillery man who went ashore on at Juno Beach on D-Day.

In its meetings in October 2002 through to March 2003, the Committee identified many areas that should be examined and reported upon, all of them flowing from the terms of reference. We were particularly interested in the progress that was being made by Garth Webb in the construction of the Juno Beach Centre. Having him as a member of the Committee was most valuable in terms of being able to understand what was being done and the amount contributed by the Government of Canada, which finally came in at about $4 million over a series of years. A million or so dollars came from the Government of France. As the matter progressed toward the opening of the Juno Beach Centre on June 6, 2003, the Government of British Columbia kicked in with a million, as did the Government of Ontario.

The Canadian Embassy in Paris indicated that the president of the Comité du Débarquement, Admiral Brac de la Perrier, had advanced ideas on what should be done before, during, and after the 2004 D-Day anniversary. It was apparent that the Admiral was a highly organized gentleman and that he had been given power by the Government of France to really run everything, in concert with General Delbouf. The Admiral would be the gatekeeper when it came to the question of getting Canadian veterans to Juno Beach on D-Day. Admiral de la Perrier had the concept of giving each veteran a medallion to identify him. It sounded to me as though it would be a potential pass that would allow a veteran to gain access to Juno Beach, which is exactly what I had been looking for in terms of overcoming the barriers that existed for all of us in 1994 (with the exception of the anointed forty-five or so Official Party veterans that Veterans Affairs had selected). Not so. We would have to devise our own "pass" system, which we did.

As we moved along with our meetings it was understood that the return to Normandy would be called that instead of a pilgrimage. A pilgrimage has for many people a quasi-religious tone that did not rest well with me or with most of the people on our Committee. What we were going to strive for was an appeal to as many veterans of D-Day and the Battle of Normandy as we could find.

To repeat, it was my objective to try to steer the Committee into making available to any D-Day or Battle of Normandy veteran the opportunity to get to Juno Beach on D-Day and also to the events before and after it.

What I wanted to avoid in 2004 — and it was clear from the very beginning — was granting just a select few veterans, out of the thousands that were eligible, access to the beach and payment by VAC. I felt that this was highly discriminatory and totally inappropriate. That was the way it had worked in 1994, but it was totally unacceptable so far as I was concerned.

My perception was not met with any resistance at all. Deputy Minister Larry Murray was really quite supportive. The man who was assigned to work with us most closely was Doug Clorey, with his assistant, Louise Wallis. I did not detect in them any contrary opinion in relation to the objective of keeping things open for all veterans.

With the consent of all I had sent a letter to Her Majesty's private secretary with a copy to the secretary of the Governor General (which was appropriate protocol) indicating that Canada wished to have Her Majesty in attendance at Juno Beach on June 6, 2004, anticipating that she would also be, as she has always been, with the British troops at Arromanches. Never had she been with the Canadians. The Brits would traditionally arrive en masse by the hundreds and then parade before Her Majesty on the sand at Arromanches in a magnificent exhibition of solidarity. But Canada had never done any such thing. I thought it was time that we could have her with us as well as have our own Canadian ceremony at Juno Beach.

I also wrote a preliminary letter to Her Excellency the Governor General, anticipating the formal invitation from the Prime Minister (whoever he was) at the appropriate time.

In May of 2003, Doug Clorey, Louise Wallis, and I did what I consider to be a fairly effective tour to the UK, Paris, and Normandy to assess the situation. When the three of us arrived in London in May, our main meeting was with a staff member of the British Ministry of Defence, John Sinfield, whose principal information was that he really didn't know how much was going on in terms of the various regiments and organizations in the UK on June 6, 2004. What he did know was that the Blair government had informed Her Majesty that 2004 was the year of the one hundredth anniversary of the Entente Cordiale between the United Kingdom and France, and that Her Majesty was expected to attend state functions in Paris for that occasion. As far as the Blair government was concerned she would be able to attend only one state function in France in 2004, and that was the Entente Cordiale affair, not the D-Day celebrations.

When I heard this, and assumed it was true, I decided to approach the Prime Minister of Canada (through the Minister of Veterans Affairs, of course) and ask him to write a letter to Her Majesty as the Queen of Canada inviting her, quite apart from the Blair government, to attend the D-Day celebrations in Normandy on June 6, 2004. I reasoned that if Her Majesty were so inclined this would be outside the purview of the British government and, if she agreed to attend, we could make all arrangements for her.

However, in our June meeting the Committee decided that it would be best if Her Majesty was not invited because if she did accept, the constraints and difficulties related to her security and all the arrangements would be "impossible." I informed the appropriate people in the office of the Governor General that no apparent word was to go across to Her Majesty until things were official in that regard.

The second stage of the May trip took us to Paris and a meeting that Admiral Brac de la Perrier had convened at his naval club, based in a ship sitting on the Seine River close to the Eiffel Tower. The military attaché of the Canadian Embassy, Colonel Houle, was our efficient preliminary liaison and made all the arrangements for our attendance. With me were

Colonel Houle, Doug Clorey, Louise Wallis, and Garth Webb's number-two man in the development of the Juno Beach Centre, Don Cooper, the son of Garth's partner, Lise Cooper. Don is in the environmental servicing business. As matters turned out, he is highly knowledgeable on all matters having to do with bureaucracy, having gone through the all the horrific negotiations for land and permits and all the necessary privileges to get the Juno Beach Centre underway and ultimately built. On top of that he is a Royal Military College graduate who is fluently bilingual. A very practical and very pleasant man who has been of great assistance to us.

At the meeting with Admiral Brac de la Perrier there were two American representatives and people from Britain, Belgium, Holland, and Poland. The Admiral went on at great length, explaining the entire situation and making it clear that he didn't want everything to happen on D-Day alone because of the impact of hundreds of people descending upon the Normandy beaches. We did not get into the details of his concept of medallions for veterans that could be used for identification and "pass" purposes. That would come later. The main exercise was to establish contact with the him and to have him know that it was our intention to focus on D-Day at Juno Beach and to have all our events around that day, a position with which he ultimately agreed.

There would have to be substantial negotiations with Admiral de la Perrier and his team in the fall of 2003 in order to work out all the details. When we did discover who our D-Day and Battle of Normandy veterans across Canada were and which of them were going to be in Normandy on D-Day, then we would be able to provide their names to the French. They could then prepare the Admiral's medallions, and we could prepare our passes.

The next stop on our tour was the Juno Beach Centre itself, where we were shown the exact status of the construction by Don Cooper. I was enormously impressed by the building and all the work that had gone into it: the concept, the design, and the architecture. Brian Chamberlain of Burlington, the head of a large architectural and building firm, had designed the building. Brian had been one of my Air Force pilots back in the days that I was commander of the Air Reserve Group. He is an excellent executive and a highly qualified pilot who operates his own aircraft. It was clear to me after our inspection of the place that this was going to be an absolutely superb achievement for Canada by Garth Webb, Lise Cooper, Don Cooper, and all associated with the project. We were then looking forward to the opening three weeks later of the Juno Beach Centre.

That opening occurred on June 6, 2003, in the presence of thousands of people. Veterans Affairs Minister Pagtakhan was in attendance with Prime Minister Jean Chrétien. Also there was Ernie Eves, the premier of Ontario (Ontario made such a substantial contribution to Juno Beach Centre) along with his life partner, Isobel Bassett. The opening ceremonies were exceptionally well carried out, complete with a flypast of a Spitfire from England, a drop of Canadian military parachutists, the marching band of the Queen's Own Rifles, and, of course, the speeches that went on and on.

The last speech was from Garth Webb and Lise Cooper, who capped it all off by giving compliments to all who had been involved in the fundraising, development, and construction of the Juno Beach Centre. Garth Webb had been a young lad on D-Day when he went ashore with his artillery unit with their 25-pounder guns. He had all the credibility of being a D-Day veteran as well as that arising from the fact that when he had started putting the Juno Beach Centre together some seven or eight years before, everyone with whom he talked said it couldn't be done. But Garth did it. It is a structure and achievement that will last many, many generations, if not forever. For his efforts he was invested with the Meritorious Service Cross by the Governor General in the fall of 2003.

In keeping with my military practice since I left the Armed Forces as Chief of Reserves back in 1981, whenever I have had occasion to appear in uniform in a military ceremony I have always asked permission from the CDS to wear my major-general's uniform. Somehow in the front of my mind I just cannot bring myself to dress up as an old veteran of the Second World War. Because no matter what my age, I am not old! To wear Air Force Association or Legion dress just turns me off. Fortuitously, every CDS has always responded positively to any request I have made in that regard.

My current general's uniform is the new blue material, a splendid rig that was brought into existence by General Ramsay Withers when he was Chief of the Defence Staff. My old friend Ramsay was always progressive and ready to change things. When he took over as CDS, he recognized that trying to meld the Army, Navy, and Air Force together was totally impossible and that the Air Force and the Navy really deserved the dignity of having their two original uniform colours rather than being compelled to wear the horrendous green uniforms that we had been forced into by Trudeau and Hellyer.

I decided to request from the Chief of the Defence Staff, General Ray Hénault, permission to wear my uniform at ceremonies associated with the sixtieth anniversary of D-Day in my role as Chair of the 60th Anniversary of D-Day Advisory Committee. The General kindly gave me that permission, and so it was that on the June 6, 2003, at the opening ceremonies of Juno Beach Centre and at other ceremonies at cemeteries in the area, I was in my Air Force general's uniform complete with my decorations and medals properly displayed, including the St. John Knight's Cross that was fondled by Princess Di on June 3, 1994, at Green Park in London when Her Majesty unveiled the Canada Memorial Monument. (See Appendix VII.)

In spring 2003, the Prime Minister shifted Larry Murray out of the job as Deputy Minister of Veterans Affairs and put him into Fisheries and Oceans. In his place he put Dr. Jack Stagg, who had come from Indian Affairs. Dr. Stagg brought with him no prior apparent association with the military, although he is a quick learner, a very intelligent, highly organized man, and easy to work with. He was in attendance ex officio for the Committee meeting in Ottawa in June where we discussed the "short" time of twelve months before June 6, 2004, and the countless matters that had to be attended to during that time. I told them then that I was aware that Doug Clorey was going to be on leave for August and September, and Louise Wallis would be away in August. So both our point people would be away during the month of August, and there was concern in the Committee that nothing would be done in that period. Jack Stagg promised that nothing would stop and there would be someone appointed to look after things while Clorey and Wallis were away.

About the only thing that was brought to the fore in August was a call from the head of the communications department, who said that he and his team were preparing finally an advertising program, something that I had been asking for for months. It was anticipated then that the proposed program would be ready for the Committee meeting scheduled for September 16. Prior to the Veterans Affairs delegation's departure for South Korea for the celebrations there, Jack Stagg asked me to come to Ottawa to meet with him and Doug Clorey so that they could present to me the proposed D-Day 2004 strategy of Veterans Affairs Canada. Over lunch at the Château Laurier, Doug Clorey handed me a July document entitled "Strategy for the 60th Anniversary of D-Day." I did not have the time then to read it, nor was I able to really get any sense of it, except that what Clorey was now proposing and the deputy minister was prepared to accept were the rewrites of the 1994 pilgrimage to Juno Beach.

The terms of reference of the Committee were not referred to.

I was upset to say the least. What I then did was this. By the end of August I had compiled a strong letter to the deputy minister outlining my perception of the non-conformity of Veterans Affairs with the terms of reference that had been agreed upon. I went item by item through the strategy paper and compared it to the terms of reference, in effect saying that the paper was not acceptable. I then listed some thirteen recommendations to be debated at the September 16 meeting, in the form of advice to be given to the minister in accordance with the terms of reference.

I compiled into a book my letter, Clorey's strategy document, the terms of reference of the Committee, and my thirteen proposed recommendations to the minister. My Collingwood print shop made sufficient copies for all Committee members, and I sent them off well in advance of the meeting.

Remember, Doug Clorey was still away on his two-month leave. But by mid-September, Louise Wallis, the able and efficient project director, was back at her Charlottetown desk.

There was much scurrying around and telephone discussion. By the time the committee meeting convened on September 16, the strategy paper was history. The original terms of reference were back in place, and my recommendations were largely accepted, including allocating five spaces in the proposed Official Party to each of the Navy and the Air Force instead of the single spot from 1994 that was carried over into the July strategy paper.

That minimal allocation to the Air Force was and is symptomatic of the prevailing Veterans Affairs mindset that the only people involved in D-Day and the Battle of Normandy were the Army troops, the soldiers. In speeches, publications, and photographs there was rarely any attribution to the Navy or the Air Force. With my limited ability I have done my very best to strongly get the message across to VAC and staff, particularly to the communications people preparing press releases and news letters. By the spring of 2004 the message was being received. Even so it was necessary to monitor the VAC product carefully.

In November 2003 Doug Clorey, Louise Wallis, and I made our third trip to Europe of that year.

In Caen we were met by the Canadian Forces pair assigned to VAC for the purpose of liaising with us and facilitating the military's planning and participation for D-Day and its surrounding events. Major Jim McKillip (the planning master) and Chief Warrant Officer Smokey Leblanc (the parade master), both highly experienced and capable men, became an integral part of the Committee and VAC's work.

Our meeting in Caen with Admiral Brac de la Perrier and the area head of security and their staffs was ultimately successful: they agreed in principle to our proposal of providing each of our veterans with a pass. Louise had prepared an example of the device, which would bear the veteran's name and be encased in a plastic holder that would hang on a cord around the veteran's neck. That pass would ensure that every veteran would be guaranteed access to Juno Beach on D-Day — which was my major objective in establishing the Advisory Committee in the first place.

We left the Admiral and went to the Juno Beach Centre, where we inspected the site to begin the seating, parade, and ceremony planning for D-Day.

Then it was back to Paris to meet Colonel Houle, who had organized a meeting with General Delbouf, the man then in charge of organizing for the Government of France the entire international ceremony, to be held at 3:30 p.m. on D-Day at Arromanches, some thirteen kilometres to the west of the Juno Beach Centre.

Colonel Houle, Doug Clorey, Major McKillip, and I met with General Delbouf (a retired four-star who was two years old on D-Day) and two of his staff. Very cordial. It was clear from the meeting with the Admiral and with the General that the French focus was totally on their international ceremony at Arromanches. Accordingly, our sideshow at Juno Beach and the special arrangements for passes and transportation were not of significant concern.

The meeting with Delbouf provided me with a startling and encouraging piece of news that triggered an entire new initiative, or rather the revival of one that I thought was dead. This was a Monday. The General informed us that on the Friday before, the President of France had sent D-Day invitations to all of the appropriate heads of state including Her Majesty Queen Elizabeth, who had accepted in advance!

Eureka! The Queen was going to be in Normandy. She would be with President Chirac at the 3:30 p.m. ceremony. Surely we could get her to visit her Canadian veterans for the first time at our (then) planned parade and ceremonies at 10:30 a.m.?

To have the Queen with us had been one of my two major objectives for the Committee as set out in its terms of reference. The information obtained from the British Ministry of Defence in our London visit in the spring had been wrong. Now I could open negotiations with the Queen's private secretary, Sir Robin Janvrin, which I did as soon as I was back in Canada.

An aside here. What General Delbouf could have told us, but probably deliberately did not, was that Chirac had also invited to the international ceremonies at Arromanches none other than his anti-U.S. partner, Chancellor Schroeder of Germany. What a political move by Chirac, one designed to stick his finger up George Bush's nose, as the Brits might say.

For myself, I had no intention of recommending that Canada invite Schroeder to Juno Beach on D-Day or any other day.

Back in Canada, I immediately wrote to Sir Robin reconfirming my unofficial "heads up" invitation suggesting the possibility of the morning of D-Day for the Queen's visit.

Talking with him in January he raised the question of whether an informal visit by Her Majesty with a walkabout might be acceptable. My response in the affirmative was immediate. In a letter to me he confirmed and advised that his office would be in touch with the Governor General's staff concerning the arrangements.

Trying to pry a formal invitation to the Queen from Prime Minister Paul Martin's office was nearly impossible. I started the process in early December. But by the end of January 2004, and with the involvement of Jack Stagg, there was still nothing. Frustrating. But she was there!

On February 16, 2004, I chaired by telephone from Tobago (Mary-O and I were there for a writing retreat to finish these memoirs and *Ultimatum 2*) the monthly meeting of the 60th Anniversary Advisory Committee in Ottawa.

During the discussions I caught some brief mention of a subject I hadn't heard about before. It was the French Legion of Honour decoration. Before the meeting finished I asked Doug Clorey what was going on. He explained that there had been overtures to Veterans Affairs from the French Embassy about the granting of thirty appointments to the Legion of Honour for selected veterans of D-Day and the Battle of Normandy. This was a matter that arose directly from the sixtieth anniversary. It was for the veterans. It should have been referred to the Committee.

Instead, the VAC staff kept the decision making (and information) to themselves. The French wanted VAC to nominate the recipients. VAC sought legal advice, which told them they shouldn't take that responsibility. In the meantime, my friend and activist Cliff Chadderton heard about the matter and submitted his own list of thirty to the French. There was also VAC contact with Jack Arsenault of ANAVETS. There was no contact with the chairman of the Committee — until that little passing mention of the Legion of Honour during that February 16 meeting.

After discussions with the resourceful Doug Clorey, the situation began to be resolved. Finally it came to this: Charles Belzile and I, with a representative of each of the Royal Canadian Legion and Cliff Chadderton's organization, would be the nominating committee, a function we performed at the French Embassy at 9:00 a.m. on March 3, 2004. We selected the deserving thirty Canadian veterans of D-Day and the Battle of Normandy and recommended them to the ambassador of France. As it turned out, all of our nominees were accepted. In addition, after a clandestine effort on the part of the valiant General Belzile, the three D-Day members of the 60th Anniversary of D-Day Committee — de Vries, Webb, and I — were added. In late May, Garth Webb and I were invested as Chevaliers of the Legion of Honour by the ambassador of France in Ottawa. Jan de Vries's investiture came later, at the hands of the President of France, Jacques Chirac, at Arromanches on June 6, 2004.

Before I move into the 2004 D-Day celebrations and how all the planning worked out, a few words about the honorary posts I have been fortunate to have, about my "literary career," and about the creation of the Ontario Veterans Memorial.

CHAPTER 75
Honorary Posts

————◆————

I HAVE BEEN PRIVILEGED TO HOLD many honorary posts.

In addition to being Chancellor of the University of Windsor, an honorary post of the highest calibre, I have had the good fortune over the years to hold other honorary titles and positions.

I was the first honorary lieutenant-colonel, then first honorary colonel of the Canadian Air Force.

In 1980, the chairman of the Metropolitan Toronto branch of St. John Ambulance, Lieutenant-Colonel Ken Robinson, asked me if I would be the Patron of Metro Toronto St. John Ambulance, the largest brigade of St. John's in the Commonwealth. I had served on the Ontario Council of St. John when I was doing the Tortola ambulance caper and so was quite familiar with the objectives and work of St. John across Ontario and as well in Metro Toronto.

There were no terms of reference nor is there any description in any of the order or regulation books of the Order of St. John, whether in the United Kingdom or elsewhere, for the term "patron." Nor has any definition been established since 1980. However, I intuitively knew what it was that Colonel Robinson wanted me to do. He had in mind that the General would be the inspecting officer at the annual parade of St. John Ambulance, wherever it might be held. I would participate at honours and awards events, be they breakfasts, lunches, or dinners. As a Knight of the Order of St. John I had a senior rank in the Order that was well recognized.

As with the chancellor's post, it was never my role to become involved in any way, shape, or form with the administrative or executive operations of Metro Toronto St. John Ambulance, nor would I attend its board meetings. On the other hand, if my advice were sought on a particular issue, I would be prepared to give it, subject to the issue's sensitivity.

I have continued in the role of Patron since 1980, rarely, if ever, missing an annual parade as the Inspecting Officer, always in full uniform as a major-general with the permission of the Chief of the Defence Staff, at least up until the time I became the Honorary Chief Superintendent of the Ontario Provincial Police.

In the year 2003, the chairman of the Toronto St. John Ambulance organization (note the change from "Metropolitan Toronto" to "Toronto" when the provincial government amalgamated all the surrounding municipalities into Toronto) decided that it would be appropriate for the patron to wear a St. John Ambulance uniform (as do all the officers of Toronto St. John Ambulance) for the annual inspection of the Toronto brigade. The result was that the uniform appeared well in advance of the annual inspection parade. They had trouble deciding on what rank to put on the jacket. Of course, the headquarters organization in Ottawa had no suggestions, so my advice to the Toronto people was simply put on my epaulettes and elsewhere the rank that is best equivalent to major-general.

The next honorary appointment took place in the year 2000, when the new commissioner of the Ontario Provincial Police, Gwen Boniface, at the urging of OPP Superintendent Bob Fitches and others, decided that she would appoint me as the Honorary Chief Superintendent of the Ontario Provincial Police. There were several honorary inspectors already in place in recognition of good work and support for the OPP over the years.

When the commissioner and I met over a breakfast meeting to discuss the possibility of my honorary involvement with her huge force of some seven thousand people she asked me about the rank that I thought would be appropriate. I suggested the rank comparable to military rank of major-general, which happened to be chief superintendent. Her response was one of approval.

At the next annual mess dinner of the Ontario Provincial Police held at the officers' mess in Camp Borden I was invested. The beloved honorary commissioner of the OPP, former Lieutenant-Governor Lincoln Alexander, PC, CC, QC, an old friend of mine of whom I have always been extremely fond (and I think he of me), presented to me my Certificate of Office with strong words of encouragement and welcome. As it happens, I am the only honorary chief superintendent of the OPP, which I am proud to say to people when I am explaining my role.

My official portrait as the Honorary Chief Superintendent of the Ontario Provincial Police.

My OPP function as honorary chief superintendent is to give advice and counsel to the commissioner when she asks for it — and even when she doesn't. I also attend various ceremonial functions in full regalia, particularly at graduating parades where new OPP personnel are sent out into the ever-expanding field operations.

And, of course, I attend the annual OPP mess dinner, wherever it is held.

I have proposed some initiatives to the commissioner that have been of interest to her and to her staff, and I will continue so to do. Should she decide that I could be of particular help in a specific area, that I will do as well.

As soon as my appointment as honorary chief superintendent was confirmed, a fine OPP superintendent whom I had met years before, and who has always been very supportive, Chris Wyatt, decided that I should be properly uniformed so that I could carry out all the functions that might be assigned to me. The result is that I have all the working uniforms of an OPP officer, including the appropriate hat and the mess kit — I took my old military mess kit and had it adapted to the style of the OPP's formal uniform. However, Mary-O thought that it didn't fit as well as it should after thirty-odd years, so I bought a new one that really looks quite elegant notwithstanding the form over which it now has to fit (not quite as slim as it used to be).

So now I have my QC gown in the closet, which I wear from time to time. I have my cap and gown as chancellor emeritus of the University of Windsor. I have my major-general's blue uniform, four OPP uniforms, and a mess kit. But that was not to be the end by any means.

Early in 2003, Ric Rangel-Bron, my St. John Ambulance friend who was my aide in St. John Ambulance for many years and who is a senior planner with the Toronto Emergency Medical Services (EMS), decided that he would recommend to the chief of the Toronto EMS, Ron Kalusky, who had been with me at many St. John functions, that it might be appropriate for the Toronto EMS to have an honorary chief to work with Ron and his senior staff. The invitation came to me from Chief Kalusky. I accepted, and on December 19, 2002, I was installed with great ceremony at the EMS headquarters on Dufferin Street in Toronto north of Downsview Airport as honorary chief of the Toronto Emergency Medical Services.

And with that post, which I treasure highly, came a new uniform and flat hat with other accoutrements, plus a mess kit that arrived in 2004.

But there's more.

In late November 2003, Collingwood's fine fire chief, Sandy Cunningham, spoke to the dynamic mayor of our town, Terry Geddes, about whether it would be acceptable to have the Town Council appoint me as the honorary fire chief. The answer was positive. Sandy asked me, and I accepted. The new fire chief's uniform arrived early in January 2004, just in time for Chief Sandy to formally present to council the new honorary in full bemedalled regalia.

I am honoured and privileged to be the honorary fire chief of Collingwood, especially since the fire station is about one hundred yards from my home, as is the OPP detachment with which I have had a close connection for several years as a member of and chair of the Collingwood Police Services Board — plus as the honorary chief superintendent!

At last count in my closet I have ten operational uniforms and two mess kits, plus seven caps/head gear. And as mentioned earlier there are my Queen's Counsel and chancellor emeritus gowns. And everything still fits!

CHAPTER 76

Literary Career, President Bush, and Brian Mulroney

———◆———

O VER THE YEARS SINCE 1970 I have written many books, both fiction and non-fiction, and even had a shot at a little poetry.

There is a list of my books and publications at the beginning of these memoirs. From it you will be able to see that I have taken the opportunity to choose a broad range of topics in the non-fiction field. As well, I have ranged over many themes with my fiction works.

Notwithstanding my extensive track record, I recognize that I am not seen, nor do I see myself, as a "literary author," nor am I a personage to be recognized in the Canadian literary establishment.

In reality, almost all my books are out of print, and they're certainly out of royalties, except *Caged Eagle*, my most recent fiction work after *John A.'s Crusade*, and the 2003 non-fiction work, *HMS* Raleigh *On The Rocks*. A novel that I am working on with the working title of *Ultimatum 2* may see the light of day fairly soon if I can find a publisher. In the fall of 2003 Dundurn Press (the publisher of these memoirs) published a trilogy of my novels, *Ultimatum*, *Exxoneration*, and *Periscope Red*, with the title *A Richard Rohmer Omnibus*.

My second book, *The Green North, Mid-Canada*, which dealt with the Mid-Canada concept, was published in 1970 by MacLean, Hunter. The book was written with Frank Oxley, who carried the bulk of the effort. It was not a best-seller but it explained the basis of my Mid-Canada ideas.

The next book, also non-fiction, was a description I wanted to write of what was going on in Canada's High Arctic at the time. I wanted to use my Mid-Canada Conference experience, my sighting of the great American ice breaking tanker, *Manhattan*, and all of the ramifications that came from that to write a book about what I thought the future of the Arctic could be.

That future promised to be bright, particularly in light of the fact that there was much talk in those early 1970s days of a natural gas pipeline from the McKenzie Delta down to market. In 2003, some thirty years later, that pipeline is moving toward to becoming a reality.

In the summer of 1972, at a meeting with Jack McClelland (after the Royal Commission on Book Publishing was finished), I told him that I had a book I wanted to write on the Arctic. I gave him the basics. He said, "You write the book, and I'll publish it." I did, and he did. McClelland & Stewart published *The Arctic Imperative* in quality paperback in the spring of 1973.

At that same time I had the concept for a novel based on what had been going on in the Arctic, particularly with the potential pipeline and the perceived American demand for Canadian natural gas. I put together about 150 pages of draft and gave it to McClelland & Stewart. But the editor-in-chief of the day, Anna Porter, now the distinguished Canada publisher of Key Porter books, rejected my submission. I then took the proposed work to Dr. Bill Clarke of Clarke, Irwin. He was very interested in the material he saw and invited me to finish the draft and then he would look at it. I finished it. He wanted to change it materially, but I fought him off. My first novel, *Ultimatum*, was published in the fall of 1973. After an enormous amount of promotion by Clarke, Irwin and a book tour across the country it went to the top of the Canadian bestsellers list and sat there for about six months. *Ultimatum* was not published in the United States at that time but went in paperback there with Simon & Schuster during the next season.

During my *Ultimatum* book tour I was lined up with a radio host in Vancouver by the name of Jack Webster. He had never heard of me, and I had never heard of him. When I sat down with him with the radio mike open this usually belligerent but great guy started hammering at me about *Ultimatum*, saying it was a book that was obviously written by a lawyer. I shot right back at him. The two of us went at it tooth and nail, something he enjoyed enormously and was totally appropriate for his audience. From that time, whenever I was on a book tour in Vancouver I was sure to be a guest on Jack Webster's show.

Another *Ultimatum* event occurred when I was approached by two young entrepreneurs who wanted to buy the film rights for it. We negotiated an option, for which they paid a reasonable price. Everything was subject to their finding a screenwriter who could produce a reasonable script. They retained the services of a Canadian working in Hollywood. He eventually produced a script that was totally different from the *Ultimatum* scenario. It was as if he had never read the book. His product was unbelievably unacceptable. The two young entrepreneurs never picked up the option. I would not have let them pick it up in any event, the script was so bad. The two young entrepreneurs? My good friends now, Moses Znaimer and, would you believe it, Garth Drabinsky. After the success of *Ultimatum* I started to produce a novel a year and gradually established a good relationship with Jack Stoddart, Sr., at General Publishing. He eventually gave me a contract for three books, which were produced and published in accordance with our agreement.

The E.P. Taylor biography I have already discussed. It was a 1978 break from the fiction run.

Back to fiction, this time *Separation*, which I produced in 1976. It dealt with the Quebec situation, what else. Shortly after *Separation* was published I had a call from my friend the great, huge John Bassett, publisher of the *Telegram* and an exceptional leader in Canadian media, including television. I was at my farm in the Mulmur Hills when John called me. When Bassett was on the phone you could hold the earpiece out well away from your head and still hear every word he was saying. John wanted to buy the television film rights for *Separation*. We negotiated then and there and did a deal. It was a condition of mine that the script produced should protect the integrity of and follow the line of the book. The negative *Ultimatum* film script experience was almost too much. John agreed. Then he informed me that he was going to have a part in the film. He was a senator in one of the scenes. I countered by saying that I too would have to have a role. I was a reporter who at the end of the film gave the results of the referendum that had taken place in Quebec — which the Parti Québécois lost.

I recently sent John's son, Douglas Bassett (with whom I sit on the advisory council of the Order of Ontario), clippings from the newspapers of the day when *Separation* was shown on television. It turned out to be an excellent production, which I think cost John about $600,000. He wanted to make a contribution to national unity. My message to Douglas was, "This film may be old but it is still highly relevant to what is going on in Canada today. Maybe you can get CTV or even City TV to show *Separation* again. After all, the reruns of the American films show productions that are forty and fifty and sixty years old, but we don't seem to have any difficulty putting them on our television screens." No response.

To people who aspire to be authors and talk to me about the book they have in mind to write I always give this advice: don't give up your day job! Until you hit with a

Toronto Star *announcement for the TV movie version of my novel* Separation, *broadcast February 27, 1978 by CFTO-TV.*

high-paying best-seller, be it fiction or non-fiction, an author should always follow that principle. I have. Which means that even at this stage I still continue to practise law, I write my newspaper columns, do television professionally, consult to various corporations and organizations, sit on boards of directors, and function as the "honorary" for many organizations. Basically, I do my book writing while I am on vacation (as I am in Tobago as this chapter is written) or when I'm driving alone in my car and I can safely use my dictating machine.

In the late 1970s I was approached by a National Film Board filmmaker who wanted to do a production based on my activities but would also adapt my official approach to writing about the potential separation of Quebec. It was to be production called, *A Day in the Life of Richard Rohmer*. Jacques Bensimon, a strong French Canadian from Quebec, was the producer. He and his video team spent weeks with me at my law office, at military parades (I was Chief of the Reserve Force in Canada), and at my farm in the Mulmur Hills. Bensimon planned and created what appeared to be a reasonable production. However, it was never shown on television, and so far as I'm aware there was no showing whatever except one in Ottawa, where the journalists for whom it was screened didn't like it. Probably they didn't like the person who was the principal subject matter. Either way, the production stayed in the can. I have a vintage copy. Bensimon is now a senior film commissioner for the government of Canada and has been a successful television executive with TVO and other organizations.

One final story flows from my book writing efforts. It features Peter Munk and former president of the United States George Bush the father.

Notwithstanding my assertions to E.P. Taylor that I would never do another goddamn biography because it was too much work, I nevertheless took on the assignment of doing a biography of Peter Munk. It was produced in 1997, just after another authorized-by-Peter biography of him was published. That book was supposed to be confined to his business skills but turned out to be a biography. At about this time, Brian Mulroney put together a prestigious advisory council for Peter's company, Barrick Gold. Through Mulroney's strong connection with George Bush, Sr., the former president accepted the post of honorary chairman of the Barrick Advisory Council. The council was composed of businessmen with international and distinctive reputations of the highest quality.

To introduce this new organization, Munk threw a cocktail reception for its members, held at the prestigious Toronto Club. I went through the receiving line and was introduced to President Bush by Peter. I shook hands with Bush, looked up at the tall man, and said, "Mr. President, you and I are contemporaries. When you were flying in the U.S. Navy in the Pacific, I was flying Mustangs in Normandy with the Royal Canadian Air Force."

He looked down at me and said, "General, nobody knows this but by the end of 1941, just before December seventh that year, I was planning to come to Canada to join the Royal Canadian Air Force and fly for

Brian Mulroney and I in conversation.

the RCAF. But December seventh arrived and I stayed and went into the U.S. Navy." It would be fiction to speculate on what would have happened if George Bush had in fact come to Canada at the end of 1941 or the beginning of 1942. Many of my classmates that year learning to fly in the RCAF were Americans who decided to stick it out in Canada after Pearl Harbor, earn their wings, and then go back to the U.S. Even so, many carried on and went overseas with the Royal Canadian Air Force.

So much for my involvement in the Canadian book industry as chairman of the Royal Commission on book publishing and as a best-selling author of fiction (sometimes) and of non-fiction (sometimes). As you can tell from these memoirs, I really do intend to continue with both fiction and non-fiction. *HMS* Raleigh *On The Rocks* was published in the fall of 2003, this work in 2004, and possibly *Ultimatum 2* in 2004. Do I expect a big money breakthrough with a best-seller? There is always hope, but it is almost always found in being able to crack the American market where the big bucks are — and they're *American* big bucks! But then there is reality.

CHAPTER 77
Chair of the Ontario Provincial Advisory Committee on a New Veterans Memorial

A S IF CHAIRING THE 60TH Anniversary of D-Day Committee wasn't enough, Ontario Premier Ernie Eves dropped another one on me at the beginning of June 2003. It was before we departed for Normandy and the opening of the Juno Beach Centre on June 6, where he was invited to be a speaker in recognition of the $1 million Ontario had contributed.

The chair of the Management Board of the Ontario Cabinet, David Tsubouchi, on behalf of Premier Eves, had asked if I would chair an advisory committee on the design and creation of a new Veterans Memorial. It would be located at the southwest area of Queen's Park near the intersection of Queen's Park Circle and College Street.

Knowing next to zero about what Premier Eves and his people had in mind, I accepted the task.

A press conference was duly held at the site. The project was announced by the premier; as well, he announced the fact that Major-General Richard Rohmer, there at the press conference, would chair the advisory committee. My colleague Garth Webb was also at the press conference, and by good and wise fortune he was also to be a member of the advisory committee.

Ultimately, the Provincial Advisory Committee judged the designs submitted to it — but then a new government was elected.

Back to square one. The McGuinty government decided to carry on with the project, but they also decided to in effect start over again by creating a new advisory committee, selecting a new Queen's Park site, and calling for a new design competition.

Under the leadership of the Honourable Gerry Phillips, chair of the Management Board of Cabinet, the project is going forward. I am chairing the new Advisory Committee, and the venerable Garth Webb is still with me.

By the time of publication of these memoirs, the advisory committee should have made much progress, but the actual design of the Veterans Memorial will be some months (and probably much controversy) away.

CHAPTER 78

D-Day, June 6, 2004, with the Queen, Governor General, and Prime Minister at Juno Beach, Normandy

———————◆———————

Back to the preparations for the sixtieth anniversary of D-Day. The next round was an end-of-March trip to Paris, this time with an enormous group of civil servants representing the Governor General, the Prime Minister, the departments of protocol and foreign affairs, and our Royal Canadian Mounted Police, with representation from the office of the ambassador in Paris. Because of the intended participation of the appropriate Canadian dignitaries, it was necessary that all those in senior staff responsible for their particular political (or in the case of the Governor General non-political) person had to take part. As chair of the Advisory Committee and the symbolic D-Day veteran, it was appropriate for me to travel with the group and attend the meetings. On this venture Mary-O was again (at our own expense) with me. As it turned out, she was able to sit in the corner at all of the meetings, all of which (starting at the Canadian Embassy in Paris) were conducted in French.

At the first meeting it was clear that the pace was going to be hectic during the week. There were meetings with senior French government officials at the seat of government in Paris, then on to Normandy for discussions with Admiral Brac de la Perrier and his security people. There were visits to the hotels at Cabourg where the Governor General was going to be accommodated and the Hotel de Golf in Deauville, where the Prime Minister would stay. There were also visits to the two prime Canadian cemeteries in Normandy and, of course, to the Juno Beach Centre.

By this time the Deputy Minister of Veterans Affairs had wisely retained the assistance of Ian McLean, who had just retired as the number two person at the Canadian Embassy in Paris. Ian's role was to be on site at the Juno Beach Centre, to work with the local French authorities and the Juno Beach staff, and fundamentally to do all things necessary to get the Juno Beach Centre ready for June 6. This would entail looking after buses, arranging locations for pick-up of veterans at Caen, obtaining bleachers to be erected, arranging for the appropriate VIP platform and other structures, and liaising with the French security authorities (which was an extremely difficult exercise all the way through). In the end, Ian performed superbly. Without his masterful presence the D-Day celebrations could not have been the success that they ultimately turned out to be.

Doug Clorey had indicated to me that he wanted to be in London for two days in order to talk with British Ministry of Defence official John Sinfield, with whom we had met the previous May. He was the man who told us the Queen was not going to be in attendance in Normandy on June 6. After we discovered otherwise during our November meeting with General Delbouf in Paris, I started up my drumbeat to obtain the presence of Her Majesty by writing to Sir Robin Janvrin, the Queen's private secretary. At the same time I pushed as hard as I could to get the Government of Canada to issue a formal invitation to Her Majesty to cover my informal invitation. Knowing that Doug wanted to be in London, I decided that Mary-O and I should do the same, and I would attempt to arrange an appointment to visit Buckingham Palace to attempt to finalize the arrangements for Her Majesty to be with the Canadians on D-Day.

After telephone discussions and exchange of correspondence with Sir Robin Janvrin, it was settled. I would go to the palace and meet with Christopher Geidt, the assistant private secretary to the Queen, who had been put in charge of Her Majesty's arrangements for June 6.

Earlier exchanges I had had with Sir Robin indicated that if Her Majesty would be able to be in attendance with the Canadians on D-Day she would do so at around 5:00 p.m., after the French international ceremonies at Arromanches.

That timing was of major concern to the Committee because after our planned main ceremony at 10:00 or 10:30 in the morning it would be a long, long wait during the day for Her Majesty to arrive. Given the age and physical abilities of the veterans, it would have been extremely difficult for them to carry on for that length of time and take part in a ceremony for her worthy of her presence.

On the advice of my Committee I opened the question with the palace before April 2 as to whether or not Her Majesty might come to us in the morning, say at around ten o'clock. That question was still unanswered when I arrived at Buckingham Palace in the morning of April 2 to meet Christopher Geidt. In telephone discussions with Buckingham Palace I had spoken with Geidt's secretary, Victoria Barrington. When we first spoke I could detect a Canadian accent. Indeed, Victoria is originally from Toronto, a most pleasant and capable young woman who was most co-operative and of great assistance through the entire D-Day negotiations.

When I arrived at Buckingham Palace and got through the security checks, Geidt met me in the reception room of the office — quite a tall young man, he was most courteous and accommodating. As he led me into his spacious office, I could see that his desk was like mine, covered with papers. To its left was a circular table with three wooden chairs and a fourth, comfortably upholstered, chair. We were to sit at the table. When I attempted to get into one of the wooden chairs I was admonished and asked politely if I would sit in the chair of distinction, namely the upholstered one. I was offered Prince of Wales cookies and coffee. Then we got down to business. The day before (April 1), the Queen had decided that indeed she would be able to attend at Juno Beach Centre at ten in the morning on D-Day. She and the Duke would be in France with friends, arriving the day before, and would travel to Courseulles by helicopter. Perfect! It couldn't have been better. I can tell you I was euphoric, walking on air, by the time I left Buckingham Palace.

On top of all that, I had the pleasure of actually meeting Victoria Barrington, another Buckingham Palace treat.

So all of the intended pieces as set out in the original terms of reference that Larry Murray and I had crafted back in 2002 were on the table. We were successfully negotiating passes whereby all Canadian veterans would be able to get to Juno Beach — which they could not do in 1994. We would have the presence of Her Majesty Queen Elizabeth for the first time and probably the last, and we would have the Governor General and the Prime Minister.

As of April 2, 2004, that was the scenario. It looked good. Could we actually pull it off?

At the next meeting of the Advisory Committee in Ottawa in mid-April, all of the details were carefully gone over. The input of Major-General Arp, Major McKillip, and Chief Warrant Officer Smokey LeBlanc (who were always in attendance at our Committee meetings) was beginning to increase with the promised input of a guard of honour from the military, a band, and other participation from the Department of National Defence. In addition, through a call from Jack Stagg to my friend "Zac"' Zacardelli, the commissioner of the Royal Canadian Mounted Police, the commitment was obtained for the presence of some twenty RCMP officers to assist in security matters as well as to have their brilliant dress-uniformed presence everywhere in the process.

The matter of passes being issued by the French continued to be a matter of major concern to the deputy minister and to myself. The plan was that Veterans Affairs would supply to the French the names of those people who had applied for passes. But the French would not give them to us until about a week before D-Day. That raised the question of whether or not they would get them to us at all. In the end, the Veterans Affairs team prepared a Canadian pass to the Beny-sur-Mer ceremony, which was scheduled to take place on June 5. The intent was that if the French didn't come through with their passes that at least the Canadians would have the Beny-sur-Mer pass, and perhaps the French would allow that to be utilized.

During my meeting with Christopher Geidt, he had informed me that he and his reconnaissance party would be visiting France, and in particular the Juno Beach Centre, on April 23. The result was that there was a reasonably fast turnaround after we arrived back in Canada on April 5. I had decided that the appropriate working team of the Advisory Committee and Veterans Affairs should as a matter of courtesy and practicality be at the Juno Beach Centre when Geidt arrived. So Doug Clorey and I were there together with Ian McLean, waiting in the large hall of the centre that faces out toward the sea. We had structured the tables and chairs in such a way that we would be able to receive Geidt and the two men with him and quickly get on with our business. At the appointed hour we could see Christopher Geidt and his two associates approach the building, but to our astonishment they were followed by a group of what I estimated to be somewhere between twenty and thirty French authorities. Unbelievable, but in the French way of doing things quite appropriate. In the group were many faces that we had met before from police to security to protocol to government. An enormous gaggle. But this time they had brought their own interpreter, so we could get English out of them if necessary.

It was a hugely successful meeting, with Christopher Geidt making several suggestions that would improve the quality of the event and facilitate the participation of Her Majesty and the Duke of Edinburgh. The size of the VIP platform was to be substantially increased, and its positioning was changed so that the television cameras of CBC-TV could get a better view. The location of the saluting stand was fixed, and the matter of microphones and lecterns was settled. At that time the sequence of events in the D-Day program was settled in principle, there being some degree of sensitivity on the part of the Governor General's representative, her assistant private secretary, Curtis Barlow, on the matter of the protocols of the Governor General being in attendance at the same time as Her Majesty.

In earlier discussions with the Governor General's private secretary, the capable Barbara Uteck, it was apparent to me that the issue of placing Her Majesty and Her Excellency together at the same time on foreign soil would produce high questions of protocol, especially when it came to the matter of who would arrive first, who would speak first, who would lay the wreath first, and how the walkabout procedures would be settled, again mainly in terms of who went first. These questions were being negotiated right up until the day before D-Day.

One of the theories advanced was that Her Majesty would be attending in her capacity as Queen of the United Kingdom, while Her Excellency would be there representing the people of Canada and accordingly she should have some degree of precedence over the Queen. At least that seemed to be the position the Governor General's staff had taken.

As we moved toward the D-Day date I found myself as the mediator between the Governor General's staff and the Queen's in relation to certain of the protocol questions.

As far as I was concerned personally, the Queen is the Queen. Her representative in Canada is the Governor General. In my mind there was never any question. The Queen goes first, no matter what. On the other hand, it was appropriate to give full consideration to the concerns of the Governor General and her staff. Indeed, as I will describe, the entire ceremony worked out perfectly.

I must say that in my opinion Madame Uteck and Curtis Barlow achieved their points of concern with determination, objectivity, and sensitivity. They performed well in the circumstances.

The same applies to Sir Robin Janvrin and Christopher Geidt. It was a privilege of this no-status person to work with all of them toward the capturing of the hearts and minds of some one thousand veterans of D-Day and the Battle of Normandy in a sequence that would last probably about forty-five minutes but at the same time would be one of the most significant ceremonial and memorial events in the lives of each and every one of us who were to take part.

During the end-of-March trip to Normandy I had heard that an arrangement had been made with the Royal Air Force Battle of Britain Memorial Flight for a flypast of a Lancaster Bomber and two Spitfires during the French international ceremony at Arromanches. That would be during President Chirac's event that had been planned starting at three-thirty in the afternoon. I immediately thought it would be marvellous if we could get those same aircraft to do a flypast over Juno beach while the Queen was doing her walkabout. After a lot of research I was able to find the telephone number and location of the flight and the name of the Commanding Officer, Squadron Leader Crowley.

On May 10, I telephoned the Squadron Leader, identified myself as Air-Vice Marshal Rohmer (in addition to major-general), explained what was going to happen on D-Day with the Queen with the Canadians for the first time, and asked what were the chances please of having a morning flypast? The Squadron Leader's response was most positive and enthusiastic. Out of that brief conversation and exchange of some fax messages, Squadron Leader Crowley made all the arrangements and got the clearances necessary from the French; weather permitting, the flight would be overhead at the exact time.

Then what about the Canadian Navy? Once again, the CDS, General Ray Hénault, came through. The plan was for the Canadian frigate

HMCS *Charlottetown* to be offshore Juno Beach at ten o'clock in the morning on D-Day. Wonderful. At the May meeting of the Advisory Committee just before we left for France I raised the question of whether *Charlottetown* might fire a royal salute, but I was told that that wasn't feasible. In the end it was, and it did occur thanks to the CDS and Major-General Arp.

Mary-O and I had booked our accommodation at the wonderful Hotel le Clos Normand at St. Aubin-sur-Mer some four years earlier during a trip to the Juno Beach area. At that time we had no idea that there would be such an involvement in the preparations for the sixtieth anniversary of D-Day, nor had we any idea that there would be a magnificent structure in place called the Juno Beach Centre in Courseulles. That booking at le Clos Normand was ideal. Instead of having to book into the Veterans Affairs hotel at Deauville, which is almost an hour's trip away from Juno Beach, our accommodation had us at the east end of Juno Beach proper and away from the minute-to-minute activity surrounding the official delegation of sixty veterans and some eighty staff.

During our visits to France in the spring of 2004, Doug Clorey and Louise Wallis had accompanied us to le Clos Normand and had been much taken by its accommodations, food, and convenience. Doug Clorey had quietly arranged for accommodation for himself during the D-Day period in a bed-and-breakfast at St. Aubin-sur-Mer. I was delighted by that news because it would mean that during the D-Day period the accommodating Doug Clorey with his vehicle would be able to give us a lift from St. Aubin to Juno Beach Centre or to Beny-sur-Mer or wherever.

On May 29, Mary-O and I were airborne out of Toronto Pearson for Paris. We spent three days there, visiting, among other places, the Louvre. Then we picked up our car and drove to Normandy. First we went to the Veterans Affairs hotel at Deauville, arriving there on the third at the same time as the Official Party of some sixty veterans and eighty much-needed staff. There was criticism because of the number of personnel dedicated to assisting the veterans, but this time they would also be required to aid in the handling of some seven or eight hundred more veterans who would get to Normandy under their own steam. We were there for the lunch and first briefing by Doug Clorey and Louise Wallis. Then we went on to St. Aubin-sur-Mer, where we were welcomed with open arms and kisses on both cheeks by Madame Dauba, the beautiful proprietor of the hotel.

There was a rehearsal on June 4 commanded by Major McKillip and the man who was in his parade square glory, Chief Warrant Officer "Smokey" LeBlanc. They were to use all of their organizational skills in orchestrating the military side of the upcoming event. Everybody had input during the rehearsal, including Ian McLean and the Prime Minister's representative, Gavin Menzies, who had come to France in advance of Mr. Martin's arrival. And, of course, the redoubtable Doug Clorey, ever efficient, ever present, was at the centre of things.

On June 5, the first major ceremony took place at the Canadian cemetery at Beny-sur-Mer, where some twenty-five hundred Canadians are buried. This was a bi-national event with Her Excellency the Governor General officiating in the company of Prime Minister Safarin of France. It was this ceremony at Beny-sur-Mer that was the centre point of the 1994 Canadian D-Day ceremonies at which Prime Minister Chrétien officiated with President Mitterand of France.

The preparations for the veterans this time were much better, with long tents covering the chairs off each side of the central cenotaph structure where the wreaths were laid and the speeches were made (including one by my old friend, Senator Duff Roblin, and, of course, one by the eloquent Governor General).

The French had abandoned the proposition of supplying the buses for the veterans from Caen to the Juno Beach Centre, so Veterans Affairs through Ian McLean had hired buses and made the appropriate arrangements for those vehicles to depart for Juno Beach Centre on D-Day morning from the single collection centre at Caen. As for the Official Party, that was not a problem because they had their own four buses. The passes that had been promised by the French had not yet materialized, so the Canadian passes that we had pressed for and that had been produced were going to be effective in terms of getting through the security issues with the gendarmes approaching Juno Beach Centre. At least that's what we thought. Those were the major concerns as we approached the countdown.

On June 4 and 5 there began a series of telephone calls between Rideau Hall on the one hand and Buckingham Palace on the other but channeled through me as a sort of mediator. The Governor General's staff became concerned about precedence issues — in other words, in the main activities, who would go first, the Governor General or the Queen? There is no need for me to get into detail here, but the reality was that there was no precedent for the Queen and the Governor General being in ceremonial activities at the same time on foreign soil. The discussions I had were with Madame Uteck, the Governor General's private secretary, and Curtis Barlow, her assistant private secretary, on the one hand, and with Sir Robin Janvrin, the Queen's private secretary, on the other. Finally, when I heard from Buckingham Palace that Madame Uteck had telephoned and talked directly with Sir Robin, I was delightedly out of the loop. I think that telephone call came on June 5. As for my activity between the two institutions, my goal was to assist in ensuring that all the issues were resolved to the satisfaction of each side. I received word on the evening of June 5 that indeed everything had been settled. What a relief!

The sixtieth anniversary of D-Day, June 6, dawned to absolutely perfect weather, not a cloud in the sky, a moderate temperature with a cool breeze blowing in off the water to ease the hot rays of the morning sun.

From his accommodation point at St. Aubin-sur-Mer, Doug Clorey picked up Mary-O and me at le Clos Normand at 8:00 a.m. Mary-O looked lovely with her "Queen's gown" on with a huge black hat. I was in my Air Force major-general's uniform replete with all my orders, decorations, and medals, with my wedge cap (not my flat hat) on my white-haired head. When we arrived at the Juno Beach Centre — having picked up our passes there the day before — all of the physical aspects were in order.

Ian McLean's bleachers were erected designed to hold some four thousand people with a place of honour at the front facing the Juno Beach Centre reserved for the veterans and their caregivers. VIPs were allocated space at the lower part of the bleachers just behind the veterans. To the west was yet another set of bleachers, and over on the right to the east was the spot reserved for Canada's military band, which would perform all of the musical pieces of the planned ceremony.

The covered platform for the dignitaries, resplendent in red from top to bottom, had the appropriate chairs in place to receive the Queen, the Governor General, and the Prime Minister, along with appropriate spouses, in the front row; there was a microphone in the centre for the speech makers.

When we arrived, large groups of veterans were already in place. It appeared that the pick-up centre at Caen was operating properly. Indeed, by the time the ceremonies began at about 9:30 a.m. all of the veterans, including those of the Official Party, were in place. To our relief we were informed after the ceremonies that not one single veteran had been left behind at Caen. That was a remarkable accomplishment in itself. The bleachers were filling up rapidly, and by the time the ceremony got underway on schedule all of the seats were filled with an estimated one thousand veterans and some three thousand spectators.

The script for the master of ceremonies, Minister of Veterans Affairs, the Honourable John McCallum, had been prepared and he was ready for his role, as were the rest of us who would take part.

In developing the format over the weeks ahead of the ceremony I had amended the program so that there would be at least some minuscule presence of veterans in the ceremonies themselves. The original plan submitted by staff made no provision for veterans whatever. All that would happen would be that the pooh-bahs would do all of the speaking and performing, even though everyone proudly announced that everything was for the veterans! What I proposed (and it was accepted) was that there should be a welcoming party of three D-Day veterans, one Navy, one Army, and one Air Force. That welcoming party would greet Her Majesty Queen Elizabeth and the Duke of Edinburgh. The Air Force veteran would escort the Queen, and Garth Webb and the Navy veteran, Ken Walker, would escort the Duke. The Queen would be taken to the saluting platform, while His Royal Highness would be taken directly to the seating platform. And that is what happened when the Queen and Duke arrived shortly after 10:00 a.m.

All of the greeters were in place at the designated drop-off point before the arrival of the Prime Minister, who was the first to get there.

Prime Minister Paul Martin and Mrs. Martin arrived on schedule at 9:45 a.m. He was escorted to the saluting platform by John

McCallum, the Minister of Veterans Affairs, then joined Mrs. Martin on the dignitaries' platform.

The Governor General and her spouse, John Ralston Saul, were next to arrive and were greeted by Chief of the Defence Staff General Ray Hénault. When she got out of the car and was met by McCallum she then came over to me, an old friend, and shook hands. We had a warm greeting. Then she was off with the CDS to the saluting base, where she received the vice-regal salute and inspected the guard. It was arranged that she would inspect the guard but that the Queen would not. His Excellency John Ralston Saul was escorted directly to the dignitaries' platform. I am told that while waiting for the Queen to arrive the Governor General and Paul Martin (in the middle of an election campaign) decided that they would go out and talk with some of the seated veterans. That was not scripted, but that's what happened. At least they were back in their seats by the time Her Majesty appeared.

It was time for the arrival of Her Majesty and the Duke of Edinburgh. Led by a phalanx of French motorcycle gendarmes, their security and personal vehicles arrived. Her welcoming trio was in place: Webb, Walker, and Rohmer.

There was my friend Christopher Geidt in the first car wearing a large straw hat. He was out and opened the door for Her Majesty, who was wearing a delightful mauve dress and one of her large off-the-face hats of the same colour. As I stepped forward to welcome her she gave me her gloved hand, which I took as I introduced myself. She and the Duke, of course, had been fully briefed as to who would be there and doing what. Next on the far side of the car came the Duke, regally dressed in his Navy blue admiral's uniform. As he came to me to shake hands I said, "I am General Rohmer," to which he replied, "I know you are. You've got more medals than I have!" What a sense of humour.

I then led Her Majesty up the path. I was on her left. We went straight up to the saluting base, which she mounted, the ever-present purse on her left arm. The Royal Salute was played, she then came back down, and I led her to her seat on the platform. I am accused from time to time of having touched her on the back as she was mounting the two steps to the platform. From the videos there is no doubt that I am rightfully accused. I was just trying to be helpful. When Her Majesty was in

*Escorting Queen Elizabeth II on her arrival at
the Juno Beach Centre on June 6, 2004.*

place in her chair I then went to the microphone, where in both official languages I identified myself to the crowd. Then on behalf of all of the D-Day and Battle of Normandy veterans I welcomed Her Majesty, the Duke, the Governor General, John Ralston Saul (whose late father had been a D-Day veteran), the Prime Minister, and Mrs. Martin. At the conclusion of my two-minute talk I invited the Queen back to speak, which she did with her usual grace and fluidity. Garth Webb introduced the Prime Minister, whose speech was appropriate and in the time allotted. Finally, our Navy veteran invited Her Excellency to say a few words, which she did with her usual thoughtful elegance.

Exactly on time, just slightly ahead of Her Majesty's and Her Excellency's walkabout, the three magnificent aircraft of the Royal Air Force Battle of Britain Memorial Flight flew over at low level, the great Lancaster Bomber with a Spitfire V on one wing and a Spit IX on the other. Wonderful, very impressive. And offshore, HMCS *Charlottetown* fired a royal salute of twenty-one rounds.

Next was the ceremony of the laying of the wreaths, which was done in the agreed to sequence of Her Majesty, Her Excellency, and then the Prime Minister followed by us three old crocks, the Veterans Welcoming

Photo courtesy Jim McGriffin.

On behalf of all veterans, welcoming the Queen, Governor General, and Prime Minister to the Juno Beach ceremony. My wife, Mary-O, is at the far right in the black hat.

Party putting our own in place, all assisted by designated young Canadians, cadets from various units.

The final activity was that specified by Her Majesty as being extremely important to her, namely her walkabout among the veterans. I had been informed that as a compromise the Queen was willing to let the Governor General get off the platform first. However, as soon as the master of ceremonies announced that the walkabout would begin, both the Queen and the Governor General stood up at the same time. I was right behind the Queen and Madame Clarkson. As soon as they were off the platform and walking toward the veterans they began chatting. Finally, I could see that they were heading for the same aisle, still talking away to each other. I had no choice; I stepped between them and said, "Ladies, you cannot go up the same aisle, you're going to have to split," which they immediately did, the Governor General going to the right and Her Majesty up the centre followed closely by me, one of her security ladies, and behind me Her Majesty's lady-in-waiting. Ahead of Her Majesty was her head of security, dressed formally but not in uniform. At some stage in the walkabout, which lasted some ten to fifteen minutes, that gentleman informed me that we were not pressed for time because President Chirac was about thirty minutes late in terms of his arrival at the luncheon he was to host at Bayeux for the heads of state. As a result Her Majesty was able to spend as much time as she thought appropriate with the veterans, most of whom related to her how privileged they were to be in her presence, many of them saying that they had met her at such-and-such an event over the past sixty years. To that kind of comment she would always say politely, "Oh, yes, of course, I do remember."

*Escorting the Queen during her walkabout
at the Juno Beach Centre.*

We came into near collision with the Duke and his party just when the Queen had finished her walkabout. She and I had a brief chat, at which time I reminded her of our meeting in Tortola and the locked ambulance. I'm not sure that she remembered, but she certainly let on that she did. It was time for Her Majesty and her party to leave. The Governor General, the Chief of the Defence Staff, and I had the privilege of escorting her to her car with the Duke close behind. With the shaking of hands and salutes and waves Her Majesty and His Royal Highness and their entourage were gone. Then it was back to the platform, where the master of ceremonies invited the Governor General and the Prime Minister to take the salute from the veterans on their march down to the beach. The veterans were invited to form up under the guidance of Major McKillip and Chief Warrant Officer "Smokey" LeBlanc, which happened in a sort of circular, disorganized way.

But finally they came together and were led off as planned by that wonderful artillery D-Day veteran Garth Webb, who gave the order to quick march. No one marched very quickly, but they proceeded under Webb's leadership. They followed a one-man colour party down to Juno Beach itself where, waiting for them, was the marvellous Burlington Teen Tour Band, over a hundred young people who played beautifully and marched exceptionally well and who had paid their own way to get over to Normandy for that exceptional celebration. On the beach the hundreds of veterans were able to mingle, talk with each other, and cast their minds back years to that very morning when many of them had come ashore at that very place and others, like me, had been with them in the air.

As I had told Garth Webb before the ceremony when he wanted me to be with him to lead the veterans to the beach, "Generals don't march!" That's now one of his favourite sayings, but contrary to my declaration, when the last of the veterans was passing by the Governor General and the Prime Minister at the saluting base — I was standing beside them during the routine — I went out, and, as the last person, I did in fact as a D-Day veteran march to the beach.

Apart from the Vin D'Honneur of wine and food served to the veterans and everyone else in tents to the west of the bleachers, that was it. The Canadian celebrations of D-Day were finished. A year and a half's planning with the input of dozens and dozens of people had culminated in forty-five minutes where everything went absolutely perfectly. As I describe the situation after June 6, on a scale of one to ten Canada's D-Day celebration with the Queen, the Governor General and the Prime Minister and all of the veterans in perfect weather — it was a fifteen.

In the afternoon, Doug Clorey led a group of veterans in buses over to Arromanches to witness the international ceremonies staged by the Government of France. Of particular interest to all of us was the splendid ceremony conducted by Chirac in which he invested fourteen veterans from various countries with the insignia of the Chevalier of the Legion of Honour. Our proud and deserving member of the Advisory Committee, Jan DeVries, resplendent in his maroon jacket and beret of the paratroopers, received his decoration from Chirac with appropriate symbolic kisses on both cheeks. We were all extremely proud of our colleague, including those of us who had received the decoration from the courteous French ambassador in Ottawa in late May. It was a long day, but a highly successful one for Canada.

Our 60th Anniversary of D-Day Advisory Committee had been working with Veterans Affairs not only in relation to the Juno Beach ceremonies but also advising in relation to what should be done across Canada on D-Day. The result was ceremonial parades and activities on D-Day at the major provincial capitals and at countless cities, towns, and villages right across the country. That segment headed by Derek Sullivan and augmented by Committee member Jack Arsenault has led me to describe the D-Day ceremonies as the single most comprehensive national and international day of celebration ever staged by Canada. Simple as that, and quite an achievement for many: the Canada Remembers Division of Veterans Affairs; Deputy Minister Jack Stagg; Director of Canada Remembers Doug Clorey and his hard-working, ever-productive Louise Wallis; the main Canadian Armed Forces participants, Major-General Jean Arp, Major McKillip, and Chief Warrant Officer Smokey LeBlanc; my 60th Anniversary Committee members, all volunteers; the marvellous Lieutenant-General Charles Belzile; the great Garth Webb; Jan DeVries; Jack Arsenault; and, in the later stages, John O'Reilly, a member of Parliament. Canada's D-Day celebration in 2004 was a unique, never to be repeated, absolutely first class achievement in which they all had a significant part. In the last months, the man who really made it happen, working on the scene, dealing with every possible problem (be it security, the bleachers, buses, gathering points, dealing with French officials) was the amazing Ian McLean, whom the deputy minister, Jack Stagg, was fortunate enough to be able to retain and who was ready, willing and able to take on the enormous task.

To conclude this D-Day 2004 story I want to go back to the man who seized the moment when he was Deputy Minister of Veterans Affairs, Vice-Admiral Larry Murray. It was he who ultimately received my memorandum recommending the creation of an Advisory Committee and setting out the proposed terms of reference. It was Larry

Murray who accepted the proposal. He and I negotiated the final terms of reference. Without his initial interest and support D-Day 2004 would never have occurred the way it did.

Let me quote from the terms of reference on the two major points we wanted to achieve: "The Committee will strive to ensure that Canadian Veterans and their families/caregivers have complete access to Juno Beach during these events (marking the 60th Anniversary of D-Day) and that the appropriate dignitaries are present to participate in the remembrance activities, including Her Majesty the Queen."

Those major objectives were accomplished in spades on June 6, 2004, at the Juno Beach Centre in Normandy.

POSTSCRIPT

———◆———

I N THE MID-SUMMER OF 2004, with the massive, highly successful sixtieth anniversary of D-Day receding in the distance, the question I often hear is "What project will you take on next?" It's as if I have nothing to do.

Actually, I have any number of windmills that I'm tilting at — all at the same time. They're the ones that I can see. Then there are those that haven't yet appeared on my horizon.

Those that I can see and that are being tilted at are my law practice, my next books, weekly newspaper columns, my weekly television program "Rohmer and Rohmer" with our gorgeous daughter Ann, keeping up with my beautiful wife, Mary-O, and our lovely lawyer daughter Catherine, doing all my honorary chores — and staying alive!

And who knows what windmill will appear on the horizon?

APPENDIX I
Design for Development

———◆———

Summary of Design for Development.

CHAPTER IV

SUMMARY

The "Design for Development" outlined in this statement of
policy is broad and comprehensive. Our aspirations cannot
be fulfilled overnight. The limitation of resources in terms
of manpower, finance, and experience means that we must gradually acquire the tools to forge ahead with regional development planning. However, the nine measures which we are about
to introduce in our regional development policy provide the
guarantee that the proper machinery for the task will be available to this government.

One is the establishment of the Cabinet Committee, with broad
terms of reference, and upon which we place great emphasis.
This Committee will be concerned with the inter-related pro-
cesses of policy, priorities, planning and coordination of
government activity. The need for such a Committee to assist
in carrying out the regional development programme is accepted
by this government. One of our principal instruments of regional development policy will be the use of government budge-
tary expenditures directed to regional needs. In this sense,
the need for priority planning of government expenditures,
which we stressed in our recent budget, and regional development planning are closely inter-related. Thus, regional development will be contained within the broader spectrum of
provincial development. Accordingly, among the broad respon-

sibilities of this Committee will be the task of directing
and coordinating the preparation and implementation of regional development plans. From this central focus flow
eight additional measures.

Two is the formation of the senior Departmental Advisory
Committee to advise and assist the Cabinet Committee, to
review plans prior to submission to the Cabinet Committee,
and to direct and coordinate the Regional Advisory Boards.

Three is the presentation of our legislation reconstituting
the present Regional Development Associations, as advisory
citizen bodies, to be named Regional Development Councils.

Four is the presentation of legislation to permit the en-
largement of the scope of activities of the Ontario Development Agency. Under new terms of reference, the Ontario Development Agency will become the Ontario Development Corporation and this new institution will assist industrial development in the province through the provision of loans for fixed
capital.

Five is the preparation for comprehensive regional economic
research through the Regional Development Branch of the Department of Economics and Development.

Six is a corollary of the above and involves establishing the
terms of reference for regionally-related research which may

- 24 -

be contracted out to Ontario universities and consulting firms.

Seven is our expectation that our comprehensive research programme will provide the necessary insight required to formu-
late development plans based on the concept that regional
growth centres are the unifying social and economic force within the region.

Eight is the establishment of a Regional Advisory Board composed of the senior civil servants in the region. These Boards
will advise the senior Departmental Advisory Committee on matters of interest in the region.

Nine is our intention to work toward the gradual establishment
of common administrative and planning regions among the operating departments and agencies of the provincial government.

CONCLUSION

We believe that this programme represents the beginning of a
comprehensive approach to regional development planning. We
also have every reason to expect that new directions and new
vistas will emerge from the operation of this programme. At

- 25 -

all times, we shall be seeking means of ensuring that people
in all parts of the province share in the benefits of economic
and social development, and that regional development will be
looked upon as an integral part of this government's contribution to the development of the province as a whole. We are
confident that this programme represents a modern, forward-
looking design for development.

APPENDIX II

Program of Mid-Canada Conference August 1969 and List of Participants

———◆———

Program of the Mid-Canada Development Corridor Conference held at Lakehead University in August 1969. I created the concept and was chairman of the Mid-Canada Development Foundation conference.

Mid-Canada
Development
Corridor
Conference

FIRST SESSION
LAKEHEAD UNIVERSITY
AUGUST 18-22, 1969

A CONCEPT IN ACTION
"Purpose of the Conference . . . to examine the advantages of establishing a nation-wide policy and plan for the development of Canada's Mid-North."

ADVISORY COUNCIL
Mr. C. P. Baker
President, Foundation Company of Canada Limited
Mr. E. C. Bovey
President, Northern and Central Gas Corporation Ltd.
Mr. N. R. Crump
Chairman and Chief Executive Officer Canadian Pacific Railway
Mr. Walter Currie
President, Indian-Eskimo Association of Canada
Mr. H. M. Griffith
President, The Steel Company of Canada Limited
Mr. C. F. Harrington
President, The Royal Trust Company
Mr. Arnold Hart
Chairman, Bank of Montreal
Dr. N. B. Keevil
President, Keevil Mining Group Limited
Brig. H. W. Love
Executive Director The Arctic Institute of North America
Mr. Donald MacDonald
President, Canadian Labour Congress
Mr. J. J. MacMillan
Chairman and President Canadian National Railways
The Honourable Keiller Mackay.
D.S.O., V.D., Q.C., LL.D., D.C.L.
President Bramalea Consolidated Developments Limited
Mr. A. Powis
President, Noranda Mines Limited
Mr. Ives Pratte
Chairman and Chief Executive Officer Air Canada

CONVENING BOARD
Professor J. Jameson Bond, University of Alberta
Dr. R. M. Bone, University of Saskatchewan
Dr. J. D. Chapman, University of British Columbia
Mr. Yves Dubé, Laval University
Dr. J. C. Gilson, University of Manitoba
Mr. Christian de Laet, Secretary-General Canadian Council of Resource Ministers
Mr. Ian Macdonald, Deputy Minister Department of Treasury and Economics (Ontario)
Mr. David Morgan, Lakehead University
Professor Peter Young, Memorial University of Newfoundland
Professor Norman Pearson, University of Guelph
Mr. James Ramsay, Department of Trade and Development (Ontario)
Mr. Richard Rohmer, Q.C., Chairman, Mid-Canada Development Corridor Conference
Dr. R. S. Thoman, Department of Treasury and Economics (Ontario)
Mr. E. F. Tonge, Executive Director, Community Planning Association of Canada (Ontario Division)
Professor Leonard Warshaw, University of Montreal
Dr. W. Y. Watson, Laurentian University
Professor F. T. M. White, McGill University
Mr. W. S. Ziegler, National Northern Development Conference

MONDAY, AUGUST 18th

9:00 AM	Registration Opens
	Place: Residence One (see map)
	(Registration continues throughout Conference)
12:00 NOON	Exhibition Pavilion opens
	Place: Centennial Building Courtyard
5:30 -	Cocktails
7:15 PM	Place: Senior Lounge
	University Centre Building
	Second Floor
7:30 PM	Opening Banquet
	Place: Great Hall
	University Centre Building
	Chairman: Dr. William Tamblyn
	President, Lakehead University
	Speaker: Richard Rohmer, Q.C.
	Chairman, Mid-Canada Development Corridor Conference
	Topic: **Mid-Canada Development Corridor Conference**
10:00 PM	Conference Task Force Committees Meet
	(Meeting rooms to be announced)
(10:30 PM	*Bar service is available, Main Floor Lounge, Residence One)*

WEDNESDAY, AUGUST 20th

7:00 AM	Wake-up call
7:30 AM	Breakfast
	Place: Great Hall, University Centre Building
	Speaker: David A. W. Judd, Esq.
	Scott Polar Research Institute, Cambridge, England
	Former Administrator of Yukon Territory
	Topic: **Administration & Northern Development**
9:30 AM	Plenary — panel discussion
	Place: University Centre Building Theatre
	Topic: **Urbanization (Human & Environmental Factors)**
11:15 AM	Discussion Groups

#1 — Room 124 east	#5 — Room 126.2
#2 — Room 124 west	#6 — Room 128
#3 — Room 126	#7 — Room 128.1
#4 — Room 126.1	#8 — Room 128.2

12:45 PM	Luncheon
	Speaker: Mr. Walter Currie
	President, Indian-Eskimo Association of Canada
2:30 PM	Buses leave for Lambert Island
3:30 PM	Reception at the Lambert Island home of Mr. R. J. Prettie
	President, Wood Preservers Limited
6:00 PM	Buses return to Lakehead University
8:00 PM	Buffet
	Place: Great Hall, University Centre Building
9:30 PM	Conference Task Force Committees Meet
(10:30 PM	Bar service is available, Main Floor Lounge, Residence One)

THURSDAY, AUGUST 21st

7:30 AM	Wake-up call
8:00 AM	Breakfast
	Place: Great Hall, University Centre Building
9:30 AM	Panel Sessions

GROUP A	GROUP B
Place: Main Bldg. Amphitheatre	Univ. Centre Bldg. Theatre
Topic: **Transportation**	**Communications**

11:15 AM	Discussion Groups

#1 — Room 124 east	#5 — Room 126.2
#2 — Room 124 west	#6 — Room 128
#3 — Room 126	#7 — Room 128.1
#4 — Room 126.1	#8 — Room 128.2

12:45 PM	Luncheon
	Place: Great Hall, University Centre Building
	Speaker: Mr. John Fisher

Centennial Commissioner for Canada, 1967 Special Consultant for International Affairs to President of Abitibi Paper Company Limited

Topic: **Canada — Development Country**

2:30 PM	Panel Sessions

GROUP A	GROUP B
Place: Main Bldg. Amphitheatre	Univ. Centre Bldg. Theatre
Topic: **Communications**	**Transportation**

4:15 PM	Discussion Groups

#1 — Room 124 east	#5 — Room 126.2
#2 — Room 124 west	#6 — Room 128
#3 — Room 126	#7 — Room 128.1
#4 — Room 126.1	#8 — Room 128.2

6:00 PM	Cocktails
	Place: Senior Lounge, University Centre Building
6:45 PM	Banquet
	Place: Great Hall, University Centre Building
	Speaker: Honourable Duff Roblin, P.C.

Executive Vice-President, Canadian Pacific Investments

Topic: **Human Factors**

8:45 PM	Plenary — panel discussion
	Place: University Centre Building Theatre

Topic: **Financing and Trade Implications**

(10:30 PM	*Bar service is available, Main Floor Lounge, Residence One)*

FRIDAY, AUGUST 22nd

6:30 AM	Wake-up call
7:00 AM	Breakfast
	Place: Great Hall, University Centre Building
	Speaker: Dr. John Conway
	York University
	Topic: **Political Planning**
9:00 AM	Conference Task Force Committees
10:30 AM	Summation of First Conference
	Conference Programme Development
11:45 AM	Luncheon
	Place: Great Hall, University Centre Building
1:00 PM	Depart for Airport
1:30 -	Air Display
2:30 PM	Participants: Canadian Air Force
	Ontario Dept. of Lands & Forests
	— demonstration water bombing by six different types of aircraft
	— JATO-assisted Hercules Aircraft take-off demonstration
	— para-drop of personnel and equipment (search and rescue demonstration)
	— helicopter fire-fighting demonstration
	Flights leave for Toronto at 2:50 p.m. and 6:05 p.m.
	and for Winnipeg at 5:00 p.m.
3:00 -	Selected films available
5:00 PM	Place: Room 122, Centennial Building

KEYNOTE SPEAKERS
ORATEURS PRINCIPAUX

Dr. W. G. Schneider,
President,
National Research Council.
His Excellency the Right
Honourable Roland Michener,
C.C., C.D.,
Governor General of Canada.
Dr. O. M. Solandt,
Chairman,
Science Council of Canada.
David A. W. Judd, Esq.,
Scott Polar Research Institute.
Mr. Walter Currie,
President,
Indian-Eskimo Association of
Canada
Mr. John Fisher,
Centennial Commissioner for
Canada 1967,
Special Consultant on
International Affairs to
Abitibi Paper Company Limited.
Honourable Duff Roblin, P.C.
Executive Vice-President,
Canadian Pacific Investments
Limited.
Dr. John Conway,
York University.

RESOURCE PERSONNEL
EXPERTS

Mr. Richard Hill,
Manager,
Inuvik Research Laboratories.
Mr. Robert Campbell,
Campbell's Limited,
Whitehorse, N.W.T.
Mr. Leo Cameron,
Community Health Worker,
Department of
National Health and Welfare.
Mr. Harold Cardinal,
President,
Indian Association of Alberta.
Mr. Hector Blake, P.Eng.,
Quebec Northshore and
Labrador Railway.
Dr. E. W. Robinson,
Frontier College.
Mr. Jack Moar,
Executive Director,
Community Planning
Association, Alberta Division.
Mr. P. W. Kaeser,
Mayor,
Town of Fort Smith.
Mr. Alan Innes-Taylor,
Whitehorse,
Yukon Territory.
Mr. E. King,
President,
Alberta Northwest Chamber of
Mines and Oils and Resources.
Mr. Isaac Beaulieu,
Secretary Treasurer,
Manitoba Indian Brotherhood.
Mr. Jim Sinclair, *Vice-President,*
Métis Association of
Saskatchewan
Mr. Jon Hopkins,
Resource Development Officer,
Western James Bay.
Mr. Victor Allan, *Driver,*
CFS Inuvik.

RESOURCES PANEL
TRIBUNE SUR LES RESSOURCES

M. Côme Carbonneau,
President,
Société Québécoise
d'Exploration Minière.
Mr. Murray Watts,
President,
Baffinland Iron Mines Limited.
Mr. Edward Pinay,
Community Health Worker.
Dr. L. I. Barber,
Vice-President,
University of Saskatchewan.

INDUSTRIALIZATION PANEL
TRIBUNE SUR
L'INDUSTRIALIZATION

Mr. Allan Moffatt,
Vice-President,
Reid, Crowther and Partners.
Dr. Geo. Jacobsen,
President,
The Tower Company (1961)
Limited.
Mr. J. Morris,
Executive Vice-President,
Canadian Labour Congress.
Mr. Gilbert Proulx,
Consultant for Special Projects,
Aluminum Company of
Canada Limited.

RICHARD ROHMER

ENVIRONMENTAL AND ECOLOGICAL FACTORS PANEL
TRIBUNE SUR L'INCIDENCE DE L'ENVIRONNEMENT ET DE L'ECOLOGIE

Professor Wm. Fuller,
Department of Zoology,
University of Alberta.
Dr. N. Kissik,
Department of Forestry,
University of New Brunswick.
Dr. R. I. Wolfe,
Associate Professor in
Geography, York University.
Dr. D. Chant,
Chairman,
Department of Zoology,
University of Toronto.
Mr. B. G. Thom,
Director,
Sub-Arctic Research,
McGill University.
Dr. G. Carrothers,
Dean,
Department of Environmental
Studies, York University.

URBANIZATION PANEL
TRIBUNE SUR L'URBANIZATION

Rev. John E. Page, S.J.,
Director,
Interdisciplinary Research,
University of Manitoba.
Brig. J. D. Christian,
President,
Cassiar Asbestos Corporation.
Mr. G. C. Hamilton,
Commissioner of Operations
and Development,
City of Calgary.
Honourable Mr. Justice
Wm. G. Morrow,
Judge of Territorial Court,
Northwest Territories.

TRANSPORTATION PANEL
TRIBUNE SUR LES TRANSPORTS

Mr. A. V. Mauro, Q.C.,
Executive Vice-President,
Great Northern Capital
Corporation Ltd.
Mr. E. P. Stephenson,
Vice-President,
Canadian National Railways.
Mr. Wm. Gilchrist,
President,
Eldorado Nuclear Limited.
Mr. W. R. Harris,
Vice-President,
Pacific Western Airlines.

COMMUNICATIONS PANEL
TRIBUNE SUR LES COMMUNICATIONS

Mr. M. N. Davies,
Vice-President,
Bell Telephone Company of
Canada.
Mr. Geo. Davidson,
President,
Canadian Broadcasting
Corporation.
Mr. Sidney T. Fisher,
Vice-President,
Radio Engineering Products
Limited.
Brig. R. S. Malone,
President,
F. P. Publications.

FINANCING AND TRADE IMPLICATIONS PANEL
TRIBUNE SUR LES QUESTIONS QUI TOUCHENT AUX FINANCEMENT ET AU COMMERCE

Mr. Ian Macdonald,
Deputy Treasurer,
Department of Treasury and
Economics,
Government of Ontario.
Dr. David W. Slater,
Dean of Graduate School,
Queen's University.

APPENDIX III
Northport and Boeing Resources Carrier Aircraft

Schematic Macklin Hancock layout of the port, townsite, and airport for the development Northport, on the west coast of Hudson Bay.

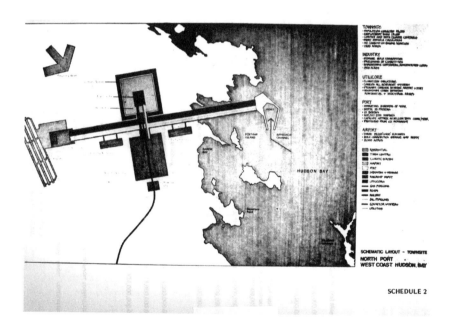

CHARACTERISTICS

WING SPAN (FT)	478
OVERALL LENGTH (FT)	338
HEIGHT (FT)	86
WING AREA (FT^2)	32,580
ASPECT RATIO	7.0
FUEL CAPACITY (LB)	600,000
POWER PLANT	(12) TURBOFANS, RATED AT 55,000 LB, SEA LEVEL, 60°F
TIRES	(44) 80 x 24
OPERATING EMPTY WEIGHT (LB)	985,000
MAX PAYLOAD (LB)	2,320,000
MAX GROSS WEIGHT (LB)	3,550,000
DESIGN RANGE (NMI)	500 TO 2,000

SIZE COMPARISON WITH 747

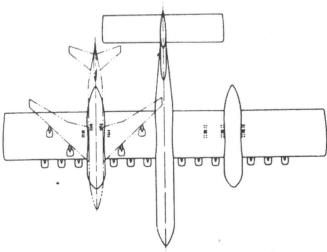

Resources Carrier Aircraft

APPENDIX IV
Royal Commission on Book Publishing

Report of the Royal Commission on Book Publishing, Canadian Publishers, and Canadian Publishing, released December 1, 1972. I was chairman of the Commission, and Dalton Camp and Marsh Jeanneret were my fellow commissioners.

ONTARIO

ROYAL COMMISSION
ON BOOK PUBLISHING

To His Honour,
The Lieutenant Governor of Ontario.

May It Please Your Honour,

We the Commissioners, appointed as a Royal Commission by Orders-in-Council OC–3991/70 and OC–3534/71 pursuant to the provisions of The Public Inquiries Act, R.S.O. 1960, c. 323, and approved by Your Honour on the 23rd day of December, A.D. 1970, and on the 18th day of November, A.D. 1971, to report upon matters relating to the publishing industry in Ontario:

beg to submit to Your Honour the following Final Report of the Commission:

Richard Rohmer, Q.C.,*Commissioner* (*Chairman*)

Dalton Camp, *Commissioner*

Marsh Jeanneret, *Commissioner*

December 1st, 1972

ORDERS-IN-COUNCIL

OC–3991/70

Certified to be a true copy of an Order-in-Council approved by His Honour the Lieutenant Governor, dated the 23rd day of December, A.D. 1970.

Upon the recommendation of the Honourable the Prime Minister, the Committee of Council advise that pursuant to the provisions of The Public Inquiries Act, R.S.O. 1960, Chapter 323, a Commission be issued appointing

Richard Heath Rohmer, Q.C.,

Dalton Kingsley Camp, and

Marsh Jeanneret,

and naming the said Richard Heath Rohmer as Chairman thereof, to conduct an examination of and report upon:

(a) the publishing industry in Ontario and throughout Canada with respect to its position within the business community;

(b) the functions of the publishing industry in terms of its contribution to the cultural life and education of the people of the Province of Ontario and Canada;

(c) the economic, cultural, social or other consequences for the people of Ontario and of Canada of the substantial ownership or control of publishing firms by foreign or foreign-owned or foreign-controlled corporations or by non-Canadians.

The Committee further advise that pursuant to The Public Inquiries Act, R.S.O. 1960, Chapter 323, the Commissioners shall have the power of summoning any person and requiring him or her to give evidence on oath and to produce such documents and things as the Commissioners deem requisite to the full examination of the matters into which they are appointed to examine.

And the Committee further advise that all Governmental departments, boards, agencies and committees shall assist the Commissioners to the fullest extent possible in order to assist them to carry out their duty and functions, and that the Commissioners shall have the authority to obtain such counsel, staff, technical advisers and clerical staff as they deem proper and the rate of remuneration and reimbursement to be approved by Treasury Board.

Certified,

J. J. Young
Clerk, Executive Council

OC–3534/71

Certified to be a true copy of an Order-in-Council approved by His Honour the Lieutenant Governor, dated the 18th day of November, A.D. 1971.

Upon the recommendation of the Honourable the Prime Minister, the Committee of Council advise that Order-in-Council dated the 23rd day of December, A.D. 1970, and numbered OC–3991/70, be amended by adding clause (d) after clause (c) as follows:

(d) the contracts or proposed contracts between any geographical wholesaler of mass market paperback books and periodicals and any retailer of such goods that creates or tends to create an obligation on the retailer to purchase all merchandise supplied by the wholesaler from that wholesaler to the exclusion of other sources of supply and, without limiting the generality of the foregoing, to inquire into the merchandising of paperback books, periodicals, and other merchandise normally carried by geographical wholesalers and sold by their retailers.

The Committee further advise that the Commission issued to Messrs. Richard Heath Rohmer, Q.C., Dalton Kingsley Camp and Marsh Jeanneret, under the provisions of the said Order-in-Council numbered OC–3991/70, be amended accordingly.

Certified,

J. J. Young
Clerk, Executive Council

Appendix

FIRST INTERIM REPORT · MARCH 23, 1971

LETTER OF TRANSMITTAL

To His Honour,
The Lieutenant Governor of Ontario.

May It Please Your Honour,

We, the undersigned, Richard Heath Rohmer, Q.C., Dalton Kingsley Camp, and Marsh Jeanneret appointed Commissioners by Order-in-Council OC-3991/70 pursuant to the provisions of The Public Inquiries Act, R.S.O. 1960, c. 323, and approved by Your Honour on the 23rd day of December, 1970 to inquire into and report upon:

(*a*) the publishing industry in Ontario and throughout Canada with respect to its position within the business community;

(*b*) the functions of the publishing industry in terms of its contributions to the cultural life and education of the people of the Province of Ontario and Canada;

(*c*) the economic, cultural, social or other consequences for the people of Ontario and of Canada of the substantial ownership or control of publishing firms by foreign or foreign-owned or foreign-controlled corporations or by non-Canadians

beg to submit to Your Honour the following Interim Report.

RICHARD ROHMER   DALTON CAMP   MARSH JEANNERET
Commissioner   *Commissioner*   *Commissioner*

23rd March, 1971

APPENDIX V

Honorary Degrees Granted by Chancellor Rohmer of the University of Windsor

List of honorary degrees conferred during Richard Rohmer's tenure as Chancellor of the University of Windsor from 1978 to 1989 and during 1996.

U N I V E R S I T Y   O F
WINDSOR

Dr. Rohmer   June 23, 2003,
32 Callary Crescent
COLLINGWOOD, ON
L9Y 4Y1

Dr. Rohmer:

Please find attached the information that you have requested. I understand that you needed all of the Honorary Degrees that were conferred during your tenure as chancellor from 1978-1989 and 1996. Please find this information listed below by year. If you require any further information please do not hesitate to contact me.

TWENTY-NINTH CONVOCATION (May 27-28, 1978)
The Hon. Jean Beetz - DCL (Justice, Supreme Court of Canada)
Mario Bernardi - D. Music (Conductor, National Arts Centre Orchestra)
The Hon. Lucien Lamoureux - DCL (Can. Ambassador to Belgium, Chancellor of Univ.)
Norbert Joseph Ruth, CSB - LLD (President, Assumption University)
William Osborn Twaits - LLD (former Chairman of Board, Imperial Oil Co.)
Maurice Lewis VanVliet - LLD (Dean Emeritus of Phys.Educ. Univ. of Alberta;
President   XI Commonwealth Games [Canada 1978] Foundation)

THIRTIETH CONVOCATION (September 30, 1978)
[Installation of Chancellor & President - No Honorary Degrees]

THIRTY-FIRST CONVOCATION (June 2 & 3, 1979)
The Hon. Reuben C. Baetz - LL.D. (Minister of Culture & Recreation for Ont.) *
Rev. J. Stanley Murphy - LL.D. (founder & director, Christian Culture Series) **
Conrad M. Black - D. Litt. (President, Argus Corporation) *
Jean Elizabeth Linton - LL.D. (District Director, VON, Windsor Branch)
David Takayoshi Suzuki - D. Sc. (scientist & lecturer) *
Robert James Tebbs - LL.D. (Senior Vice-President & Director, Hiram Walker; Past
Chair, Board of Governors)

THIRTY-SECOND CONVOCATION (September 29, 1979)
Abram Bergson - LL.D. (George F. Baker Prof. of Economics, Harvard Univ.)
The Hon. Donald R. Morand - LL.D. (Ombudsman, Ontario) *

CLERK OF THE SENATE
401 SUNSET • WINDSOR ONTARIO • CANADA N9B 3P4 • 519/253-3600

THIRTY-THIRD CONVOCATION (May 31, 1980)

Jacob David Geller - LL.D. (Windsor businessman & lawyer)
Antonine Maillet - D. Litt. (Canadian writer & educator) *
The Hon. George Alexander Gale - LL.D. (former Chief Justice of Ontario)
Timothy R. Pryor - D. Sc. (President & Director of marketing, Diffracto Ltd.) *

THIRTY-FOURTH CONVOCATION (October 4, 1980)

John Wendell Holmes - D. Litt. (Research Dir., Can. Inst. of International Affairs) * **
Gordon Murray MacNabb - D. Sc. (President, Natural Sciences & Eng. Research Council)

THIRTY-FIFTH CONVOCATION (June 6, 1981)

Therese Casgrain - LL.D. (Member of Senate of Canada) **
Peter John Sereda - D.Sc. (Division of Building Research, NRC of Canada) *
Pierre Berton - D. Litt. (Canadian author, journalist & historian) *
Judge Bruce J.S. Macdonald - LL.D. (lawyer, soldier, author) **

THIRTY-SIXTH CONVOCATION (October 3, 1981)

Jack Longman - LL.D. (Chairman, Ont. Advisory Council on the Physically Handicapped)
Virgil Thomson - D. Music (composer & critic)
Francesco Paolo Fulci - LL.D. (Italian Ambassador to Canada) *

THIRTY-SEVENTH CONVOCATION (June 5, 1982)

Roy Bonisteel - LL.D. (creator & host of "Man Alive") *
Edith Margaret Bowlby - D. Music (musician & philanthropist)
William Ormond Mitchell - D. Litt. (Canadian dramatist & novelist) *
William Arthur Wilkinson - LL.D. (Founder of Green Shield Prepaid Services Inc.)

THIRTY-EIGHTH CONVOCATION (October 2, 1982)

Frederick Kent Jasperson - LL.D. (Military leader & judge) **
Roger Lemelin - LL.D. (Canadian author, president & publisher "La Presse") *

SPECIAL CONVOCATION (November 20, 1982)

Allan Ezra Gotlieb - LL.D. (Canadian Ambassador to the United States) *

THIRTY-NINTH CONVOCATION (June 2, 1983)

John W. Adams - LL.D. (President, Emco Limited) *
Leon Z. McPherson - LL.D. (former chairman, Board of Governors)
Albert H. Weeks - LL.D. (former Mayor, City of Windsor) * **

FORTIETH CONVOCATION (October 1, 1983)

Edward Baillargeon - LL.D. (past president, Windsor & District Labour Council)
The Hon. Herbert Eser Gray - LL.D. (M.P. Windsor-West) *
The Hon. Mark MacGuigan - LL.D. (MP Windsor-Walkerville)
The Hon. Eugene Whelan - LL.D. (MP Essex-Windsor)

FORTY-FIRST CONVOCATION (June 2, 1984)

Len Cariou - D. Litt. (Canadian actor)
Thomas Shoyama - LL.D. (Prof. of Public Admin., Univ. of Victoria)

William Hugh Kenner - D. Litt. (Literary Critic)
James Gordon Parr - LL.D. (Chairman & CEO, TV Ontario)

FORTY-SECOND CONVOCATION (September 29, 1984)
Larkin Kerwin - D.Sc. (President, National Research Council)

FORTY-THIRD CONVOCATION (June 2 & 9, 1985)
John Michael Sherlock - LL.D. (R.C. Bishop of London)
J. Wilfrid Dwyer - LL.D. (educator, Assumption Alumnus)
John H. Maus - D.Sc. (retired Director, Windsor Regional Cancer Centre)
The Hon. Thomas Wells - D. Litt. (Agent General for Ontario)
Anthony Adamson - LL.D. (Architect, Planning Consultant)
Carl Beigie - LL.D. (Political Economist)
Burton Jacobs - LL.D. (Band Councillor, Walpole Island Indian Reserve)

FORTY-FOURTH CONVOCATION (October 13, 1985)
Madeleine Parent - LL.D. (retired Quebec Union leader)
Sir William Stephenson - D. Sc. ("A Man Called Intrepid")
Hon. Bertha Wilson - DCL (Justice, Supreme Court of Canada) *
Selma Huxley Barkham - D. Litt. (Canadian historical geographer)
John Howie McGivney - LL.D. (past chairman, Board of Governors)

FORTY-FIFTH CONVOCATION (June 1 & 8, 1986)
J. Mavor Moore - D. Litt. (Can. playwright, actor, past Chair of Can. Council) *
Marie-Josee Drouin - LL.D. (Exec. Director of Hudson Inst.) *
Canon Robert S. Rayson - LL.D. (first principal, Canterbury College) *
Valerie Kasurak - LL.D. (former member of Board, retired Citizenship Court Judge) *
Claudette MacKay-Lassonde - D. Eng. (President-elect, Assoc. of Prof. Eng. of Ont.) *
Pierre Camu - LL.D. (VP, Lavalin Inc., Canadian geographer) *
Mitzi Dobrin - D. Sc. Bus. Admin. (Exec. V.P. Steinberg's)
Diane Dupuy - D. Litt. (founder of Famous People Players) *

SPECIAL (October 5, 1986) conferred in People's Republic of China
Ao-qing Tang (Auchin Tang) - LL.D. (past President Jilin Univ.)

FORTY-SIXTH CONVOCATION (October 5, 1986)
Elizabeth Kishkon - LL.D. (former mayor of Windsor)*
Florence Irene Henderson - LL.D. (past Executive Director, Federation of Women
Teachers Association of Ontario)
Violet Balestreri Archer - D. Music (Canadian composer)
Frank Anthony DeMarco - D. Education (Sr. Univ. administrator & professor) *

FORTY-SEVENTH CONVOCATION (June 14 & 15, 1987)
Maurice F. Strong - LL.D. (former Undersecretary General, UN) *
Sylvia O. Fedoruk - D. Sc. (Chancellor, Univ. of Saskatchewan) *

Walter S. Tarnopolsky - DCL (Justice of Supreme Court of Ontario) *
Frances Hyland - LL.D. in absentia (Canadian actress & director)
Sylvia Ostry - LL.D. (Canadian economist) *
Peter Gzowski - LL.D. (Canadian radio & television host) *

FORTY-EIGHTH CONVOCATION (October 4, 1987)
Alton C. Parker - LL.D. (retired police officer & community worker) * **
Anna Russell - D. Music (international concert comedienne) *

FORTY-NINTH CONVOCATION (June 5, 8 & 12, 1988)
Stephen Lewis - LL.D. (Can. Ambassador to the United Nations) *
Maureen Forrester - LL.D. (Chair, Canadian Council; international concert artist) *
John Francis Leddy - D. Litt. (former President, Univ. of Windsor) *
Rosalie Silberman Abella - LL.D. (chair, Ont. Labour Relations Board) *
Brian Dickson - DCL (Chief Justice of Canada) *
Amintore Fanfani - LL.D. (President, Italian Senate) *
Peter Lougheed - LL.D. (former Premier of Alberta) *
Pauline McGibbon - LL.D. (former Lieutenant Governor of Ontario)
Ramsay Cook - D. Litt. (Professor of History, York Univ.) *
Rosalie Bertell - D. Sc. (Dir. of Research, International Institute of Concern for Public Health) *

FIFTIETH CONVOCATION (October 23, 1988)
Frederick Kenneth Hare - D. Sc. (Chancellor of Trent University) *
Paul A. Charbonneau - LL.D. (Director, Brentwood Recovery Home) *

FIFTY-FIRST CONVOCATION (June 4 & 18, 1989)
Malcolm Ross - D. Litt. (Canadian critic & essayist) *
Maurice Joseph Closs - LL.D. (Pres. & Chief Exec. Officer, Chrysler's) *
Ralph Mellanby - LL.D. (Exec. Producer, CTV 1988 Winter Olympics) *
Wm. Henry Somerville - LL.D. (Past Pres. & Chief Officer, National Victoria & Grey Trustco) *
Jon Vickers - D. Music (Canadian operatic & concert singer) *
The Hon. Florence Bird - D. Litt. (former Can. Senator, author & broadcaster) *

FIFTY-SECOND CONVOCATION (September 24, 1989)
Robert White - LL.D. (President, CAW) *
Boris Stoicheff - D. Sc. (Exec. Director, Ont. Laser & Lightwave Research Centre)
James K. McConica - D. Litt. (Pres. University of St. Michael's College) *
Phyllis Lambert - LL.D. (Director, Canadian Centre for Architecture)

SIXTY-FIFTH CONVOCATION (June 8 & 9, 1996)
Kamel Ajlouni, D. Laws, President Jordan University of Science & Technology.
Stephen Bellringer, D. Laws, President BC Gas Utility.*
Olive Patricia Dickason, D. Litt., Amerindian Authority.

Gary Parent, D. Laws, Financial Secretary/Treasurer, CAW Local 444.*
Allan M. Rock, D. Civil Law, Min. of Justice & Attorney General of Canada.*
Shirley Thomson, D. Litt., Director, National Gallery of Canada.*

LAW CONVOCATION (June 15, 1996)
Patrick LeSage, D. Civil Law, Supreme Court Judge.

SIXTY-SIXTH CONVOCATION (October 19, 1996)
Domenic A. Alfieri, D. Laws, President, Ontario Casino Corporation.*
Michael D. Hurst, D. Laws, Mayor, City of Windsor. *

Sincerely,
Maria Giampuzzi
Assistant to the Clerk of the Senate
Ext. 3317
woody@uwindsor.ca

APPENDIX VI

Terms of Reference of 60th Anniversary of D-Day Advisory Committee

———◆———

60th Anniversary of D-Day Advisory Committee terms of reference.

60th Anniversary of D-Day Advisory Committee

Terms of Reference

Context

The responsibility for organizing the Government of Canada's remembrance activities to mark the 60th anniversary of D-Day is assigned to the Minister of Veterans Affairs.

Purpose

The purpose of the 60th Anniversary of D-Day Advisory Committee (hereafter referred as "the Committee") is to provide advice and guidance to the Minister of Veterans Affairs regarding the events to mark the 60th Anniversary of the D-Day landings on Juno Beach, Normandy, France. The Committee will also be responsible for facilitating Veterans' participation in the events associated with marking the 60th anniversary of D-Day. The Committee will strive to ensure that Canadian Veterans and their families/care givers have complete access to Juno Beach during these events and that appropriate dignitaries are present to participate in the remembrance activities, including Her Majesty the Queen.

Timing

The 60th anniversary of D-Day landings will be celebrated on June 6, 2004.

Scope

Remembrance activities will be conducted both in Canada and overseas. The 60th Anniversary of D-Day Advisory Committee will focus its attention on all matters associated with the anniversary.

Membership

- Major-General (retired) Richard Rohmer (Chair)
- Royal Canadian Legion representative
- Army, Navy and Air Force Veterans Association representative
- National Council of Veterans' Associations representative
- Garth Webb, Juno Beach Centre Association
- LGen (retired) Charles Belzile, Battle of Normandy Foundation
- Deputy Minister, Veterans Affairs Canada (ex-officio)
- Director General, Canada Remembers Division, VAC (secretary)

Committee Responsibilities

- to advise on and participate in the development of plans necessary to ensure the full and appropriate participation of Canada's D-Day Veterans in the June 2004 celebration at Juno Beach, Normandy, France;
- to provide guidance in determining the number of living D-Day Veterans and to advise on methods to encourage their participation in activities organized to mark this anniversary;
- to review and advise on options for marking the 60th Anniversary of D-Day including such topics as the invitation of all still operating D-Day units (regiments, squadrons, ships), the participation of dignitaries -such as the Queen - at the Canadian celebrations on Juno Beach, etc.;
- to review and comment on the budgets proposed for submission to the Minister of Veterans Affairs;
- to provide advice on and participate in the liaison and coordination with appropriate French authorities, the central D-Day organizing body in the United Kingdom, the Canadian embassy in Paris and the office of the Canadian High Commissioner in London; and
- to provide advice on and participation in the liaison and coordination with DND and Canadian Heritage regarding matters related to their preparation and participation in the 60th Anniversary of D-Day celebrations in Normandy.

Veterans Affairs Responsibilities

- to provide secretarial support to the Advisory Committee;
- to cover travel and accommodation costs of Committee members associated with their participation in committee meetings, as well as participation in France at the opening of the Juno Beach Centre (June 6, 2003) and the 60th Anniversary of D-Day events in June, 2004;
- to conduct initial research into international and Canadian plans regarding participation at the 60th Anniversary of D-Day ceremonies and events;
- to prepare options/proposals for the Committee regarding the planning and conduct of the 60th Anniversary events at Juno Beach;
- to prepare cost estimates and budgets associated with marking this anniversary, to submit these to the Committee, and to obtain appropriate budget approval;
- with the appropriate participation and approval of the Committee, to plan and carry out communications activities including official media involvement;
- with the appropriate participation and approval of the Committee, to organize and execute VAC's involvement in the 60th Anniversary of D-Day celebration events;
- with the appropriate participation and approval of the Committee, to conduct liaison with other federal government departments and agencies involved in the planing and organization of the events (e.g. DND, DFAIT, Canadian Heritage, Chancellery, RCMP); and
- with the appropriate participation and approval of the Committee, to conduct liaison and coordination with appropriate French authorities, the central D-Day

organizing body in the United Kingdom, the Canadian embassy in Paris, and the office of the Canadian High Commissioner in London.

Operation of Committee

- operates until June 30, 2004
- meetings to be held quarterly

APPENDIX VII
My Decorations and Medals, Wings Room, Royal Canadian Military Institute, Toronto

My decorations and medals on display in the Wings Room of the Royal Canadian Military Institute in Toronto. Missing are the Chevalier of the Legion of Honour and the 2002 Jubilee Medal.

Orders, Decorations, and Medals of
Major-General Richard Rohmer

Order of Military Merit, Commander
Order of Canada, Officer
Order of Ontario, Member

Distinguished Flying Cross
1939–1945 Star
1939–1945 Aircrew Europe Star w/ France and Germany Clasp
1939–1945 Defence Medal
1939–1945 Canadian Volunteer Service Medal w/ Overseas Clasp
1939–1945 War Medal
1967 Centennial Medal
1977 Queen Elizabeth II Silver Jubilee Medal
Canadian Forces Decoration
Service Medal Order of St. John
Order of Leopold (Belg.), Officer

Tour of Operations (Ops) Wings RCAF

Order of Lafayette (American)
Combattant Voluntaire (French)
Maltese Order of St. Lazarus
Order de Cobra (Maltese)
American Medal of the Association of Military Surgeons
L'Ordre de Confrerie Equestre Internationale de Saint Georges de
France
Normandy Commemorative Medal

Knight, Order of St. John
Chevalier of the Legion of Honour
2002 Jubilee Medal

INDEX